Ethnography and the City

The only collection of its kind on the market, this reader gathers the work of some of the most esteemed urban ethnographers in sociology and anthropology. Broken down into sections that cover key aspects of ethnographic research, *Ethnography and the City* will expose readers to important works in the field, while also guiding students to the study of method as they embark on their own work.

Richard E. Ocejo is Assistant Professor of Sociology at John Jay College of Criminal Justice of the City University of New York (CUNY), where he teaches research methods and urban sociology. His research uses ethnographic methods to analyze urban and community issues, culture, public space, and work in the contemporary city.

THE METROPOLIS AND MODERN LIFE

A Routledge Series
Edited by **Anthony Orum, Loyola University and Zachary P. Neal,
    Michigan State University**

This series brings original perspectives on key topics in urban research to today's students in a series of short accessible texts, guided readers, and practical handbooks. Each volume examines how long-standing urban phenomena continue to be relevant in an increasingly urban and global world, and in doing so, connects the best new scholarship with the wider concerns of students seeking to understand life in the 21st-century metropolis.

Books in the Series:

Common Ground: Reading and Reflections on Public Space edited by Anthony Orum and Zachary P. Neal

The Gentrification Debates edited by Japonica Brown-Saracino

The Power of Urban Ethnic Places: Cultural Heritage and Community Life by Jan Lin

Urban Tourism and Urban Change: Cities in a Global Economy by Costas Spirou

The Connected City by Zachary Neal

The World's Cities edited by A.J. Jacobs

Ethnography and the City edited by Richard Ocejo

Also of Interest from Routledge:

The Community Development Reader, Second Edition edited by James DeFillipis and Susan Saegert

Housing Policy in the United States, Second Edition by Alex F. Schwartz

Neobohemia: Art and Commerce in the Postindustrial City, 2nd Edition by Richard Lloyd

China and Globalization, 3rd Edition by Doug Guthrie

Foodies: Democracy and Distinction in the Gourmet Foodscape by Josée Johnston and Shyon Baumann

Branding New York: How a City in Crisis Was Sold to the World by Miriam Greenberg

City Life from Jakarta to Dakar: Movements at the Crossroads by AbdouMaliq Simone

Ethnography and the City

Readings on Doing Urban Fieldwork

Edited by
Richard E. Ocejo
John Jay College of Criminal Justice, CUNY

Routledge
Taylor & Francis Group

NEW YORK AND LONDON

First published 2013
by Routledge
711 Third Avenue, New York, NY 10017

Simultaneously published in the UK
by Routledge
2 Park Square, Milton Park, Abingdon, Oxon OX14 4RN

Routledge is an imprint of the Taylor & Francis Group, an informa business

Library of Congress Cataloging-in-Publication Data
Ethnography and the city : readings on doing urban fieldwork / [edited by] Richard E. Ocejo.
    p. cm. — (Metropolis and modern life)
    1. Urban anthropology—Fieldwork. I. Ocejo, Richard E.
    GN395.E7 2012
    307.7'6—dc23
    2012022256

ISBN 13: 978–0–415–80837–8 (hbk)
ISBN 13: 978–0–415–80838–5 (pbk)

Typeset in Sabon and Helvetica Neue
by Swales & Willis Ltd, Exeter, Devon

CONTENTS

From his classic work *The Urban Villagers*, in this selection Herbert Gans analyzes how an Italian-American community reacts to impending displacement. By living in their Boston neighborhood Gans discovers how the primacy of the family and peer group in the lives of these working-class Italians and the "urban village" community that they constructed influences their inaction against displacement and the destruction of their neighborhood.

This piece showcases how Philippe Bourgois immerses himself in East Harlem ("El Barrio") to understand the daily struggles and hardships of families and children in this dangerous and unstable environment. From living in the neighborhood and having a young son, Bourgois learns both the important role that children play among residents, as well as the harsh realities that they and their mothers face.

In this selection Richard Lloyd takes us inside the gentrifying Chicago neighborhood of Wicker Park to show how a bohemian aesthetic and work ethic gets contested within and integrated into a commercial nightlife scene. By living in Wicker Park and participating in its arts scene, Lloyd discovers the importance of leisure spaces in its construction and in transforming it into a postindustrial neighborhood of cultural production.

Seeing herself as a gentrifier in North Kenwood-Oakland, Mary Pattillo examines the intra-racial conflicts between newcomers and existing residents that emerge in a neighborhood experiencing "black gentrification." As one of the newcomers against whom working-class residents show wariness and hostility, her work demonstrates the difficulties ethnographers face in immersing themselves in their field sites.

This piece pushes the community study beyond the boundaries of the urban neighborhood as Gina Perez goes to Humboldt Park in Chicago as well as San Sebastián in Puerto Rico to examine the transnational lives and identities of Puerto Rican migrants. An example of "multi-sited ethnography," Perez's study highlights the importance of immersion across spatial boundaries to experience and understand the impact of social contexts and spatial and cultural distance on people's lives.

Introduction
Richard E. Ocejo

Along with his extensive observations of vendors, Mitchell Duneier also gets behind the table to see the sidewalk from their perspective. In this selection he demonstrates the complex relationship between the police and the vendors when he creates a situation through which an officer confronts him.

Peter Moskos in this study goes through the Baltimore police academy and becomes an officer for a year. He provides a first-hand account of the varying perspectives and interpretations of their duties and decisions that officers make while policing in the inner city.

In this study David Grazian discovers the multiple interpretations that different actors have of "authenticity" in blues clubs. This piece shows how he uses his own musical abilities on the saxophone to reveal how a community of blues club regulars construct notions of authenticity and socialize people into the group.

PART II: RELATIONSHIPS WITH PARTICIPANTS

Introduction
Richard E. Ocejo

to reveal the importance of non-blood kin relations for impoverished families. Her identity as a mother with a young son aids her in overcoming social distance and forming a close relationship with her main informant.

Ethnographers are trained to analyze the thoughts and perceptions that their participants have about their own lives, but rarely do they consider the thoughts and perceptions their participants have about them. In this piece Sudhir Venkatesh discovers that the "hustle" principle that permeates life in the Chicago housing project he studies is also applied to him and his fieldwork by its residents. Such reflection casts a critical lens on the ethnographer's role in the field at the same time as it aids him in his own analysis.

Along with race, gender is often another important social boundary between ethnographers and their participants. In this study from the 1960s, Sherri Cavan examines gender relations in pickup nightspots. She often uses her gender to position herself in the world of male-dominated bars and analyze how social interaction between men and women works in them.

In this co-authored study on the people in an impoverished and highly contaminated shantytown and their reactions to their hazardous surrounding conditions, Javier Auyero and Debora Swistun use the "photo-elicitation" method with the town's children to learn how they understand their environment. Through this method they overcome the age gap that exists between them while remaining sensitive to the vulnerability of their population.

Introduction
Richard E. Ocejo

This controversial work by Laud Humphreys is among the most mentioned in courses and textbooks that discuss ethics in sociological research. This selection showcases the actual data that Humphreys gathered and the analysis he conducted on impersonal homosexual sex in public places.

It is not uncommon for ethnographers to engage in illegal activities with their participants, and in this piece Jeff Ferrell joins a group of graffiti writers in Denver as they reveal the importance of style in constructing their subcultural community. Ferrell argues that he engaged in illegal activities with his participants to experience their world and validate their claims, but places limits on doing so for all activities.

In this work, Randol Contreras deals with a number of ethical issues from studying drug robbers who regularly engage in violent acts. In this piece he focuses on their mistreatment and exploitation of women in their robberies. Contreras's work exemplifies situations when participants engage in behaviors that fieldworkers are morally against.

SERIES FOREWORD

Ethnography and the City: Readings on Doing Urban Fieldwork, by Richard E. Ocejo

This series brings original perspectives on key topics in urban research to today's students in a series of short accessible texts, guided readers, and practical handbooks. Each volume examines how long-standing urban phenomena continue to be relevant in an increasingly urban and global world, and in doing so, connects the best new scholarship with the wider concerns of students to understand life in the 21st century metropolis.

In this addition to the series, Richard Ocejo collects selections from urban ethnographies written over the past 70 years to illustrate how to "do urban fieldwork." The intricate art of ethnography cannot be taught by a textbook, but must be learned through observation and experience. Thus, Ocejo immerses the reader in the urban worlds of 21 leading ethnographers, both past and present, to teach through demonstration. In the first part, the selections illustrate their varied strategies of embedding themselves in their settings, either by living among or working alongside their research participants. In the second part, the readings illustrate how researchers negotiate two challenging boundary issues in this type of work: crossing social boundaries to gain entry into the participants' lives, and not crossing ethical boundaries while in the field. Throughout the book, Ocejo incorporates a series of original essays that serve as a roadmap that guides the reader through these glimpses of the streets, and links them into a coherent strategy for adopting this approach to understanding the modern metropolis. Both engaging and instructive, this volume brings together some of the very best examples of urban ethnography and thus provides both students and scholars a window into what Robert Park once described as the city's "little social worlds."

Anthony Orum
Zachary Neal
Series Editors

PREFACE

This is a collection of readings by some of the most well-known and up-and-coming urban ethnographers in sociology and anthropology. There are several readers that gather examples of ethnographic work. But these volumes do not focus on urban ethnographies, which have been an indelible part of ethnographic research in the field of sociology since the discipline's inception in the United States. There are also several collections of classic and contemporary works in urban sociology. But these texts are geared toward urban sociology courses, rather than qualitative research methods courses, and not all of their selections are works of ethnography. *Ethnography and the City*, on the other hand, is the only collection of readings dedicated to urban ethnographies on the market.

I break this reader down into two parts with two sections in each part. Part I deals with two data collection strategies of immersion, namely living in the same neighborhoods as participants and working alongside participants in the field. Part II deals with issues relating to establishing and maintaining relationships with participants, namely by crossing social boundaries and ensuring ethical conduct. I introduce each section with an essay that discusses several key issues for each theme that are found in its readings, provides background on the larger work from which the pieces are excerpted, and summarizes the pieces themselves. My intention for these themes and for the original introductory essays is to provide students with a background in urban ethnography and guide them in their own research.

Ethnography and the City will be primarily suitable for courses on qualitative methods, including ethnographic, observational, and interviewing methods, at the graduate level. The readings in *Ethnography and the City* will teach students about ethnographic research, expose them to integral works in the field, and serve as models for their own work. Since most graduate courses on qualitative methods offer in-depth readings of book-length monographs, I feel that this reader will serve as a highly useful complement to such courses by providing a broad array of examples of key aspects of ethnographic research. (And while they are less common, this reader will also be helpful for undergraduate qualitative research courses.) Secondarily, *Ethnography and the City* will also be suitable for urban sociology, urban anthropology, and other urban studies courses that are fieldwork-driven. These courses will benefit from having a text that covers studies in numerous cities (New York City, Buenos Aires, Chicago, Baltimore), urban environments (ghettos, downtowns, ethnic enclaves, bars), and urban situations (street corners, workplaces, walking tours, shantytowns). Finally, because of the broad range of topics covered by its selections, it will also be suitable for such courses as proseminars that introduce students to sociological research and topics such as race, ethnicity, and social class.

Introduction

Sociology's Urban Explorers

On a Saturday afternoon in the early spring of 2010 I walk into Milano's Bar. I began my dissertation research at Milano's, an old neighborhood bar on the Lower East Side of Manhattan, more than six years ago. Since I had expanded my project beyond the doors of the bar to examine whether and how the conflicts of change and gentrification that I was witnessing among its regulars occurred among residents in the neighborhood four years ago, I did not have as much time to spend there. But I have still occasionally gone in to get some updates and catch up with people. Jackie, the regular Saturday day bartender in her mid-40s, greets me warmly, as she does whenever I come in. Originally from Northern Ireland, Jackie has been bartending at Milano's for fifteen years. She always works the day shift, when the older regulars are there, for whom she serves as a den mother of sorts. Teases and playful insults usually characterize her banter with them, which is loud enough for the whole bar to hear. Regular customers highly respect Jackie, and she provides them with compassion and discipline in equal measure.

I take a seat next to Kevin, a retired fireman in his 50s. Originally from the Bronx, he now lives upstate. He used to work at a fire station around the corner on Lafayette Street, which is how he got introduced to Milano's ("Back when there were Bowery men [homeless men] and Italian men, who still lived with their mothers"). Despite the distance, he still makes a point of traveling down to the Lower East Side to visit Jackie and other regulars at the bar. He also does not get what Milano's provides where he lives. "People in my town are suburban," says Kevin. "They don't really go out to the bar to sit and have a drink. Instead they have you over at their homes, which I'm not really into." Kevin commutes through four counties to get to his neighborhood bar.

I then notice Dick sitting a few seats away from me. Dick is in his mid-50s and moved to the Lower East Side in the late 1970s, after graduating from the University of Minnesota, in his home state. He came to New York City to pursue a career as an artist, and the affordable Lower East Side with an art and music scene was an obvious destination. "When you're famous in New York, you're global," he says. "When you're famous in Minneapolis, you're famous in Minneapolis." While his art career never completely took off, Dick often makes and sometimes sells paintings and collages. He returns to Minnesota to visit his family once a year, and wears a purple suit for the occasion, always stopping at the bar for a pre-flight drink (or drinks) to take the edge off his fear of flying. Dick describes himself as "the best regular this bar has," and could be seen at Milano's every day. Usually when something around the bar breaks or needs repairs, such as light fixtures or the swinging bathroom door, he fixes it, and gets compensated in alcohol. Early on when we met I asked Dick what he did for a living.

"A bartender, a handyman, a carpenter, a dressmaker, a sewer, a draper, uh, I think I've been a babysitter, I've been a nanny, umm, that's all I can think of. There are precious few things that I haven't done. Oh, I'm a pretty good engineer. I fix things. I fix machines."

"What would say your central occupation is?" I asked.

"I would say a carpenter. No, I would say fixit man."

Given his "best regular" status, Dick and I saw each other at the bar and talked very often about a wide range of topics like books, politics, old films, and world history, or we would just work on the *New York Times* crossword puzzle. Sometimes he would give me a complaint letter to a corporation over a product or a letter to the editor of a newspaper about a recent article he had read that he was drafting to read over. Dick lives alone in a rent-regulated apartment nearby (he is divorced with two teenage kids, who live in the neighborhood with their mother), and the bar serves for him what it once did exclusively for the Bowery men: employment center and place to sustain his addictions. As we start talking today, Jackie comes over to us.

"What can I get for ya, Rich?"

"I'll have a Smithwick's."

"A Smithwick's," she repeats.

"I'll have another vodka grapefruit," says Dick, on top of her.

"You wait your turn! I'm talking to Rich!"

I asked Dick how he is doing and he asks me how my dissertation is going. He had forgotten that I told him the last time I saw him that I had graduated and now had an academic job. I remind him.

"Wait, psychology?" he asks.

"Sociology."

"Oh. Like Durkheim?"

"Yeah, Durkheim."

"I hate Durkheim."

"What do you hate about him?"

"Terrible writer."

"Well, he wrote in French more than a hundred years ago."

"Well, it must be the translation. Only sociology course I ever took, Soc 1-0-0-1. The professor starts talking about Durkheim, and some other guy, and he acts like we're supposed to know who they are."

Dick always asks me what I am studying. He always forgets. And then he always talks about Durkheim. Our usual conversations begin with him asking a question, me answering it, and then a stream of consciousness reply. For instance, later on he asks me, "Are you an atheist?"

"I suppose something like that."

"I mean, you have to be. It's just too logical. I mean, you say there's a creator. Well, who created him? And what about heaven? If you say everyone goes to heaven, do animals go to heaven? And if animals go to heaven then black widow spiders go to heaven. And why would I want to sit next to a good guy for the rest of eternity? Wait, so, are you writing a book?"

"Yes, I am."

"Am I going to be a character?"

"Yeah, you might be."

"Ok, well, if I'm a character, I want to be called Phil Simms."

After Kevin and Dick leave, Jackie and I get to finally chat one-on-one. She comes over to where I am sitting.

"So, Jackie, how is everything around here?"

"Ah, Rich, it's the same. Everyone's the same. Nothing ever changes around here."

* * *

I wrote this field note while working on a book based on my dissertation research (Ocejo, forthcoming). In 2004 I first walked into Milano's Bar as a graduate student in search of a field site. After going there several times and meeting some of the customers and bartenders, I realized how much character they had and how important and meaningful the bar was to them. I decided to examine the social world of the bar, the lives of its people, the relationships among regulars and between regulars and bartenders, and the different ways in which they interpreted and defined community by becoming a regular customer and embedding myself in its everyday life. I gradually learned that Milano's consisted of three waves of clientele: old-timer Bowery men who had been going to the bar since the neighborhood's days as a slum; people who had moved to the neighborhood at the start of its gentrification; and young newcomers and visitors. Each group used the bar at different times and in different ways. Each also understood their role in the bar differently, with some of the longtime regulars and bartenders expressing negative attitudes toward newcomers. Since Milano's was an old bar in a gentrified neighborhood with a large nightlife scene, it had become a destination for young revelers in search of an authentic, working-class bar (Grazian, Chapter 8, this volume). I realized from exploring the social world of Milano's that its story was part of a larger development taking place on the Lower East Side. The more I looked inside the bar, the more I was drawn outside its doors. Two years into my fieldwork I decided to expand my project to examine conflicts over the commercial gentrification of the Lower East Side by examining how people in the neighborhood defined and acted upon their definitions of community.

I tell this brief story of how my project developed from walking into a bar to becoming an in-depth examination of people in a neighborhood as an introduction to this reader because it touches on both the goals of urban ethnography and some of the key themes of this volume. Ethnographers seek to analyze how people understand their own situations in their lives, examine the connections between their micro-level thoughts and actions and macro-level social structures, and provide generalized explanations for their behavior and for what makes them distinct or similar to other social groups by studying them as they behave in their natural settings. In many cases ethnographers do not know what they are going to study before they enter a field site. But by embedding themselves in a place and among a group and forming relationships with people, fieldworkers give themselves the opportunity to learn new phenomena and expand existing knowledge.

Herbert Gans, whose classic work *The Urban Villagers* is featured in this reader, says of learning ethnographic fieldwork, "I believe to this day that the method almost teaches itself … I sometimes feel that the instructor is dispensable. Anybody who has done fieldwork can teach this course by letting students do their work and supervising them, saying 'This is what you should do better next time'" (2009, 381). While Gans makes a valid point about the experiential nature of ethnography, or the importance of going out and getting the "seats of your pants dirty in real research" (Park, cited in McKinney 1966, 21), learning and understanding the method requires more than supervision. Ethnography consists of a set of practices, strategies, and philosophical assumptions for examining society. Primary among these assumptions is the notion that ethnographers can understand the socially constructed meanings of people's social worlds and lives by examining them as they act within their natural contexts.

Examining people's behavior in a manner that will effectively reveal and explain how they interpret their situation and make sense of their lives requires guidance as well as reflection on the part of the fieldworker. Because of the breadth and depth of interactions with which ethnographers engage and the myriad interpersonal complications that arise from them, the method lends itself to reflection. Learning how to conduct ethnographic research requires not just supervision and practice, but also reflective engagement with its actual practices and strategies. Providing students and burgeoning practitioners with examples and models of these practices and strategies to help them think about and conduct their own work is an aim of this reader.

A BRIEF HISTORY OF URBAN ETHNOGRAPHY

Scholars from many disciplinary backgrounds use ethnographic methods to study people in a wide range of settings. Anthropologists traditionally focus on indigenous populations in non-Western societies. Sociologists have conducted studies on people in rural areas and small towns (Bell 1994; de la Pradelle 2004; Erikson 1976; Vidich and Bensman 1958), on workers and workplaces (Bearman 2005; Fine 1996; Hochschild 1983; Katz 1982; Van Maanen 1978), and on members of social institutions such as schools, asylums, and places of worship (Garot 2010; Goffman 1961; Khan 2010; Marti 2008; Nelson 2004). They have also studied processes such as aging (Myerhoff 1978) and experiences such as driving and committing crimes (Katz 1988; 1999). There is no shortage of groups or settings for ethnographers to examine.

This volume focuses on ethnographers who have conducted research on people and places in cities. In most cases the social problem under investigation occurs in urban as well as non-urban environments. Gentrification and displacement occur in rural areas as well as cities (Brown-Saracino 2009), poverty, homelessness, immigration, and drug activity are hardly exclusive to urban environments, and religious talk and informal economies exist in all settings. But we cannot ignore the fact that the empirical examples under investigation in this volume's readings, or the actual people and places that these scholars studied, are in cities. The people whose perspectives are examined here live and act in specific urban contexts where unique urban forces have significant impacts on their lives. What distinguishes urban ethnographies such as many of the pieces in this reader is that their authors take the larger forces of urban life into account in their analyses. In their work, urban ethnographers recognize the importance of the city, its political economy, inequalities, cultures, and conditions of size, density, and diversity in the lives of their participants. The social problems they examine do not just happen to exist within cities. The urban contexts within which the people they study live influence ethnographers' understanding, because these contexts play key roles in shaping people's lives.

Many ethnographers work within a long-standing tradition of sociological fieldwork in urban environments. The city—its people and social problems, and the ways its "physical environments shape and are shaped by social life" (Kasinitz 1995, 10)—was one of early American sociology's main topics of research and analysis. Sociologists who pioneered ethnographic research in the United States did so in cities, particularly in Chicago. Greggor Mattson (2007) documents that the first two published examples of ethnographic research in a sociology journal were by the husband and wife Ernest and Dorothea Moore in 1897 in the *American Journal of Sociology*. At that time sociologists did not write a considerable amount about the methods they used and the issues they faced in the field. In his article on Chicago saloons, Moore says that,

The *laboratory method* was employed. The saloons were visited, an attempt was made to escape that bane of social investigation—the psychologist's fallacy. In so far as possible, conditions were exchanged. Purse and scrip were left behind. The saloon became an integral feature of life. It was a loafing place, news center, and basis of food supply in its free lunch counter; a complete orientation was made into its life. Trammeled neither by an abstinence pledge nor by a predisposition for its wares, it is believed that the freedom necessary to unbiased judgment was obtained.

(1897, 2–3; emphasis added)

Indeed, the metaphor of the "laboratory method" that saw places in the city as objects of investigation was not an uncommon way in which fieldworkers understood sociological research. Scholars in the young discipline formed an identity for sociology as a social science through which "unbiased judgment" could be obtained from observation. They did so as significant social forces like industrialization, immigration, and migration were transforming cities and urban life. Albion Small, who chaired the first sociology department in the United States, at Chicago, describes the city's influence on his thinking about research,

The most impressive lesson which I have learned in the vast sociological laboratory which the city of Chicago constitutes is that action, not speculation, is the supreme teacher. If men will be the most productive scholars in any department of the social sciences, let them gain time and material by cooperating in the social work of their community.

(1896, 581–582)

The "Chicago School" was a group of scholars from the 1910s to the 1930s who built upon these early efforts and developed strategies to systematically examine a broad range of topics in the city. They influenced many subfields and disciplines, such as criminology, juvenile delinquency, social deviance, the family, immigration, race, ethnicity, and community studies. The common element in all of their studies is the city and urban conditions, and the School is primarily known for contributing to our knowledge of cities and urban life in the early twentieth century.

Robert Park, a co-leader of the Chicago School, implored his students to get their bodies and minds out of libraries and books and out into the field, or out in the city. Sociologists at the University of Chicago had already been conducting fieldwork, often alongside the reformist-minded settlement house workers, like those at Jane Addams's Hull House, in immigrant communities and ethnic neighborhoods (Mattson 2007). But it was not until Park's arrival that the department developed a methodology based on objectivity and a theoretical approach that emphasized locating social actors in their contexts (i.e. specific times and locations) to analyze them (Abbott 1997; Bulmer 1986). As a former journalist in Chicago and other cities, and as an adherent of pragmatism, the philosophical tradition that bases theoretical insights on actual behavior, Park emphasized that researchers must immerse themselves in urban environments and get up close to people. In one of his best-known quotes Park tells his students to,

Go and sit in the lounges of the luxury hotels and on the doorsteps of the flophouses; sit on the Gold Coast settees and on the slum shakedowns; sit in the Orchestra Hall and in the Star and Garter Burlesque. In short, gentlemen, go get the seats of your pants dirty in real research.

(McKinney 1966, 21)

With such guidance from Park and his colleague Ernest Burgess, students at the University of Chicago produced dozens of case studies and monographs on the city's marginalized groups and places and their picaresque social worlds. Jewish and African-American neighborhoods, hobos, youth gangs, taxi-dancers, bohemians, and jack-rollers were just some of their subjects, and a city undergoing the tremendous transformations of urbanization and industrialization was their context (Anderson 2009).

Robert Park expanded the "laboratory method" metaphor. He considered the city to be like a "social laboratory," "or clinic in which human nature and social processes might be conveniently studied" (Bulmer 1986, 92). As a social laboratory the modern city was a place of constant change and mobility. Sociologists in the Chicago School saw cities as people's natural habitat, where social orders were reflected in and shaped the built environment. As Park says,

> The city magnifies, spreads out, and advertises human nature in all its various manifestations. It is this that makes the city interesting, even fascinating. It is this, however, that makes it of all places the one in which to discover the secrets of human hearts and to study human nature and society.
>
> (1929, 19)

Park and Burgess supported a multi-method "case study" approach to studying urban life, which included up-close observation (Anderson 1923; Zorbaugh 1929), personal documents (Thomas and Znaniecki 1918), autobiographical life histories (Shaw 1931), and maps (Cressey 1932).

While practitioners of the case study method in the early twentieth century made significant contributions to our understanding of numerous social groups, neighborhoods, and deviant behaviors in the modern city, they have been criticized for being too socially detached and distant from the people they studied (Emerson 2001). In particular they relied too much on their own pure observations and the personal documents of their participants, and not enough on analyzing the perspectives of others. In the period spanning pre- and post-World War II sociologists adopted the methodological approach of participant observation. As its name suggests, this methodological approach emphasizes that researchers simultaneously serve as both observers of and participants in the action in their field sites. It demands that ethnographers get up close to their participants for long periods of time to understand the social meanings they construct and attach to their behavior: "Participant observation asserted that by emphatically participating in an intimate and sustained fashion, the fieldworker gained privileged access to the meanings that infuse the daily lives and activities of those studied" (Emerson 2001, 13). Following William Foote Whyte's classic example of participant observation research, *Street Corner Society* (featured in this volume), urban ethnographers gradually embraced this approach to examining city life. Social detachment and distance from the web of meanings and interpretations that people construct was replaced by immersion, or becoming embedded in the social life of the field site and its communities, into the places and situations in which they construct them.

Robert Emerson (2001) identifies several reasons for the shift to the participant observation model. First, anthropological approaches that already emphasized immersion in field sites began to get incorporated into sociology studies, with Whyte's work serving as an important example. By the mid-twentieth century sociologists also began to come from different social backgrounds from their participants. Many early urban ethnographers at the Chicago School were "insiders," or people from or familiar with the people they studied, such as Nels Anderson, who had been a hobo and studied this group, Clifford Shaw, who was a probation officer and studied juvenile delinquents, and Louis Wirth, who was a social worker and studied a Jewish ghetto. In the decades following World War II many urban ethnographers were different from their participants (such as Whyte, an upper-middle-class WASP who studied working-class, first- and second-generation Italians). Immersion became a necessity for fieldworkers to understand unfamiliar social worlds. Since immersion requires overcoming and managing the social boundaries that divided them from their participants, urban ethnographers who conducted participant observation also began to reflect on the obstacles they faced in doing so, the relationships they formed with their participants, and the ethical decisions they made.

As participant observation developed through the late twentieth century and into the twenty-first, ethnographers have become more reflective and self-conscious of their role in the field and in the lives of the people they study. Part of this reflection includes understanding that fieldwork is highly experiential and personal. Conducting ethnographic research involves realizing that an important basis of fieldworkers' analyses is their own experiences of the situations within which people construct meaning. Ethnographers therefore seek to not just embed themselves within their field sites to learn how people make sense of their lives. They also reflect on how being embedded influences and is influenced by the site and its people. By immersing themselves ethnographers enter into the lives of their participants in direct and sometimes intimate ways. They listen to them tell their stories, watch them work and raise their children, see them behave as friends and lovers, mothers and fathers, husbands and wives, and work and live alongside them. The social boundaries that divide people and complicate communication in everyday life are present and highly salient in fieldwork between ethnographers and their participants. However, just as important as crossing these social boundaries to make communication and understanding possible is maintaining a critical distance from participants, or not getting so close as to glamorize or misrepresent them. Early ethnographers were too detached from the interpretations of their participants, but getting close to their subjective meanings threatens to bias an ethnographer's explanations, which in the end does not contribute to empirically-based, generalizable knowledge. As such, reflection over immersion and relationships in the field, particularly as these aspects of research aid or interfere with data collection, has become an important aspect of ethnographic research.

Not all, but many of the authors in this volume work within the Chicago School tradition as participant observers, or their methodological decisions and practices demonstrate several elements in common with the School. Some learned how to conduct ethnographic research while at the University of Chicago (Duneier, Gans, Grazian, Lloyd, Pattillo, and Venkatesh). Robert Emerson (2004) identifies three themes of Chicago-style fieldwork that characterize it as a distinctive approach to ethnographic research. First, ethnographers working in the Chicago tradition emphasize discovery, or "identifying and analyzing new, unappreciated, or mis-appreciated processes that have important effects on social life" (9). Second, they demonstrate "loyalty to the phenomenon" under investigation, or examining what is actually happening among the people in the setting. Both of these themes emphasize using the data collected from fieldwork as the primary source of theoretical explanations, rather than entering the field with theoretical explanations in hand. The final theme of the Chicago tradition of fieldwork is the collection of original data in original ways, with the quality of originality stemming from an ethnographer's choice of setting, population, and angle. In other words, the decisions that ethnographers make on the people and places they study, the strategies they pursue, the relationships they form and manage, and the analytical angle they take all contribute to the originality and innovative nature of the data they collect. As we will see, each author uses the practices and strategies of participant observation in their own specific way to generate knowledge that builds from existing ideas.

THEMES AND ISSUES

This unique collection of readings serves two purposes. First, it introduces students to classic and contemporary works in urban ethnography by some of the field's well-regarded practitioners. It also includes more recent works by up-and-coming scholars in the field conducting their first major ethnographic research projects, as many student readers of this volume will also be doing. While hardly exhaustive, these pieces cover a wide array of urban issues in several cities to give readers a sampling of urban ethnography's scope. Hopefully reading these excerpts inspires readers to explore the larger, original works by these authors.

Second, it provides guidance to students by discussing and demonstrating models of and issues with strategies of data collection and maintaining and managing interpersonal relationships between them and their participants that ethnographers use. Through these readings this volume seeks to foster discussion over these themes. No two ethnographic projects or sets of experiences in the field are ever the same. In fact, since exploring un- and under-explored populations, places, and processes are among ethnography's "warrants" (Katz 1997), uniqueness can and should be an ethnographer's intention (Small 2009). There is also not a best way to conduct ethnographic research. But as readers will see, even though fieldwork does not follow strict rules and many strategies are considered legitimate, it is still a methodology with generally agreed-upon, though sometimes debated, procedures, standards, and codes of conduct.[1] By exposing students to how some urban ethnographers have designed their projects and conducted themselves while in the field among the people they study, this reader will show them how ethnography can be done and help them think about their own work.

To achieve these objectives I have placed each reading into one of four themed sections, with two sections focusing on strategies of data collection, specifically forms of immersion, and two focusing on issues of handling relationships and interactions with participants. These four themes—being there by living in the same neighborhoods as participants, participating in the same activities as participants, crossing social boundaries, and ensuring ethics in fieldwork—represent some of the key *choices* that all ethnographers make in their research. When they design their projects ethnographers decide on the level of participation they will take. The people they meet and the situations they find themselves in in their field sites constantly influence the decisions they make. There are many other themes that a reader on urban ethnography could cover, such as data collection techniques (e.g. field note taking, audio and video recording, photography, using participants as co-researchers), scrutinizing what is a "field," discussing the distinctions between deductive and inductive approaches to fieldwork, exiting the field, analyzing data, and ethnographic writing, to name just a few. This does not make the themes that I have chosen more important than others, and readers should use the readings to examine various themes. I chose these themes because of their importance to the method and their relevance for my own early development as an urban ethnographer. These themes also should not be seen as their own isolated categories. They regularly influence each other in ethnographic work, such as when ethical matters interfere with data collection or when crossing social boundaries intersects with immersion. I try to make these points in my introductory essays.

In each section I have tried to combine classic and contemporary works so readers can see how ethnographic research has changed over time. It is often the case that a chosen piece fits under more than one theme and sometimes each one (and certainly the larger works from which these excerpts originate) cover multiple methodological themes. For instance, an excerpt from Mary Pattillo's book, *Black on the Block*, appears in this reader under the theme of being there by living in the same neighborhood as participants. As an urban ethnographer examining the disparate understandings and experiences of gentrification among middle- and working-class African-Americans and the tensions that emerge between them in a Chicago neighborhood, Pattillo chooses to become a gentrifier in her own field site. She buys a house and participates in community groups as both a researcher and a neighbor. I could have easily placed her work in the section on establishing, maintaining, and managing relationships with participants, but decided to put it with others who choose to live among the people they study. I composed the sections based on the specific methodological issues within the themes that each piece addresses, my own experiences reading and teaching them, and on how they have aided me in thinking about my own work. Readers should consider each piece for both how it illuminates issues within its section as well as how it reflects other themes.

As mentioned, the methodological themes and issues discussed and explored in these readings are not specific to urban ethnographies. Fieldworkers who study people in other places or who focus on social phenomena such as social institutions or social processes must also deal with data collection strategies of immersion, establishing and maintaining relationships with their participants by crossing social boundaries while balancing social closeness and critical distance, and ensuring ethical standards through project design and prudent decision-making in the field. As examples of urban ethnographies, however, these readings deal with empirical phenomena that present fieldworkers with the challenges and obstacles that emerge from conducting research in cities. Despite covering a broad range of urban issues these studies are all explorations of how people make sense of their situations in specific contexts. They share a methodological connection of examining slices of urban life through sustained participation observation. I introduce each section with a short essay that discusses its theme, each piece within it, the larger work from which it comes, and the specific issues within the theme that it highlights. Below is a brief synopsis of the major issues of each section's theme and readings.

Being There, Up Close

Among the principles of participant-observation research, "being there, up close," or being immersed in the daily life of field sites, is paramount. The level of immersion that fieldworkers reach is an important data collection strategy. By choosing how immersed they will be in their field sites and in what manner ethnographers select an angle for examining their participants' social world. A common example of immersion in urban ethnography is living in the same neighborhoods as participants. City neighborhoods have always been a central focus for urban ethnographers (see Kornblum 1974; Suttles 1968; Wirth 1928; Zorbaugh 1929). Living among their participants as a form of being there allows researchers to base their analysis on first-hand experience of everyday life in the neighborhood. But as a data collection strategy living in a field site raises important methodological as well as practical issues.

Urban ethnographers have conducted fieldwork in many different types of neighborhoods, and this section consists of readings on a range of them. These include an Italian-American enclave (Herbert Gans), a Puerto Rican barrio (Philippe Bourgois), a gentrifying black neighborhood (Mary Pattillo), an artists' neighborhood (Richard Lloyd), and a transnational Puerto Rican community in Chicago and San Sebastián, Puerto Rico (Gina Perez). Each reading also features several issues and obstacles that relate to immersion and data collection. For instance, since participant-observation research is a personal process of data collection, ethnographers living among their participants often have experiences that compromise their critical distance. In his classic work *The Urban Villagers* Herbert Gans studied an Italian-American community in Boston that was in the process of getting displaced. While his intent was to examine the community itself and not the displacement, he discovered that its grave implications for the community did not elicit significant action from its members. Gans then uses his academic background in sociology and city planning to advocate on behalf of the community to city leaders, thus expanding his data from objective scholarly inquiry to politically-oriented action agenda. In his research on crack dealers in "El Barrio" Philippe Bourgois experiences the issues of immersion on a more personal level. He acknowledges practical issues of living in an impoverished neighborhood such as dealing with crime, violence, and public drug activity with a young family. His extreme closeness to his participants served as a benefit to his data collection in the sense that he feels comfortable to ask them probing questions that are very direct and confrontational, but he sometimes finds himself reacting very emotionally and defensively to the responses he received. Again, these issues are not specific to the strategy of living among participants and can arise in all forms of immersion. From this section's works readers will learn some of the benefits and challenges that come from being there and getting up close to people by living among them in their neighborhoods.

Being on the Job

An additional data collection strategy that exemplifies immersion and is common to urban ethnography is when researchers engage in the same activities and do the same work as their participants. This strategy also reflects the experiential nature of the participant-observation approach. For ethnographers the aim of working and performing alongside their participants is to learn how to "take the role of the other," or to experience their situations by entering into the same meaning-making processes that are central to their lives. As with living among participants, engaging in the same activities as participants provides ethnographers with an original angle for analyzing their empirical phenomena.

Urban ethnographers have developed a wide array of skills to supplement their data collection method of sustained observation. This section includes works by researchers who have become a sidewalk book vendor (Mitchell Duneier), police officer (Peter Moskos), and walking tour guide (Jonathan Wynn), and who have performed the blues onstage (David Grazian), apprenticed as a boxer and trainer (Lucia Trimbur), and volunteered in a charity's kitchen preparing meals (Courtney Bender). An important aspect of "taking the role of the other" by participating and working with people in the field is that ethnographers are in a position to simultaneously collect and generate data to analyze. As a vendor, Mitchell Duneier does not just learn the scavenging and sales techniques that are necessary for gathering and selling used books. He also creates interactions that reveal significant dynamics of race and social class that play out on the sidewalk between vendors and the police. Similarly, David Grazian, an amateur saxophonist, learns about and contributes to the socialization process for newcomers in the community of blues musicians and fans who he studies by performing alongside professionals. Along with living in the same neighborhood, in-depth participation allows ethnographers to experience participants' situations for themselves and discover the processes they use to construct meaning beyond observing or talking to them.

Crossing Boundaries

Ethnographers undergo a series of steps to get into their field sites and develop relationships with their participants, and once there they must constantly work to maintain and manage these relationships. The experience starts with "getting in," or contacting or getting introduced to a social group's members or leaders to obtain permission to conduct research on them. Following this basic but crucial step is establishing trust and a rapport with participants through communication. For ethnographers who study people who are from different backgrounds from them and identify with different groups, key obstacles in the way of communication and understanding are the socially constructed boundaries and stratifying categories that create social distance. Along with establishing trust, fieldworkers must learn how to cross social boundaries and balance social closeness and critical distance between them and their participants.

Many urban ethnographers have been faced with this obstacle and the issues that emerge from it, and many have reflected on its importance in their work. Among the social boundaries that fieldworkers have had to cross are ethnicity (William Foote Whyte), race (Elliot Liebow, Carol Stack, Sudhir Venkatesh), gender (Sherri Cavan), and age (Javier Auyero and Debora Swistun), with other categories such as class combining with these to increase social distance. Among the many issues that arise from crossing boundaries featured in these readings are the limits of immersion, the importance for ethnographers to use their own social identities for data collection within the field site, and the usefulness in reflecting on how participants understand their role in the field. Elliot Liebow discovers that while he managed to get close to and gain the trust of many of the poor black corner men in the Washington, D.C. neighborhood that he studied, the social category of race remained a salient quality in his relationships with them. He concludes that fieldwork allows people from diverse backgrounds to get close to each other to the point of touching, while boundaries ultimately prevent researchers from completely immersing themselves in these populations. Both Carol Stack and Sherri Cavan use categories through which they self-identify (young motherhood and gender, respectively) to overcome limitations that other social boundaries create for them in their field sites. By reflecting on how his participants in a Chicago housing project interpreted him and his fieldwork as an academic "hustle," Sudhir Venkatesh learns the impact of his immersion on his relationships and is able to reinforce his finding of the hustle metaphor as a central organizing principle in the community. For many ethnographers, crossing boundaries serves as an important challenge for establishing and managing relationships with people in the field. Overcoming social distance while maintaining critical distance between them and their participants also has important implications for data collection.

Doing the Right Thing

Ethics is a central aspect of all empirical research that involves collecting data from people. Since ethnographers collect their data from sustained participation in people's lives and from developing and managing relationships, they must be careful that their decisions in the field do not cause their participants harm or put them at risk. Among the potential harms that people could experience from participating in an ethnographic study are emotional and psychological damage, such as from recalling traumatic episodes or sharing sensitive information, reputational damage, such as to one's occupational and family status, and even the risk of imprisonment and deportation, such as in studies on criminals and undocumented immigrants. Ethnographers must clearly communicate the nature of their project to their participants, and ensure that their decisions in the field during their interactions and outside the field when they are analyzing and writing up their data protect their participants from harm.

Like all fieldworkers urban ethnographers face and must contend with ethical dilemmas that arise from their interactions. They also attempt to minimize potential sources of harm through their project's design. Like the subject of ethics itself, this section features works that are intended to spark discussion and debate. As Laud Humphreys argues in defense of his decisions, what is and what is not the right thing to do while in the field is situational and not clear-cut. Jeff Ferrell defends his own participation in illegal activities by minimizing them (crimes against property, not people) and emphasizing the importance of directly experiencing the behaviors of participants for gaining an understanding of their social world and testing their claims about their own behavior. Randol Contreras, on the other hand, emphatically chooses to not engage in the illegal activities of his participants, which consist of personal theft and violence, while highlighting the importance of maintaining confidentiality and critical distance from them. While the ethical perspectives of other actors factor into ethnographic research, ethnographers are ultimately responsible for ensuring that participants are not harmed because of their involvement in their projects.

* * *

Ethnography presents sociologists with a unique set of methodological tools to analyze social worlds, and urban ethnographers have used them to examine complex urban issues, demystify city settings, and portray misunderstood and misrepresented groups in ways that provide details and explanations that stretch beyond common conceptions and stereotypes. I hope these readings guide and encourage students to discuss and reflect on their themes and issues and ultimately to follow in their authors' footsteps into the city's innumerable social worlds.

NOTE

1. One of the most well-known recent debates occurred in a review symposium in the *American Journal of Sociology* in 2002. Sociologist and ethnographer Loic Wacquant critically reviewed three recent books in urban ethnography, Mitchell Duneier's *Sidewalk* (1999), Elijah Anderson's *Code of the Street* (1999), and Katherine Newman's *No Shame in My Game* (1999). Along with criticisms of each piece that were as harsh as they were specific and, at times, selective in terms of evidence, Wacquant also argued that each exemplified an American style of ethnographic research that favors moral tales of heroic figures, ignores such subjects as social class, power, and the state, and disconnects theory from evidence. Each author was given the opportunity to respond to Wacquant's lengthy essay (Anderson 2002; Duneier 2002; Newman 2002), and each takes exception to his specific critiques of their own work as well as to his larger points about urban ethnography in the United States.

REFERENCES

Abbott, A. 1997. "Of Time and Space: The Contemporary Relevance of the Chicago School," *Social Force*, 79, 4: 1149–1182.

Anderson, E. 1999. *Code of the Street: Decency, Violence, and the Moral Life of the Inner City*. New York: W.W. Norton.

Anderson, E. 2002. "The Ideologically Driven Critique," *American Journal of Sociology*, 107, 6: 1533–1550.

Anderson, E. 2009. "Introduction," *Ethnography*, 10, 4: 371–374.

Anderson, N. 1923. *The Hobo: The Sociology of the Homeless Man*. Chicago: University of Chicago Press.

Auyero, J. & Swistun, D., 2009. "The Compound and the Neighborhood," *Flammable: Environmental Suffering in an Argentine Shantytown*. Oxford: Oxford University Press: 28–31; 32–44.

Bearman, P. 2005. *Doormen*. Chicago: University of Chicago Press.

Bell, M.M. 1994. *Childerley: Nature and Morality in a Country Village*. Chicago: University of Chicago Press.

Bender, C. 2003. "What We Talk about When We Talk about Religion," *Heaven's Kitchen: Living Religion at God's Love We Deliver*. Chicago: University of Chicago Press: 92–103.

Bourgois, P. 1995. "Families and Children in Pain," *In Search of Respect: Selling Crack in El Barrio*. Cambridge: Cambridge University Press: 259–267; 272–276.

Brown-Saracino, J. 2009. *A Neighborhood That Never Changes: Gentrification, Social Preservation, and the Search for Authenticity*. Chicago: University of Chicago Press.

Bulmer, M. 1986. *The Chicago School of Sociology*. Chicago: University of Chicago Press.

Cavan, S. 1966. "The Marketplace Bar," *Liquor License: An Ethnography of Bar Behavior*. Chicago: Aldine Publishing Company: 171–177; 193–200.

Contreras, R. 2009. "'Damn, Yo—Who's That Girl?' An Ethnographic Analysis of Masculinity in Drug Robberies," *Journal of Contemporary Ethnography*, 38, 4: 465–466; 474–483.

Cressey, P.G. 1932. *The Taxi-Dance Hall: A Sociological Study in Commercialized Recreation in City Life*. Chicago: University of Chicago Press.

de la Pradelle, M. 2004. *Market Day in Provence*. Chicago: University of Chicago Press.

Duneier, M. 1999. "A Christmas on Sixth Avenue," *Sidewalk*. New York: Farrar, Straus and Giroux: 253–256; 260–279.

Duneier, M. 2002. "What Kind of Combat Sport Is Sociology?" *American Journal of Sociology*, 107, 6: 1551–1576.

Emerson, R.M. (ed.) 2001. *Contemporary Field Research: Perspectives and Formulations*. Prospect Heights, IL: Waveland Press, Inc.

Emerson, R.M. 2004. "Introduction," *The ANNALS of the American Academy of Political and Social Science*, 595: 8–13.

Erikson, K. 1976. *Everything in its Path: Destruction of Community in the Buffalo Creek Flood*. New York: Simon & Schuster.

Ferrell, J. 1993. "Denver Graffiti and the Syndicate Scene," *Crimes of Style: Urban Graffiti and the Politics of Criminality*. Boston: Northeastern University Press: 21–26; 49–53.

Fine, G.A. 1996. *Kitchens: The Culture of Restaurant Work*. Berkeley: University of California Press.

Gans, H.J. 1962. "Redevelopment of the West End," *The Urban Villagers: Group and Class in the Life of Italian-Americans*. New York: The Free Press: 281; 288–298.

Gans, H.J. 2009. "The Chicago School and the Roots of Urban Ethnography: An Intergenerational Conversation with Gerald D. Jaynes, David E. Apter, Herbert J. Gans, William Kornblum, Ruth Horowitz, James F. Short, Jr., Gerald Suttles and Robert E. Washington," *Ethnography*, 10, 4: 375–396.

Garot, R. 2010. *Who You Claim: Performing Gang Identity in School and on the Streets*. New York: New York University Press.

Goffman, E. 1961. *Asylums: Essays on the Social Situation of Mental Patients and Other Inmates*. Garden City: Anchor Books.

Grazian, D. 2003. "Like Therapy: The Blues Club as a Haven," *Blue Chicago: The Search for Authenticity in Urban Blues Clubs*. Chicago: University of Chicago Press: 87–90; 105–116.

Hochschild, A.R. 1983. *The Managed Heart: Commercialization of Human Feeling*. Berkeley: University of California Press.

Humphreys, L. 1975. "The People Next Door," *Tearoom Trade: Impersonal Sex in Public Places*. Piscataway: Aldine Transactions: 106–111; 114–122.

Kasinitz, P. (ed.) 1995. *Metropolis: Center and Symbol of Our Times*. New York: New York University Press.

Katz, J. 1982. *Poor People's Lawyers in Transition*. New Brunswick: Rutgers.

Katz, J. 1988. *Seductions of Crime: Moral and Sensual Attractions in Doing Evil*. New York: Basic Books.

Katz, J. 1997. "Ethnography's Warrants," *Sociological Methods & Research*, 25: 391–423.

Katz, J. 1999. *How Emotions Work*. Chicago: University of Chicago Press.

Khan, S.R. 2010. *Privilege: The Making of an Adolescent Elite at St. Paul's School*. Princeton: Princeton University Press.

Kornblum, W. 1974. *Blue Collar Community*. Chicago: University of Chicago Press.

Liebow, E. 1967. "Men and Jobs," *Tally's Corner: A Study of Negro Streetcorner Men*. Boston: Little, Brown, and Company: 61–71.

Lloyd, R. 2006. "The Celebrity Neighborhood," *Neo-Bohemia: Art and Commerce in the Postindustrial City*. New York: Routledge: 123–143.

Marti, G. 2008. *Hollywood Faith: Holiness, Prosperity, and Ambition in a Los Angeles Church*. New Brunswick: Rutgers University Press.

Mattson, G. 2007. "Urban Ethnography's 'Saloon Problem' and its Challenge to Public Sociology," *City & Community*, 6, 2: 75–94.

McKinney, J.C. 1966. *Constructive Topology and Social Theory*. New York: Appleton-Century-Crofts.

Moore, E.C. 1897. "The Social Value of the Saloon," *American Journal of Sociology*, 3: 1–12.

Moskos, P. 2008. "The Corner: Life on the Streets," *Cop in the Hood: My Year Policing Baltimore's Eastern District*. Princeton: Princeton University Press: 64–66; 77–80; 83–88.

Myerhoff, B. 1978. *Number Our Days: A Triumph of Continuity and Culture Among Jewish Old People in an Urban Ghetto*. New York: Simon & Schuster.

Nelson, T. 2004. *Every Time I Feel the Spirit: Religious Experience and Ritual in an African American Church*. New York: New York University Press.

Newman, K. 1999. *No Shame in My Game: The Working Poor in the InnerCity*. New York: Russell Sage Foundation.

Newman, K. 2002. "No Shame: The View from the Left Bank," *American Journal of Sociology*, 107, 6: 1577–1599.

Ocejo, R.E. Forthcoming. *About Last Night: Nightlife, Conflict, and Community on the Lower East Side*. Princeton, NJ: Princeton University Press.

Park, R.E. 1929. "The City as a Social Laboratory," in T.V. Smith & L.D. White (eds.), *Chicago: An Experiment in Social Science Research*. Chicago: University of Chicago Press: 19.

Pattillo, M. 2008. "The Black Bourgeoisie Meets the Truly Disadvantaged," *Black on the Block: The Politics of Race and Class in the City*. Chicago: University of Chicago Press: 87–100.

Perez, G. 2004. "*Los de Afuera*, Transnationalism, and the Cultural Politics of Identity," *The Near Northwest Side Story*. Berkeley: University of California Press: 92–94; 96–110.

Shaw, C.R. 1931. *The Jack-Roller: A Delinquent Boy's Own Story*. Chicago: University of Chicago Press.

Small, A.W. 1896. "Scholarship and Social Agitation," *American Journal of Sociology*, 1: 564–582.

Small, M.L. 2009. "'How Many Cases Do I Need?': On Science and the Logic of Case Selection in Field-based Research," *Ethnography*, 10, 1: 5–38.

Stack, C. 1974. "The Flats," and "Swapping: What Goes Around Comes Around," *All Our Kin*. New York: Basic Books: 11–16; 32–43.

Suttles, G.D. 1968. *The Social Order of the Slum: Ethnicity and Territory in the Inner City*. Chicago: University of Chicago Press.

Thomas, W.I. & Znaniecki, F.W. 1918. *The Polish Peasant in Europe and America: Monograph of an Immigrant Group*. Boston: Richard G. Badger, The Gorham Press.

Trimbur, L. 2011. "'Tough Love': Mediation and Articulation in the Urban Boxing Gym," *Ethnography*, 12, 3: 334–336; 339–343; 346–350.

Van Maanen, J. 1978. "On Watching the Watchers," in P.K. Manning & J. Van Maanen (eds.), *Policing: A View From the Streets*. Pacific Palisades: Goodyear: 309–349.

Venkatesh, S. 2002. "'Doin' the Hustle': Constructing the Ethnographer in the American Ghetto," *Ethnography*, 3, 1: 91–92; 96–103.

Vidich, A.L. & Bensman, J. 1958. *Small Town in Mass Society: Class, Power and Religion in a Rural Community*. Princeton: Princeton University Press.

Wacquant, L. 2002. "Scrutinizing the Street: Poverty, Morality, and the Pitfalls of Urban Ethnography," *American Journal of Sociology*, 107, 6: 1468–1532.

Whyte, W.F. 1943. "Doc and His Boys," *Street Corner Society: The Social Structure of an Italian Slum*. Chicago: University of Chicago Press: 14–25.

Wirth, L. 1928. *The Ghetto*. Chicago: University of Chicago Press.

Wynn, J.R. 2005. "Guiding Practices: Storytelling Tricks for Reproducing the Urban Landscape," *Qualitative Sociology*, 28, 4: 399–400; 404–413.

Zorbaugh, W.H. 1929. *The Gold Coast and the Slum: A Sociological Study of Chicago's Near North Side*. Chicago: University of Chicago Press.

PART I

*D*ata Collection Strategies

SECTION I

Being There, Up Close

The sections in Part I feature readings that deal with two data collection strategies that urban ethnographers choose, specifically strategies that represent being immersed in a field site. The decisions fieldworkers make in designing their projects play a key role in the type and quality of the data they collect and analyze. The theme of this section is the importance of spending long periods of time in the field with participants. It specifically focuses on ethnographers who decide to live in the same neighborhoods and communities as the people they are studying, the benefits to data collection that this decision provides, and the obstacles they face in doing so. Such a theme would sound unusual to anthropologists, since living among participants, traditionally tribes and other indigenous groups in remote villages and rural areas in non-Western societies, has been a common disciplinary requirement in anthropology since its inception. And many anthropologists have used their training to focus on and live within urban environments in Western cities, some of which are featured in this volume (Liebow and Stack, Chapters 13 and 14) and in this section (Bourgois, Chapter 2). Living with the people they are studying is less a decision for anthropologists than it is a foregone conclusion.

But sociologists who use field methods do not necessarily face this disciplinary pressure. Much of sociological research uses quantitative forms of inquiry or other qualitative methods such as interviewing and content analysis. Still, many of sociology's urban ethnographers have used the data collection strategy of living among participants to great effect, that is, in a manner that turns them into an expert of the setting and its social worlds who can then communicate the experience of "being there" upon leaving the field. The principal idea behind choosing to "be there, up close" for urban ethnographers is to learn details about a population, a place, and a culture that they would not from just being there most of the time or only at times when the "action" takes place. Neighborhoods and communities contain their own hidden rhythms that field researchers must directly observe and experience to fully understand. Behavior in the "backstage" areas (Goffman 1959) of private homes and leisure settings (and even the "backstage" time of night or off hours) often offers deeper insight into the public "front stage" lives people lead. As David Grazian (Chapter 8, this volume) notes in his research on the search for authenticity in the social worlds of blues clubs, it is in private spaces or backstage regions that "we reveal what we imagine to be our most authentic selves to our intimates and confidants" (2003, 11). Ethnographers also regularly seek out the back areas where their participants engage in "real" interactions, or those that reflect deeper meanings beyond their public displays. Embedding themselves in a field site for a sustained amount of time allows ethnographers to focus and narrow their analytical lens to reveal otherwise hidden dimensions of their field site and population. It provides a unique angle for collecting original data.

Many scholars have used being there as a central tenet of ethnographic research. Some have focused on its importance for data collection. In his introduction to a 2004 special journal issue entitled "Being Here and Being There: Fieldwork Encounters and Ethnographic Discoveries," Robert Emerson points out the theme of discovery, or "'bring back the news' from unknown or misknown social worlds" (8), that ethnographers seek to accomplish by being among specific groups of people. As he states, this falls within the Chicago School tradition of fieldwork that places researchers up close to their participants. Andrew Abbott (1997) extols Chicago School scholars' assertion that "no social fact makes any sense abstracted from its context in social (and often geographic) space and social time" (1152) as a significant intellectual foundation in sociological thought and research. By studying social facts within actual locations, sociologists uncover and develop theoretical explanations for the "constellation of forces" (1160) that influence social life.

Others have examined the importance of being there for analyzing data. Clifford Geertz (1988) entitles the first chapter in his book on anthropological writing "being there," arguing that an ethnographer's goal should be to provide readers with the experience of a place and its people. Ethnographic writing for Geertz is more than just reporting from the field. It is where "thick description," or the researchers' interpretations and explications of people's meanings and social contexts, and the scientific endeavor of ethnography take place (see Geertz 1973). Reacting to the critiques of fieldwork within their discipline as a form of power over and domination of objectified groups (see Clifford and Marcus 1986; Marcus and Fischer 1986), anthropologists John Borneman and Abdellah Hammoudi (2009) focus in their volume on the practices of anthropology, rather than issues dealt with by textual analysis. Instead of continuing with or adding to the discursive analyses of the discipline, they instead look at how these critiques have affected experienced-based field research. While in need of self-reflection, Borneman and Hammoudi argue that looking at "being there," as a set of knowledge- and power-generating practices, yields important insights into understanding such methodological concerns as truth, reflexivity, and objectification.

While being there is a fundamental element of ethnographic research, we should not forget that living among participants is a decision that fieldworkers make, not a requirement for obtaining good data. For some ethnographers doing so may not be possible or even necessary for answering the questions they have about their social problem or population. The nature of the field site and participants often factor into a researcher's decision. For instance, Jonathan Wynn (Chapter 9, this volume; also see 2011) studies the practices and career paths of walking tour guides by going along on their tours and extensively interviewing them (and by, as we will see later in this volume, becoming a tour guide and leading walking tours himself). While settings are integral to them, walking tours traverse multiple places in the city, and tour guides are obviously not a spatially definable group. Following his intellectual focus, Wynn's strategy for being there places him squarely in situ, on the actual tours, where he can experience and examine how the guides put their attitudes toward their work into practice on the city streets.

But for urban ethnographers such as those featured in this section, living among participants was a decision that allowed them to understand their subjects' lives within their social contexts more clearly, to blend into the environment more easily, and to experience life in the place. Each of the following works deals with a specific population living in a neighborhood that is either mostly homogenous or experiencing a transition, such as displacement or gentrification. Among the themes of living with participants that these pieces feature are the benefits of discovering unknown and hidden meanings from experiencing daily life in a neighborhood, becoming too embedded in the lives of those studied such that a researcher's critical distance and objectivity are compromised, and the potential issues of conducting research in multiple field sites.

This section starts with a piece by Herbert Gans from his classic work *The Urban Villagers*. Trained in fieldwork at the University of Chicago in the post-World War II "Second Chicago School" (Fine 1995), Gans ultimately received his Ph.D. in city planning. He used his background in ethnographic research to shed new light on what was an important issue in cities at the time. From 1957 to 1958 Gans lived in Boston's West End neighborhood, which was predominantly first- and second-generation working-class Italian. The city slated it for demolition and redevelopment after declaring it a slum in 1953. An urban renewal strategy, slum clearance was a federally-supported attempt to improve city conditions through the demolition of existing buildings, the relocation of their residents, and the redevelopment of the area with new projects. City planners and policymakers labeled areas slums based on the presence of such physical conditions as substandard housing, which they assumed gave rise to deviant behavior. But Gans noticed that the *social* conditions of the people in the neighborhood did not factor into their assessments or plans. As he states in the book's preface:

> Contemporary city planning and professions such as education, social work, public recreation, public health, medicine, and psychiatry . . . use middle-class values to help low-income populations solve their problems and improve their living conditions. As a sociologist and city planner, I wanted to test the validity of this approach. I wanted to know what a slum was like, and how it felt to live in one, because many planners and caretakers believe that it is the source of much of the low-income population's problem.
>
> (1962, ix–x)[1]

By experiencing life in the West End, as no city official or developer in a position of power had done, Gans discovers that not only is it not a slum (as the book's title suggests, he describes it as an "urban village," or a small community within but separate from the city), but that the Italian residents did not possess deviant forms of middle-class values. Rather, they had their own working-class values that derived in part from a lack of access to the city's resources. Their urban village situation of a community based on family, peer groups, and social class rather than ethnicity or an ethnic identity contributed to their reaction to urban renewal.

The piece featured in this volume deals with this very issue. Most of *The Urban Villagers* is a report that Gans made on life in the neighborhood, such as the importance of family and peer groups, not on urban renewal. But the Epilogue, where this piece comes from, focuses on how residents failed to take action against the relocation and redevelopment that loomed over their community throughout the fieldwork period. Gans finds that residents mostly went on with their normal daily lives despite impending displacement. They were confused by the redevelopment process, which bred skepticism that it would ever even take place, and felt socially disconnected from the outsider community leaders who spoke for them against slum clearance.

Being and living there among the working-class Italians at a vulnerable time in their lives affected Gans. Later in the Epilogue he remarks on what living and conducting research in the neighborhood did to change his feelings toward the people and their impending relocation: "I began to develop that identification with the people, and sympathy for their problems which is experienced by many participant-observers" (1962, 305). From living with and learning from the West End's residents, Gans used the sociological findings in his report to take action and speak informatively on their behalf. Getting "up close" did not just result in an informative monograph on the importance of peer groups and social class in the formation of a conception of community that provides an explanation for their relative inaction in the face of displacement. Gans also used his empirical knowledge to "persuade renewal officials to reverse any still reversible policies to help the West Enders who were about to be displaced" (2007, 232). His example demonstrates the power and potential of this data collection strategy, while also raising the issues of maintaining critical distance and intervening in the lives of participants.

"I was forced into crack against my will," states Philippe Bourgois in the first sentence of his book on crack dealers in New York City's mostly Puerto Rican neighborhood of East Harlem, or "El Barrio," in *In Search of Respect*. Bourgois moved into a tenement building in El Barrio in 1985 to study poverty and ethnic segregation in the middle of a wealthy city (in fact, the Census tracts immediately south of East Harlem, on the Upper East Side where Bourgois happened to grow up, rank among the nation's wealthiest). The underground drug economy was one of many themes he wished to explore. It was not long after he moved into the neighborhood and actually lived among the real conditions that statistics of poverty and violence represent that Bourgois realized how important crack dealing and use were in shaping daily life on the street. His opening line is an example of the influence that living in the neighborhoods of the people they are studying has on urban ethnographers.

Highly character-driven, *In Search of Respect* focuses in particular on two crack dealers named Primo and Caesar. Bourgois used his tape recorder to capture his experiences and conversations with them, on the street, in the Game Room (their crackhouse), and in schoolyards. The narrative regularly pauses as guns fire in the distance and the two men drink and do drugs. Since he makes himself a central character, we learn much about the neighborhood from Bourgois's retelling of how he gained entry in the crack dealers' ring. As one of the only white men on the street the dealers assume he is either an undercover cop or a drug addict. After getting introduced through a neighbor, over time he gradually earns the men's trust and gets close to them and their drug-dealing enterprise.[2] He gets so close, in fact, that he sometimes challenges the men's self-reflections to their faces (e.g. 1995, 116–117). The closeness and familiarity allow him to probe deeper into the hidden meanings they hold about their lives. Bourgois also breaks an ethnographic aim of remaining objective and not making moral judgments about participants' behavior. In an especially poignant moment, Caesar and Primo brag with their typical macho attitude about how they used to beat special education students in school. Bourgois, whose infant son had just been diagnosed with cerebral palsy, rebukes them for their behavior and fights back tears (1995, 188–189).

This section's piece focuses on how children and mothers deal with the realities of living in a neighborhood where crack is a way of life. From living in El Barrio Bourgois learns that children are important to its inhabitants' daily life as well as clear examples of the impact crack has on them. He introduces Angel and Junior, two youths who struggle with the conditions of their segregated neighborhood, and Maria, Primo's girlfriend, who is overjoyed by her pregnancy despite Primo's impending court case and lack of legal employment, which will potentially make her and her baby's lives a struggle from the outset. Bourgois brings his infant son around with him in the neighborhood, and the affection that strangers show heartens him. However, overall the chapter presents a sad, difficult environment for children and mothers to achieve and gain respect.

Urban ethnographers do not just study the conditions and lives of people in poor neighborhoods. They also focus on how neighborhoods are changing and how their residents deal with these changes. Many, for instance, have been attracted to the phenomenon of gentrification that has characterized cities around the world since the late twentieth century. Gentrification is the process of middle-class people moving into and investing in lower-income neighborhoods and industrial areas, which often results in the displacement of existing residents, businesses, and cultures (Brown-Saracino 2010). In many cases it has been artists who have first moved into these areas and signaled their transformation from low-income slums to hip and profitable destinations (Zukin 1982). But how do residents experience these changes? How do these neighborhoods fit within the larger structural changes taking place in the contemporary city?

To answer these questions, Richard Lloyd decided to move to Wicker Park, a gentrifying neighborhood in Chicago with a popular arts scene, to examine this social problem in the 1990s and early 2000s. He coins the term "neo-bohemia" "as a heuristic to examine the changes that took place in Wicker Park during the 1990s and beyond" (2006, 12). Neo-bohemia refers to a neighborhood that continues the urban bohemian tradition of living the artists' lifestyle by linking the aesthetics, tastes, flexible work ethic, and cultural products of local artists with the postindustrial economy of the contemporary city. Lloyd shows how global corporations benefit from the content that local artists produce and how such figures as city leaders and real estate investors benefit from the interest that the neighborhood has garnered as a result.

Living in the neighborhood allowed Lloyd to discover how Wicker Park functioned as an artists' enclave and how it transformed into a neighborhood of cultural production. In this piece he argues that bars, clubs, cafes, and restaurants initially served as community venues for artists and artistic works. Today these leisure spaces are themed around Wicker Park's "juxtaposition of grit and glamour" and have helped transform the neighborhood into a destination for nightlife consumption and entertainment for young adults around Chicago. Unlike Bourgois, Lloyd does not reflect on his position in the neighborhood (in fact, without a discussion of methods in the book, readers wouldn't know with certainty that he lived there) and as a character he recedes into the background of the narrative, presenting his descriptive experiences and the neighborhood's people and places in the foreground. However, in line with Geertz's (1988) discussion of the importance of ethnographic writing, Lloyd demonstrates in this piece to be a well-informed authority on the neighborhood and its people. The details, data, and perspectives he presents could only be gained through extensive participation, careful observation, and deep embeddedness.

We have already heard a bit about Mary Pattillo's work on gentrification in this volume's Introduction. While Lloyd focuses on the experiences of gentrifying artists in his study on gentrification, Pattillo looks at the conflicts between African-American gentrifiers and existing residents. Her book raises a significant issue among urban ethnographers who study this topic. When field workers, who are often well-educated members of the middle class, move into a gentrifying neighborhood, they contribute to its transformation. As a black woman moving into a black neighborhood, Pattillo is sensitive to and reflective of her status as a "middleman," or what she defines as those middle-class blacks who "[span] the space between established centers of white economic and political power and the needs of a down but not out black neighborhood" (2008, 3). In 1998 she buys a house in her field site, North Kenwood-Oakland, which in 1990 was the poorest community area in Chicago. As she notes, her purchase contributes to the rising real estate prices in the area that threaten to displace the existing working-class residents (her house's sellers made a 44 percent return on their investment after just two years of ownership, and Pattillo was not ripped off). Pattillo becomes simultaneously an objective participant observer, a gentrifying homeowner, and an active member of community groups whose aim is to advise and monitor issues in the neighborhood such as housing and schools. Like Gans, she uses her privileged position as an informed academic and the knowledge she gains from her data and theorizing to bring to bear on those decisions that would negatively impact low-income blacks in the neighborhood. However, she also finds herself sometimes supporting these measures, or favoring "the man," such as when she votes against increasing density levels for housing, which would raise real estate prices but reduce traffic.[3] In this case her own values interfere with her greater desire to improve conditions for existing residents.

In this piece Pattillo analyzes the complex relationship between the "black bourgeoisie" and the "truly disadvantaged" in North Kenwood-Oakland. She borrows these terms from the classic works of E. Franklin Frazier (1957) and William Julius Wilson (1987), respectively, but argues that neither truly explains how "race, class, and place" (87) intersect through heated interaction over critical urban issues. Pattillo provides several examples of what happens when middlemen and middlewomen, who return to the neighborhood confident in their status as role models and in their ability to improve conditions for poor blacks, meet disadvantaged residents, who react defensively to the threatening changes. The result is an examination of core debates in the black community, of which Pattillo and her experiences living in North Kenwood-Oakland are examples.

The final piece in this section is an example of "multi-sited ethnography," or fieldwork that "moves out from the single sites and local situations of conventional ethnographic research designs to examine the circulation of cultural meanings, objects, and identities in diffuse time-space" (Marcus 1998, 79). The classic ethnographic monograph predominantly features a researcher studying a single field. Intense globalization has put people, goods, cultures, and ideas in rapid motion, while borders that traditionally separate these phenomena have become highly porous. Ethnographers must often examine the linkages and exchanges across multiple locations to fully understand a social problem and a group of people. Ulf Hannerz (2003) points out that multi-sited ethnography tests some of the assumptions behind the practices of being there. For instance, working in multiple fields potentially creates issues of breadth and depth for fieldworkers. If we accept, as classic interpretations of ethnography assert, that a researcher's goal is to study the "entire culture and social life" (202) of a people, then would time traditionally devoted to a single site that gets broken up to cover two or three diminish an ethnographer's experience and interpretation of the place and the people's relationship to their social context? Hannerz concludes that it depends, but cites his own work on the lives of foreign news correspondents as an example of a multi-sited ethnographic project for which such an issue did not arise. He was more interested in examining the people who work within the global news landscape, focusing on correspondents in three cities, and not the "entire culture and social life" of those places.

In probably no other subfield is multi-sited ethnography more relevant than immigration and migration research, particularly those studies that focus on issues of transnationalism, or the connections and lines of exchange immigrant groups form between their home and host countries. In her book, *The Near Northwest Side Story*, Gina Perez undertakes a multi-sited ethnographic study on Puerto Rican migrants who have established strong links and social networks between Chicago and San Sebastián, in Puerto Rico. Set in motion by economic need and facilitated by the ease of entry into the United States, Puerto Ricans began migrating to cities like New York and Chicago in the 1940s. Since then several generations of families have established roots in both American urban neighborhoods and Puerto Rican towns, with considerable movement and exchange between the two places. By choosing to live in Humboldt Park, in Chicago, and in San Sebastián, Perez sets out to examine how these migrants deal with issues of family and identity and manage their often precarious economic circumstances as they travel between and maintain ties in both societies.

This piece comes from a chapter that focuses specifically on transnationalism and migrants' struggles that result from being one of *"los de afuera,"* Spanish for "those from outside." Locals in San Sebastián use this term derogatorily, but it also represents a discourse that they use to "resist the ways in which 'progreso' (progress) threatens 'authentic' or 'traditional' Puerto Rican culture" (2004, 96). The cultural attitudes of resistance that greet migrants cause conflicts and uncertainty in their lives upon their return, such as in situations concerning gender roles and identity. In addition, while migrating to American cities provides enormous economic opportunities for Perez's families, they uphold a belief that Chicago is no place to raise their children, which lures them back home. In spite of their admiration for the child-raising benefits of Puerto Rico, their experiences in an American metropolis have altered their understanding of who they are. By living among Puerto Rican families in two countries, Perez uncovers the impacts that migrating between them has on their lives. Without "being there . . . and there . . . and there" (Hannerz 2003), we miss knowing how important linkages influence people's experiences and help shape social contexts.

Being there and experiencing a place provides ethnographers with the data they need to explain a group's situation and make connections between them and larger structures in society. Living in the same neighborhoods as participants is one among several data collection strategies that exemplifies immersion in a field site. We then turn in the next section to another strategy that raises several more issues of being up close to participants.

NOTES

1. Unless noted, all quotes from an author's featured book or article (or, of course, from another source entirely) do not appear in this volume. I intend such quotes to provide background on the piece and the author as part of the summary of the work and discussion of the issues that pertain to the section's theme.
2. Bourgois's book is an example of a work that features and engages with each of this volume's four major themes. Here is a brief mention of "getting in" and establishing trust, which will be taken up in Section I of Part II.
3. Pattillo directly confronts these issues in a section entitled "Middleman Me" (2008, 141–146).

REFERENCES

Abbott, A. 1997. "Of Time and Space: The Contemporary Relevance of the Chicago School." *Social Force*, 79, 4: 1149–1182.

Borneman, J. & Hammoudi, A. (eds.) 2009. *Being There: The Fieldwork Encounter and the Making of Truth.* Berkeley: University of California Press.

Bourgois, P. 1995. "Families and Children in Pain," *In Search of Respect: Selling Crack in El Barrio.* Cambridge: University of Cambridge Press: 259–267; 272–276.

Brown-Saracino, J. (ed.) 2010. *The Gentrification Debates.* New York: Routledge.

Clifford, J. & Marcus, G.E. (eds.) 1986. *The Poetics and Politics of Ethnography.* Berkeley: University of California Press.

Emerson, R.M. 2004. "Introduction." *The ANNALS of the American Academy of Political and Social Science*, 595: 8–13.

Fine, G.A. (ed.) 1995. *A Second Chicago School? The Development of a Postwar American Sociology.* Chicago: University of Chicago Press.

Frazier, E.F. 1957. *The Black Bourgeoisie.* Glencoe, IL: Free Press.

Gans, H.J. 1962. "Redevelopment of the West End," *The Urban Villagers: Group and Class in the Life of Italian-Americans*. New York: The Free Press: 281; 288–298.

Gans, H.J. 2007. "Remembering *The Urban Villagers* and its Place in Intellectual Time: A Response to Zukin," *City & Community*, 6, 3: 231–236.

Geertz, C. 1973. *The Interpretation of Cultures*. New York: Basic Books.

Geertz, C. 1988. *Works and Lives: The Anthropologist as Author*. Palo Alto: Stanford University Press.

Goffman, E. 1959. *The Presentation of Self in Everyday Life*. Garden City: Doubleday.

Grazian, D. 2003. "Like Therapy: The Blues Club as a Haven," *Blue Chicago: The Search for Authenticity in Urban Blues Clubs*. Chicago: University of Chicago Press: 87–90; 105–116.

Hannerz, U. 2003. "Being there . . . and there . . . and there! Reflections on Multi-Site Ethnography," *Ethnography*, 4, 2: 201–216.

Lloyd, R. 2006. "The Celebrity Neighborhood," *Neo-Bohemia: Art and Commerce in the Postindustrial City*. New York: Routledge: 123–143.

Marcus, G.E. 1998. *Ethnography Through Thick and Thin*. Princeton: Princeton University Press.

Marcus, G.E. & Fischer, M. 1986. *Anthropology as Cultural Critique*. Chicago: University of Chicago Press.

Pattillo, M. 2008. "The Black Bourgeoisie Meets the Truly Disadvantaged," *Black on the Block: The Politics of Race and Class in the City*. Chicago: University of Chicago Press: 87–100.

Perez, G. 2004. "*Los de Afuera*, Transnationalism, and the Cultural Politics of Identity," *The Near Northwest Side Story*. Berkeley: University of California Press: 92–94; 96–110.

Wilson, W.J. 1987. *The Truly Disadvantaged: The Inner City, the Underclass, and Public Policy*. Chicago: University of Chicago Press.

Wynn, J.M. 2011. *The Tour Guide: Walking and Talking New York*. Chicago: University of Chicago Press.

Zukin, S. 1982. *Loft Living: Culture and Capital in Urban Change*. New Brunswick: Rutgers University Press.

CHAPTER 1

Redevelopment of the West End

Herbert J. Gans

INTRODUCTION

When I began this study, the West End was facing destruction as a slum under the urban redevelopment program. For more than seven years, federal and local agencies had been preparing the plans, and getting the necessary approvals for tearing down the old structures and for building a new neighborhood—not for the West Enders, but for high-income tenants of luxury apartment buildings. One of the original reasons for making a study was to discover how the West Enders as individuals and as a community were reacting to the eventual—and then imminent—destruction of their neighborhood

Had the West Enders exhibited the expected stress, the book might have dealt with these phenomena in much greater detail.[1] *As it turned out, however*—for reasons to be described below—most *West Enders did not react in this fashion and continued to follow their normal routines.*[2] Because of this and because of my greater interest in the workings of the peer group society, the discussion of redevelopment has been limited to this epilogue.

THE WEST ENDERS' PERCEPTION OF THE REDEVELOPMENT PROCESS

To the West Enders, the many years between the announcement that the area would be redeveloped and the actual clearing of their neighborhood appeared quite differently than it did to the city and its officials. No one with whom I talked was quite sure when the West Enders had first heard about the plans for redeveloping their neighborhood. The Planning Board's recommendation in 1949 had been made public, of course, and the press had also carried stories of the preliminary planning studies that had begun in 1951. At that time, the residents were opposed to the redevelopment, but did not feel themselves sufficiently threatened to be alarmed.

The initial announcement, however, did have some more important consequences. During the postwar era, the West End—like most other inner city districts—had begun to lose some of its recently married couples to the suburbs. The announcement itself undoubtedly spurred additional moves, and it seems also to have discouraged other people from moving into the West End. Whatever the causes, the vacancy rate in the area began to climb, especially in buildings owned by absentee landlords, who then began to have a change of heart about the redevelopment. Eventually, in fact, they became its most fervent adherents, and in later years urged the city and federal government to hasten the process, since they were losing money on vacant apartments that they could no longer rent.

Tenants, and resident owners whose buildings were still occupied, were almost unanimously opposed to the redevelopment. Some of the tenants in the most dilapidated structures were hopeful that government action would provide them with better places to live. But the vast majority of West Enders had no desire to leave. As I have tried to show throughout the book, they were content to live in the West End, and were willing to overlook some of its physical defects in comparison with its many social advantages. Those who had been born there cited the traditional belief that "the place you're born is where you want to die." Even criticism of the area would sometimes be stilled by the remark, "never disparage a place in which you've grown up." Many of the people who had left the West End at marriage would come back occasionally—if only to shop—and one man whose family had left the area shortly after his birth twenty years earlier insisted that "you always come back to the place of your childhood."

Most people were not very explicit at that time about their feelings toward the area. Since the West End still existed, and since they had never known anything else, they could not estimate how its disappearance might affect them.[5] "What's so good about the West End? We're used to it," was one quite typical comment. Subsequently, however, I heard more anguished remarks that indicated how important the area and its people were to the speaker. In December, 1957, the day after the federal government gave the city the go-ahead, one young Italian man said:

> I wish the world would end tonight. . . . I wish they'd tear the whole damn town down, damn scab town. . . . I'm going to be lost without the West End. Where the hell can I go?

Another West Ender told me: "It isn't right to scatter the community to all four winds. It pulls the heart out of a guy to lose all his friends." Shortly before the taking, a barber in his early sixties ended a discussion of death that was going on in the shop with these comments:

> I'm not afraid to die, but I don't want to. But if they tear the West End down and we are all scattered from all the people I know and that know me, and they wouldn't know where I was, I wouldn't want to die and people not know it.[6]

Perhaps because most people were opposed to the redevelopment, they could not quite believe that it would happen. Over the years, they began to realize that the redevelopment plans were in earnest, but they were—and remained—skeptical that the plans would ever be implemented. Even on the day of the taking, the person just quoted told me: "I don't believe it; I won't believe it till it happens. I'll wait till I get my notice. . . . You'll see, they'll start at the lower end, and they'll never come up here."

There were several reasons for the West Enders' skepticism. *First*, they had considerable difficulty in understanding the complicated parade of preliminary and final approvals, or the tortuous process by which the plans moved back and forth between the Housing Authority, the City Council, the Mayor, the State Housing Board, and the federal Housing and Home Finance Agency. Instead of realizing that each approval was one step in a tested and finite administrative procedure, the West Enders saw it as merely another decision in a seemingly purposeless, erratic, and infinite series. Thus, when the federal housing agency did give its final approval in the winter of 1957, most West Enders did not understand that this was the last step in the process. They recalled that the same agency had approved it several times before, without any visible result. Thus, they felt certain that there would be more meetings, and more decisions, and that twenty-five years later, the West End would still be there.

Their failure to understand the process can be traced back partly to the poor information that they received from the press and the city agencies. The latter, assuming that West Enders understood the nature of the process, did not attempt to describe it in sufficient detail. Moreover, city officials did not see that to West Enders, all government agencies were pretty much the same, and that notions of city-state-federal relationships were strange to them. The West Enders in turn paid little attention to the press releases, and were more receptive to distorted facts and the many rumors that they could hear from friends and neighbors.

Moreover, they noted that official announcements were vague about when things would begin to happen in the West End, and that if estimates were given, they were usually wrong. In January, 1956, for example, the Housing Authority's pamphlet pointed out that it was impossible to predict when the various agencies involved would give their approval, but that it might happen within eight months, and that relocation would begin in the winter of 1956–1957.[7] This estimate turned out to be false.

Nor could West Enders really conceive of the possibility that the area would be torn down. They had watched the demolition of parts of the North End for the Central Artery—the city's expressway system—and while they disapproved, they realized that a highway was of public benefit and could not be opposed. But the idea that the city could clear the West End, and then turn the land over to a private builder for luxury apartments seemed unbelievable.

Their skepticism turned to incredulity when the city awarded the redevelopment contract to the second highest bidder. The lawyer's ties with the Mayor convinced them that the redevelopment was a politically motivated plot to take the West End for private profit with government help. The idea that a private builder could build apartments then estimated to rent for $40 to $50 a room—more than they were paying for five- and six-room apartments—was hard to believe. And that the government could encourage this venture seemed incomprehensible except as a result of political corruption, the exchange of bribes, and the cutting in of politicians on future profits.[8] As one West Ender among many pointed out:

> The whole thing is a steal, taking the area away from the people, and giving it to some guys who had paid off everyone else. . . . It is just someone making money at our expense. There are many areas lots worse than this one. Look at [the Mayor], a city clerk once, and now he's rich enough to buy up Boston itself. Yes, just a city clerk and look at him now.

Thereafter, all of the steps in the process were interpreted as attempts to scare the West Enders out of the area, so that the values of the buildings would be reduced and the private developers could buy them more cheaply. But even then, people were skeptical that this scheme would come to fruition, partially because it was so immoral. Many West Enders argued that only in Russia could the government deprive citizens of their property in such a dictatorial manner.

Also, West Enders found it hard to think far ahead. Even if they could admit to themselves that the area might eventually be "thrown down"—as they put it—it was still difficult to think about what might happen years hence, especially in the absence of incontrovertible evidence. As already noted, Housing Authority announcements were not considered reliable. Nor were announcements and newspaper stories generally accepted as evidence; people had to see more concrete examples of the city's plans before they would believe that the city was in earnest. For example, the registered letters, which the Redevelopment Authority sent to all West Enders indicating that it had taken over the area, were less persuasive than the announcement that as of May, 1958, rents were to be paid not to landlords but to the city's relocation office. Only when people saw their neighbors—and especially their landlords—going to that office to pay their rents did all of them realize that the end had come. Conversely, a few weeks earlier, when the announcement of the taking was imminent, West Enders were much cheered by the city's repaving of streets immediately outside the project area and by the gas company's installation of more modern gas meters in West End apartments. These were concrete actions that could be taken as evidence, especially since they seemed to prove what West Enders wanted to believe—that nothing was going to happen—and were considered much more reliable than official announcements or news stories.[9] And finally, of course, West Enders simply denied the possibility of redevelopment because they did not want it to happen. They were content to live in the West End, and could not imagine living elsewhere, or going about the city looking for "rooms."

As a result, life in the West End went on as always, with relatively little overt concern about the redevelopment, and with even less public discussion of it. On the days following the announcement of another decision in the process, people would talk about it heatedly, but then it would be forgotten again until the next announcement. There had been so many announcements, and so many meetings, and nothing ever seemed to happen afterwards. Surely it would be safe—and easy—to assume that nothing would ever happen.

As a result of this attitude, the oncoming redevelopment had little impact on the lives of most West Enders until the very end. The daily routine continued as before, the evenings were given over to peer group life, and holidays were celebrated as always. Some gradual changes could be noticed by the more observant. For example, landlords had been advised early in the decade not to make extensive repairs, and this increased the friction between them and their tenants when something went wrong in the building. People also noticed that, over the years, vacant apartments did not fill up again, or that they were rented to people who had not been seen previously in the West End: Gypsies, newcomers to the city, and people from the South End—the city's most transient district.

And the local parish began to cut down on its school operations—admitting new students only to the first grade. But all this had no major impact on the long-term residents of the area. Community organizations, such as the Holy Name Society, continued to function as before.

Only the merchants and the caretakers were directly affected. As empty apartments were not rerented, storekeepers, whose total receipts were never large, began to find their incomes shrinking even further, and some of them closed down. Even so, I would estimate that only about 10 per cent ceased operations in the year before the onset of relocation. And there were always rumors that some would reopen soon.

The caretaking agencies knew, of course, that the area would be redeveloped, and were not in doubt over the outcome of the long process. This knowledge, the gradual reduction in the number of their clients, and the appearance of some of the lower-class newcomers, sapped their morale. For although most of the agencies and their staffs were in favor of the redevelopment, they were also sorry to see the neighborhood torn down, and its residents dispersed. They did not voice their feelings in public, but at the annual board meeting of one of the settlement houses, the staff put on a skit about the redevelopment which reflected its ambivalence toward the destruction of the West End. The caretakers also tried, with little success, to prepare the West Enders for what was about to happen.[10] Some of them urged the redevelopment agency to improve its relocation procedures, but by then it was too late.

The best illustration of the lack of impact of the redevelopment process on the West Enders was the failure of the Save the West End Committee to attract their overt support, and the absence of other forms of protests noted earlier. The Committee came into being in 1956, when a handful of West Enders met with a local civic and political leader who had long been interested in the West

End. An upper-class Bostonian whose family and forebears had been active in caretaking projects in the area since the turn of the century, he helped to build the park, pool, and boating area along the banks of the Charles River and had participated in other improvement projects since the 1930s.[11] He felt that the West End was not a slum and also argued that the city had no right to take private property—especially that of poor people—for luxury apartment buildings. He promised to support the group politically and financially, and, with his help, the Committee rented a vacant store in the area. Over the year, it held a number of meetings, spoke at public hearings, published pamphlets and leaflets, went to Washington to try to overturn the decision, and eventually took its case to the courts. The Committee sought of course to enroll the neighborhood in its work, but attracted only a small—although loyal—group of members, who kept up a steady barrage of protest over the years. Not until the very end, however, did they gain a wider audience.

One of the major obstacles to the Committee's effectiveness in its own neighborhood was its outside leadership. Although many West Enders had heard of the civic leader who helped to guide the Committee, they knew also that he lived outside the area, and that however strong his sympathy, he was in class, ethnic background, and culture not one of their own. Nor was he at ease among the West Enders. While he identified with the neighborhood, he often seemed to feel more strongly about the facilities on the River bank—which were of little interest to the West Enders—than about the tenement streets and their occupants.

Moreover, the other active members—and the people who originally asked for his guidance—were neither typical West Enders, nor the kinds of people who could enroll them. Among the most active were an Italian writer and an artist, a young Jewish professional, a single Polish woman, and a number of elderly ladies who lived in the Charlesbank Homes.

While some of them did have leadership ability, almost all of them were in one way or another marginal to their own ethnic groups in the West End. Thus, they could not attract these groups to their cause.

This inability had nothing to do with the Committee's point of view, for that was based on the beliefs shared widely by a majority of the West Enders: That the redevelopment was motivated by political chicanery and individual greed; that government actions to scare the West Enders into leaving stemmed from sympathy or collusion with the builders; and that until definite proof was available, there was no reason to believe the West End would actually be torn down.

The Committee, however, did not develop a program that would require West Enders as a whole to take action. Its pamphlets and speeches expressed the same indignation and incredulity felt by all, but it did not ask them to act, other than to come to meetings, help the Committee in its mailings, and stay in the West End.

Yet all of these considerations for the Committee's lack of success in gaining active neighborhood support paled before the most important one: *the inability of the West Enders to organize on their own behalf.* Indeed, other causes were only effects of that basic inability. Had the West Enders flocked to meetings in larger numbers, the leadership would probably have gone to someone whom the residents would have followed. As it was, they watched the activities of the Committee with passive sympathy. Some were suspicious: they argued that the Committee consisted of people who had been left out when the graft was distributed; that the leadership was Communist; and that a Jewish officer of the Committee was related to one of the developers. The majority, however, did agree with all that the Committee claimed, and shared its anger. But even then they could not break out of the peer group society, and organize in common cause. It was impossible to fight City Hall; this was a function of the local politician. If he failed, what else was there to do? Action-seeking West Enders would have relished a march on City Hall to do violence to the officials principally associated with the redevelopment, but the act of joining with neighbors to work together for halting the redevelopment was inconceivable. At the meetings at which West Enders spoke, they spoke as individuals, about their own individual cases. The local politicians who appeared at these meetings spoke *to* the West Enders rather than *for* them; they convinced the audience of their own opposition to the redevelopment, and tried to display themselves as loyal representatives of the West End. But they too were unable—and perhaps unwilling—to organize an effective protest movement.

Even the resident leaders of the Committee—notably those of Italian background—were ill-at-ease about guiding a protest group which called for citizen participation. They realized that their Beacon Hill supporter could not attract the West Enders, but they were also skeptical as to their own ability to rally them. In addition, they were ambivalent about their personal involvement. They were able to make speeches, and to share their anger with an audience, but other activities came less easily. Being a leader without any proof of results, spending time away from family and friends, or from second jobs and other individual pursuits was difficult. When Committee members were asked to carry out the routine tasks of organization, and failed to come through—as was often the case—the leaders who gave the orders resented having to carry out these tasks themselves. They were hurt that they should give up their own free time, and extend themselves for the group if no one else did, and if there was no reward for such self-deprivation. Thus, the Committee itself was constantly split by bickering, by people withdrawing from activity when no support was forthcoming, and by individuals offering new solutions and making speeches to each other when more prosaic activity was called for.

The leaders were also hampered by lack of information. The politicians claimed—with some justification—that since they were opposed to the project, they had not been kept properly informed by redevelopment officials. Also, they and the leaders of the Committee were unable to deal properly with what information was available. Like most other West Enders, they believed that the project's fate was in the hand of one individual, the Mayor, and that it could be overturned simply by persuading him of its immorality. As unable as the rest of the West Enders to follow the series of steps that led to the final taking of the land, some of them believed until the last moment that the redevelopment would never take place. They accepted the rumors that swept the area like everyone else, and could not detach themselves sufficiently from their neighbors to look objectively at the doings of the outside world. Thus, none of the prerequisites or minutiae of organizational activity came easily to the Committee leaders. Much of the time, only their anger at the outrage they felt was being perpetrated against themselves and their neighbors kept them going.

The truth was, that for a group unaccustomed to organizational activity, saving the West End was an overwhelming, and perhaps impossible, task. Indeed, there was relatively little the Committee could do. The decision to redevelop the West End had been made early in the decade, and it had received the blessings of the city's decisive business leaders and politicians. The West End's local politicians all opposed the redevelopment, but were powerless against the unanimity of those who favored it. As noted in Chapter 8, the election of city councilors at large rather than by wards since 1951 had reduced the influence of individual districts. Smaller areas, with few voters, were especially hard hit; and the West End, which was losing population at this time, was virtually disenfranchised. Nor did the West End have other attributes of power such as those displayed by the neighboring North End, which had successfully repulsed efforts toward its own redevelopment. This area had a larger population and a much larger business community—some of it politically influential. Most important, the North End was the center—and symbol—of Italian life in Boston. Its destruction thus would have been a threat—or at least an insult—to every Italian voter in Boston, and the city's politicians simply could not afford to alienate this increasingly influential vote. Conversely, although the Italians were also the largest group in the West End, they were not in the majority. And since they had attained a plurality only comparatively recently, the area had never really been considered an Italian neighborhood. Thus, it is doubtful whether even a unanimous turnout in opposition by the West Enders would have been sufficient to set in motion the difficult process of reversing years of work by local and federal agencies, and giving up the large federal grant that financed the clearance of the area.

NOTES

1. When I use the term West Ender in this chapter and the next, I mean all of the people in the area, regardless of ethnic background. Even so, most of my observations about redevelopment were made among the Italian West Enders. Whenever I refer to someone of Italian background, however, this will be indicated.

2. At least they did so as long as I remained in the area. I left in May, 1958, shortly after the city had taken title to the land, but before people had begun to move. The chapter deals with events up to that time only. The full impact of the redevelopment will be described in considerable detail, of course, by the long-term study being conducted by the Center for Community Studies.

3. Since I was highly critical of the redevelopment

process, my sociological analysis is affected by my point of view. The reader is therefore advised to look over the introduction to the concluding chapter for a brief statement of that point of view.

4. These activities are discussed in detail in the next chapter.

5. For a more detailed discussion of the West Enders' reactions, see Marc Fried and Peggy Gleicher, "Some Sources of Residential Satisfaction in an Urban 'Slum,'" *Journal of the American Institute of Planners*, vol. 27 (1961), pp. 305–315; and Marc Fried, "Grieving for a Lost Home," in Leonard J. Duhl, ed., *The Urban Condition*, New York: Basic Books, 1963, pp. 151–171.

6. I should note that I have selected the most demonstrative comments of the many I heard about the destruction of the area. That they are not atypical is supported by findings—and even more poignant statements—reported in Fried, "Grieving for a Lost Home" *op. cit.*

7. Boston Housing Authority, "West End Progress Report" Boston: The Authority, January, 1956, p. 1.

8. I heard from several disparate sources that one of the city councilors had asked for a sizable "campaign contribution" in exchange for a favorable vote on the redevelopment. Since his vote was not needed, he did not get the money. Eventually, he voted for it anyway.

9. These feelings even affected me. Although I knew enough about redevelopment procedures to realize that the process was moving toward its inevitable climax, I was opposed to the redevelopment, and hoped it would not take place. Since I was not in touch with city officials, occasionally I would begin to share the West Enders' beliefs that "our children will still be here when they break it up," and wondered whether the rumors that the project had collapsed might not be true. It is thus understandable that West Enders, who knew much less about the process, and could not call city officials to get the facts, would hold these beliefs more stubbornly.

10. For some examples, see Chapter 7.

11. His father had been a founder of the public playground movement in America; and his relatives, who included all of the famous names of Boston's aristocracy, had helped to build the West End settlement houses. They also supported the charities and social welfare agencies that served the area and the larger community.

CHAPTER 2

Families and Children in Pain

Philippe Bourgois

> You know what's wrong with these girls nowadays? They only think of themselves. They only think of their sexual pleasures, their fun and their happiness. But they don't think of their kids first.
>
> Candy

Developmental psychologists and psychiatrists are generally considered to be the "experts" on early childhood socialization and family violence. Most of their large-scale, multimillion-dollar, cross-generational epidemiological surveys of "children at risk" conclude that the bulk of an adult's character is determined in infancy. Their statistical studies demonstrate that most battered children are virtually irremediable by the ages of six to eight. Furthermore, they assure us that a child does not have to be the object of physical violence to be emotionally scarred for life. Simply witnessing violence can induce long-term trauma.[1]

In other words, according to the standard psychological theories of early childhood socialization, most people living in El Barrio, and certainly everyone in Ray's network and the crackhouses I frequented, might be dismissed as antisocial sociopaths because of their early childhood socialization experiences. Certainly, the gun-and-knife-wielding, knockdown fights between Candy and Primo that unfolded in front of twenty-year-old Tabatha, fourteen-year-old Junior, ten-year-old Jackie, four-year-old Mina, and one-

year-old Lillian must have inflicted profound emotional scars. But once again, an individualistic, psychological determinist approach misses the larger political economic and cultural context. It ignores historical processes and the effects of unequal power relations around class, ethnic, or gender and sexual categories. Developmental psychologists tend to focus only on the epiphenomenon of individual neuroses. Their data and analytic tools are also limited by the cultural and class biases of their survey methods. White middle-class families are overrepresented in their epidemiological samples because of the very logistics of collecting reliable statistics.

The restructuring of New York City's economy and the history of Puerto Rican immigration have profoundly changed the ways East Harlem families are organized. For many of the poorer households these changes have been disruptive, and children, of course, are the ultimate casualties when households disintegrate. The problem is integrally related to the contradictory shifts in gender power relations discussed in Chapter 6. Motherhood roles have remained fixed, while women's rights and the structure of the traditional family have undergone profound, long-term transformations. Mothers, especially heading single-parent households, are still saddled with the exclusive responsibility for nurturing their children, even though they may no longer be willing to sacrifice unconditionally their individual freedom for their progeny.

This results in a parenting vacuum when mothers take to the streets. It expresses itself statistically in the dramatic increase in child neglect and abuse, and in poisoned fetuses over the past generation.[2] By default, street culture becomes a more important socializing force when fragmented families force children to take refuge in the streets.

Politicians, the press, and the general public in the United States interpret the visible problems faced by poor urban children as evidence of "a crisis in family values." Structural problems of persistent poverty and segregation, as well as the more complex issues of changing gender power relations are rarely addressed in public discussion. The most immediately self-evident policy interventions, such as offering affordable, developmental appropriate day care for the children of overwhelmed or addicted mothers, are not even part of most policy debates. Similarly, effective drug treatment facilities, or meaningful job training and employment referral services, remain off-limits to women who live in poverty.

STREET CULTURE'S CHILDREN

Children have always faced difficult lives in East Harlem. The neighborhood has always been a poor, segregated home for first- and second-generation immigrants. As the historical chapter documents, academic and social service denunciations of the "worsening" plight of youth and the exacerbation of violence on the street merge over the past century into a pastiche of clichés portending imminent doom. In the late 1920s, for example, the Italian priest of the Catholic Church two blocks down from the Game Room told a graduate student that "the reckless destructive spirit of youth is getting worse and there is less and less consideration of property rights. This is due to the want of religion and the lack of respect for authority."[3]

Similarly, in the mid-1950s, a Community Service Society report on the conditions of the

blocks opposite the Game Room complains of children "feeling unsafe in a fermenting neighborhood." The authors conclude:

> From parents, teachers, Bureau of Attendance and Youth board workers came the same response: "These children don't have much of a chance!"
>
> . . . Living constantly in an environment filled with disorder and destruction . . . provoke[s] these youngsters to acts of aggression. . . . they strike out in anti-social behavior.[4]

On a personal level, the most stressful dimension of living in El Barrio's street scene was witnessing the wholesale destruction of the children of my friends and neighbors. I lived in the neighborhood long enough to witness dozens of little girls and boys fall apart as they passed from childhood to adolescence. I watched energetic, bright-eyed children get ground up into what the United States calls its underclass. Within five short years, my little neighbor Gigi metamorphosed from being an outgoing, cute, eager-to-please eight-year-old who gave me a construction paper Valentine's card every year, into becoming a homeless, pregnant, crack-using thirteen-year-old "teenager." Meanwhile, her older brother Hector was transformed from a shy, giggling undersized twelve-year-old into a juvenile inmate, guilty of "assault with a dangerous weapon."[5]

Upon first moving onto the block, I found it heartwarming to see gleeful children running, jumping, shouting, and laughing in front of my apartment window at all hours of the day and night. Once again, ethnographic description of these same blocks from the 1920s applies almost verbatim to the 1990s:

> The cross streets . . . become the chief playgrounds of children. Hordes of them are seen . . . playing ball, craps, and cards. They become expert in dodging traffic. . . . During 1927, fifteen children were killed by traffic accidents principally on Second and Third Avenues.[6]

My early fieldwork notes revel in the warmth of the dozens of pre-teenage friendships I was able to make within my first few months on the block:

[May 1985]

I love the way the kids run up to me with excited smiles whenever I come home. They shower me with hugs, stories, and questions at any hour of the day or night. Whenever a mother walks by with a newborn it's considered normal for me to bend over it and bless it tenderly, "Que Diós lo bendiga," even if the mother doesn't know me. I hope someday soon I'll be comfortable enough to pick up these newborns and hug them like most other people do.[7]

In dissonance with my public celebration of street culture's relationship to children was the omnipresent underlying wail of crying babies that competed with the salsa and rap music pulsing from my neighbors' windows.

Two years later, with my own newborn, Emiliano, in my arms generating countless blessings and constant cooing, I remained convinced that El Barrio had special energy and love for children. I even learned to appreciate my local supermarket's inefficiency and decrepitude, when every time I walked by on the sidewalk in front, at least three of the four teenage cashiers ran from their machines to tap on the display window and to throw kisses and grimaces at my appreciatively giggling baby. Downtown society's industrialized Taylorist logic would have long since obliged the manager to fire those affectionate wannabe mothers. When I took Emiliano to Anglo-dominated parties downtown, I noticed that he was disappointed with the adults. He expected a more appreciatively physical reaction from them. Very few of my white friends and acquaintances even knew how to hold my baby comfortably; none of them grabbed him spontaneously out of my arms for a cuddle and a blessing the way my acquaintances regularly did on the street uptown. In fact, some of my downtown friends even requested I leave my son at home with a baby-sitter when they invited me to their homes.

My love affair with street life's intergenerational affection and integration began to sour when my son's first words at sixteen months of age turned out to be "tops, tops, tops." I had been trying to penetrate a new and particularly active crack-copping corner, and had been taking him along with me to allay the suspicions of the sellers that I might be an undercover cop. That corner had four competing "spots," each selling three-dollar vials. The sellers on duty shouted or hissed at their prospective clients to advertise their particular brands, delineated by the color of the plastic stoppers on their vials: "Graytop, graytop, graytop! Pinktop, pinktop, pinktop! Blacktop," and so on. A few weeks later, I found myself in the midst of an angry crowd surrounding two white police officers who had just killed an African-American man high on angel dust. It was only when the crowd had begun chanting "Open season on the black man! Murderers! Murderers!" that I noticed that the only other whites present were the two "killer cops" frantically shouting into their walkie-talkies for help.[8] Emiliano, perched on my shoulders, caused the tense crowd to burst into laughter by clapping his hands gleefully in time with the angry chanting.

As a parent, I was learning the lesson faced by all the working mothers and fathers on my block. Either I had to abandon public space and double-lock my child inside my cramped tenement apartment and assume a hostile attitude toward street culture, or I would have to accept the fact that my child would witness drugs and violence on a daily basis. My perspective on the future of the children living around me further soured when Iris, the mother of ten-year-old Angel and eight-year-old Manny, my two favorite shiny-eyed street friends, fell apart on crack and became pregnant. My wife and I stopped dropping by their apartment unannounced after finding them one evening sitting in the dark (because the electricity bill had not been paid), scraping the last corners of peanut butter out of an empty jar. Their mother was passed out on the bed, recovering from last night's "mission."

I began organizing biweekly trips for them, and whoever else happened to be hanging out on the block, to cross New York's invisible apartheid barriers to visit museums and other world-renowned bourgeois havens like the FAO Schwartz toy store and Trump Tower. They loved the Andy Warhol exhibit at the Museum of Modern Art, and Angel even assured me that the Frick Museum's collection of Dutch masters was "not boring at all." In contrast, they were not impressed by the Whitney Museum's "alternative" multimedia rap/break-dance/graffiti/skateboard extravaganza.

The full force of the racial and class boundaries confining the children of El Barrio became glaringly clear on these outings. In the museums, for example, we were usually flanked by guards with hissing walkie-talkies. Often I was eyed quizzically, as if I might be some kind of pedophile, parading my prey. Angel was particularly upset at the Joan Miró exhibit at the Guggenheim when he asked one of the guards—who himself was Puerto Rican—why he was being followed so closely, and was told, "to make sure you don't lift your leg."

On our way home from the Miró exhibit, I brought Angel and his friends to my mother's apartment in the Upper East Side's Silk Stocking district, located less than twenty blocks from our tenements.[9] I was sobered by Angel's simple but naive wish, "I'm planning on moving my mother into a building like this when I grow up too. I wish my mom lived here." When he added that "the schools probably be better down here too," I pounced on the opportunity to engage him in a discussion of the structural inadequacies of the education system. His response, however, focused on the destructive behavior of the victims themselves:

Philippe: What's the matter? You got mean teachers?

Angel: No, It's the kids I'm afraid of. They be mugging people in the hallways.

Later that evening Angel complained to me that his mother's boyfriend had broken open his piggy bank and taken the twenty dollars' worth of tips he had saved from working as a delivery boy at the supermarket on our block. He blamed his mother for having provoked her boyfriend into beating her and robbing the apartment when she invited another man to visit her in her bedroom. "I keep telling my mother to only have one boyfriend at a time, but she won't listen to me." I was forced to recognize in these guileless expressions of vulnerability on the part of the children surrounding me, the brutal dynamic whereby tender victims internalize the social structures that dominate them, to the point that they eventually take charge of administering their own mutual self-destruction. This was even more forcefully portrayed in the hauntingly sad and violent pictures that they drew, when I provided them with paper and crayons on the car hoods in front of my tenement after dark.

As my youthful friends grew older, places like the Game Room or the Social Club gradually emerged as central institutions in their lives. They were socialized into the "normalcy" of drug dealing. In El Barrio, the crackhouse is virtually the only adolescent space that is heated in the winter and air-conditioned in the summer. There are simply no other healthy social scenes to frequent if one has limited resources and wants to be where the action is. Many—if not most—East Harlem apartments are overcrowded, plagued with vermin, poorly heated in the winter, and stiflingly hot in the summer. The street or the crackhouse consequently offers a more comfortable alternative living room.

Candy's son, Junior, was the first boy I watched graduate into crack dealer status.

When I first asked him at age thirteen what he wanted to be when he grew up, he answered that he wanted to have "cars, girls, and gold chains—but no drugs; a big roll [of money], and rings on all my fingers." In one of these conversations, Junior had even dreamed out loud of wanting to be a "cop." It was midnight and we were sitting on the hood of Ray's Lincoln Continental parked in front of the Game Room.

Primo: [with a drunken slur] Naah! You're going to be an idiot like me and Caesar. A no-good, good-for-nothing *desperdicia'o envicia'o* [vice-ridden, life-wasting man].

Junior: [earnestly] Unh, uhh! I could be a cop if I wanted to be.

Primo: Yeah, yeah! A cop sexaholic—rape women, too—because you got authority with your badge [howling laughter in the background from Caesar].

Angelo: [an eleven-year-old friend of Junior's enthusiastically giggling] Right, right!

Junior: [still earnest] Naah, just be a cop and that's it. Bust people.

Primo: [seriously] Yeah, bustin' people like me.

Junior: Naah, only like, if they rob somebody. If they do crime and stuff.

Philippe: [turning to Angelo] What do you want to be when you grow up?

Primo: [interrupting] A pimp or a drug dealer, right?

Angelo: No, a rapper.

As the years progressed, Junior became increasingly involved in Game Room activities. Literally before he knew it, he became a bona fide drug courier. He thought of it as simply "running errands." Junior was more than eager to be helpful, and Primo would send him to pick up ten-dollar packets of powder cocaine from around the corner, or to fetch cans of beer from the bodega two doors down. Junior was not using drugs; he was merely behaving like any eager teenager flattered by the possibility of hanging out with grown-ups. Before his sixteenth birthday, Junior began filling in for Caesar as lookout, when Caesar's crack binges kept him from coming to work on time. Soon Ray promoted him to working at the Social Club as permanent lookout on weekends, replacing Luis, whose crack use was making him an unacceptably erratic employee. Although Junior had dropped out of school by this time, and already had a juvenile record for hot-wiring a car, he was a strict teetotaler, and an obedient worker. He was only available to run errands and work lookout at night, however, because Candy often made him baby-sit his little sister during the day.

When I tried to make Junior realize that he was being sucked into a life of drug dealing, the conversation merely degenerated into a display of how crackhouse logic maintains its hegemony in the daily lives of even those children who want to be good:

Philippe: So Junior, if you don't wanna be a drug dealer what are you doing working here for Primo tonight?

Junior: Nah, I'm only lookin' out. I ain't touching no product. My moms knows about it; she said it was okay.

Besides, I know drugs is wack. They just put you in the hospital.

Philippe: [smiling at Primo] Junior, what's gonna happen to you? Are you just gonna turn into another scum-of-the-earth drug dealer like Primo? [in a serious tone] And keep on selling drugs, and get yourself arrested?

Junior: No, not no more, 'cause if I get busted again, I get in a lot of trouble.

Primo: [interrupting] No, not the first time Junior.

Junior: But I could get sent to a home, 'cause of that shit with the car.

Primo: [condescendingly] If you get busted selling drugs now, you'll be all right. It's the second time that you'll get fucked.

[turning to me reassuringly] He'll have someone lookin' out for him; someone who will send him bail—[giggling] most likely.

In Search of Meaning: Having Babies in El Barrio

Witnessing the maelstrom consuming children on the street in their most vulnerable years, one cannot help wondering why mothers continue to bear so many babies into so much suffering. During my five years of residence, virtually all my friends and acquaintances in El Barrio had at least one baby. This was the case with Primo's girlfriend Maria, who refused to have an abortion when she became pregnant, even though Primo was in the midst of a felony trial for his second arrest for selling crack to an undercover officer. Only two months earlier, Maria and Primo had been thrown out of the project apartment belonging to Maria's sister, who had fled to Bridgeport, Connecticut, when her husband's drug-dealing partner was found murdered in their car. At the time Maria became pregnant she was living with her deeply depressed, alcoholic, 250-pound mother. I described it in my fieldwork notes:

[March 1990]
Primo took me over to Maria's house: strewn with garbage, broken furniture, and empty quarts of Bacardi. It smells of vomited alcohol, and is crawling with cockroaches. Plates full of boiled cabbage, and boiled meat, from Maria's stepfather's unfinished meals lie spilled around the living room, where Maria has to sleep on a broken couch that hurts her back.

Primo assures me that this is nothing compared to the howls, wails, shouts, and sobbings of Maria's bruised mother after she finishes her evening bottle of Bacardi. Apparently, she

fights with her husband, accusing him of infidelities. According to Primo, on some nights she actually stabs him, "but she just jigs him a little bit."

Today she has a swollen face, because last night her husband—an equally alcoholic janitor at a public school—retaliated and "clocked her."

Maria was overjoyed to be pregnant. It was the happiest I had ever seen her, and it took me a long time to realize that it was precisely her wretched living conditions that made motherhood so appealing. It offered a romantic escape from her objectively difficult surroundings. The pregnancy also cemented her deep love for Primo, who we all expected would receive a four- to six-year prison sentence. Having Primo's baby was going to be her way of demonstrating her solidarity with him during his incarceration. Maria began writing poetry to celebrate her relationship with Primo and their future progeny. Maria's high self-esteem during this period in her life literally springs from the pages of her diary, which she showed me. In the following excerpt, for example, her appreciation for the beauty of her body both internalizes and overcomes racist and sexist stereotypes:

I have light brown eyes, sexy cat eyes, and a nice big butt and big juicy balangas . . . and I have big bubble lips that cover my face just right; and I have hair, curly, and I could put it anywhere I want to.

She was also filled with appreciation for *hetjavao'*[10] boyfriend.

I'm eighteen years old; he's twenty-six. He has light brown eyes, big eyes. He has beautiful lips too, nice teeth; and he has juicy buns . . . and he has nice curly hair.[11]

Primo, in contrast, was anxious and angry at Maria. He was overwhelmed with anxiety over his court case, and he was at the height of his personal disillusionment at not being able to find a legal job. He begged Maria to have an abortion, and even went out of his way to abuse her verbally when she showed him her love poems, calling her a "fucking crazy bitch that looks like a negro Michelin man; like Black-a-Claus . . . like Blackula."

Maria also had a concrete material interest in bearing a child. It represented her most realistic chance of establishing an independent household given the extraordinary scarcity of affordable, subsidized public housing in New York City. During the years I lived in El Barrio, the waiting list for New York City Housing Authority apartments was eighteen years long.[12] Homeless pregnant teenagers, however, were given priority in obtaining apartments under a special outreach program designed to relieve crowding in emergency homeless shelters and welfare hotels. The "only" negative in Maria's strategy to forge an independent household was that she had to survive for three long months in a homeless shelter before being placed in a "youth action" renovated tenement for homeless teenage mothers. As a matter of fact, Primo Jr. was born while she was still in the shelter.

During this same period, Maria's sister Carmen also became pregnant with her boyfriend, Caesar. Caesar's abusive tendencies did not dampen her joy and love. At the time, Caesar had obliged Carmen to make her oldest sister the foster mother of her six-year-old daughter, Pearl. He also frequently beat her two-year-old son, Papo, claiming that he lacked discipline and was "slow in the head."[13] Just before Carmen's pregnancy, Caesar gave her an ultimatum, "choose between Papo or me." She was negotiating with her older sister to adopt Papo as well.

Carmen's pregnancy solved her immediate crisis. Not only did Caesar agree to become Papo's stepfather, but his grandmother invited Carmen to move into their apartment and live in Caesar's bedroom. Caesar's grandmother even formalized Carmen's status by registering her officially on the Housing Authority lease. Caesar himself had never been legally registered as living in the apartment, to avoid having his SSI payments included in the rent calculation.

Carmen and Maria were following the traditional path of escaping from a troubled home by falling romantically in love with an idealized man, and embracing motherhood wholeheartedly. Carmen showed me her journal entries shortly after becoming pregnant. She was even more infatuated with Caesar than Maria was with Primo, describing her relationship with Caesar as "paradise on an island":

> The years that I've seen Caesar, I've always had a crush on him. But when we first got together, it was like love at first sight. And still to this day I feel the same. I guess you could say I fell in love with him. But when I see him, my heart skips a beat, and when he gets near, I just want to faint.
>
> I really love him and care for him always, no matter. And as for my son, Benito Jr., [Papo], he loves Caesar, as far as I know.

Both Maria and Carmen were young, but their enthusiastic embrace of motherhood should not be dismissed as the fleeting romantic whims of immature women. The dearth of alternative scenarios for female adulthood on the street not only normalizes motherhood at an early age but also makes it attractive.

In Candy's case, for example, when her love affair with Primo ended violently, it was her love for her children that stabilized her and restored meaning to her life. By wholeheartedly reassuming the traditional "jíbara role" of being a self-abnegating mother at age thirty-four, Candy saved herself and her household from terminal self-destruction in Ray's street-dealing scene.

Candy: I used coke for five months to kill myself. Then I woke up and said, "I love my kids too much to kill myself." Because if you love your kids that makes you do nothing wrong.

I was real skinny, and I was like neglecting my kids, in the way of not paying mind to them. I didn't hit them, but I didn't want to be bothered with them. Like, I was [gruffly], "I don't want to hear no noise."

They used to tell me, "Mommy, what's wrong with you? Mommy, please! People are going to think you are on crack." And yes God is with me, because I had a dream back then. I was dying. I saw my son Junior, my only boy, crying that I was dead. And I saw my other two daughters looking very different, [stopping abruptly] I wish to God I wouldn't even think about it, 'cause I'm against drugs. I think my children would've gone into drugs.

But don't get me wrong. I'm a strict mother where I believe in the best education. I believe in being a strict, strong, good, loving parent.

You know, Felipe, what it is? When you see your kids everyday telling you, "I love you." And you know I've been through a lot—a beating every day, three times a day, from the age of thirteen. Why you gonna make that baby pay for your mistakes? No!

That's why I'm crazy about my kids. And I still want twelve. Because a baby means purity to me—innocence. And a baby can't come and smack you, and say, "Mommy, don't abuse me." But you do it. And I'm against child abuse.

But I'm thirty-four now, and I still wish I could have five more now. Because my kids come to me, kissing me, saying, "Mommy, love you, love you."

You hardly see that in kids now. You see kids streetwise, like my sister's kids—Angelo, for example—

where they don't have a lovable parent.

But I did my best. My children all went to Catholic school from first grade to now. And I have paid for it all.

NOTES

1. Farrington 1991.
2. During the 1980s, child abuse statistics in New York City escalated almost 700 percent. From 1985 to 1994 they increased 232 percent (cf. *New York Daily News*, November 19, 1990:5, 10; *New York Times*, December 28, 1988:63; *New York Times*, December 19, 1989:61). It is impossible to know how much of this increase reflects a real increase or is the result of improved reporting procedures and changing social definitions of child abuse.
3. Marsh 1932:361.
4. Community Service Society 1956:25.
5. For more examples of the destruction of children, see the life scenarios of Manny, Angel, Lestor, Junior, and Angelo in the epilogue.
6. Marsh 1932:48.
7. Coincidentally, a few years later, I noticed a photograph of this same corner in the *New York Times* depicting a shrine of flowers commemorating the murder of a fifty-two-year-old woman caught in crossfire while accompanying her five-year-old grandson home from school (December 1, 1993: A20).
8. I found out the next day in the *New York Times* that the victim was forty-four years old (*New York Times*, November 16, 1989:112).
9. I grew up seven blocks from the border between Manhattan's Upper East Side and El Barrio. As noted in Chapter 1, note 16, the median household income of my childhood neighborhood was more than thirteen times higher than that of the two census tracts surrounding my apartment on the Game Room's block. Less than 1 percent of the residents in my childhood neighborhood lived below the poverty line in 1990, compared to approximately 47 percent in the two census tracts surrounding my tenement in El Barrio. Only three Puerto Ricans lived in my childhood census tract in 1989 despite its being a five-minute walk from the neighborhood with one of the highest densities of Puerto Rican residents in the entire United States (*1990 Census of Population and Housing Block Statistics*).
10. In Puerto Rican Spanish, *javao'* refers pejoratively to someone with African features and "white" skin.
11. I significantly edited or, rather, censored these excerpts of Maria's poetry for fear of portraying decontextualized racist and sexist material as well as excessively private perspectives.
12. In 1991, there were as many people waiting for public housing (189,000 families) in New York City, as there were living in public housing (approximately

600,000 individuals) (*The Christian Science Monitor*, August 19, 1991:14).

13. Caesar confided to Primo that he sometimes grabbed the toddler by his feet as he lay sleeping and spun him in the air over his head. When Carmen would come running to the bedroom, Caesar pretended he was comforting Papo, who had just woken up, shrieking, from a nightmare. On another occasion, Papo had to be taken to the municipal hospital's emergency room when Caesar ripped his foreskin while bathing him.

I began fretting over whether or not I should file a child abuse report against Caesar, but simultaneously the *New York Times* began running exposes on how overwhelmed the foster child system had become with 45,000 children flooding into its care in 1990 alone. According to one reporter, children were sleeping on the desks of the intake officers at the Bureau of Child Welfare headquarters. Brothers and sisters seized by the foster care program were routinely split apart (cf. *New York Times*, July 3, 1989:B21–22; *New York Times*, October 23, 1989:A1, B4; *New York Times*, December 19, 1989:61, B4; *New York Times*, March 29, 1992:A1, A20; *New York Times*, February 9, 1989:A1, B9; *New York Times*, October 19, 1990:B3).

I also wondered how to interpret the shrieks of crying children that regularly rose through the heating pipes in my tenement. Was I ethnocentrically misreading the expressively aggressive child-rearing practices of inner-city families, or should I go downstairs and intervene?

Someone else eventually reported Caesar for child abuse, but the investigator took no action; on the contrary; she provided Caesar with enough information to be able to figure out who had reported him, leading to long-lasting enmity.

CHAPTER 3

The Celebrity Neighborhood

Richard Lloyd

Bohemians go everywhere and know everything; sometimes their boots are varnished, sometimes down at the heel, and their knowledge and the manner of their going varies accordingly. You may find one of them one day leaning against the chimney-piece in some fashionable drawing room, and the next at a table in some dancing saloon.

—Henri Murger, Scenes from the Bohemian Life, 1848

It's after 1 A.M. on a February night in 1999, and Allan Garland and I descend the stairs to the bowels of the multilevel nightclub Stardust. We can hear the muted sounds of Chicago-style house music from the other side of its heavy doors as we are confronted by the gatekeeper, a pixyish young woman with two-tone dyed hair and a long vintage coat. Sprayed-on glitter sparkles on her cheeks in the dim light. "It's $10 [to get in]," she informs us. Allan, a slender black man in his middle twenties, rocks on his heels, dreadlocks bobbing. We had just left the downtown café Third Coast, where Allan, an aspiring club DJ and West Side resident, works. He's still dressed in his work-mandated white shirt, now untucked and mostly unbuttoned. "Does it matter if I'm industry?" he asks, with a conspiratorial smile.

She squints. "Where do you work?"

"I work at Third Coast," Allan explains. "And I spin." He rattles off a résumé detailing venues where he has subbed as a DJ.

Her squint turns to recognition and a beaming smile. "I know you!" she says happily. "You're Norman's friend." Allan nods, and the door swings open. "Go in," she instructs, forgetting our cover charge obligation. Allan bounces through the door. I hesitate, since my own affiliation, with the University of Chicago, seems likely to have less resonance here. But she nods me along. I am to be the beneficiary of Allan's "industry" aura.

This club, a popular hangout with hip kids and affluent young professionals about a mile southeast of Wicker Park, is lodged in what Ernest Burgess called the city's "zone in transition," near the terminus of railroad tracks that long exported the city's impressive industrial output. Just past the western fringe of the Loop, the area is thick with warehouses and low-rise factory buildings. But the zone's contemporary transition involves the proliferation of living lofts, high-end restaurants, and hip nightclubs. This transition is far from total. During the day, this stretch is still thick with big trucks and prowling forklifts. But where the night once saw it mostly deserted, now its nocturnal sidewalks are lined with stylish young people and its streets patrolled by yellow cabs. And in this after-hours world, "industry" work refers to mixing drinks, serving food, or spinning records.

Sections of Chicago's West Side are evolving into a glamour zone of warehouses-turned-nightclubs, new-wave restaurants, and noir-themed bars. Chicago's new nightlife integrates the former industrial neighborhoods of the West Side into the global city that is also an "entertainment machine,"[1] satisfying consumer demands made by a young, relatively affluent, and well-educated workforce. As an industry, the entertainment scene has less in common with the manufacturing that once dominated the West Side, often in the same structures, than it does with Hollywood—it is a culture industry, and the contributions made by its workers are significantly, but not only, aesthetic.

In the past, serious urban scholars have minimized or ignored the city's leisure economy. But the ongoing decline of heavy industry in U.S. cities has been accompanied by an increase in the scope and impact of tourism and consumption on urban fortunes. Terry Nichols Clark indicates that "Chicago's number one industry has become entertainment, which city officials define as including tourism, conventions, hotels, restaurants, and related economic activities."[2] Urban tourism is fast becoming a central, not a tertiary, object of academic study. But by and large, new theories emphasize consumption districts that operate at a radical disjuncture from the everyday life of residents[3]—in Chicago, themed attractions like Navy Pier, or the phantasmagoric shopping spectacles along the Magnificent Mile. Dennis Judd calls such districts "tourist bubbles,"[4] and, as in Fredric Jameson's famed analysis of the Bonaventure hotel, the postmodern manifestation of culture as capital is indifferent to and alienated from the quotidian space of the city.[5]

Disneyland has become a central symbol of this new style of consumer space. Critics see Mickey Mouse as symbol of bleak postmodern dystopia—the absolute triumph of artifice over reality.[6] Argues Michael Sorkin, a leading critic of theme-park urbanism, "The empire of Disney transcends [its] physical sites; its aura is all-pervasive."[7] But whatever its postmodern features, the actual production of the Disney aesthetic adheres

to the Fordist principles that Adorno and Horkheimer saw in the culture industries of midcentury,[8] with a routinized labor process and standardized output. Indeed, arguably the one place where Adorno and Horkheimer's analysis is today repeated uncritically is in the new urban criticism of Sorkin and other Disneyfication theorists. In their totalizing scope, adherents to this paradigm often seem to forget Jean-François Lyotard's admonition: "Eclecticism is the degree zero of the contemporary general situation."[9] Wicker Park challenges the "all-pervasive" saturation of these models, as flexible, post-Fordist arrangements of cultural production and labor-force exploitation characterize its entertainment economy. While Disneyland generates its aesthetic "from above," imposing rigid standards of appearance and performance on its workforce, the bars and restaurants in neo-bohemia piece out image construction to individual employees steeped in the local neo-bohemian subculture.

Moreover, the assumption of a homogenized urban landscape inherent in the Disneyfication thesis misses the extent to which urban tourism draws upon distinctive features of local history. In a richly textured ethnographic study, David Grazian examines how Chicago's legacy as the "home of the blues" is tapped in the active construction of the contemporary tourist economy.[10] As Grazian demonstrates, visitors to the city seek out blues clubs as a central feature of the Chicago experience, with club musicians duly offering rote performances of weathered stand-bys in order to satisfy tourists' reified expectations of authenticity. This presentation of a well-seasoned tradition does not tell the whole story, however. City residents also frequent blues clubs (often favoring those that are off-the-beaten-track), striving to distinguish themselves from tourist dabblers through their superior knowledge of the musical tradition, as well as their superior competence in nocturnal comportment.

As the residential profile of Chicago changes, city dwellers do not leave entertainment only to visitors, but use their own city "as if tourists,"[11] aggressively pursuing urban consumption opportunities. This is particularly true of the young urban professionals who fill jobs in the high-rise offices of the global economy and also drive neighborhood gentrification.[12] This "new class" is quite different in character from the blue-collar workers of Fordism; their consumption habits reflect not only their affluence but also their occupations, education, and age.[13] The ability of the global city to capture and retain "talent" hinges in part on responsiveness to their aesthetic dispositions,[14] typically "omnivorous" tastes[15] that include fondness for the Chicago Bulls as well as off-Loop theater, or at least the idea of off-Loop theater. As sophisticated city dwellers, they seek out diverse consumption opportunities beyond mass attractions like Navy Pier, Chicago's number one visitor destination.[16] For some, a neighborhood like Wicker Park brokers fantasies of a hipper, more authentic urbanism, available to discerning insiders but not the tourist hoard.

THE WICKER PARK SCENE

As Wicker Park achieved celebrity status, promoted by sustained notice in the local media of its many hip attractions, the number of entertainment venues expanded dramatically. New bars and restaurants opened regularly in the neighborhood throughout the decade and beyond, although, as is often the case with small businesses, many of these survived only a short while. The staples of the emerging hipster scene were the Rainbo Club, Bop Shop, Phyllis' Musical Inn, Borderline, Czar Bar, Innertown Pub, Artful Dodger, Sweet Alice's, Hothouse, North Side, Dreamerz, Subterranean, Red Dog, and Gold Star. Later arrivals in the neighborhood area include Lava Lounge, 1056, Double Door, Holiday, Nicks, Mad Bar, Bigwig, Davenport's, Eddy Clearwater's, Pontiac, and the Note. Thus, by 2000 the neighborhood, while not completely bereft of its older industrial character, had become a hub of culture and entertainment, as an examination of the location quotients for relevant industries reveals (table 3.1).

The patronage of these bars is hardly limited to committed participants in the neighborhood arts scene; for the most part they are populated today by college students and young professionals—individuals with enough disposable income to actually make these businesses viable. Nonetheless, the hip, neo-bohemian ethos of the neighborhood remains thematized in this nightlife scene. Several of these bars feature live music, and

Table 3.1 Concentration of Selected Industries in Bucktown and Wicker Park Relative to the Chicago MSA, 2000

Industry Code	Industry	Location Quotient
31–	Manufacturing	1.3
711110	Theater companies & dinner theaters	3.1
711130	Musical groups & artists	2.0
711510	Independent artists, writers & performers	1.7
722110/211	Full and limited-service restaurants	1.6
722410	Drinking places (alcoholic beverages)	1.8

Source: U.S. County Business Patterns, 2000. The Location Quotient (LQ) statistic can be used to measure how concentrated an industry is in a particular geographic area at a point in time. An LQ greater than one indicates that the concentration exceeds the average for the Chicago Metropolitan Standard Area. Thus, Drinking places has an LQ of 1.8, indicating that the share of drinking places in Wicker Park is eighty percent greater than in the MSA.

others host open-mikes for local poets and writers to read their work. Walls are often decorated by murals or hanging pieces created by local visual artists. Interiors are typically kept deliberately unpolished and are decorated with retro furnishings like old couches and lamps. Usually, they are dimly lit, with lighting strategically deployed to produce the shadowy, chiaroscuro effects associated with film noir.[17] Moreover, the connection to the arts community in these bars is displayed through the personae of the bartenders and wait staff, which disproportionately consists of young cultural producers and aspirants.

In addition to these watering holes, the neighborhood is now also thick on the ground with restaurants that often cater to an affluent as well as stylish clientele. These venues are representative of the various types of "new wave" restaurants that Zukin notes began to multiply in big cities during the 1980s,[18] reflecting the cosmopolitan tastes of professionals in a globalizing economy. "Restaurants have become incubators of innovation in urban culture. . . . For cultural consumers, restaurants produce an increasingly global product tailored to local tastes."[19] Spring, a popular and high-priced restaurant on North Avenue, serves Pan-Asian cuisine, a style that quotes ethnic culinary traditions rather than reproducing them. For several years in Wicker Park only the decidedly mediocre Pacific Café served sushi, a pricey bill of fare that is extremely popular with young professionals. By 2001, there were five sushi restaurants in the neighborhood: Blue Fin, Mirai, Bob San, Papajin, and the inexplicably still-open Pacific Café. Moreover, a range of other regional and ethnic cuisines are readily available: Thai (Thai Lagoon), Persian (Souk), Italian (Babaluci), Soul Food (Soul Kitchen), and many more. Lodged in converted industrial spaces and retail storefronts, these restaurants display the dramatic juxtaposition of grit and glamour that is a key modality of neo-bohemian

value. And despite the cosmopolitan cultural influences, the restaurants' public face is presented by servers who are American-born artists, marrying exotic cuisines to the hip and funky ambiance of the local bohemia. Thus, many of these restaurants thematize, all at once, culinary tastes emblematic of postmodern globalization (simulacra of "authentic" ethnic traditions), the adaptive recycling of postindustrial symbols and spaces, and the creative vibrancy of an artists' community.

Both bars and restaurants cluster along the neighborhood's main drags of Milwaukee, North, Damen, and Division, interspersed with new retail outlets, as well as the check-cashing stands and discount furniture stores that endure from a less high-profile period. They are key pieces of the "retail renaissance" that includes shops selling antiques, art supplies, records and CDs, and fashionable (even edgy) attire, along with some two dozen art galleries.[20] Actual artists, as well as young professionals, live above these establishments in Milwaukee Avenue lofts, for example. These mixed uses produce just the kind of lively and eclectic pedestrian traffic that Jane Jacobs lauded with so much enthusiasm in her description of Greenwich Village;[21] they belie dystopic imaginations of the dead inner city. Thus is the "scene" constituted in neo-bohemia, through the activities of artists, entrepreneurs, consumers, and service laborers, categories of social actors that bleed into one another.

The popularity of the neo-bohemian scene, taken as whole, demonstrates its ongoing appeal to a new class of urban consumers even though, or perhaps because, the gritty motifs discussed in chapter 3 increasingly belie the reality of a more upscale residential and consumption profile. For all the demographic changes of the past ten years on Chicago's near West Side, there persists the allure of the cutting edge on which local entrepreneurs capitalize, making use of local artists as standard-bearers in the process.

Hiring artists keeps the businesses tapped into an ethos of hip creativity. Moreover, entrepreneurs in the neighborhood justifiably view themselves as creative scene makers in their own right. By opening and maintaining establishments that express the neo-bohemian place ethos of Wicker Park, they do not merely appropriate elements of the scene—they are integral components of the scene.

FROM THE NORTH SIDE TO MIRAI

By examining the cases of two establishments, opened at opposite ends of the 1990s, we can see the continuity in strategies of scene production in the neighborhood. When Cyril Landise opened the North Side Café in 1988, it was among the first new businesses in Wicker Park clearly banking on neighborhood change. In contrast to the dense entertainment scene depicted above, Landise recalls, "All the storefronts from North Avenue to the tracks were vacant, every single storefront." Although the bar, with its fake fireplace and beer garden, resembles many such venues catering to comparatively affluent professionals in the city's lakefront communities like Lincoln Park, Landise insists that the relative underdevelopment of the neighborhood allowed him to go for a funkier vibe, consistent with the emerging neo-bohemia, and predictive of subsequent neighborhood designs. When I interviewed him in 1995, he recalled:

The advantages were that it was a little more free form. Since the neighborhood wasn't sedate . . . there weren't a lot of restrictions on what we could do. So it just felt freer, we could make a little more noise, we could have a little more bizarre [attractions]. We could book bands once in a while, and they would play out in the garden. We'd try different kinds of music, we'd try more bizarre menu items. We were able to do a lot of things you didn't do at Bennigan's because it wasn't done. We didn't

care if it wasn't done, in fact we liked it better if it had never been done.

Like Urbus Orbis' owner, Tom Handley, Landise liked to think of his bar as far more than a business opportunity. Though he did not explicitly mention Oldenberg's book *The Great Good Place*, Landise may as well have been quoting from it when describing his aspirations for the North Side. Oldenberg argues that third places serve as social levelers, and Landise asserts, "The most distinctive expression that I try to put in every fiber of the place is a sense of equality, that is the fact that I want this to be a respite from any sense of the caste system. . . . My idea of a really interesting place to be is somebody with purple spiked hair sitting next to a guy in a suit talking about some topic of interest at the bar."

For Landise, as for many other subsequent local entrepreneurs, the growing population of neighborhood artists made available a workforce consistent with his goal of a more "free-form" environment:

Everyone who worked here really saw it as a mixture of lifestyle and income. Anybody who sees it as just income doesn't last long. They tend to come in—the corporate waitress types, the bartenders, the managers who are looking for a gig—[but] for some reason don't stay here. The ones who stay here are people who are artists and actresses, writers. There's almost a sense of community here. And they get to talk with people, there's much less distinction between a patron and a server here.

Landise claims that the high number of artists employed by his establishment did not occur by conscious design. He concedes that "people who are artists are more interesting and intelligent than those who aren't"—presumably an advantage in the interview process. But he adds, "I never consciously sought out artists. They'd come in here and they'd apply, [but] we never said 'Are you an artist?' We'd hire them for totally different reasons and then find out that they are."

Landise claims to hire both artists and non-artists, while conceding that artists are easier to retain since they are more likely to buy into the employment culture that he seeks to maintain. In doing so they become part of the scene: not just passive servers catering to the whims of patrons, but active participants in the production of the overall ambiance, the creation of a "really interesting place."

Granted these workers differ from the other participants in the scene by virtue of having to take orders, serve food and beverages, and mop counters in addition to engaging in spirited, third place-style exchanges. But Landise is right to note that they contribute more than base servility. Being "more interesting and intelligent than other people," and almost always possessing exceptional competence at the key leisure pursuit of fashionability, the artist as service worker contributes to the production of the bar's ambiance in an outsize way. This double duty comes at a cost to Landise of minimum wage, which, as he proudly points out, is twice what he is legally mandated to pay employees who work primarily for tips. The vaunted ideology of "community" and "creativity" becomes the coin with which this labor is secured. Landise tells the story of an employee who came to the North Side from a much swankier and more remunerative restaurant job:

> The waitress right there in fact came here from Charlie Trotter's, a very high-end restaurant on Armitage, $250 for two people to eat. It's one of the few four-star restaurants in Chicago, and she was a waitress there, and she said, "No, that's not for me. That's a lifestyle commitment to servitude that I'm not interested in subscribing to, even though the money's great." So she can come here and make less money, but not be a server: she can be a co-equal in the community.

And yet, service workers at the North Side and other neighborhood bars are not co-equals with either Landise or the bar's patrons—within the structure of the social situation, they remain subordinates, although the way that subordinate status plays out can be complicated.

This is not to presume that Landise is being insincere, and as Erik Olin Wright points out, small capitalists occupy structurally contradictory positions with regard to relations of production.[22] Unlike in large corporations, the owners typically toil in close proximity to their employees, often realizing small and precarious financial rewards for their labor. While the corporate form allows top executives to insulate themselves from risk that is passed on to shareholders and employees, this is not case for entrepreneurs like Landise. His personal stake in the venture far exceeds that of his employees, who do not view their employment as a permanent commitment, and who typically move from one service job to the next with some regularity before departing the service "industry" altogether. While Landise may yearn for community, in order to be viable in a competitive arena, his business must eventually extract significant surplus value from the labor of its employees, and therefore must direct its strategies toward that end. As it happens, this is a goal many small businesses fail to achieve, leading to short average life spans for new enterprises. Landise points out that for the first two years of the North Side's existence it was not profitable, a fact that created enormous personal strain:

> I got a developer to essentially lend me a couple of hundred thousand dollars on a handshake, and that worked, and within a couple of years we were a viable business. In two years I was actually paying myself regularly. For about a year and a half I didn't get paid so often. The staff always got paid. The owners didn't always get paid. So I lived off credit cards. I was very much in debt. . . . So you learn to lay awake at night and watch the trees blow, and say, "My God."

His employees have much less invested in the success of the venture; they view their employment as temporary, and therefore, while most would wish him the best of luck, they have far less personal commitment to the business. Genuine desire to produce a harmonious workplace intersects with the requirement that Landise control his workers, however soft and apparently benign the strategies directed to this end may appear. And the hard fact remains that Landise has the privilege of being able to terminate the employment relationship, a decisive source of power asymmetry. At the North Side, as with other bars and restaurants in the neighborhood, rates of employee turnover are quite high, despite the ethos of community and collective enterprise.

The North Side persists in its Damen Avenue location, now surrounded by a host of trendy competitors, and it continues to employ a rotating cast of colorful employees linked to the arts in Chicago. For all the changes in the local retail ecology, new businesses continue to echo the strategies articulated by Landise, actively striving to construct a sense of cutting edge ambiance. Mirai, a sushi restaurant, opened in 1999 at the opposite end of the neighborhood, on what was then a lightly developed stretch of Division Street just west of Damen. Like the North Side, it helped to initiate what has become a fairly dramatic retail expansion in its immediate vicinity. When Mirai opened, the development on the street was still decidedly uneven, with a Laundromat across the street and vacant lots and shuttered storefronts interspersed on the block.

Mirai is a chic, two-story venue catering to the beautiful people, as Matt Gans, its initial manager, indicates:

> Mirai is crazy, man. It plays to this obsession with the Asian culture. They have the finest sushi chefs in the country. They put this funky nightclub upstairs and the whole thing was designed by this crazy French guy François, so it was ultra-swanky. But it's a restaurant, not a nightclub; people go upstairs to wait [for a table]. They don't mind [waiting] because the upstairs bar is this totally swank fancy hangout, [people in] great clothing. They come dressed to kill. It's a stomping ground, it's a place they want to come to be seen at before they go out to be seen. . . . It's an insanely good location. This area had not had that caliber of restaurant, as long as everybody's been living here. They had Pacific Café, which is also sushi, [but] awful sushi. So they'd been kind of waiting for something to come to the neighborhood. In a way, it's completely different for Wicker Park, it's not grungy—it's not anything you would expect around here.

But the juxtaposition of Mirai's posh atmosphere with the underdeveloped local landscape serves to heighten the drama for its patrons, and allows them to imagine that they are consuming a product unavailable to those too timid or uninformed to venture into the wilds of the new bohemia.

Geared to hip and well-heeled party people, rather than greasy slimy artists, the link to the neighborhood neo-bohemia is manifested in the staff. Says Gans:

> [The staff] is very representative of Wicker Park. The girls are very artistically inclined, very imaginative, very creative. The guys are the same, they're musicians. We specifically hired very funky-looking people because of wanting to appeal to Wicker Park. Meia [the owner] specifically hired these girls that looked crazy. They looked totally different than everybody else. It's eye candy. It's something you don't normally get up close and personal. Piercings, different colored hair, no bras. *It's what's going on.*

This hiring strategy was thus directed explicitly to producing the desired ambiance at Mirai—that is, to making the scene. As with Landise at the North Side, the hiring of artists is also a move toward securing employee loyalty and engendering the kind of soft control associated with the post-Fordist workplace. Gans elaborates: "It was strategic for us to hire from this neighborhood, people who live here that can walk to work. We thought they would be very prone to give us their souls because they lived here." As for their artistic interests, he says, "I think it makes a difference, because a lot of these people are so passionate about what they do, as far as their creativity and what they do personally, and [they like] being able to come to a place where they can kind of express that, where they feel they can be who they are."

Neighborhood resident and musician Brent Puls was an early employee of Mirai. A vocalist and saxophone player in the local funk and hip-hop band Bumpus, Puls is a handsome, hip-looking man in his mid-twenties with spiked blonde hair. Previously he had bartended at the Note on Milwaukee Avenue. Puls confirms Gans's observations concerning Mirai's hiring strategy:

[The owner] hired people more for their looks than their experience. Like I'm pretty sure one girl she hired because she had dreads and was a little bit weird. It's very eclectic. We have the most handsome guy I've ever met. And then there's Larissa who has pink hair. And everyone is doing art of some kind. . . . Look at the restaurant itself. It's very sleek, somewhat elegant, but not overly fancy. And sort of contrast all the [employees] dressed in black, and there's something weird about them. The restaurant is called Mirai because it means future in Japanese. Meia wanted to be really cutting edge, the cutting-edge place to get sushi in the city, to have this really elegant place that also had these hip kids working at it.

Unlike most neighborhood venues, Mirai features an employee dress code, albeit a minimalist one. Employees were required to sport a strict ensemble consisting of a solid white shirt and solid black pants or skirt, items they were expected to supply themselves. This stark ensemble serves to highlight the striking features of the individual employees, from stunning good looks to dreadlocks or pink hair.

Gans concedes that Meia, the owner, evinces a highly driven and authoritarian

style. He saw his managerial role as requiring that he soften Meia's demands for efficient performance in communicating them to the employees, since, being artists, they are often sensitive sorts. He is an extremely affable and likable individual, and he presents a laid-back persona even when giving strict instructions. Still, he also points out that his effort to cajole employees' hard work in a friendly fashion was backed up by the power to fire them if they failed to go along:

Meia, she's the Gestapo owner, the Fuhrer, the drive, y'know; she's relentless. But she also has the respect of everyone who works there because she's a woman in this business by herself that's made a name for herself, and they're making good money. I took everything she said and put it in terms that they could understand. And I always had a smile on my face. But I was also the person who fired every single person [who got fired] in that place. I was your best friend, and I would help you out as best I could, but if you weren't doing your job, I was also the person to fire you. I would cut you off right away.

Precisely because Wicker Park and the surrounding neighborhoods remain beacons for young aspirants in the arts into the 2000s, there is more than enough slack in the labor market to swiftly replace those who are "cut off" with similarly colorful new workers.

SCENE MAKERS

The neighborhood demography and the elective affinity between the flexible lifestyle dispositions of young artists and service work connect entrepreneurs to a steady stream of applicants from the arts community. Established bars and restaurants rarely take out ads for new employees. Information about new openings travels by word of mouth, and preference is given to the acquaintances of current staff in further hiring, buttressing the sense of community. Hiring quickly becomes a closed loop, dominated by artists and their friends, a state of affairs that generally suits the interests of employers nicely.

Thus, new employees typically enter into these jobs by leveraging contacts that they have made in the arts community. For example, Amy Teri, who worked first as a cocktail waitress and then as a bartender for almost a decade at the Borderline, was invited to apply by a classmate at Columbia College. "I got the job when I was 21. Do you remember Amy Novack? The staple of the Borderline. Actually I had a photography class with her. They needed a cocktail waitress, and I started working as a cocktail waitress." Tall and extremely striking, Amy Novack worked at the Borderline throughout the 1990s, leaving a gaping hole in the local scene when she eventually departed for New York toward the end of the decade. Together, the two Amys (known by regulars as "Big Amy" and "Little Amy") were fixtures behind the bar, with their outsize personalities a key part of the ambiance. By hiring their friends, they stamped the place with an enduring personality. Amy Teri eventually took charge of the hiring herself, and she adopted a strategy similar to Amy Novack's when it came to recruitment: "It's pretty much, people that get hired here are regular customers or they know someone, it's a friend-of-a-friend kind of thing. We never, ever hired anyone who has walked in off the street and said, 'Here's my application.' I just throw them in the garbage. . . . Everybody who works here now knew somebody, and that's how they have the job here."

This pattern not only keeps the Borderline's owners (three Macedonian brothers who also own Café Absinthe, Red Dog, and the Blue Dolphin) tapped into a labor market comprising cool kids with high neighborhood profiles, but it also buttresses the kind of "soft control" that prevails in the post-Fordist workplace. Amy Teri adds, "It's nice, all the bartenders are pretty close and hang out after work, and it's a pretty tight family

here. That's about all we have going on right now. If you don't have that behind the bar, then forget it, then otherwise it will drive you crazy."

These employees also improve the ambiance by serving as magnets for their friends, who likely possess hip cultural capital, and by frequenting the bar on their off nights. Young artists and service workers like to visit establishments where they know members of the staff, as the special attention they receive is one way insider status in the scene is confirmed. Many bartenders in the neighborhood are a source of attraction by virtue of their exalted position in the service status hierarchy. Local writer and bartender Krystal Ashe describes them as "the Startenders," a common phrase in the industry. "There are bartenders that work at three or four different clubs, [and] that promote their own nights, and people go there because they are working there." This dimension can be crucial to the bar's ambiance, since patrons measure one another in determining the coolness of the bar or restaurant.

DEALING WITH THE AMATEURS

Most bars and many restaurants are only open during the evening; in any event, nighttime is usually where the bulk of activity occurs and the most money is made, for owners and staff alike. If they are available at all, day shifts are comparatively unprofitable and undesirable. They can also be depressing. Krystal remembers, "I had a day shift [in a neighborhood bar], and people would be coming in five days a week. That lasted three weeks for me because it's just so sad." The Borderline opens at 2 o'clock in the afternoon, and each member of the permanent staff must work one afternoon shift a week. Most of the work on this shift consists of stocking and preparing the bar for the evening, a duty carefully attended to out of a sense of obligation to the co-workers who will replace them on the evening shift. What patronage there is generally consists of older men from the neighborhood drinking cheap beers, often regular customers who bring the bartender face to face with the unhappy consequences of a lifetime of alcoholism. These shifts are endured grudgingly as a necessary sacrifice for the right to work the far more lucrative evening hours, especially on Friday and Saturday.

Though night shifts are where the money is, they are not without drawbacks. Evening patrons do not typically produce the sadness inspired by day-shift alcoholics, but they do animate a host of status antagonisms. The night brings servers into contact with urban dwellers who are not involved directly in the arts and who hold 9-to-5 jobs, a group often lumped together under the pejorative of "amateurs" by the savvy industry professionals. This is especially true as the neighborhood demographics shift, and the vaunted entertainment scene receives constant advertisement to the metro area in the daily newspapers. Patrons who are presumed to hold professional jobs and live outside the neighborhood are especially reviled for their multiple inadequacies in the performance of bar etiquette.

The bohemian dispositions of workers can lead to a reversal of the ordinary patterns of age, race, and gender discrimination, as Landise indicates:

It's funny, in a lot of venues you have to remind the staff that they have to treat someone who's dressed in an unusual way with respect and dignity. Here you have to give the other admonition. Just because they have suits on doesn't mean they're jerks. You have to treat them politely, and if they behave properly—I don't care who they are, how old they are, what color they are, I don't care if they're white fat businessmen in suits—you've got to be nice to them. . . . And it's a kind of atypical admonition, usually it's the other way around. With the staff we have attracted, the tendency is not to want to wait on a woman in a fur or a guy in a suit. They don't treat them very nicely.

While a clientele of professionals improves the profitability of the establishment, these "outsiders" displease bar and restaurant workers by failing to tip in an extravagant manner, despite the fact that they presumably command fabulous wealth. Shortly before she quit and moved to New York, I asked Amy Novack how business was at the Borderline. She rolled her eyes: "These fucking yuppies that come in now, they don't know how to tip."

These "yuppies" also offend bar professionals by failing to "handle their liquor," often becoming "sloppy drunks," especially on Friday and Saturday nights, the big nights out for those who hold 9-to-5 weekday jobs.[23] In addition to incompetent drinking, they are considered to operate at a significant style deficit compared to the superhip kids that fill service positions. Says Puls of the Note:

You start getting the suburbanite yuppie crowd. Tight jeans. The big over-polished white people. The Note was a big meat market, and it became even more of a big market with Gold Coasters and actually a lot of suburbanites coming in. Arco, the bouncer, at the end of the night he would start kicking people out, and he would yell, "The bus to Schaumberg [a North Shore suburb] is leaving now!"

The Borderline continues to draw a very diverse crowd, one that is inflected by the presence of the Red Dog nightclub upstairs. Because Red Dog remains a hip spot on the club kid circuit and showcases different musical styles on different nights, it draws patronage to the corner from the black and Latino communities and from the gay community. The latter especially come in on Monday nights, which Raul refers to as "a supreme queen scene" popular with transsexuals and drag queens. Still, Borderline rests at the heart of the West Side entertainment scene on the six corners, and its patronage has also shifted from mostly artists and scene makers to increasing numbers of young professionals. While many of these may actually now live in Wicker Park or nearby, given the levels of gentrification, they are nevertheless ordinarily presumed by the staff to come from even more gentrified neighborhoods like Lincoln Park or from the suburbs, as Anne, a former cocktail waitress, indicates:

> I guess you get a lot of people from the suburbs. There was a pub-crawl the other night. Are you fucking kidding me? These guys come in: "Yeah, I want five pitchers, can we get a discount on this? Do you have plastic cups?" "No. Drink your beer and go." I hate to be a bitch, but it's like, you get these people. This girl comes in Friday night, right when I got to work, and she was drunk already. She was like, "I lost my wallet." She thinks it fell under the table. I don't know what I can do. . . . They want me to get down on my hands and knees to get their fucking wallet.

The claim that these outsiders demand inordinate, and demeaning, servility recurred often in my conversations with Wicker Park's service workers.

Nina Norris once managed the Note and later bartended a couple of blocks down on Milwaukee at the Holiday Club. She described the differences between "yuppie" patrons in her bar and cooler kids "from the neighborhood": "There's a certain kind of dress thing. The people from Lincoln Park have this weird kind of college thing. They all wear their little uniform with their sweatshirt and jeans, or their oxford and jeans, it's really kind of odd. . . . The people that live in [Wicker Park] tend to be funkier and trendier; they have their goatees, nail polish on the men, earrings and tattoos, that stuff." These descriptions show us once again that presumptive spatial affiliation becomes shorthand denoting normative distinctions around style and demeanor: people from Lincoln Park are conformist and unhip, and people from the suburbs are even worse. Of course, the 2000 census shows that half of Wicker Park's employed population was made up of young professionals. It is unlikely that more than a small number of

the customers ever actually disclosed to Anne or Nina where they lived, but that doesn't matter, since "people from Lincoln Park" or "people from the suburbs" is less a geographic than a species distinction. Many of the Wicker Park artists and food and beverage service workers were themselves born and raised in the suburbs, but they have repudiated this pedigree to live *la vie bohème.*

In contrast to Milwaukee Avenue bars like the Holiday Club and the Note, Mirai tends to get a more stylish crowd, although their style is not necessarily of the variety that Wicker Park artists personally identify with. Recalls Brent: "It's definitely a Gold Coast crowd. It's gonna be trendy club kids, everybody shops at Club Monacco, everyone probably on weekends does [the drug] Ecstasy at the clubs, and is probably twenty-five to thirty-five and has a lot of money. That's pretty much the clientele in a nutshell. At first it was entertaining, now it all kinds of grates on me. It's not my crowd. I can't relate to them at all." With the Gold Coast, we get another geographic designation that stands in for social type. "Gold Coast" patrons, whether or not they actually have an address in the ultra-expensive lakefront district, are trendier and flashier; they also are "better behaved." That is, they're comfortable with and well versed in norms of comportment in places such as Mirai's. Still, they are resented for their presumptive entitlement compared to the plight of "starving artists" toiling to serve them.

Nonetheless, they are better than those typed in the "suburban" and the "Lincoln Park" phyla, which err in multiple ways. Brent indicates that as well as lacking style, many patrons at the Note were clueless when it came to reading the cues of social interaction in the bar, often because of their incompetent handling of alcohol: "I saw so many things that depressed me when I was working. You know, some girl just sitting there by herself, and some guy walks over and starts talking to her, and they're both like sloppy drunk, and she's not talking to him, and he's not getting the hint."

Krystal worked at the now-defunct Mad Bar in Wicker Park when I interviewed her in 2000, and she indicated the crowd was far better behaved there, a fact that she attributed to the patronage of artists and service workers—categories that overlap:

KA: The people that come in [Mad Bar], even if they drink a lot, I hate to say they're probably alcoholics which is why they're so well controlled, it's definitely a nicer crowd. A better tipping crowd. I had to do a lot less work to make the same amount of money.

RDL: How do you account for that?

KA: More service industry, being in the middle of an artists' neighborhood, which is service industry. Here, you have people, even if they're in college, they are probably working at a restaurant to make ends meet, whereas in Lincoln Park, those people were being funded by their parents. There's a whole different respect there.

Krystal's emphasis on "respect" alerts us to patterns of behavior among some patrons that prove far more threatening to the bar workers' sense of selves than simple bad drinking and bad outfits. It is widely agreed among service workers in and around Wicker Park that "yuppies" are more likely to force workers to confront the servility that is, after all, the nature of their jobs. Says Rainbo bartender Jimmy Garbe of the "new class" of patrons at the Rainbo that appeared with increased gentrification and neighborhood notoriety, "Maybe I'm a little paranoid, but there's a definite sense that the newer clientele looks down on us a little bit. I don't want to be looked down on like I'm a servant to the person because they're dropping cash in here."

NOTES

1. Lloyd and Clark, "City as an Entertainment Machine."
2. Terry Nichols Clark, "Trees and Real Violins: Building Postindustrial Chicago," working paper, University of Chicago, 2000, p. 12.
3. Bart Eeckhout, "The Disneyfication of Times Square: Back to the Future?," Critical Perspectives on Urban Redevelopment 6 (2001): 379–428; John Hannigan, Fantasy City: Pleasure and Profit in the Postmodern Metropolis (New York: Routledge, 1998).
4. Dennis Judd, "Constructing the Tourist Bubble," in The Tourist City, ed. Dennis Judd and Susan Fainstein (New Haven, CT: Yale University Press, 1999).
5. Jameson, Postmodernism, pp. 39–44; for a critique of Jameson's deracinated perspective, see Robert Fairbanks, "A Theoretical Primer on Space," Critical Social Work 3 (2003): 131–154.
6. Jean Baudrillard, America (New York: Verso, 1989); Umberto Eco, Travels in Hyperreality (New York: Harcourt Brace Jovanovich, 1986).
7. Michael Sorkin, Variations on a Theme Park (New York: Hill and Wang, 1992), p. 205.
8. Adorno and Horkheimer, Dialectic of Enlightenment.
9. Jean-François Lyotard, The Postmodern Condition (Minneapolis: University of Minnesota Press, 1979), p. 76.
10. David Grazian, Blue Chicago: The Search for Authenticity in Urban Blues Clubs (Chicago: University of Chicago Press, 2003).
11. Lloyd and Clark, "City as an Entertainment Machine," p. 357.
12. Sassen, Global City, pp. 286–287.
13. Clark and Rempel, Citizen Politics in Postindustrial Societies; Lloyd and Clark, "City as an Entertainment Machine."
14. Clark et al., "Amenities Drive Urban Growth"; Leonard Nevarez, New Money, Nice Town (New York: Routledge, 2003).
15. Richard A. Peterson and Roger Kern, "Changing Highbrow Taste: From Snob to Omnivore," American Sociological Review 61 (1996): 5.
16. Lloyd and Clark, "The City as an Entertainment Machine."
17. See James Naremore, More Than Night: Film Noir in Its Contexts (Berkeley: University of California Press, 1998).
18. Zukin, Culture of Cities, p. 154.
19. Ibid., p. 182.
20. Jacquee Thomas, "Transitional Areas Attracting Renters," Chicago Sun-Times, Sept. 20, 1998, p. NC2.
21. Jacobs, Death and Life of Great American Cities.
22. Erik Olin Wright, Classes (New York: Verso, 1985).
23. David Grazian makes a similar observation about the boorishness of dabblers in Chicago Blues clubs. Grazian, Blue Chicago.

CHAPTER 4

The Black Bourgeoisie Meets the Truly Disadvantaged

Mary Pattillo

When the black bourgeoisie meets the truly disadvantaged face to face as neighbors, the issues are as crucial as keeping a roof overhead, raising a healthy and productive child, and feeling like you belong.

Gladyse Taylor easily felt that she belonged when she bought her home in Oakland in 1989. She was literally coming back, not to the block on which she grew up, but not too far from it. She was born in the Ida B. Wells projects a stone's throw away from her new home. Her journey from the projects to a five-thousand-square-foot, three-story house was, she believed, what public housing was all about: a stepping-stone—or in her case a launching pad—on the way to success. Bringing her talents and experiences back to the block felt right, and welcomed. "I've not had any problems with people in the community Actually I think for the most part, they were kind of excited. Even though they realized that the gentrification was taking place, they were happy and pleased that it was someone black." Taylor has a hypothesis that when the black bourgeoisie meets the truly disadvantaged it is more amicable than an encounter between the white gentry and the black poor. An assumption underlies her statement that black gentrification is distinctive, maybe even strange, and is smoothed by the common skin color of old-timers amid newcomers.

Ms. Taylor's comment suggests a set of research questions: Is "pleased" how old-timers feel about the blackness of the gentrifi-

ers? Or is it contempt? ambivalence? appreciation? a sense of betrayal? Or does it provoke different sentiments in different contexts? When in the late 1990s Paul Knight and his family sold the home that his grandparents bought in 1949 they were worried about severing the generational legacy that the house represented. "The neighborhood is alive in some kind of way. Like this house. This house is what we wanted, and it didn't want us to leave. But now it's okay. It likes Tracey and it likes her husband." Something about the buyers calmed Mr. Knight (or the house). Maybe it was that the buyers were married, or that Tracey had helped Knight with his resume a few years before. Or maybe it was that Tracey and her husband were black. Mr. Knight did not say specifically, but other cues—like the pride he expressed about his uncle, who was the first black graphic artist for the Chicago Police Department, or his outfit by Sean John, a popular black clothing company—made it plausible that he was more "pleased" to sell his house to a black couple than he would have been had they been white.

In a different context, Rosie Foster was bothered by a community meeting in which residents maligned public housing, of which she herself was a resident. Having heard enough in the meeting, she rose from her chair and interjected, "[It's] like you don't want the projects in this community. I thought this was a community thing? Maybe I'm getting the wrong vibe here. Some of the questions just seemed like people have a problem with things. Always acting like you don't want to live next to people in CHA." Whereas Paul Knight's soul was soothed by the blackness of the couple that bought his house, Rosie Foster got the *wrong* vibe from African American newcomers who seemed allergic to public housing and its residents. The reality is that a range of emotions and sentiments characterize the interaction in North Kenwood-Oakland as the settings change and communication styles are practiced and perfected. Exploring and analyzing the variable tenor of these exchanges provides a rich depiction of the forging of a black community, and an empirically informed theory of the intersections of race, class, and place.

THE ENCOUNTER

Emmett Coleman moved to North Kenwood with his wife and daughters in 1983. He was a bit ahead of the real rush, but his boss, who was well connected with higher-ups in city planning, advised him that the move would pay off financially. "Everyone else was saying don't do it, you know. Hoodlums and thugs, you know. And dope. And it's slum and blighted." Twenty years later he concluded that his decision to buy the house was a good one. He also recognized how common it was to be torn by contradictory advice from the optimists and the naysayers. "Each buppie family that I talked with tells the same story. Their friends were apprehensive at first and then in recent years, you know, recent months [their friends ask], 'Are there any more properties around?'" Coleman also got confirmation of what he expected: all the supposed hoodlums and thugs weren't as bad as they were rumored to be. His early "encounters," like the one narrated below, went off without a hitch.

> Like I said, I was working in a corporate setting, so I had to wear a suit. So the first day

I moved over here, my wife was out of town with the kids and I got off the bus at 43rd and Berkeley and all the brothers were out there. You know what I mean. There was a tavern up there, so you know. I looked kind of conspicuous because in those days people would dress, you know, rebelliously and what not . . . [So] I'm in a business suit and I get off the bus. And this wasn't pretended, it was just instinctive. When I got off the bus, I said, "Hey fellas! I got some time on the transfer. Anybody need a transfer?" [And they responded,] "Yeah, mellow. Thanks, man." And [I] went on down the street. And I thought about that afterwards. I said, "Hey, you fell right in.". . . And my point is, it wasn't pretended. It was just automatic. It was just, you know, it was just there.

The lilt of Coleman's voice is not perceptible on the written page, and it's hard to re-create how the word "fellas" fit into the black slang of the 1980s. When read, the exchange makes Coleman sound kind of square. But this is misleading. Coleman told this story to make a point about how he "knew something about urban problems and urban living," having grown up in Chicago's Black Belt in the 1940s. As an adult moving up the corporate ladder he lived in integrated Hyde Park, but he had not forgotten how to maneuver the social worlds of working-class and poor black neighborhoods. It was in his body. It was in his voice. "It was just there." In the conceptual framework of anthropologist John L. Jackson, it was "sincere." His performance required "trust over proof"—the trust of the "fellas" who accepted the transfer, and the trust of me and my readers (you) that it was as heartfelt and comfortable as he claimed and experienced it to be.[1]

Coleman might have exaggerated, but only a bit, in saying that his suited presence was a conspicuous anomaly in North Kenwood in the 1980s. The unemployment rate in 1980 was over 20 percent, but nearly 40 percent of those who did work worked in white-collar occupations, a broad category for sure, but one that could include workers who wear suits. He did likely catch the eye of the young men on the corner when he got home from work, but as much for his newcomer status as for his suit. And just as he naturally pulled out the appropriate words and delivery to make the interaction work, so too did the young men he greeted.

George Wade wasn't, but could have been, one of those men standing in front of the tavern as Coleman came home from work. He lived only a few blocks away from Coleman's house when he was a young teenager in the 1970s. He was not in a gang, but his older brother was and Wade remembers sneaking to watch the older guys fight, sometimes using homemade zip guns. When I met George Wade, he was unemployed and having difficulty finding work due to chronic health problems. He had moved from apartment to apartment in the neighborhood, once because the house he was living in was sold to someone who planned to convert it back into a single-family home. That experience made him acutely aware of the changes going on around him. The plan, as he saw it, was to "balance the budget. We tryin' to make the poor live with the rich. The whole idea is to make the neighborhood comfortable. That's what all this is about. To make the whole neighborhood comfortable." Wade liked the idea of mixing rich and poor, and even mixing black and white. And when new people like Emmett Coleman moved in, he knew how to act. He told me, "Like me, I don't think of myself as poor, poor, poor. I see myself as a little bit above poor. And I can hang in with them and get along with them 'cause I know how to talk to people. And then I can get a good response and they get a good response. But [with] some of us, it's not that way, you know. It's just, we wanna do it the hard way." Wade welcomed the changes in the neighborhood and committed himself to holding up his part of the bargain to make the mixed-income community experiment work. But he also recognized

that other longtime residents might not be so inclined and might take a different route, "the hard way." "If we live in this neighborhood together, everybody help one another, [then] I'm sayin' it's no need of me to take from you when I can ask from you." As the neighborhood changes and the new groups come in contact with one another, Wade sees the options as aggression or accommodation, crime or solicitousness, and both are possibilities.

Envision Emmett Coleman alighting from the bus, an exemplar of the black bourgeoisie with his suit and his briefcase. He meets George Wade with his truly disadvantaged friends, drinking and having a good time right where they've been drinking and having a good time since well before Coleman moved in. Coleman offers his bus transfer. Wade accepts it and adds a cordial greeting and maybe a handshake to show his appreciation. They go their separate ways with a subtle sense of accomplishment. The encounter took work on both sides. If it had not, neither man would be so cognizant of and pleased with his ability to make such interactions go smoothly. As North Kenwood-Oakland experiences the transition from being a predominantly poor neighborhood to one where rich, middle class, and poor live side by side, most (but not all) meetings fall within this type. In the public sphere tolerance is the norm.[2]

For newcomers who sociologist Japonica Brown-Saracino would call "social preservationists," socioeconomic diversity is also part of the allure of the neighborhood.[3] Reflecting on what she enjoys about North Kenwood-Oakland, resident Soeurette Hector commented:

> I like it in the sense where I'm able to touch the poor right on 43rd Street, and the store that was there, [and] the alcoholics. I like that in a sense. In a sense that as long as they don't dirty it, they don't throw their bottles and everything, it doesn't bother me. It doesn't bother me to see older fellows sitting at the corner of

43rd Street talking about old times and listening to the blues. It made me feel good. Or the older guy that sits over here and he blasts his music, his blues, and he sits there with his cane just contemplating nature, whatever, the sun. It doesn't bother me. I think it's a beautiful thing. That's me. He's not dirtying anything. He's cleaning his flowers by himself. He's sitting in his chair, nobody bothers him, he's not bugging anybody, he's not screaming, he's not yelling. He's just outside.

"The poor" that Hector likes to "touch" are a reality in the neighborhood, and both Mr. Coleman and Ms. Hector congratulate themselves on their ability to get along in such a diverse context. The brothers and alcoholics display the same ability. Both sides draw on their repertoire of experiences to communicate respectfully with one another. If this were not the case, the neighborhood would be nothing more than a boxing ring of scorn and suspicion. It is not that at all, even if such feelings and perspectives do lurk beneath the agreeable surface. The facility with which the haves and have-nots negotiate each other is based partially on having been trained in all-black settings that were also mixed-income, not necessarily by design but because of the circumstances of racial discrimination and disproportionate poverty that impact black residential America.[4]

This easygoing public face notwithstanding, the subterranean mutual critiques that stem partially from class differences are equally important for understanding the interactional milieu and the political battles in North Kenwood-Oakland. At the most basic level, the two groups just do things differently. John Mason, a bank supervisor, did not have to think long to answer my question: "Any stories to share about your neighbors?" "I guess in my upbringing we didn't have a lot of traffic through the house," he began. "They're the exact opposite. I mean it's like they have relatives, daughters and cousins, who come over every day, seven days a week. To me it'd be nauseating because there's no privacy. I mean, when do you kind of regroup to do what you need to do?" Mason's discomfort with the comings and goings of extended family next door is an example of Frazier's characterization of the black bourgeoisie as removed from the traditions of the "folk." But it's more complicated than that. The evidence shows that middle-class blacks still engage with their extended families and tend to have more contact with their mothers and siblings than middle-class whites have.[5] I doubt that the practice of visiting relatives is so foreign to Mr. Mason. Instead, Mason was commenting as much on the *performance* of the family gathering as the contact itself. It was the congestion that he would have found nerve-wracking, especially given the fact that all of his siblings were financially stable enough to own separate homes, which were scattered across the Chicago metropolitan area.

Randall Van Dyke, a lawyer, was also occasionally bewildered by the things his neighbors did:

We didn't always see eye to eye with what our block club wanted to do. A lot of the members of the block club were the—I shouldn't say the older residents 'cause some of 'em are probably no older than I am—it's probably 50–50, new residents versus residents who have been here prior to the "gentrification.". . . One of the residents wanted to get the block club behind him to allow him to run his own car wash down the street here. He lost my interest right away because, you know, I'm like, I would have moved next to a car wash if that's what I was wanting to do. You know, we have zoning laws for a reason. And all the older residents were on his bandwagon. And when I would sit there silent in the meetings they just couldn't understand. [They would think] what is wrong with him? I just had no interest in it whatsoever, or things like that.

The block club is supposed to be a mechanism for bridging differences, but in this instance, and many others like it, it only made more glaring the lifestyle clashes that occur in a changing neighborhood.

Of course, the puzzlement goes both ways. Just as Van Dyke could not relate to his neighbor's plan to run a car wash on the street, some poor and working-class residents find the ideas of their middle-class neighbors curious. At a community meeting, the owners of a local gas station presented remodeling plans that called for the removal of the pay phones. This decision was based on more than aesthetic considerations; the owners had been advised by community leaders (most of whom are middle-class home owners) that pay phones create a security problem. Basically, drug dealers use pay phones. One resident protested, "So everybody has a cell phone now? What's up with the people? So say you're just lost and you just need directions. For people people!" This resident argued that all pay phone users are not up to no good. There are *people* people—as opposed to *cell phone* people or *drug dealing* people—who still need the convenience of public phones. She was astonished at how the people making the decisions—who were apparently all cell phone people—were oblivious to this fact.

Anne Boger is a bit less critical of the actions of the more affluent newcomers. This is perhaps because she is not a member of the truly disadvantaged, even though she grew up in the neighborhood and lived through its hard times. Because of this experience, she sees herself as apart from the middle-class blacks now moving in. But she appreciates their sense of style, the fact that "people [are] renovating, remodeling inside, a kitchen or a bath or something. You know, I think bit by bit people are trying to put, you know, wrought iron fences on the front. The windows, there were people doing things like leaving the curtains open more now. I would just love to just have mine open because I like that look." If there ever was doubt that people are acute readers of social class, Anne Boger's attention to the positioning of curtains should erase it. It only makes sense to keep the curtains open if you have something worth showing off, especially given the oversize picture windows that adorn many of the houses in North Kenwood-Oakland. In homes where the drapes are elegantly pulled back, they often frame things like a piano, an ornate flower arrangement, a piece of stained glass, or a decorative vase. Pulling the curtains back is a way to display and convey material wealth. Boger did not have any of these showpieces and thus viewed the practice with a mix of envy and admiration, imbuing it with a bit of mystique.

A most straightforward display of difference exists in the juxtaposition of the neighborhood's two grocery stores. One Stop Foods has been in operation since 1928, and at its current location at 43rd and Lake Park Avenue, on the border between North Kenwood and Oakland, since 1978. It was just a few blocks west before that. On its facade are the mottos "Buy the Can, Buy the Case" and "From Our Trucks to Your Shopping Carts." The messages: bulk buying is more economical, and there's no point in paying for frills. One Stop's market is the shopper with a larger family and a tight budget, and the store passes on to its customers the money it saves by keeping things simple. Four blocks south is the Co-op Market, which opened in 1999 in a new mini-mall at 47th and Lake Park, at the southeastern corner of North Kenwood and closer to racially integrated Hyde Park. It was the third store location of the Hyde Park Co-op, a cooperative grocery store that opened in 1933 and has served Hyde Park ever since. This store displays the motto "A Love Affair with Wonderful Foods" and offers such items as exotic fruits and vegetables, a fresh salad bar, and live lobster. The two places are like night and day. "The Co-op is for people that have money," felt Emma McDaniel whose part-time salary did not land her in that category. "If you go down there and catch their sales, you got something. But other than that, honey, that's not the place for me." McDaniel's MBA neighbor had exactly the opposite orientation. "Every now and then I'd go to One Stop, like if I needed, whatever, some collard greens or something. Not very often, because the brands that they have there aren't ones that I necessarily like. But there's some stuff that I would go and get there. Like if I need to get some, whatever, neck bones, stuff like that. But I would not do general shopping at One Stop." Each store had its niche and exploited it. The Co-op carried high-end brands and a wide selection of fresh foods, and One Stop stocked basic canned and boxed goods along with black ethnic food staples. As a resident myself, and a black bourgeoisie newcomer, I've been in One Stop no more than three times and then mostly for research purposes.[6]

This all seems harmless enough. The market efficiently allows for two grocery stores to serve distinct market segments, and residents look across the class divide with a bit of wonderment or confusion. But such observations of difference often morph into a rhetoric of condescension, which when empowered can turn into exclusion. "The biggest problem in the Co-op was the people working and the people shopping," explained Kirk Clemons, who should know a little something about groceries since he has worked as a brand manager for a major food manufacturer. "They wanted community hiring, but these folks wasn't ready to be the may-I-help-you type of people. . . . Oftentimes they'd engage a conversation within themselves. Some of the language wasn't becoming of a professional environment. I'm a customer—if I want to cuss, I can cuss. You're getting paid—you have to say, 'Yes, sir. No, sir.'" Clemons grew even more agitated when talking later about various social programs, like the ones that placed these purportedly unpolished workers in their jobs in the first place. His next target: indigent sick people who use free health clinics. "If you're going to go to the doctor, you go to the doctor. Why do they

have to put a clinic there for you?" he asked, referring specifically to a new health clinic in the neighborhood that took clients of all economic means. I answered, "Because you don't have health insurance." Not a good enough answer for Clemons, who had a logical free-market solution to everything: "[Then] why are you living over here? You need to downgrade the living, take the profits, and buy you some health insurance. If you're sitting on a property and let's say you're an indigenous resident—and this may be a totally vain thing—you got your house paid for. You might have bought it for $10,000 or $20,000. You got an opportunity to turn around and sell this house for $180,000. I'm sorry—it's not for me to put a social net for you. You sell your home, you downgrade." Ironically, when I interviewed Clemons, he no longer lived in the neighborhood, having cashed out for a cheaper house in the suburbs when it made financial sense for him. He was not being callous, but rather articulating principles that he too lived by.

The issue of the safety net is at the center of many of the more consequential debates in the neighborhood. While there are occasional references to racism, an inhospitable labor market, or a crumbling educational system as the causes behind an array of behaviors that the middle class finds objectionable, most explanations instead focus on the deficient internal states of the families that haven't been able to make it out of public housing, into steady full-time work, or on to college. The culprits are "questionable values," "not being responsible," an insufficient "work ethic," "welfare recipients and other kinds of recipients that couldn't really do without someone assisting them," as one resident put it, echoing Kirk Clemons's reluctance to assist those who cannot solve their problems through personal initiative. But while I found few hard-line structuralists among North Kenwood-Oakland's middle class, there were many environmentalists. Individuals are products of their environments, this perspective holds. People's imme-diate surroundings have a greater impact on their lives than the more distant notions of a capitalist economy that feeds on inequal-ity, or of racist whites with their foot on the necks of black folks.[7]

Given the primacy that residents attribute to the environment, of which the neighbor-hood is a key part, the task of the black bour-geoisie has always been to model a different set of behaviors and provide a new spate of resources to create a different environment. The return to North Kenwood-Oakland is as much about reclaiming a poor black neighborhood with the flag of middle-class behaviors as it is about striking it rich with a smart financial investment this regard, the arguments in *In The Truly Disadvantaged* resonate with the beliefs of North Kenwood-Oakland's newcomers. As if using Wilson's book as his text, Robert Blackwell lectured, "If you look at the 70s, I'd say in the 70s and '80s, blacks wanted to be out of black neigh-borhoods. I mean, so there's a flight from black neighborhoods. There has not been a major flight into [black neighborhoods]. I don't think blacks who I have seen anyway would look at somebody poor, a poor black person, and say, I am somehow very con-nected to that person. I need to make sure that this group is protected." In *The Truly Disad-vantaged*, William Julius Wilson emphasizes the spatial and thus social out-migration of the black middle class. Other public intellec-tuals like Henry Louis Gates also promulgate this notion of racial detachment, going so far as to say that black America is divided into "two nations"—what author Michael Eric Dyson has critiqued as gross divisions into an Afristocracy and Ghettocracy. From Gates's position as a Harvard professor, one black man he encountered on the other side of the class divide "seemed like a Martian."[8] Is the gulf that wide?

Mr. Blackwell makes a point that sounds something like Gates's—"I don't think blacks who I have seen anyway would look

at . . . a poor black person, and say, I am somehow very connected to that person"—but his behavior charts a different direction, and thus critiques the position staked out by Gates, and by Frazier before him. The black middle class is *not* without cultural roots, is *not* mired in racial self-hatred, and (despite the drama of this chapter's title) is *not* so detached from the black poor that the latter seems to be from an alien world. Blackwell's move to North Kenwood-Oakland *contra-dicts* contemporary arguments that there are two nations within black America by refus-ing to allow such a development. And Rob-ert Blackwell is not alone. His emphasis on the individual ("I need to make sure that this group is protected") is contradicted both by the swell of returners like himself and by the social science research.

William Julius Wilson's theories about out-migration seem to have made a greater mark on everyday rhetoric in the black com-munity than those of other researchers who find actual connections between poor and nonpoor black folks, and a widespread sense of group identification and responsibility among blacks. My own research with col-league Colleen Heflin shows that just over 40 percent of middle-class blacks have a poor sibling (compared to 16 percent of similar whites), and a third of middle-class blacks grew up poor themselves. As John L. Jackson writes in his ethnography of Harlem, "The black people I met in Harlem have lives that shoot through overly rigid, static, either-or designations of class." This familiarity with poverty is unlikely to support the contention that there are "two nations." It might also explain why, as political scientist Michael Dawson shows, two-thirds of blacks believe that their fate is linked to that of other black people. And Dawson finds that this is even *more* true among better educated African Americans.

Measuring the propensity of middle-class blacks to, as Blackwell put it, "protect" poor blacks is trickier. On the one hand, blacks with higher incomes (but not those with more education) are more likely to *oppose* policies aimed at economic redistribution, the safety net of which Kirk Clemons was so critical. On the other hand, more middle-class blacks than poor blacks think that the black middle class has an *obligation* to help the black poor. That is, middle-class blacks feel even *more* responsible than poor blacks think they should feel. Hence, if protection means calling for government funds to help black families in need, then Blackwell is right that black professionals are more likely to shun such advocacy. But if protection is more straightforwardly measured as personal obligation, then he is readily joined by other professional African Americans like himself.[9]

Given the prevalence of belief in the "linked fate" of African Americans across the class spectrum, the emphasis that middle-class African Americans put on the "environment" makes sense. The neighborhood, the schools, and the symbolic "black community" are all parts of the environment and are places in which individual middle-class blacks can actually make a difference. It takes concerted and collective action to redirect the economy or politics at the local or national level, whereas it only takes parking your BMW in front of your house to be an example of financial success for your less well-off neighbors. When Oakland resident Sharon Liberty's neighbors played their music too loudly or trampled her lawn or double-parked too many cars, she would politely go outside and say something. After a while, her concern for neighborhood decorum was taken up by the same people who used to violate it.

> For some of the neighbors that have been here for years, it's just that they haven't had the same exposure. They're still people. If they had the same exposure they would do the same. And to show the value [of exposure]: these neighbors that live on our street, all of their friends would come over and they visited in the street. It's the craziest thing. People don't come in their house. They have cars around and all that kind of stuff. But now you don't hear them out in the street any more. The street is quiet. Because there was a time when I'd get up in the morning and the street was like a graveyard. When I come home at night they'd get it perked up. And when it was time for me to go to sleep they were full scale. But now you don't hear that. And what was so amazing, one night I was just sitting here getting in bed 'cause I sleep in this front bedroom. And I won't use her vernacular, but one of the persons that you always knew [was] out there, [whose] voice was very prominent, I heard her tell 'em, "Don't bring that stuff over on Ellis, now take that stuff over where you live. Don't come over here with that."

When her neighbors took responsibility for policing themselves and each other, Ms. Liberty felt that her work was done, that she had successfully exposed them to what a block *should* look and sound like.

There is also a notion among newcomers about what the vanguard of neighborhood activism should look and sound like. It is commonly assumed that because poor residents, and public housing tenants in particular, have lacked exposure to good schools and orderly civic engagement, they are often not the best representatives of neighborhood demands. "We were at the Chicago Planning Commission discussing why these projects are a problem and why, you know, [residents] have this type of mentality," said Ruby Harris, explaining the fight she and many others waged to lessen the concentration of public housing in North Kenwood-Oakland. Zeroing in on the importance of environment, she continued, "We're not fighting the fact that the people have this mentality. The fact is that a lot of times it has been because of their surroundings. We understand what environment is, you know. It's 50 percent of who you are." In other conversations, Harris made it clear that many public housing residents go on to be highly successful, but here she emphasized that too many are left behind. The latter category was a sobering reminder of the incomplete project of black advancement. When public housing residents spoke up in meetings, she wanted to "get up under a chair somewhere, you know, the lowest point that I could, and just try and hide, you know." Long-term residents of the projects, who had proven unable to use public housing as the temporary support it was meant to be, were for that reason neither suitable nor effective representatives of this changing black neighborhood. I pushed Harris on her desire to have her poor neighbors take a backseat in community leadership, to disappear to ease her discomfort.

"But she represents a real population," I interjected about one woman who Harris thought was particularly outspoken but not well spoken.

"Yes, she does," Harris agreed.

"And she should have a voice," I added, making my ideological position clear.

"They have had too much voice" was her even clearer response. When the black bourgeoisie moves back on the block, they mean business.

It must be emphasized that Ruby Harris's comments addressed the *voice* of public housing residents, not necessarily their presence. With a few exceptions (as in Kirk Clemons's advice that poor home owners should cash out of the neighborhood to be able to afford health care), new residents to North Kenwood-Oakland do not *want* to displace anybody. If all the poor people moved out, there would be no one who needed role modeling, no destitute neighborhood to reclaim, nobody to "protect." Julius Rhodes, for example, worried that school improvements would come only after existing residents had been moved out. "I would hate to think that the reason that they became successful schools is because the neighborhood changed and, as a result, there was a recognition that those schools needed

to be able to do more. They need to be able to do more now." Norman Bolden had the same critique of the multimillion-dollar renovation of the local high school. "King High School should have been revamped fifteen years ago," he said, implying that the poor children who attended the school in the past had been ignored by the Chicago Public Schools. He used the high school example to express an even larger point: "Let me be real clear about my perception of success. Who were they developing King for? When four years ago you stopped accepting students and flushed them out, that's no success. I can't think of the words but I can clearly tell you that that was not a success. All that's being done is not being done with the intent to serve the existing community. That's urban planning." As discussed further in the next chapter, the newcomers want the old-timers to benefit from the investments in the neighborhood stimulated by their presence. Yet for all their good intentions, some of the strategies used to improve the neighborhood have exclusionary results. As Carolyn Hobbs commented with sadness about the prospects for young people who could not qualify for the new high school: "We just gotta kinda deal with some of the realities, you know, that this place is changing. And if you can't change with it then they're not looking to accommodate you."

Hence, when members of the black bourgeoisie meet the truly disadvantaged, the former hold two simultaneous convictions about their roles in the neighborhood: First, they intend to serve as both behavioral models and resource magnets to alter the environment of their less fortunate neighbors. Second, their efforts presume the superiority of their behaviors and resources. The assumption is not wholly unreasonable given the prevalence of hardships among old-timers and poor residents and the elation that many of them express now that things are turning around, but neither is it uncontested.

These debates—over how to be black and what black people need to do to prosper—are what binds the black community into one nation, rather than two.[10] When those debates subside—when Bill Cosby no longer cares about or comments on the family choices of poor blacks, and when the next generation of Robert Blackwells decides not to move into black neighborhoods—then the black community is no more. For despite Ruby Harris's trenchant critique of black public housing residents, the general gist of her argument was strongly problack. The point she wanted to convey to any public official who would listen was that in building and then neglecting public housing, "you're creating an environment that is destroying our people. And we're very serious about that." However obnoxious her words may have sounded, the public housing residents in whom she was so disappointed were but flesh and blood examples of such racist destruction. Harris's approach required the concerned participation of middle-class blacks who would stop city bureaucrats from foisting bad policies on the black community and who would then become leaders in the quest for community control. Control, in this framework, is not a possession that can be evenly divided among the residents of North Kenwood-Oakland—or, to broaden the analogy, among the national black community. Instead, it should be wielded by those best equipped, most qualified, most able to wield it: the black middle class.

This is not, of course, a new insight. It summons DuBois's "talented tenth," Frazier's black politicians with a "middle-class outlook," and the racial uplift ideologues who believed strongly that overshadowing what was seen as a more embarrassing contingent of black folks would prove to whites the fitness of all blacks for full citizenship. This historical backdrop helps to frame the cross-class encounter in North Kenwood-Oakland.

NOTES

1. Jackson 2005, 87.
2. A 1999 survey of North Kenwood-Oakland residents (Metro Chicago Information Center 1999) found that 93 percent of residents thought that the people moving into the neighborhood were people they felt "comfortable with as neighbors," and only two of the eighty-nine respondents reported having had a "bad encounter" with new neighbors.
3. Brown-Saracino 2004.
4. Pattillo-McCoy 1999.
5. Raley 1995; White and Riedmann 1992.
6. In January 2005, the Co-op closed due to "struggling sales and hefty operating costs." Alderman Toni Preckwinkle also believed the store had been poorly managed and had suffered from ongoing construction on Lake Shore Drive, which limited access by commuters. See Kat Glass, "Bleeding Money, 47th Street Co-op Shuts Doors," *Chicago Maroon*, February 12, 2005, http://maroon.uchicago.edu/ news/articles/2005/02/12/bleeding_money_47th_.php.
7. National surveys show that African Americans do see the problems of blacks as stemming from systemic causes. Hughes and Tuch (2000) find that African Americans are more likely than whites, Asians, or Hispanics to cite structural causes such as discrimination and poor educational opportunities for the "economic and social problems" of blacks. African Americans were not, however, any less likely to also suggest individual explanations, such as lack of motivation. In the spontaneous discussions that I describe in North Kenwood-Oakland, I picked up more of the latter, individualist sentiments. In the Hughes and Tuch study, the surveyor offered a list of explanations for economic and social problems and asked respondents to state their level of agreement or disagreement. Had I initiated a discussion about racism or the labor market, perhaps I would have heard more such arguments. Also see Schuman et al. 1997.
8. Wilson 1987; Gates 1998; Dyson 2005. Gates is quoted in Burnham 1998.
9. Heflin and Pattillo 2006; J. L. Jackson 2001, 86. To measure African Americans' sense of linked fate, Dawson asked respondents for their level of agreement with the following kind of question: "Do you think that what happens generally to the black people in this country will have something to do with what happens in your life?" (Dawson 1994, fig. 4.1). The percentage of African Americans agreeing "somewhat" or "a lot" has not changed much since the 1980s: 63 percent in 1984, 66 percent in 1988, 67 percent in 1993–1994 (Dawson 1994, fig. 4.1; Dawson 2001, table A1.1). On more educated blacks' feeling more linked to blacks, see Dawson 1994, 81–82. On middle-class support for economic redistribution,

see Dawson 1994, table 8.3. On middle-class blacks' sense of obligation to the black poor, see Hochschild 1995, table 4.6. Also see Billingsley 1992; Tate 1993.

10. Simpson 1998.

11. Demo and Hughes 1990. Positive feelings toward other blacks were measured on the basis of agreement with statements such as "black people keep trying" and "black people love their families." On support for black autonomy not affected by education or income, see Dawson 2001, tables A2.1 and A3.1. On income and economic nationalism, see Dawson 2001, p. 130 and table A2.3.

12. Hochschild 1995; Gay 2004; Schuman et al. 1997, 276–77. Also see Cose 1993; Hughes and Thomas 1998; Simpson 1998.

CHAPTER 5

Los de Afuera, Transnationalism, and the Cultural Politics of Identity

Gina M. Perez

"El Pepino siempre llama" (Pepino always beckons), Mercedes Rubio quietly explained as we sat together in her small living room in Humboldt Park one cold October evening. "I was born in Aguadilla, but my parents were from Pepino. I was born August 1, 1951, delivered by a midwife—just like the Indians—right beside the sugarcane. I didn't go to school—well, I only went until I was ten years old. We were very poor. And even though I am still poor, compared to before, I live like a millionaire."

As Mercedes shared her life story with me, I was struck by how her narrative reflected the rhythm of her daily life with its quiet moments, unavoidable interruptions, interludes of resolution and calm, and even more periods of uncertainty and concern. One of nine children, she has moved between Chicago and San Sebastián at least four times since 1971, when she first left Pepino to live with a sister in Chicago. Each trip, she explains, "is like starting all over again. But if it all goes well for me, I'll stay a few years. Even if I lose everything, I do it for them. My children."

I met Mercedes and her family through Evelyn Trujillo, a thirty-one-year-old G.E.D. student from Humboldt Park. The Rubios were Evelyn's downstairs neighbors, and she had featured them in several in-class essays about her neighborhood and its people. One September morning, a student asked me about my ongoing research in Humboldt Park. When I explained that I was conduct-

ing interviews with people who had lived in Puerto Rico for varying lengths of time, including those who moved many times between Chicago and the island, Evelyn laughed, saying that I should talk with her downstairs neighbors. "You know the ones. The ones that play the loud music." Even though Evelyn complained about the salsa music blaring from Mercedes's apartment day and night, the families were quite friendly and spent a lot of time together, a fact due largely to the friendship between Evelyn's younger daughter, Bianca, and Mercedes's children and grandchildren.

Their friendship was strengthened through the daily struggle of living in a neighborhood divided by feuding gangs and riddled with gunfire, and sharing a deteriorating two-story house near the corner of California and Armitage Avenues, near the border of Humboldt Park and Logan Square. Like many Puerto Rican families in the area, they battled with the landlord—usually unsuccessfully—to provide adequate heat in the winter; repair faucets, broken Light switches, and windows; and rid the apartment of rats. Evelyn's husband, Frank, worked with Mercedes's husband and son-in-law to fix those things the landlord refused to repair. And Evelyn, Mercedes, and her oldest daughter, Yamila, often borrowed household items from each other or sent their daughters to each other's apartments with prepared food. Both families lived month to month, depending on public aid, income from the informal economy, and their husbands' sporadic wages as day laborers.

When I met Mercedes, one of her daughters had just graduated from Clemente High School, and the entire family was preparing to move back to San Sebastián. Their large extended family—twelve members total— shared the first floor and basement of the two-story house, and like Evelyn, Frank, and their two daughters, Mercedes's family lived in extremely cramped conditions. Yamila and her husband and their two children slept together in the basement, while Tamara (Yamila's younger sister) and her two children shared one bedroom, and Mercedes, her husband, and their youngest son slept in another on the first floor. The other two daughters slept on a neat, plastic-covered couch in the living room. Although the family was excited about returning to Pepino, Mercedes expressed a great deal of anxiety because she knew they would have to live with either her sister or her son's family until they could find their own place. The last time she was in San Sebastián, she lived in one of town's *caseríos* (public housing), but she was sure that she would not be as fortunate this time, given the limited availability of *caseríos*.

For Mercedes and other Puerto Ricans in Chicago and San Sebastián, moving between "dual home bases" is stressful and often fraught with uncertainty.[1] Most worry about where they will live, a reasonable concern given the paucity of affordable housing for large families in Chicago and the unavailability of public housing both in Chicago and in San Sebastián.

Others are concerned with whether they will adjust to their new environment and find stable employment. Like thousands of other poor and working-class Puerto Ricans, Mercedes's movement between Chicago and San Sebastián can be understood as a "flexible survival strategy" used by migrants to negotiate the changing political-economic realities circumscribing their lives and to

enhance their economic status. Puerto Ricans living in Chicago, for example, may move to the island in search of a safer environment for their children and families or to improve their living conditions. They may subsequently return to Chicago for better health care, jobs, or schooling. The decision to move rests partly on migrants' assessment of which place offers the best opportunity to meet household needs, but it is also conditioned by decades of migration practices that have become woven into the fabric of Puerto Rican island and mainland community.

The back-and-forth movement of Puerto Ricans has received critical attention from academics and policymakers interested in understanding the scope, causes, and consequences of this movement, which challenges traditional views of migration as a unidirectional phenomenon, offering instead a more complicated portrait of migrant life and practices that involves multiple dwellings and, at times, high rates of mobility. Some writers have argued that Puerto Ricans' circular migration is a disruptive process that prevents migrants and their children from establishing strong roots and attachments in local communities, labor markets, and institutions such as schools. Others have countered these claims, emphasizing the structural forces underlying these multiple movements, such as deteriorating labor possibilities as a result of economic restructuring in northeastern cities like New York or changes in minimum wage legislation in Puerto Rico in the 1970s. Still others have demonstrated that only a specific type of migrant engages in circular migration and that most are settled in particular communities. One study notes, for instance, that despite the absence of legal barriers, Puerto Rican migrants are less likely to engage in recurrent migration than are undocumented Mexican immigrants in the United States, who show surprisingly high mobility rates.[2] Over the years, public and academic attention to Puerto Ricans' circular migration—the *vaivén* tradition—has obscured the rootedness of the lives of most Puerto Ricans on the island and the mainland. Thus, while "ir y venir" (going and coming) has become an almost unquestioned cultural trope of the Puerto Rican nation, new work on Puerto Rican communities reveals that "quedarse y sobrevivir"—remaining and surviving—is perhaps a more appropriate way of describing the experience of most Puerto Ricans.[3] Indeed, most Puerto Rican migrants lead deeply local lives, although they do so transnationally, either by actively maintaining political, economic, and social links with another community or by nurturing affective ties connecting them with other places through ethnic celebrations, cultural events, sports, and even stories.

That the lives of so many Puerto Ricans continue to be bound up with events, people, communities, and imaginings from places they left long ago, or perhaps have never even visited, attests to the profound way in which state-sanctioned migration policies from decades earlier have shaped the social, economic, and political landscapes of Puerto Rican communities. The policies guiding Puerto Rico's industrialization program not only succeeded in globalizing the island economy; they also stimulated a variety of migration patterns and social practices that gave initial form to transnational social fields in which people "take actions, make decisions, feel concerns, and develop identities within social networks that connect them to two or more societies simultaneously."[4] Over time, these transnational social fields have matured through the active participation of migrants, returnees, and even nonmigrants whose daily practices in particular places and historically determined times intersect with "transnational networks of meaning and power" in the contested process of "place-making"— that is, the dynamic process whereby local meanings, identities, and spaces are socially constructed within hierarchies of power and difference operating at both a local and a global scale.[5] Place-making is a critical feature of

transnational social fields: It is a process that locates transnational phenomena in "specific social relations established between specific people," while simultaneously providing a lens for analyzing instances of conflict, resistance, and accommodation among differently situated individuals and social groups that occur within transnational social fields. For example, community groups, labor unions, and grassroots activists may organize against the presence of global businesses—such as coffee shops or clothing stores—that "from above" threaten to transform a town's distinctive economic and social life. But they may also viciously resist the ways in which migrants, returning with different kinds of cultural knowledge and social remittances, challenge "from below" ideas of group membership, identity, and belonging.[6]

In San Sebastián, this process of place-making has been particularly conflictive since the 1960s, when both the town and the island experienced high levels of return migration. Over the past three decades, many *pepinianos* have echoed Mercedes Rubios's feelings about San Sebastián, saying that it always calls you back home. They have also discovered that returning "home" is not always easy. After years of living *afuera*, many *pepinianos*—particularly women and children—have a difficult time adjusting to their new life in rural Puerto Rico.[7] Return migrants are commonly derided as *Nuyoricans,* a culturally distinct group whose members are usually born and raised *afuera*. While most return migrants eventually overcome such a stigma, the idea of *los de afuera*—literally "those from the outside" or "outsiders"—continues to define membership in the Puerto Rican nation and is used as shorthand to refer to everyone from Dominican immigrants to *Nuyoricans* and "criminals" allegedly terrorizing the island. This *los de afuera* discourse is also employed in local community politics to resist the ways in which "progreso" (progress) threatens "authentic" or "traditional" Puerto Rican culture.

Ultimately, these conflicts remind us that place-making within a transnational social field is fundamentally about power—the power to make place out of space, the power to decide who belongs and who does not—and that imagining and forming transnational identities is a historically contingent process circumscribed by power relations operating on local, regional, and transnational levels.

RETURN MIGRATION TO SAN SEBASTIÁN

When I began my fieldwork in San Sebastián, I went to live with my *tía* Cristina in Barrio Saltos. I was not sure at first if I would live with my *tía* and her family throughout my fieldwork or if I would eventually look for my own apartment in town, approximately two miles away. I quickly realized, however, that *despachar en la tienda*—serving customers in the store—was probably one of the best places for me to learn about the community's migration history, since almost all of the people frequenting Cristina's store have lived for a year or longer in a major U.S. city like New York, Newark, or Chicago. My *tía* soon convinced me that living with her would benefit us all. Not only would I be able to do my field research *para terminar la tesis* (finish my dissertation), but I would also be able to help in the store and *servir de compañía* (be good company) for her and my father's cousin, who also lived with Tía Cristi and her husband, Bernardino.

Like most of their neighbors, Cristina, Bernardino, and their two children had returned to San Sebastián in the 1960s after nearly two decades of living in New York City. Cristina had migrated alone to Brooklyn in 1945 and had worked in a garment factory while living with a maternal aunt until she could afford her own apartment, where her brothers and sisters eventually joined her. Shortly after her arrival, Cristina sent for six of her brothers and sisters—including my grandfather—to live with her in Williamsburg, Brooklyn,

where much of the family continues to live today. In Brooklyn, Cristina married Bernardino Robles, also from Pepino. And in 1964, they moved back to San Sebastián with their two children, residing with extended family until they were able to establish themselves in the town. Cristina and Bernardino lived the Puerto Rican dream: After living and working *afuera* for many years, they returned to their hometown, bought some land, built a home, and raised their children in Puerto Rico. They also built a *tiendita*, next to their two-story home. In the course of many months of selling food, soda, beer, and shots of rum—and playing countless games of dominoes—I learned that *la tiendita*, like many institutions and homes throughout San Sebastián, is very much a product of the town's long and complicated migration history. It is also an important barrio institution that mediates transnational practices in a number of significant ways.

First and foremost, *la tienda* is a public gathering place for neighbors and friends. While it is primarily frequented by older men, teenage boys and young men mix with this older crowd to share stories, discuss politics, and play dominoes. It is also a customary final stop before one goes *afuera*. During my fieldwork and my tenure *despachando* at the store, every person who left to work and live in the United States spent time there the night before they were to leave. In addition to saying their goodbyes to friends and neighbors, they listened to stories and were given advice and money by my *tía* and anyone else who could afford it, "por si acaso" (just in case) anything went wrong. These discussions, it seemed, were always the most fun for the "old-timers". Who enjoyed telling shocking stories of life in American cities and reminiscing about "los tiempos de antes"—the old days.

The *tienda* is also one of the first places one visits upon moving into the neighborhood, a place to meet neighbors and catch up with people one hasn't seen in years.

Newcomers visit the store to buy food, use the phone, get information about the area, and initiate a good relationship with Cristina, who almost always provides food on credit despite the large, weathered sign in the store stating "No se fía bebidas alcohólicas" and "No se fía, ni preguntar" ("We do not sell alcohol on credit" and "There is no credit, do not even ask").

The *tienda* also provides critical services for family members, neighbors, and close friends: ready cash in emergencies, check cashing for older residents who are unable to go to *el pueblo* to do so, a place to sell or exchange locally grown fruits and vegetables for nonperishable goods, and a place to buy food and necessary household items on credit until one's check arrives at the beginning of the month. In short, the *tienda* functions as a kind of bank that operates on the basis of personal relationships and connects households in a web of reciprocal arrangements. For residents in Barrio Saltos, this kind of economic safety net is extremely important.

Like other rural municipalities in the island's central region, San Sebastián is quite poor. Its per capita income is one of the lowest on the island, a phenomenon some scholars have referred to as Puerto Rico's "deep regional inequality."[8] Cash-strapped households therefore often make ends meet by raising small animals and growing minor crops—*plátanos*, *guineos*, and a variety of tubers—for their own consumption or to sell locally. In this context, *la tiendita* emerges as an important economic institution for poor families who don't have banks, credit unions, or credit cards to carry them from month to month.

While working in the *tienda*, I met men and women who had lived *afuera*, returned, and frequently moved to the United States again for short periods of time. In this most appropriate space symbolizing the migration, they shared their stories with me about life in U.S. cities, the difficulty of return, and their dreams and hopes for the future.

Although my research focuses specifically on these people's lives, census data suggest that their migration experiences are typical. Between 1970 and 1980, the population of San Sebastián increased by more than 20 percent, a remarkable demographic shift following two decades of population decline in the 1950s and 1960s. This trend, however, is not surprising, and in fact reflects population increases throughout the island. While return migration to the island began in earnest in the 1960s, it reached a peak in the 1970s and continued at a steady although diminished rate through the 1980s.[9] The life histories and stories of the residents of Barrio Saltos reveal myriad economic and noneconomic factors informing migration decisions. They also paint a complicated portrait of life in San Sebastián and the ways in which migration, identity, and the politics of place remain emotionally charged issues in their daily lives.

RETURN OF THE NATIVE

> *This* coquí *represents the spirit of struggle of those* pepinianos *who leave their natural habitat in order to contribute from afar the best of their talents and their lives to the unfolding of history and the development of our dear land.*
> "El Coquí Pepiniano," a poem accompanying the bookmark and pin distributed to visitors by the Municipality of San Sebastián

As I began identifying barrio residents who had lived in Chicago, several men at the *tienda* insisted I speak with Carlos Arroyo, a deeply religious man who attended the local Adventist church. But Carlos's whereabouts were disputed by some men stopping in the store for an afternoon beer. "Carlos Arroyo? He's not here. *El anda pa' Chicago*" (He's over in Chicago). "He's here," another man replied. "He lives on the street with the Flamboyán on the corner." And the debate continued until a local schoolteacher offered to take me to meet Carlos to prove that he was indeed living in San Sebastián. This, of course, didn't settle the disagreement—I was told by some of the regulars in the store that they wouldn't believe Carlos was in town until I returned with an interview—but the discussion did highlight the mobile lives of the residents in Saltos. Neighbors take great pride in knowing who lives in the community, their extensive kin networks, and when people come and go. And they are not surprised when people move back and forth between San Sebastián and the United States, because *ir y venir* (coming and going) is embedded in the town's history. As the distinguished writer Luis Rafael Sanchez eloquently explains, the "airbus" carries a floating nation smuggling hope between two ports.[10]

When I finally did meet Carlos and his wife Nilda, they laughed at my description of the confusion about where they lived. Their family had in fact recently lived in Chicago, but they had been back in Saltos for almost three years. The neighbors probably assumed Carlos's recent visit to his sick mother in Chicago was "permanent," an understandable conclusion given that most people leaving the town usually buy either one-way or open-ended fares just in case they decide to stay.[11] Our first meeting appropriately coincided with the beginning of the 1998 NBA finals featuring the Chicago Bulls playing—and eventually defeating—the Utah Jazz. Luckily, we were able to watch the game in his home, since he had recently installed a satellite dish for this very purpose. I was immediately impressed by all the household objects signaling their links to Chicago: a large photograph of the city on the wall, Chicago Bulls memorabilia throughout the home (although, with Michael Jordan and the Bulls' international fame, almost everyone in the town wears Chicago Bulls hats, T-shirts, and jerseys, regardless of where they lived in the United States), and other trinkets stamped with "Chicago" and the city's recognizable skyline.

Carlos began his migration history by describing his life in San Sebastián before he moved to Chicago,

I was born in San Sebastián, in Barrio Guatemala, in the sector Central La Plata. We were very poor. The house where we lived, well, we closed the door with only a little rope. We didn't have doors like we now have today. I studied until the sixth grade—until the fifth grade here in Puerto Rico—and then in 1957 I went to Chicago. My father took me there supposedly for a vacation, which lasted until 1975. . . . I was ten years old [when I left].

Carlos and another brother moved in with their father and his wife, leaving their mother and other siblings in San Sebastián. In 1960, his mother sold their house in Pepino to pay for airfare to Chicago, and they all moved into a small apartment on Milwaukee Avenue and Racine, then to an apartment on Chicago Avenue, where they lived until Carlos and Nilda married in 1966.

Like other return migrants I interviewed, Carlos and Nilda worked in a number of different factories in the Chicago area. In 1965, he joined his father and brothers at the Merrit Casket Company, but he quickly left to make more money at a nearby rubber factory, where he worked for almost four months. On November 11, 1965, Carlos went to work for the Teletype Corporation in Skokie, where he stayed until the factory closed in 1975. Nilda first arrived in 1965, when she was eighteen years old, and initially worked caring for her cousin's three children. This arrangement quickly soured, however, when Nilda, like many other immigrants, discovered that the social networks on which she relied provided "grounds for cooperation but at the same time bred conflict."[12] She explains,

The first job I had was I took care of my cousin's three children while she [worked]. She was supposed to find a job for me, right? But time went by and she didn't find anything for me at the factory where she worked. My mom finally told me, "Look, your cousin tricked you. You'd better find another job yourself." So I went and found a factory job at night. A candy factory, the Holloway Company. I had a shift from 12 a.m. to 7 the next day. It was horrible because

I was always tired. I would also eat some of the chocolates [she laughs]. . . . That was my second job. . . . After that, I wanted to find a day job, because that job was too hard. I went to work at Freddy Hope Lamps, a lamp factory, but I didn't speak English. The girls would ask me, "Do you speak English?" And I said, "Just a little bit." [She laughs again.] . . . When I would go to work, I looked like a model because I would do my hair, put on make-up and I looked like a model. I worked sanding wood, and I worked at a long table with a lot of black women who had liquor and would drink. The owner was an old man who finally took me out of there. He saw me, I was like a flower, he said, so he put me in a cleaner place working with a Japanese man named Frank . . . and I worked with [him] assembling lamps. It was a really nice job and clean. And I liked it a lot.

Nilda later worked at a plastics factory, the last job she had before she and Carlos married. After marrying and having children, Nilda worked sporadically in a number of clerical positions.

When I asked Carlos and Nilda why they returned to San Sebastián, they responded with what would soon become a familiar refrain among migrants: "We always thought we would return here to raise our children. The younger [they are], the easier [it is for them]." In Puerto Rico, it is a truism that the island is a better place to raise children. My first encounter with this virtually unquestioned belief was a conversation I had with a taxi driver the day I arrived to do fieldwork in Puerto Rico. As he drove me from the airport in Carolina to the nearby town of Rio Piedras to catch a *carro público* to San Sebastián, he explained to me that Puerto Rico was the best place to raise children. It was okay to live in the United States in order to work and save some money. But the moment a couple has children, he assured me, they should return to Puerto Rico, where life is "menos complicada y más sana" (less complicated and healthier). When I asked him if he thought San Juan was safer and healthier than other American cities, he said yes, adding, "There

is simply no comparison between the life here and *afuera*. In fact, it would be *irresponsible* for people to raise children *afuera* if they could come back and live in Puerto Rico." This sentiment was echoed by almost everyone I met and interviewed in San Sebastián, and it was one of the most popular explanations for a family's return.

When Carlos and Nilda decided to return to San Sebastián in 1975, Carlos came first and began looking for work. Although it was difficult finding work and a place for his family to live, he believed they were making the best decision for their children. When I asked why they decided to return to San Sebastián, Carlos replied,

C: I believe that my roots called me back here. The family—well, I thought that it would be easier to find work here. We never really considered living in the metropolitan area [San Juan] because we thought that we were going to be faced with the same problems that exist in all big cities, like Chicago.

I: And how did you—did you have problems when you were living in Chicago? Did that also [influence your decision to leave]?

C: We didn't have problems per se. But we did have a vision for our children. And we wanted them to study in a better environment. For that reason, we wanted to come to the countryside.

N: Yes, because here they had a place to play and everything.

C: They had more room to run. And that's how it was. They grew up like little wild children. [He smiles.] In the open country they could go outside every day and there was no fear and it wasn't even slightly dangerous [*ni estaban calientito*]. And little by little, they were able to adjust well.

Carlos and Nilda's concerns are similar to those of parents in both San Sebastián and

Chicago, who use migration as a strategy to protect their children from urban dangers—like gangs, violence, drugs, and overcrowded schools—which disproportionately affect residents in poor and working-class neighborhoods. Their decision also highlights the ways in which places like Chicago and San Sebastián are increasingly imagined as mutually exclusive spheres of productive and reproductive labor. As the taxi driver said, you go to the United States to work, but you live and raise your children in Puerto Rico.[13]

Like Carlos and Nilda, Juan and Carmen de Jesús were concerned about potential dangers in Chicago, and returned to San Sebastián in 1977 shortly after their three children were born. One of my father's cousins introduced me to Juan and Carmen one hot afternoon in March. They were *hermanos de la iglesia* (church brethren) who attended one of the growing number of evangelical churches in San Sebastián. As we sat in front of their small, neat home, Carmen, Juan, and their daughter Laura asked me questions about my family and Chicago, and they eagerly shared with me their stories about life *afuera* and in Pepino. As Carmen described her life in Chicago, she grew increasingly animated and repeated several times how happy she had been there. Her various factory jobs and extensive social network of family, friends, and neighbors provided a stable, rich life. But she suddenly became serious when I asked why they had moved back. "[We returned] because of the children, you know. It was best for our children." They were afraid that their son might have problems with gangs when he was older, she explained. So they bought some land in San Sebastián, cashed in Juan's profit shares from the paint company where he worked, and returned to Puerto Rico.

Angie Rubiani, a quiet woman in her early fifties whose husband, Rubén, is a regular at Cristina's store, also said their family returned once they had children. She liked Chicago, she explained to me one night, as we talked in the living room of her small

wood house. The balmy, almost uncomfortably warm evening—pleasantly interrupted by the melodious songs of the *coquís* nearby—provided a fascinating contrast to her stories of the gray, bitter-cold Chicago winters that assaulted her daughters' frail health.

> They were always sick. . . . The winter was very bad for them. And it was like, when one wasn't sick, the other was. The winter really affected them, you know? Problems with their throats, their ears. And my oldest even got bronchitis twice. . . . The doctor who treated them—no, not the doctor, it was the pharmacist. I would always see him because of my medical plan, he would see the girls and he told me to come back to Puerto Rico. For the girls' health.

When I asked her if they would have stayed if her daughters had been healthier, she shook her head, saying that their neighborhood and the local elementary school "se estaban dañando" (were deteriorating), and she was scared to send her kids to school. So in 1978 they moved back to San Sebastián, although Rubén returned to Chicago to work for six months before settling permanently with his family in Saltos.

What is striking about these and other narratives of return is the way in which people privilege concern about raising their children in explaining why they left Chicago. In fact, their stories are checkered with myriad reasons for return, including sick relatives in Puerto Rico, housing problems in Chicago, battles with depression exacerbated by long, isolated winters, and, not surprisingly, job loss. Thus, immediately after Carlos and Nilda explained that they wanted to raise their children in Puerto Rico, Carlos mentioned that he had been laid off after ten years of working for Teletype Corporation. This was the best time to move, he explained, since the company gave him a severance package that paid for airfare and allowed him to ship his belongings back to Puerto Rico. Juan similarly confided that he was afraid that the paint factory where he worked just before leaving Chicago might relocate, like other blue-collar jobs in Chicago at that time. These narratives of return, however, are consistent with a migration ideology that anticipates that people will return to Puerto Rico to live a better life. According to this logic, migration is an economically motivated decision to "mejorarse y progresar"(better oneself and progress), while return is largely informed by "place utility" and sentimental attachments to home and nation. The assumption is that one returns to Puerto Rico to retire or enjoy life after many years of hard work *afuera*.[14]

Migrants often feel the pressure to succeed *afuera* and return with enough money to buy land, build a home, own cars, and consume at a level commensurate with their new economic and social status. These pressures are reinforced by people's remarks and good wishes before one leaves. For example, the night before eighteen-year-old Willy left to work in Atlantic City, he talked with old-timers who had lived and worked abroad decades earlier. Not only did they congratulate him for leaving and being an example to the other youth, who are constantly reviled as lazy and ignorant of the honor of hard work, but they each patted him on the back, shook his hand, and said, "Suerte. Y vuelve con mucho dinero" (Good luck. And come back with a lot of money). Willy laughed nervously and assured them all that that was the idea. These interactions confirm other scholars' accounts of the social pressure migrants face to succeed abroad and alter their social status upon return. As Grasmuck and Pessar point out, the popular refrain "If things go well for you over there, write" not only reinforces the expectation of succeeding abroad, but it is also a key mechanism in mythologizing migrant success by erasing failures.[15]

Many *pepinianos* explained that they never adjusted to life *afuera*. In fact, they often compared themselves to the *coquí*, the tiny, melodious frog native to Puerto Rico that popularly represents "Puerto Ricanness." Like the *coquí*, I was repeatedly told, *true*

Puerto Ricans cannot thrive outside of Puerto Rico. They might be able to live, *pero no cantan afuera* (but they don't sing outside). For that reason, many proudly reminded me, to really live your life, you must return to your native land. But for many, returning to San Sebastián is not easy. Although most of the people I interviewed had been back in the town for at least fifteen years, they recalled in vivid detail the difficulties they had faced in adjusting to life in San Sebastián again. Women and children were particularly clear about how they suffered during this transition. As I demonstrate below, these narratives reveal that migration is often a conflictive process, in which *women and children* contest and resist new gender and generational ideologies and culturally prescribed behaviors that circumscribe their lives.

THE SUFFERING OF RETURN

The past decade has witnessed a dramatic shift in migration research, as feminist scholars have theorized the role of gender in migration processes. As many of these writers have demonstrated, migration decisions are guided by kinship and hierarchies of power based on gender and generation within households and among migrant social networks, which are often sites of struggle and contestation. Return migration in particular raises troubling questions, since women frequently fear losing independence gained in the United States.[16] My research among return migrants in San Sebastián revealed similar concerns, as women described *el sufrimiento* (suffering) involved in returning to the island after living and working in Chicago. Family and community pressure to stay at home, a renewed dependency on husbands because of inadequate public transportation, and limited job opportunities all contributed to women's dissatisfaction upon returning to Puerto Rico.

Elena Rodriguez is the energetic pastor of an evangelical church who has lived in San Sebastián for more than twenty years. Born in Aibonito, in the southeastern region of Puerto Rico, Elena was raised in Chicago with her nine brothers and sisters. At the age of seventeen, she married Lolo. Shortly after they were married, they went to live in San Sebastián. When I asked her if she wanted to return to Puerto Rico, she smiled and said, "This is where the story begins! You cannot even imagine how much I suffered in that change!" When she first arrived in Puerto Rico, she lived with her mother-in-law for a month, while her husband remained in Chicago with plans to eventually join her there. She explained:

I came to Puerto Rico before [my husband] to set things up. And in that month, well, for me, that month was terrible for me, because there weren't the same facilities you could find [in Chicago]. When I began to stay in my mother-in-law's house and she would say to me, "There's no water," . . . and I saw that the stores were far away, that there weren't any stores close or pharmacies close . . . and when one left the doctor's office worse than when they arrived . . . I saw all this and I wrote a letter to my husband saying, "Send me a ticket home fast because I'm leaving. I am not going to live here." . . . Well, he sent me [and our two children] tickets and I left.

Shortly after Elena returned to Chicago, however, her sister-in-law died in San Sebastián, and her husband decided it was best for them to return to Puerto Rico to take care of his mother. Because they didn't have their own home, they lived with Lolo's mother, which only made a difficult transition worse.

You know the saying "Quien se casa, casa quiere" [Everyone who marries wants a home]? And living in another's house, no matter how well they treat you, you want your own home. I lived in a room next to the carport [marquesina] and I already had two children, and I felt uncomfortable in my mother-in-law's home. And seeing that there was never any water—I had to go with buckets to get water from the neighbors. And carrying that water in order to do something to help my mother-in-law. And

my husband was only making sixty dollars a week. [With that] we had to pay the bank, feed our children—it wasn't easy. And I'm telling you, for me it was so traumatic. I cried every night because I wanted to leave. Every night. And I told my compañero, "If you want to stay, you stay. But I'm leaving. I can't take this anymore." Because I saw how if my children got sick here—in Chicago, [the doctors] took care of them quickly, but here I had to wait to be called, sometimes almost three hours, while my children suffered from fever, pain, and they still made me wait. . . . I finally wrote to my father . . . and I told him, "Papá, send me tickets because I'm leaving. I'm going to leave my husband because life here is full of suffering (muy sufrida) . . ." This is how I lived. It was so traumatic. And honestly, honestly, I cried to leave [Puerto Rico] for ten years.

Elena's husband begged her to stay, and he eventually convinced her to use the money her father sent for tickets back to Chicago to begin building a home of their own. She stayed in San Sebastián, but regretted her decision for a very long time.

Like Elena, Nilda vividly recalls her difficult transition to life in San Sebastián. Even though she disliked the weather in Chicago, she preferred living there because life was easier in the city and there was more to do. They lived near museums and parks, and they had access to public transportation. She adapted to her new life in San Sebastián slowly, she explained, and she was much happier once they had their own home. She still complains, however, about the town's lack of public transportation, a common lament among almost all the women in the town. Unless one owns a car and knows how to drive, one has to depend on the town's earns públicos, which run irregularly until 2 p.m., and they often have to wait until drivers have a full car of five or six people before they go on their routes. Women complained bitterly about this new dependence on husbands, friends, and family, and were frustrated that these transportation problems limited their movement, largely confining them to their homes.

Women's isolation was further heightened by their failure to work outside the home, a remarkable difference from their lives in Chicago. When I asked women about their jobs on the mainland, they were extremely animated and provided great detail about all the places where they worked, what they enjoyed about their jobs, the people with whom they worked, and frequently the racial/ethnic politics of the workplace. In San Sebastián, their labor history changed dramatically. Nilda worked irregularly when she first arrived, but she decided to collect unemployment after she began to have back problems. Carmen also stayed at home collecting unemployment while her husband worked in a series of factory jobs in San Sebastián, Isabela, and Aguadilla. Angie has been employed sporadically since her return and currently cares for an old man, cleaning his house and cooking his meals. For some women, working outside the home became a necessary condition for agreeing to stay in Puerto Rico. Elena, for example, became very involved in her local church. She eventually studied to be a pastor and now leads her own community. And Yahaira, a young woman who, like Elena, was born in Puerto Rico but raised in Chicago, decided to stay in San Sebastián only after her husband agreed to help her open a small cafetería in the town.

Women rarely complained about their new domestic roles when I asked them directly about how the demands and expectations in their households had changed upon their return to San Sebastián. Rather, they often explained that they enjoyed staying home to care for their children. But in daily conversations, they frequently expressed frustration with how much more difficult domestic tasks were in San Sebastián. In addition to the problem with water—which continues to be a problem even today—women complained that in Puerto Rico they had to cook more often, it required more time to buy food because of poor public transportation, and there were fewer entertainment venues.

The women also noted that because their husbands earned less money and the cost of living was higher in Puerto Rico than in the United States, they had to be creative in stretching their money. These new responsibilities increased women's *sufrimiento* and prompted some to advise their sisters to resist their husbands' efforts to return to Puerto Rico. Elena explained to me one day:

> It wasn't easy. After living in Chicago where you have your good job, and you would eat out on Fridays and maybe Saturdays too . . . and to come to Puerto Rico I had to get used to cooking breakfast, lunch, and dinner. . . . It wasn't easy. . . . After one has lived in Chicago, it's not easy to adjust to life here. . . . I would never tell anyone to come to Puerto Rico [to live]. No one, no one, no one. When my sisters would come to visit, [I would take them aside and tell them], "Don't come to Puerto Rico to live. Leave me here, it's okay since I'm more settled here now. . . . My husband is here and I have a house. . . . But I would advise you not to come to live in Puerto Rico."

Return migration influenced domestic arrangements, making housework less egalitarian. While none of the women explicitly discussed their husbands' willingness to share in domestic chores, they implied that housework was primarily their responsibility and expressed great discontent with the amount of housework they had to do and the fact that it usually involved more labor-intensive chores than in Chicago. In Chicago, most of the women worked outside the home and had more disposable income, allowing them a reprieve from some cooking duties. Their lack of wage labor in San Sebastián, as well as their husbands' reduced earnings, circumscribed the household's disposable income and contributed to women's feelings of being overwhelmed by domestic tasks.

While Elena, Yahaira, and Nilda admit that they eventually adjusted to life in San Sebastián and, in retrospect, believe it was the best move for them, they also describe their children's difficulty adjusting to life in San Sebastián. Language problems, different norms for dress, and the stigma attached to being *de afuera* alienated migrant children from their peers, especially in school. Yahaira worried about her son's performance in school because of his language acquisition. When I asked her if Tito had problems with other students, she assured me that he got along with everyone. Overhearing our conversation, Tito politely corrected his mother, saying in Spanish, "I like it here, I like being in the open air and everything. But at school they bother me. They call me 'the gringo.' Well, they used to call me that, because I didn't speak Spanish. I spoke English too much. I used to get really mad." Yahaira was surprised by her son's response and sympathetically added that there were certain words *she* still couldn't pronounce correctly, being English dominant. Then, slipping into English, she complained, "There are some things that I'll never get used to here. People are so *nosey* here. Everybody *quiere saber la vida de uno*" (wants to know about your life).

Language has long been a lightning rod for debates about Puerto Rican identity, culture, and nationalism. In the early twentieth century, a language policy that promoted English as the official language of instruction at all grade levels was a key feature of the Americanization campaign that sought not only to cement loyalty to the U.S. colonial project by inspiring "admiration for 'American' history, polity, and symbols," but also to "uplift" the Puerto Rican people, who were regarded as racially inferior and mired in a language and culture devoid of democratic vocabulary and ideals.[17] Mandatory English instruction in the schools was reversed in 1952, but debates regarding the extent to which Puerto Ricans should be bilingual, the social meanings attached to English and Spanish use, and the relationship among language and cultural and national identity continue to incite impassioned responses.

Not surprisingly, return migrants, whose social identities and linguistic practices challenge the assumption that *a* language corresponds to *a* culture, have become embroiled in these debates and represent for some the unsavory consequences of globalization and transnational living. According to linguistic anthropologist Ana Celia Zentella, island writers, intellectuals, and government officials have expressed profound concern about the ways in which return migrants and their use of Spanglish and code-switching—alternating Spanish and English words, clauses, and phrases—threaten Puerto Rico's linguistic, and therefore cultural, integrity. Puerto Rico's distinctive colonial history with the United States has reinforced the persistent coupling of Puerto Rican identity with the Spanish language, contributing to what Zentella describes as a belief held by many island intellectuals that "English has had a continuously deteriorating effect on the Spanish of Puerto Rico and that, as a result, Puerto Rico's national identity itself is being threatened."[18]

The presence of return migrants and transnational actors throughout Puerto Rico requires an understanding of citizenship and nation that transcends the island's borders, although many dismiss these challenges "from below" as illegitimate, a source of corruption and danger. Puerto Ricans also resist efforts to use language to mobilize ideas of nation "from above," a source of great debate. This became particularly evident in March 1998, when the U.S. Congress debated the Young Bill, the statist-backed legislation promoting Puerto Rican statehood. Almost every night in March, residents in Barrio Saltos argued in *tía* Cristina's store about Puerto Rico's political status and the PNP's attempts to forge *la estadidad jíbara*—the Creole state, based on the idea that Puerto Rico could become a U.S. state while maintaining its cultural and linguistic integrity. One evening, Gonzalo, an octogenarian who had lived for more than thirty years in Brooklyn and a loyal *popular*, asked me if I preferred to speak English or Spanish. When I told him I preferred to speak Spanish in Puerto Rico, he smiled and warned me, "If we vote for statehood, they are going to impose English as the official language. And you know, I ask myself why. Why? If there are more countries that speak Spanish than English, why English? In the United States, wherever you go, people speak Spanish. Even the Chinese speak Spanish. They speak it badly [*mata'o*], but they speak it."

The topic came up again the next night as I played dominoes at the store, but this time it generated a much more heated debate. My uncle Bernardino and Ramón, a regular at the store who eventually migrated to New Jersey as a temporary agricultural worker, agreed that there was no reason for English to be the official language in Puerto Rico. Another man who joined our domino game disagreed, saying that it was good for English to be the official language because it was the international language of trade, politics, and commerce. Ramón answered angrily, "Why don't the Americans just learn Spanish? Or why can't we just be bilingual?" To which the old man replied, "Just look at Canada. Over there, everything is in English and French, and look at how many problems they're having now," referring to problems surrounding Quebec's nationalist movement. As in most discussions of politics and Puerto Rico's political status, the debate quickly degenerated, with the old man ending the argument by saying that the problem with "us Puerto Ricans" is that "we're not prepared" (*preparado*): "If we accept English as the official language, we would be able to overcome our problems and better ourselves."

It is of particular interest that in these debates, language represents cultural authenticity. Adults who returned to San Sebastián as young children—especially as teenagers—still agonize over their ability to speak Spanish not only correctly, but with a Puerto Rican accent, very quickly, and with clipped endings. One thirty-seven-year-old man confided that he is self-conscious about speaking Spanish because he believes he still has an accent betraying his U.S. upbringing. When he first arrived from the Chicago area back in the 1960s, Wilson was teased constantly about his language skills, a painful memory that reinforced his resolve to stay and raise his children in Puerto Rico. In order to compensate for his linguistic failures, he devotes his free time to traveling around the island attending each town's cultural festival and learning everything he can about Puerto Rican history and folklore. It wasn't easy living in San Sebastián after growing up in the United States, Wilson admitted. But in an interesting twist, he and other adults who were once subjected to teasing now readily condemn today's youth, using the same racialized language of contamination, disorder, and pathology that was directed at them when they occupied a similarly ambiguous cultural position. Wilson, like other returnees and nonmigrants, believes that many of Puerto Rico's problems—and San Sebastián's in particular—can be attributed to *los de afuera*, outsiders who not only refuse to assimilate to life in Puerto Rico, but who dare to transform its cultural, social, and political-economic landscape as well.

NOTES

1. Alicea 1990.
2. Duany 2002, 234–35 He bases these findings on a study surveying four communities in Puerto Rico in the summer of 1998. The surveys used were adapted from those used in the Mexican Migration Project (MMP) of 1999 at the University of Pennsylvania and the University of Guadalajara, which were designed by a research team led by Douglas Massey. Comparing his findings with that of the MMP, Duany reported that only 13 percent of Puerto Ricans who had moved abroad were multiple movers, compared with nearly 44 percent of all migrants in the MMP study (22).
3. I would like to thank Isa Vélcz and Patricia Zavella for helping me to clarify this point. Alicea 1997; Bourgois 1995; Glasser 1997; Ramos-Zayas 2003; Rúa 2001; Souza 2000; Stinson-Fernández 1994; and Whalen 2001 are examples of research focused on specific Puerto Rican communities on the mainland.

4. Glick Schiller, Basch, and Blanc-Szanton 1992a, 2.

5. Smith 2001, 106, 144; Massey 1994.

6. Smith and Guarnizo 1998.

7. Kerkhof (2000, 144) makes similar observations about children's difficulty in adjusting to life in Puerto Rico.

8. Francisco L. Rivera-Batiz and Carlos E. Santiago (1996) have noted this regional inequality, arguing that the income gap between municipalities on the island is increasingly polarized. "This inequity," they write, "follows closely along metropolitan/nonmetropolitan lines. Most of the *municipios* with the lowest per capita income were in nonmetropolitan areas" (83).

9. Rivera-Batiz and Santiago 1996, 55.

10. L. Sánchez 1994, 22. Popular references to "la guagua aérea"—the airbus—reveal the ease and frequency with which Puerto Ricans move between the island and the mainland, although such metaphors background the rootedness of people's lives in particular communities. Acclaimed writer Luis Rafael Sánchez explores the complexity of this movement in a provocative and humorous way in *La guagua aérea* (1994).

11. A travel agent in San Sebastián pointed this out to me in an interview. She also said that of the three most popular destinations—New York, Chicago, and Newark—most travelers went to Newark en route to Perth Amboy, New Jersey, the city many *pepinianos* refer to as the mini-San Sebastián on the mainland.

12. Menjívar 2000, 174. Menjívar's research among immigrant women from El Salvador provides important analysis of the conflicts, cleavages, and limits to immigrant social networks, the ways in which gender shapes them, and the prevailing "structures of opportunities" in which these social networks are embedded. Hondagneu-Sotelo 1994; Kibria 1993; and Mahler 1995, 1999 also provide critical attention to the conflicts surrounding immigrant social networks.

13. Alicea (1997, 619) makes similar observations, explaining that Chicago Puerto Ricans regard the island as a site for investment (buying land and a home, for example), recreation, and a safe place to raise children, while American cities are productive sites for work and reliable social services. Using Goldring's work (1992) among Mexican transnational families as an important comparison, Alicea explains that this differentiation of social space is largely a result of global and political restructuring.

14. Ellis, Conway, and Bailey (1996) describe four categories of return/circular migration: those who return because of the labor market, "tied" migration (a move precipitated by a partner's migration or family need), to improve place utility (a better place to live due to improved housing or preferred climate and culture), and other reasons, such as religious or political reasons.

15. Grasmuck and Pessar 1991, 92. Works by Goldring 1998; Levitt 2001; and Mahler 1995 explore similar issues of migrant success and the social pressures they face in sending communities. It is important to note here the difference between the kind of advice given to Puerto Rican migrants and that given to other Latin American immigrants bound for the United States. Because Puerto Ricans are American citizens and do not have to navigate die bureaucratic—and sometimes illegal—waters of international migration, my observations of old-timers' advice and even light-heartedness regarding migration is striking compared to other scholars' accounts of warnings and *consejos* (advice) given to Mexican and Central American immigrants. See Chávez 1992; Hondagneu-Sotelo 1994; Mahler 1995; and Menjívar 2000.

16. Examples of this work include Grasmuck and Pessar 1991; Goldring 1998; Hagan 1998; Hondagneu-Sotelo 1994; Levitt 2001; Mahler 1999; and Menjívar 2000. Research on the gendered dimensions of return migration include Grasmuck and Pessar 1991; Levitt 2001; and Pessar 1986.

17. Negrón-Muntaner 1997, 259; Urciuoli 1996, 47–48.

18. Zentella 1990, 85. The literature on language, bilingualism, and Puerto Rican cultural identity is extensive. Notable examples of this work include Flores 1993; Flores and Yúdice 1983; Zentella 1990, 1997; Negrón-Muntaner 1997; and Urciuoli 1991, 1996.

19. The conflicts arising from return migration provide an interesting counterpoint to Anderson's notion of an imagined community (1983) and point to the different ways in which this imagined community is constructed differently over time. Here I have borrowed from David A. Hollinger's notion of "the circle of the 'We'" (1993) to discuss how different groups are included and excluded in popular understandings of the nation.

20. Many scholars have carefully documented the ways in which returnees and Spanglish-speaking Puerto Ricans on the island and the mainland are charged with corrupting Puerto Rico's linguistic integrity. Citing island writers, intellectuals, and government officials, Zentella (1990) reveals widespread concern for the deterioration of the Spanish language. Puerto Rico's extinctive colonial history with the United States has reinforced the "consistent identification of Puerto Rican identity with the Spanish language." As a result, "many of the island's intellectuals and others believe that English has had a continuously deteriorating effect on the Spanish of Puerto Rico and that, as a result, Puerto Rico's national identity itself is being threatened" (85). Negrón-Muntaner (1997) masterfully maps the gendered politics of language onto enduring debates regarding Puerto Rican identity, nationalism, and migration. For some island academics and politicians, bilingualism is often a metaphor for "ambiguity, cultural disorders, and political passivity." Similarly, defenders of the Spanish First legislation—an attempt to make Spanish the official language of government in Puerto Rico—regard

bilingual Puerto Ricans on the island and the mainland as "a race of *tartamudos* [stutterers], unable to communicate either in English or Spanish." She writes, "For many intellectuals on the island, U.S. Puerto Ricans serve as a 'futuristic' projection of what all Puerto Ricans will/have become: culturally 'impure' or hybrid, racially *mestizo* and bilingual (that is, having two 'national' loyalties). The notion of 'hybridity' is important since given the nation-building narratives' concern with reproduction, a hybrid cannot reproduce; it is sterile. The possibility that the elite's destiny will be explicitly tied to the U.S. diasporas (the *hampa*) or be displaced by the 'lower classes' partly fuels these groups' writing off of two-thirds of the Puerto Rican population" (279). Kerkhof (2001) makes similar observations about the struggle over language and Puerto Rican return migrants as well.

In addition to linguistic corruption, return migrants are also popularly regarded as diseased, physically contaminating the body politic with AIDS and other diseases. A controversial *New York Times* article described the migration between Puerto Rico and New York as an "air bridge" transporting sick and polluted migrant bodies. "New Yoricans [*sic*]" are blamed, according to the article, for importing AIDS from the mainland, further cementing their marginal status (quoted in Sandoval Sánchez 1997, 203). Sandoval Sánchez writes, "The metaphorical construct of an 'air bridge' constitutes a space of continuity and contiguity that makes possible the passage of those condemned by Puerto Rican society: the sick, the infected, the contaminated, the marginal (IV drug users, homosexuals, gay tourists, prostitutes)" (203).

SECTION II

Being on the Job

Continuing with the topic of immersion, the theme for this section's readings is "being on the job," or when ethnographers engage in the same activities and do the same work alongside their participants. Like living among participants this strategy's primary strength for data collection and analysis is how it enables researchers to experience social life in their field sites. As discussed in the Introduction, through the course of the twentieth century and into the twenty-first ethnographic research has featured greater participation and immersion into the lives and practices of people in their settings by researchers. As Robert Emerson (2001) documents in his history of the method, early fieldwork emphasized that researchers be socially detached and distant from their subjects for the purposes of maintaining objectivity and examining people sociologically. These scholars saw direct observation by the fieldworker and informal interviewing as the paramount techniques for studying people, as such classic works as Nels Anderson's *The Hobo* (1923) and Paul Cressey's *The Taxi-Dance Hall* (1932) demonstrate. They valued the researcher's objective observations, and did not consider the subjects' subjective meanings as important. Participant observation's emergence as a model of fieldwork in the mid-twentieth century shifted this relationship. As its name implies, participation in the lives and activities of subjects on the part of the researcher became as important as in situ observation for conducting field research. In contrast to social detachment and distance from subjects and their settings "participant observation emphasized gaining access, creating trust and rapport, getting close—in short, immersion" (Emerson 2001, 17). Similar to the strategy of living in the same neighborhoods and communities as participants, working with participants enables ethnographers to see and understand the embedded meanings in a setting and the constructed meanings of a group by doing what they do.

There are many philosophical underpinnings to the data collection strategy of engaging in the same activities as participants. Laying the foundation for the theoretical tradition of symbolic interactionism, George Herbert Mead (1934) claims that people develop a social self by learning how to take the roles of others, knowing the attitudes and roles of others in the group (or the baseball team, in Mead's example), and understanding what others expect of them in their own roles. Building from Mead, Herbert Blumer (1969) focuses on how people form meaning through interaction and language. Stemming from this line of thought, ethnomethodologists contend that taken-for-granted and shared meanings form the basis for interaction and make everyday life possible (Garfinkel 1967). People can and regularly do make and assign their own interpretations of others' behavior and of the meanings behind it (Becker 1996). Ethnographers do not rely on their own suppositions when these are not based on actions or derived from direct observation in settings where people construct meanings.

They seek to learn how others actually understand and interpret their own behavior. Taking the role of the other, learning others' attitudes toward their own role, and seeing the world from others' viewpoints through immersive and participatory fieldwork is how they uncover and gain an understanding of these meanings. Doing what their participants do provides fieldworkers with the opportunity to experience and perform the behaviors that are central to the meaning-making processes with which people regularly engage and interpret.

A significant benefit for ethnographers of taking the role of the other by engaging in the same activities and doing the same jobs as them is that they gain personal insight into the social worlds of their participants by making meaning alongside them. Since the late twentieth century participant observation as a fieldwork model for uncovering and explaining local meanings has experienced a "reflexive turn" (Emerson 2001, 20–24) in which researchers have begun to understand ethnography as an experiential process. With this realization some ethnographers undertake "embodied sociology," or research that uses the body as a central instrument for and subject of ethnographic research. For these researchers behavior is not just a strategy for gathering data on local meanings, but also for generating data. In his research Lee Monaghan (2002) becomes a bouncer to study the bouncing profession and the regulation of unruly bodies inside and outside of commercial establishments. He uses his own interpretations of and experiences with bouncer work as well as his own observations of other bouncers to examine how systems of social control and surveillance operate in the night-time economy. Other scholars have used their fieldwork to reveal the hidden meanings behind practice. Erin O'Connor (2005) takes up glassblowing to learn the tacit understandings of the craft and discover how people develop practical knowledge. Without learning the trade, O'Connor would not have entirely understood how people actually progress from novices to skilled practitioners of a craft through acquiring embodied, tacit knowledge. By surrendering to the requirements of the trade and becoming an amateur boxer, Loic Wacquant (2004) gains an understanding of the commitment and sacrifices that the African-American members of the gym in the black ghetto he examines make. Through what he calls "carnal sociology" Wacquant reveals what it means to experience the painstaking daily routines and mundane rituals of training and preparation that boxing entails. Through understanding people primarily as flesh and blood and sensory organisms and by immersing their own bodies into the activities of their field sites, these scholars demonstrate the power that doing the same work as their participants has on researchers' data and the depth of their understanding.

This data collection (and data generation) strategy raises several issues for doing ethnography, which come up in this section's readings. One is the matter of gaining trust and establishing rapport. Ethnographers often use the activities in their setting to deepen their relationships with their participants. William Kornblum (1996), for instance, recalls an episode when he was studying Boyash gypsies in a shantytown on the outskirts of Paris. At that point the group accepted him as an observing researcher, but did not respect him as an active participant in the group. One evening a neighboring group of Serbian immigrants attacked their camp with stones. The Boyash gypsies armed themselves with knives and guns for battle, and one of them, Persa, thrusts a heavy stick into Kornblum's hands and shoves him to the front line. While filled with deep ambivalence and fear, Kornblum proved to the group that he would stand with them in the face of danger (the standoff did not result in violence). He notes that Persa's attitude about him changed after this incident from disdain to guarded respect. Engaging in the same activities as participants can elevate an ethnographer's status among a group and reveal to fieldworkers the importance of these activities.

All of this section's readings are by fieldworkers who engage in the same forms of work, action, and performance as their participants. However, the notion of embodying and practicing a specific role to learn about participants' lives and meanings is not limited to formal activities. Behavior in the field takes many forms, and urban ethnographers benefit from reflecting on how they acclimate to life in their settings, regardless of the formalness of the activities taking place there. For instance, in *In Search of Respect* Bourgois does not engage in the same drug selling and buying activities as his participants, nor does he join them in their rampant drug use (although he regularly hangs out and consumes alcohol with them until late at night). But he writes often of how learning the "code of the street" in his everyday behaviors helped him understand and navigate hierarchies in his fieldwork. For instance, after some early missteps he learns how to identify the coded meanings behind why some of the men drink certain beers over others (Ray, the crackhouse owner, drinks pricier imports while members of the rank and file drink cheaper Budweiser and malt liquor). Bourgois also adjusts his own behavior, such as how he talks, to confer respect upon and establish rapport with the crack dealers. Along with everyday behavior the realms of work and performance offer clear examples of how learning certain practices, taking on certain roles, and immersing themselves through action helps ethnographers understand their participants' lives, surrounding urban conditions, local understandings, and processes and activities with which they construct meaning.

The first piece comes from Mitchell Duneier's book *Sidewalk*. Like many urban ethnographers featured in this volume, Duneier has an interesting story about how he "got in", or gained access, to the group he wanted to study. Walking through Greenwich Village one day, he passed a table on the sidewalk with books for sale, and saw his first book, *Slim's Table* (1992), lying on it. Curious, he asked the vendor where he got it. The vendor reluctantly gave a vague answer, and when he asked for Duneier's phone number and address for his Rolodex, Duneier was taken aback and intrigued ("This unhoused man has a Rolodex?" he puzzled; 1999, 21). He found the subject for his next book.

Duneier expanded his work on this single vendor, Hakim, who serves as his guide and the book's principal character (and who turned out not to be homeless), into an examination of sidewalk life from the perspective of the book and magazine vendors as well as the panhandlers and other homeless characters who inhabit a unique social world in public space. By working alongside these black men (and one Filipina) at their tables and joining them on "hunts" throughout the city for used books, magazines, and other paraphernalia to sell, Duneier shows how they construct a moral order, earn a living, provide a public service, and gain self-respect on the sidewalk in spite of difficult personal and social circumstances. In the 1990s Mayor Rudolph Giuliani implemented numerous "zero tolerance" policies against such public figures as street vendors, graffiti artists, and squeegee men. Based on the "broken windows" theory these policies labeled such people as symbols of disorder whose public presence indicated a breakdown of moral order and an invitation for further disorder. Throughout *Sidewalk* the vendors deal with these laws and the police who have to enforce them.

This section's piece comes from a chapter that Duneier mainly devotes to a single incident between the vendors and police. He uses it to represent how these two groups negotiate their relationship on the sidewalk through strategies that confer respect. The scene is a black police officer telling Ishmael, a black vendor, to break down his table, citing his captain's orders not to sell on Christmas Day. Lacking the legal knowledge to argue, Ishmael defers. Hearing this, Duneier, who is white, at this point a seasoned vendor himself, and a confident professor with knowledge of the municipal law (which he keeps a paper copy of in his pocket), decides to conduct a "natural experiment" by setting up a table, to the chagrin of the police officer. The result is a dramatic and rare confrontation between an ethnographer and the police that demonstrates how the intersecting factors of race and social class influence interactions on the sidewalk. Duneier experiments with the officers to see how they would react, but the vendors must deal with them on a daily basis. By becoming a vendor, Duneier does not just learn the practices that the men use to gain self-respect and their interpretations of their situation (i.e. honest work selling recycled reading material), but also uses his knowledge to create a social situation that highlights the dynamics at play in a fundamental relationship in the men's lives.

There may be fewer misconceived occupations than the city police officer. Popular media produces numerous images and myths on officers and police work, while urban police departments are notorious for their hostility toward external investigations, which may or may not dispel some of their existing stereotypes. Following in the footsteps of ethnographer John Van Maanen (1978), Peter Moskos wanted to learn about the culture of policing from the perspective of the beat police officer. The best way to do this, he surmised, was to become a police officer himself. He proposed his research plan to several cities, and only one, Baltimore, accepted it. He entered the academy in 1999 and spent a year policing Baltimore's Eastern District, an area with a high crime rate and significant drug activity.

People often view bureaucracies such as the criminal justice system as culturally monolithic, with workers who move in lockstep with official administrative positions. In this piece Moskos demonstrates that in fact police officers differ widely in their perspectives toward the law and their own duties, which translates into how they perform on the job. He focuses in this chapter on how different officers interpret and approach street corner drug dealing in their work. Superiors measure police officers in Baltimore by the number of their arrests, and officers feel the pressure from their supervisors to make them. Many officers, however, recognize that arresting street-level drug dealers is largely ineffective in combating drugs and drug-related violence. Their reasons for making these street-level arrests, even when they are for loitering, range from sending a message to the area's criminal element to keeping the streets safer, at least temporarily, to moral reasoning (i.e. it is the right thing to do). As a police officer Moskos is in a privileged position—literally sitting in uniform next to officers in squad cars, making arrests, and dealing with people in the community—to learn policing culture and experience the interpretations that officers have about their work, while also generating his own attitudes toward drug enforcement policies by working on the corners and streets. His analyses and conclusions of contemporary urban policing are highly informed by his experiences engaging in everyday police tasks.

Among the many changes in contemporary cities since the late twentieth century is the rise of consumption, culture, and tourism as significant contributors to urban economies (Zukin 1991; 1995). Many scholars have examined how this has influenced daily urban life. Peter Eisinger (2000) documents that city leaders who market versions of their city's cultural and physical attributes to attract visitors and investors risk alienating residents. Others show that the rise of consumption, tourism, and entertainment has resulted in public spaces that resemble theme parks rather than places that promote egalitarianism and democracy (Sorkin 1992). Sharon Zukin (2010) argues that middle-class people who come to cities to live or visit seek out "authentic" places and experiences found in them as opposed to sites for homogenized mass culture and inauthentic experiences. David Grazian explores this "search for authenticity" among urbanites in his book, *Blue Chicago*. By examining the social worlds of Chicago's blues clubs and its rich history as a center for blues music, Grazian reveals the various ways in which people define and seek out authenticity. As Chicago blues culture has become commoditized in House of Blues chain restaurants and as city leaders promote its legacy through sanitized tours and corporate-sponsored blues festivals, Grazian discovers how a group of blues fans and musicians construct their own interpretations of the art form's authenticity that differ from more popular sources.

After analyzing tourists and casual fans who seek out the authentic blues in these clubs, in this chapter Grazian focuses on the local regulars and professional and amateur musicians who treat them like their second homes. For these people, the weekly "jam sessions," or those behind-the-scenes events where the "real" music takes place, are moments for sharing cultural knowledge, receiving psychic rewards, and establishing community. They are also situations in which experienced musicians socialize newer, inexperienced ones into the culture of the club and teach them how to become competent members of the group. Grazian demonstrates this process by taking the stage himself. An alto saxophonist, Grazian had some background in music from high school, but considered himself an amateur (and one who was out of practice at that). But performing live allowed him to gain the trust of the musicians (2003, 23–24) as well as generate data that reveals the meanings they construct in the clubs. By taking on this role, giving what he feels is an embarrassing performance among professionals and in front of a discerning blues audience, and receiving feedback on his performance, Grazian demonstrates the gradual and sometimes painful socialization process of learning the group's standards of authenticity.

Grazian's work is part of a growing literature on urban tourism (Hoffman et al. 2003; Judd and Fainstein 1999; Judd 2003). He shows how urban culture can be produced "from above," or created by large-scale corporations, city leaders, and the media, as well as "from below," or created by people on the ground (see Gotham 2007). Examining this dynamic within the tourism industry is Jonathan Wynn's work on walking tour guides in New York City. As the tourism bureau and business actors promote specific places in and images of the city, walking tour guides provide entertaining information on some of its hidden history and social worlds. They combine historical facts with lore, myths, and legends to weave unique tales of the city while walking through the built environment. Their tours vary depending on the group members and the random people and uncontrollable situations that they encounter. Wynn refers to guides as "urban alchemists" (2010; 2011) who "re-enchant" a city whose public spaces have grown more and more homogenous.

In this piece Wynn focuses specifically on the "tricks" that guides use to create a narrative about their tour's theme. When taking a tour, people are generally not aware of how the guide constructs it, or what about it has been planned or improvised. Wynn combines observation and interviews to show how guides use certain practices to get tour members to think about the city differently. The piece contains numerous examples of tour guides in action, and includes vignettes that serve as guides to the central analysis. While he does not show it in these episodes, Wynn became a walking tour guide to supplement his extensive participant observation fieldwork. He therefore put these tricks into practice, which serves as a form of "triangulation," or a beneficial validation technique (Bloor 1997; Denzin 1978). Because of the impossibility of replicating social circumstances in society, as opposed to replicating conditions in a laboratory, qualitative research proves difficult for establishing validity. But using different research methods or different strategies within the same method on the same empirical phenomena helps fieldworkers minimize the prospect of their conclusions resulting from problems in their measurements. Wynn shows how the strategy of engaging in the same activities as participants allows ethnographers to test the validity of their participants' claims and of their own assessments, in this case the legitimacy and effectiveness of strategies that guides use to weave a story. Had the tricks that he observed not been effective or relevant on his own tours, Wynn may have had to reassess his explanations of their behavior and perhaps find new insights that match the reality of their situation.

Ethnographers regularly study people who are less educated and in a lower social class than they are. The following section deals specifically with the issues that arise from such relationships, but the next author demonstrates how urban ethnographers sometimes engage in activities not typically associated with their social identities. For her research, Lucia Trimbur, a female graduate student, studied a Brooklyn boxing gym mostly populated by people of color from poor neighborhoods. To understand how the gym's members deal with racial oppression in the contemporary city, Trimbur used her role as participant observer to immerse herself in the world of the boxer. She learned many boxing-related activities like wrapping hands and putting in mouth guards, apprenticed as an assistant second, and even trained to box, undergoing the grueling workouts and lacing up the gloves. Boxing is known as a "manly art," and the boxing gym is commonly seen as a male domain of hypermasculinity where women are forbidden (Wacquant 2004). We must question this somewhat since Trimbur managed such in-depth access and her gym has 200 women out of 1,000 total members. However, as she shows in her work, trainers constantly impress a strong sense of masculine toughness upon their pupils. Her very position and participation in the gym raise enormous issues of the obstacles of overcoming gender and sexuality in the field. But Trimbur's decision to learn how to box and participate deeply in the world of the gym informs her of the bodily rigors and commitments to grueling tasks that boxing entails. The strategy allows her to experience and explore the meanings that trainers and fighters at the gym attach to the "manly" practice.

In this piece Trimbur focuses on the competing discourses that the gym's trainers use to advise their amateur fighters. While they espouse individualism and personal responsibility in the ring, they cite combatting systemic inequalities and anti-black racism that exist outside the ring as motivations for their work. Far from being a protected island that shields its members from the chronic problems found in the black ghetto (Wacquant 2004), Trimbur finds that the boxing gym is a place where trainers and fighters negotiate the social conditions of racial, class, and gender hierarchies in the postindustrial city. From her experience as a boxer and assistant Trimbur is able to discern the distinctions between the types of advice and guidance that the trainers give the fighters inside compared to outside the ring. She discovers variation in the setting, and from her discovery provides an explanation for how underprivileged groups make sense of and deal with their oppression and personal obstacles.

When we think about religion and where people who consider themselves religious talk about their beliefs, we normally think about particular locations, such as places of worship, certain voluntary organizations, and private settings like the home. In this section's final work, Courtney Bender aims to demonstrate how religion and religious talk happens in daily life outside of these traditional locations and explain why it matters when it does. Her field site is God's Love We Deliver, a nonprofit organization that cooks and delivers hot meals to homebound people with AIDS in New York City. Unlike the scholars we have seen who work within the Chicago School tradition, Bender did not discover religious talk by "following the phenomenon" in the setting. Rather, she chose this organization as an empirical case for an analysis of religious talk in everyday life and to discuss theoretical insights regarding social practice. Indeed, the fact that God's Love We Deliver is not a "typical" setting for examining how people talk about and perform religion in public life supports her argument for the need to examine such behavior in locations besides places of worship (2003, 3). However, while in the field Bender learns about the people and setting beyond religious talk and meaning.

Despite its name, God's Love We Deliver is not a religious organization, although the founder's impetus and certain aspects of the agency were spiritually oriented (2003, 25–33). Food is love, food is therapy, and food is charity became the organization's mission statements and cultural repertoires, each subject to multiple and shifting interpretations and meanings. Though it hires professional chefs to manage the kitchen and make sure recipes meet nutritional requirements for people with AIDS, volunteers do the bulk of the preparing and cooking. The volunteers vary widely in terms of their backgrounds and motivations for volunteering. They assume that other volunteers love to cook and have had experiences knowing and caring for people who have died of AIDS. The volunteers also do not share the same religious backgrounds or the same interpretations of the agency's mission statements. To analyze how a diverse group of people tries to communicate sensitive topics such as religion with others who do not share their own understandings, Bender becomes a volunteer and immerses herself in the daily life of the kitchen, its mundane tasks of food preparation, and, most importantly, the ongoing talk.

Through her participant observation Bender learns how the volunteers practice religion in the kitchen, such as by interpreting their work chopping vegetables as a form of prayer. In this piece she presents the ways in which the volunteers talk about religion with people who they assume do not share their religious symbols and codes. They do not discuss religion directly, such as by openly talking about faith or morals, but they weave religious subjects into their regular conversations. Average talk about daily events is not unimportant among the volunteers, but a way in which they assess their "footing," or the grounds for discussing religion, all while going about their business of preparing and providing food for people with AIDS. The tasks of the kitchen are routine and most of the conversations between the volunteers comes off as idle chatter. Neither would seem to be evocative of religious practice or talk. Without immersing herself in the setting by doing the work and entering into the flow of conversation, Bender would not have learned the deeper religious meanings that are embedded in everyday life.

Ethnographers today are engaging in more and more activities in the field for the sake of immersing themselves deeper in their participants' lives. Each level of immersion provides a new analytical angle for fieldworkers to understand the perspectives and meaning-making processes of their participants and validate their claims. With these two data collection strategies in mind, we will then turn to the next Part, which focuses on the relationships that urban ethnographers form with people in the field.

REFERENCES

Anderson, N. 1923. *The Hobo: The Sociology of the Homeless Man*. Chicago: University of Chicago Press.

Becker, H.S. 1996. "The Epistemology of Qualitative Research," in R. Jessor, A. Colby, & R. Schweder (eds.), *Ethnography and Human Development*. Chicago: University of Chicago Press: 53–71.

Bender, C. 2003. "What We Talk about When We Talk about Religion," *Heaven's Kitchen: Living Religion at God's Love We Deliver*. Chicago: University of Chicago Press: 92–103.

Bloor, M. 1997. "Techniques of Validation in Qualitative Research: A Critical Commentary," in G. Miller & R. Dingwall (eds.), *Context and Method in Qualitative Research*. London: Sage: 37–50.

Blumer, H. 1969. *Symbolic Interactionism: Perspective and Method*. Englewood Cliffs: Prentice Hall.

Cressey, P.G. 1932. *The Taxi-Dance Hall: A Sociological Study in Commercialized Recreation in City Life*. Chicago: University of Chicago Press.

Denzin, N.K. 1978. *The Research Act: A Theoretical Introduction to Sociological Methods*. New York: McGraw-Hill.

Duneier, M. 1992. *Slim's Table: Race, Respectability, and Masculinity*. Chicago: University of Chicago Press.

Duneier, M. 1999. "A Christmas on Sixth Avenue," *Sidewalk*. New York: Farrar, Straus and Giroux: 253–256; 260–279.

Eisinger, P. 2000. "The Politics of Bread and Circuses: Building the City for the Visitor Class," *Urban Affairs Review*, 35, 3: 316–333.

Emerson, R.M. (ed.) 2001. *Contemporary Field Research: Perspectives and Formulations*. Prospect Heights: Waveland Press, Inc.

Garfinkel, H. 1967. *Studies in Ethnomethodology*. Englewood Cliffs: Prentice Hall.

Gotham, K.F. 2007. *Authentic New Orleans: Tourism, Culture, and Race in the Big Easy*. New York: New York University Press.

Grazian, D. 2003. "Like Therapy: The Blues Club as a Haven," *Blue Chicago: The Search for Authenticity in Urban Blues Clubs*. Chicago: University of Chicago Press: 87–90; 105–116.

Hoffman, L.M., Fainstein, S.S., & Judd, D.R. (eds.) 2003. *Cities and Visitors: Regulating People, Markets, and City Space*. Oxford: Blackwell Publishing.

Judd, D.R. (ed.) 2003. *The Infrastructure of Play: Building the Tourist City in America*. Armonk: M.E. Sharpe.

Judd, D.R. & Fainstein, S.S. (eds.) 1999. *The Tourist City*. New Haven: Yale University Press.

Kornblum, W. 1996. "Introduction," in C.D. Smith & W. Kornblum (eds.), *In the Field: Readings on the Field Research Experience*. New York: Praeger.

Mead, G.H. 1934. *Mind, Self, and Society*. Chicago: University of Chicago Press.

Monaghan, L. 2002. "Regulating 'Unruly' Bodies: Work, Tasks, Conflict, and Violence in Britain's Night-Time Economy," *British Journal of Sociology*, 53, 3: 403–429.

O'Connor, E. 2005. "Embodied Knowledge: Meaning and the Struggle Towards Proficiency in Glass-blowing," *Ethnography*, 6, 2: 183–204.

Sorkin, M. (ed.) 1992. *Variations on a Theme Park: The New American City and the End of Public Space*. New York: Hill and Wang.

Van Maanen, J. 1978. "On Watching the Watchers," in P.K. Manning & J. Van Maanen (eds.), *Policing: A View From the Streets*. Pacific Palisades: Goodyear: 309–349.

Wacquant, L. 2004. *Body & Soul: Notebooks of an Apprentice Boxer*. New York: Oxford University Press.

Wynn, J.R. 2010. "City Tour Guides: Urban Alchemists at Work," *City & Community*, 9, 2: 145–164.

Wynn, J.R. 2011. *The Tour Guide: Walking and Talking New York*. Chicago: University of Chicago Press.

Zukin, S. 1991. *Landscapes of Power: From Detroit to Disney World*. Berkeley: University of California Press.

Zukin, S. 1995. *The Cultures of Cities*. Oxford: Blackwell.

Zukin, S. 2010. *Naked City: The Death and Life of Authentic Urban Places*. New York: Oxford University Press.

CHAPTER 6

A Christmas on Sixth Avenue

Mitchell Duneier

In 1996, for the second consecutive winter, the holiday season came to New York City without snow. In the towers above Rockefeller Center, men and women who were engaged in international transactions and the coordination of global production could look down on sidewalks packed with tourists glimpsing the ice skaters and the famous Christmas tree. The sidewalks throughout midtown were so congested that it took five minutes to make one's way the length of a city block. There on the streets of the influential Fifth Avenue Association and Grand Central Partnership Business Improvement District, no vendors, panhandlers, or unhoused people could be seen.

A few subway stops south, on Sixth Avenue in the Village, the Volunteers of America had their Sidewalk Santas ringing bells near Eighth Street, asking people to "help our neediest neighbors." Halfway down the block, a Santa from the Salvation Army rang his bell. A few steps away, Keith Johnson cried out from his wheelchair, "Help the homeless," and then complained about the institutional panhandlers, who were cutting in on his proceeds this holiday season.

On Greenwich Avenue, next to Hakim's table, the florist had taken over the sidewalk space where Conrad usually puts his magazines, setting up a dozen Christmas trees for sale.

And across the avenue, Balducci's market had taken over the sidewalk in front of its store with straw baskets filled with gourmet items. The lines flowed outside and around the block as local residents waited for their chance to buy fancy cakes, imported cheeses, and other delicacies.

Meanwhile, Ishmael was raising hell on the sidewalk.

"You heard they took my table, Mitch?" he says when I arrive on the blocks around eleven on the morning of December 23. He continues telling Hakim and Alice that all of his belongings had been seized by officers of the New York City Police Department between two and two-thirty that morning.

He says, "They took my magazines and they took my personal belongings, too. I went shopping, bought some new clothes, had a receipt and everything. They took all that. And they didn't give me no summons for my stuff, nothing. They just took it."

Ishmael says that he is being punished because two other men on the street, Joe Garbage and Al, had placed their goods for sale on the ground, in violation of local laws; in response, the police had punished them by removing everything that was out on Sixth Avenue, not merely Joe's and Al's belongings. "If the problem's down there," he says, "don't take *my* stuff."

Ishmael does not have anywhere else to keep his belongings, so the bags underneath his table can contain anything ranging from a family photograph to clothing. Often men will say that everything they own is under their table, that a certain bag is their survival bag: "That bag is my life," Warren once said. "That bag can do nobody any good than me. It had my clothes, my ID, my toiletries, just things that I need to survive on the street. Some people out here stay in the same clothes, don't care about their hygiene. But that's not me. I wasn't brought up like that."

A few weeks earlier, Ishmael had met a young Japanese woman named Tina, a graduate student in music who was trying to support herself as a singer, and she had begun to visit him regularly on the block. After many conversations, they developed an amorous relationship, and they had planned to go out on a date that very evening. Ishmael had used his earnings the day before to purchase new trousers and a shirt on 14th Street so that he could look neat and clean on the date. "He [the officer] took my new clothes that I went shopping for," Ishmael explained. "I have nothing to wear on my date tonight."

* * *

If we look closely at this incident and others like it, we can better understand how unhoused vendors are regulated in New York City. After his election victory, as we have seen, Mayor Rudolph Giuliani advanced a change in the strategy of the police department that was already taking place, from responding to 911 calls to maintaining order and eliminating public disorderly behavior.[1] The new model of policing, again, began with the assumption that felony crimes spring from environments in which forms of nonviolent deviance are tolerated—aggressive panhandling, scavenging, and "services" such as opening car doors, flagging taxis, locating parking spaces, and washing motorists' automobile windows at intersections without their permission.[2] The laws and their enforcement have been made part of a quality-of-life campaign that is widely described as intended to "clean up" the city.[3] It is accompanied by offical disparagement

of "street people." In this climate, as we will see, individual police speak as if the vendors occupy places on the street at the discretion of the police; their presence is a privilege bestowed by the community and regulated by the beat-patrol officers. The police engage in a kind of micromanagement—making sure vendors set up within precise lines, stay close to their tables, and keep merchandise off the sidewalk.

On Sixth Avenue, fixing broken windows entails constant face-to-face relations between police and vendors. The police must rely on the cooperation of the vendors, and the vendors must rely on the police not to abuse the law. As we shall see, this is hardly an optimal set of expectations for either side to rely upon.

The system of sanctions police have at their disposal to regulate the vendors consists mainly of civil penalties. Whereas under a penalty of criminal law someone might be put in jail for an infraction, in controlling minor offenses (like putting merchandise on the ground) police rely on summonses and tickets, which bring fines. The difficulty people working the sidewalks have in not committing minor infractions, and the failure of these tickets and summonses to have any lasting effect on their behavior, lead to crises of personal respect between police and those who do not comply. These crises lead to abuses of law on the part of both vendors and police.

Advocates of "broken windows"-style policing acknowledge that such regulation puts more power in the hands of the patrol officer on the beat, and that in their discretion the police will occasionally harass the poor. They also contend that, through effective education,[4] such abuse of discretion and harassment can be minimized. But the problem is not merely one of discretion or education. Rather, it inheres in the very structure of such a policing process.

Let us look more closely at the way this all works.

TAKING THE LAW INTO THEIR OWN HANDS

"Broken windows" policing places great faith in the discretion of individual police officers in the field—on their ability to regain control of the street, and to establish orderly, conventional standards of conduct.[5] Although police always have enormous discretion, the attention paid to minor infractions broadens the scope of situations over which they have authority. It also increases the number of situations in which police and people working the streets have direct interaction, times when issues of respect must be faced. And when other methods seem to fail, it encourages police to take the law into their own hands.

Every day, some vendors, scavengers, and panhandlers violate the Municipal Code by setting up in illegal spots, laying miscellaneous scavenged items for sale out on the ground ("laying shit out"), or leaving their tables unattended. With the mayor directing the police department to focus on "quality of life" issues, every day the police issue summonses for these code violations. The summons requires a vendor to appear before the Environmental Control Board, a civil tribunal. If found guilty, he will be fined.

According to the Environmental Control Board's statement of purpose, fines and other civil penalties are incentives meant to encourage violators to change their behavior. The vast majority of civil fines are leveled against property owners for building- and fire-code violations, excesses of air and noise pollution, and sanitation and asbestos violations. If the owner of a building does not answer such a summons, the city can put a lien on his or her property.

Civil penalties like fines are not likely to be effective against the people working on Sixth Avenue, however. Many don't carry identification. (When asked by the police for some form of ID, a scavenger or vendor will, not uncommonly, pull out a wad of other summonses he has received.) Some give the police false names, and often a police officer has known the same vendor by the wrong name for years. Moreover, only 10 percent of those summoned appear before the Environmental Control Board. The other 90 percent of summonses go unanswered, and fines against vendors mount.

All this is frustrating to individual police officers, who are pressured by their commanders to do something about the "quality of life." When the police officer must repeatedly tell vendors on the block to pick up their stock-in-trade from the sidewalk, when every time the policeman turns his back the vendor puts his materials where they do not belong, the officer feels he is not being treated in a way that is consistent with how he is entitled to be treated. Inevitably, from time to time an officer seeks to avenge this—for example, by throwing a person's table, crates, and goods into the back of a garbage truck.[6] As we shall see, the officer's sense that he has been disrespected may be the variable most likely to lead him to go beyond the official limits of his discretion and take the law into his own hands.

A lieutenant in charge of policing the vendors has told me that, rather than write a ticket, officers sometimes prefer to wait for a person to leave his table unattended, and then confiscate his goods. In such an instance, the officer can claim that the goods were abandoned and take the vendor's belongings to the nearest dump truck or Dumpster in the trunk of the squad car. Such punishment serves to achieve a measure of social control by getting vendors to stay close to their belongings; more important, such measures are moralistic, bringing personal satisfaction and a sense of justice to police officers who have been embarrassed or shamed by vendors' attitudes or behavior.[7]

In ordinary life, when we speak of people taking the law into their own hands we are referring to situations in which citizens settle their own grievances without resorting to law enforcement.[8] But just as many citizens who take the law into their own hands do not want to depend upon the police to settle their disputes, many police officers do not want to be entirely dependent on the law. The law can be frustrating. For example, the local law states that when an officer seizes a vendor's merchandise he or she is supposed to issue a summons, label the goods, and bring them back to the precinct house; this can take an hour or more. Many officers see it as wasted effort, since the vendor can recover his goods from the property clerk by paying a small storage fee, without appearing before the Environmental Control Board. And it makes the property clerk a kind of warehouse for recycled trash. Besides, most scavengers never come to collect their goods at all—it is easier for them to replenish their stock by picking through a new round of trash.

These incidents are repeated over and over again, so that the relationship between the vendor and the police officer is ritualized. The individual police officer who methodically labels trash that has become merchandise, takes it to the precinct house, and then returns to the street only to see more trash for sale as merchandise feels that he has not been treated with the level of respect to which he is entitled. Though the street person is inconvenienced by the enforcement of civil penalties, they have little or no effect on his behavior. It is much easier for an officer to throw a man's belongings away than to place them in storage at the precinct. And since the officer knows that so much of the merchandise comes from the trash anyway, he sees the Dumpster as the proper place for it. From the officer's point of view, throwing away Ishmael's stock of magazines while he is away from the table—taking the law into his own hands—is a way of moving beyond penalties that have no effect and toward penalties that do.

THE "LEGITIMACY" OF RETALIATION

After Ishmael and I arrive back on the block from the police station, Marvin asks, "So

what happened? Was I right? Did you learn that you should get a lawyer?"

"Get a *what?*" Ron asks.

"Get a *lawyer,*" Marvin repeats. "They took Ishmael's stuff. They fucked with him."

"He wasn't there, though," says Ron. "How you going to do it? By fucking lying?"

Even though vendors will complain about the police's behavior, there are times when they will recognize in talk among themselves that their own misdeeds may have brought on the results they are frustrated about. In so doing, they show awareness that taking a man's belongings is a prescribed method of punishment. In this case, Ishmael was unwilling to admit that he was away from his table, a denial that didn't make sense to Ron:

"I *was* there, man."

"You was there, Ishmael?" asks Ron.

"Yeah," says Ishmael.

"You wasn't there."

"You gonna tell me yesterday they took my stuff and I wasn't there?" says Ishmael.

"How you gonna have a case if you wasn't there?" says Ron. "What if the man at the newsstand left his stuff and someone took all his shit? You think he could say anything?"

Turning to Marvin, Ishmael defends himself. "Marvin, what Ron's saying is irrelevant right now. He don't know nothing, because he just got here today. He's just going by earsay."

"That's what everybody says, Ishmael," responds Ron. "That you wasn't there. So you need a witness to say you was there. Nobody said you were there."

"You know what your problem is, Ron? You want to be so right. At the moment you are wrong. I got a witness there."

"You was there?" asks Ron. "So why did you let them take it?"

"Why I let them take it? They took it because they wanted to take it. Because the motherfuckers throwing shit on the ground like you doing right now. They say every time they see shit like that they taking everybody's table."

"That's not why they took yours!" says Ron.

"They came from down here and took my fucking table because Joe laid shit all over the fucking ground."

"How come they didn't take Grady and them's table?" asks Ron. "How come they only took your table?"

"Look, Ron, right now I don't need you to get me upset. You got your shit. You here. Be happy with that. I got my shit tooken and I'm not too fucking happy. Leave it alone, okay? The whole issue is based on you laying your stuff on the ground and the officer specifically saying, If I see anything on the ground, I'm going to look for anybody's table and take it."

"That's what the issue is," says Marvin.

"You right, Marvin," continued Ishmael. "But the issue remains that the same officer took the table spoke to me and said, 'I'm not gonna mess with your stuff at all.' I said to him, 'I'm gonna walk off, I'm gonna go to the bathroom, get some food and stuff.' He said, 'You don't have nothing to worry about.' See, that's a form of entrapment."

An Asian woman, about twenty-five years old, has been standing a few feet away, waiting for us to finish talking. When Ishmael sees her, he says to me, "Look at this. That's my wife," using the word loosely to describe in a possessive way the woman with whom he has begun to have a romantic relationship. "What's up, Tina?"

"Hey!" she says.

"They took my stuff, Tina!"

"I heard it," she says. "You have to tell me! Because I was waiting, waiting, waiting, waiting. And I went outside and I was standing outside. . . ."

"That's the one I was supposed to take to the movies," Ishmael says to me in a low voice.

"The reason they took my stuff, Tina, is just because another guy put his stuff down on the ground," Ishmael continues. "They took every last thing that I had."

"So you ain't working today?"

"I don't know. I've just been taking care of business all day, dealing with the law all day. . . . I went to the precinct to get my stuff."

"They want to keep it? They don't want to give you back?" asks Tina.

"They didn't even give me a summons for it, hon!"

"What's that?" asks Tina.

"A paper where they write up the stuff that they take from you. It's like a receipt. Tina, I've been busy all day."

After another minute of conversation, Tina leans over and kisses him on the lips. "Well, I'll come back and see you tomorrow, Ishmael."

"I be thinking about you." They embrace. Then she goes away.

Marvin and Ron turn to their customers. Ishmael goes for a slice of pizza, and then on a hunt to find a new supply of magazines.

* * *

Whatever the facts may be (recall that Ishmael told the desk sergeant that he was approaching the table when the officer removed his belongings), the argument illustrates that Ishmael and Ron understand the rule of the street: that police can seek vengeance under certain circumstances. By refusing to admit that he was away from his table, Ishmael shows his assumption that a table left unattended can be taken *legitimately*, even though there is no municipal ordinance to this effect. Police are free to control the "quality of life" through routine discretionary acts that they establish in the minds of vendors as legitimate.

WHEN THE LAW "MEANS NOTHING" TO THE POLICE

Two days later, on Christmas afternoon, I saw Ishmael again. When I arrived, Hakim was standing on the corner. Ishmael had set up his table in his usual spot on the corner of

Sixth Avenue and Eighth Street. Ten minutes later, Officer X (as I'll call him) approached and said something to the effect of: "Ishmael, you have to break down, guy."[9]

"I'm not breaking down, man," he responded.

Ishmael clearly was not showing the kind of deference the men on the block normally observe. I took out my tape recorder and turned it on, though neither Ishmael nor the officer saw me do so.

"You have to break down," the officer insisted.

"But I'm not. Because there's no such thing as a law telling me that. I'm not gonna break down, man. If I can't work, what the hell you working for?"

"Step over here for a second. Ishmael . . ."

"I'm not, man. Come on, that's my food. . . ."

"Listen to me," said the officer.

"I'm the only one out here."

"Listen!"

"I'm not doing nothing wrong!"

"Listen. Listen, Ishmael. The captain says he don't want anybody out here. Now, by all means I should be out here closing the table down, putting your stuff in the car, but I'm not gonna do that to you. I want you to voluntarily do it yourself. 'Cause, listen, if he comes out here and you out here, he's just gonna take your shit away, probably collar you or something like that. And you know, it's not a good day for it."

"Collar me?"

"Listen. Of all days, I don't want to break you down today, because it's Christmas, but I've got to do what I'm told. All right. So, please, don't give me a hard time."

"I'm not giving you a hard time. You giving me a hard time."

"I know. It's just something he said I have to do out here. That's all."

"But do you think it's right?"

"No, I don't think it's right. But I have to follow his orders, man. You know. 'Cause he is my boss. And if I don't follow his orders,

the guy could fucking do anything to me. Do you follow me?"

"You saying he could write you up?"

"Yeah, for not following orders. Listen, you know what, why don't you go set up across the street? But not on Sixth Avenue. That way he's not gonna say shit to you. Thank you."

With that, the officer walked away. Ishmael called after him.

"What is the thing about Sixth Avenue?"

"Ishmael, it's a lot better to be over there. Maybe you'll sell a few books. It's better than having your shit broken down and being locked up."

"I'll be locked up for that, too?"

"Listen! For not complying with orders, right? Take your stuff across the street. Take your chances over there. It's better than over here right now. All right?"

"All right."

The officer walked away. Ishmael walked over to Hakim and me. We were standing on the corner.

"You heard that, Mitch."

"What happened?" asked Hakim.

"He said I could be locked up for not complying with the orders."

"With what orders? What law?" asked Hakim.

"The captain's law," said Ishmael.

"The captain said you can't be here today? There's something in the Municipal Code that says you can't work on Christmas Day?"

"He didn't tell me that," said Ishmael.

"Is there exigent circumstances, an emergency circumstance that does not allow you to be here?" asked Hakim. "Is that what he said to you?"

"It's just his captain telling him this. And I asked him, What do you think? And he said he know it isn't right, that he gotta go along with what his captain says. . . . Right now he's saying that, if I don't comply with what he's saying, then I can be collared."

"You can be arrested?"

"For not complying."

"In other words, they gonna take you *and* the table?"

"Yeah."

"That's deep," said Hakim, and went on: "What is the legal basis for him telling you to leave? You in a legal vending space. Unless he say there's an exigent circumstance going on that has millions of people walking down the street. But what did he say?"

"He said that I can't be on Sixth Avenue today because there's no vendoring on Sixth Avenue today. If you choose to stay on the block, the captain will take you and your stuff. There's no law to find out. But I don't want to go through this procedure with these people. I'm gonna have to break down. I don't feel like getting locked up for nobody today."

"Well, if you feel that way, then break down. But I'm just saying to you, they make up the law today, they make up the law tomorrow. So you gotta put him in check. You see, he don't have nothing to say to me. Because, the last time, I let his ass have it down here. If you don't know the law, they abuse you."

"Well, this is what I don't know," said Ishmael.

* * *

Ishmael began packing up his magazines. After a few minutes passed and about half the material was packed up, the officer returned.

"You know, it really affects me," Ishmael told him as he continued packing. "Because this is first year out of seven years out of all the Christmases that I've worked out here and this is the first time that I've heard something like that. And I don't know where that captain comes off at saying that statement that I know for sure is not documented in no kinds of papers. They've got vendoring up there on 14th Street. And it's a holiday weekend. So what's the difference? If I'm being shut down, what about the newspaper stand [pointing]? Why isn't he being shut down? He's on Sixth Avenue."[10]

The officer stood silently as Ishmael continued. "That's like taking the bread out of my mouth, man. And that's something that I have to go and confirm with this captain. It's not right, man. And if it's allowed to be done this time, it will keep being done. It's not right. Lawfully, it's not right." Ishmael continued: "That's like superseding over everything, man. That's like violating my rights for trying to make my livelihood of money. Come on, man. I'm not saying it's you. It's that individual who's sending that law down that you have to do that. Out of seven years, this is the first time that I've ever heard of some crap like that, man!"

"You the only one out here, Ishmael," said the officer.

"They see me is the only one out here. Other people choose not to be out here and work. If they had a table, I guarantee the tables would have been set up today. But since their tables got tooken from them . . ."

"Those guys got their tables taken from them?" asked the officer.

"Yeah, they had their tables tooken from them!"

"When was that?"

"The other morning."

"Did they have their shit all over the floor?"

"No. It was unattended. And legally it can be tooken when it's unattended."

"You know how many times I've warned them about that, too?" the officer asked rhetorically as he walked away.

* * *

As Ishmael packs up his belongings, I read and reread my own crumpled copies of the municipal ordinances that govern the sale of written matter. I am certain that Hakim is correct. Barring some special circumstance that makes it dangerous to remain on the street at a particular time—a parade, say, or a demonstration—the officer has no legal reason to insist that a vendor move from a legal space.

I have spent years studying these laws and spoken to experts on the codes. It seems to me that I may be witnessing an example of the discretion taken by police officers as they engage in policing against "quality of life" infractions. The officer had justified his actions in a variety of ways (my captain says to close you down, you are the only one out here today) without making reference to the law—because, indeed, the law would not have stood behind him. But since Ishmael does not know the law, and so has no confidence that he is correct ("That's what I don't know," he told Hakim), he was afraid to stand up to the officer and risk arrest or a summons. Perhaps, he thought that as an unhoused black male, even if he was in the right, the officer would not necessarily acknowledge it.

I wanted to see what else I could learn by setting up in the very spot Ishmael had just vacated. As he was hauling tables away, I asked him to loan me a small table and a set of *National Geographics*.[11]

Five minutes later, I stood behind a table just as Ishmael had earlier in the day. I was wearing a leather winter jacket, with the microphone from my tape recorder sticking out the front pocket. I wondered what I might discover about the police's use of their own discretion to improve the "quality of life."

Alice walked up to the table. "You see, Mitch, that's the thing. These cops is full of shit. Because they don't have nobody else to bully around."

The vendors moved away from the table against the front of the B. Dalton bookstore about twenty feet away. "If they take you in, we're going with you," Ishmael called out to me.

At two minutes after five (I checked), a Sixth Precinct police car drove by and a white officer stared at me from the passenger seat. When the car had passed, one of the vendors yelled, "As long as it's a white guy out here it's okay."

If this was a test designed to find out whether an upper-middle-class white person would be treated differently from an unhoused, poor black vendor, I thought to myself, then it was not a good one. To begin with, the officer had just closed Ishmael down. The odds were very small that a black police officer who had to enforce the law against black vendors every day would let himself be seen as one who would allow a white man to stay in the same spot. Furthermore, he might notice the microphone sticking out of my pocket, and this would probably affect what he'd say to me.

I had been standing at the table for about ten minutes when I saw the officer and his beat partner walking toward me.

As I waited, approximately ten black vendors, including Hakim and Ishmael, stood by, offering their support.

"It's showtime!" yelled Ishmael.

"Yo, if they take you in, Mitch, we're coming down there," offered Al.

Then the police were at my table—or, as the vendors would say, "on my ass."

"My man. There's no selling here today. Break it down."

"Excuse me," I said.

"No selling here today. Break it down."

I took a copy of the municipal law out of my pocket. "I'm exercising my right under Local Law 33 of 1982, and Local Law 45 of 1993, to sell written matter."

"Break it down," said the officer. "There's no selling here today."

"Am I within the spaces?" I asked.

"I'll tell you one more time."

"Am I within the spaces?"

"I'll tell you one more time. Break it down."

"Under what law?" I asked.

"No vending here today. Break it down."

"For what reason?"

"Listen. There was somebody here who broke it down, all right? Break it down or I'm gonna take your table away."

"Just tell me the reason I'm being broken down. I have the law right here. I just want to know what reason I'm being broken down."

The officer grabbed the copy of the municipal law out of my hands. "*This*, listen to me, *this* means nothing to me right now."

"But *this* is the local law!"

"I don't care. Break it down."

"Can I please have my copy of the local law back?"

"After you break it down."

"No. I'm not breaking down. How can you say the law means nothing to you?"

"Because *he* broke it down," he said loudly, pointing to Ishmael, who was out of earshot on the corner.

"I'm set up within the lines. Correct or not?"

"Listen," the officer responded, "vending on Sixth Avenue is a privilege that is bestowed on you guys by this community over here."

"A privilege?"

"Yes."

"I'm set up under the law. Can I have my copy of the law back?"

"Listen."

"You just confiscated my property."

"Listen. Break it down."

"Officer, give me back my property."

"You can have it back when I give it to you."

With that, he walked away from the table and conferred with his beat partner on the corner. Then they put in a call on their radio.

"What are they telling you?" Al cried out. "That they're gonna give you a ticket?"

"No. He confiscated my copy of the law and he won't give it back to me."

A few seconds later, the same patrol car that had passed by earlier pulled up to the curb behind the table.

"Listen, man. We gonna be with you, man," one of the vendors called out.

Officer X walked over to the car and conferred with the officer in the passenger seat for a full minute. Then that officer, a white man of about fifty, got out of the car and slammed the door behind him. He walked around my table and inspected its contents.

Another patrolman appeared on the block,

walked up to the table, inspected the magazines closely, and said to Officer X, "This guy looks good."

At the same time, Officer X pulled me aside and said, "What's your name?"

"Mitchell Duneier."

"Mitchell Duneier. Can I talk with you over here, please. Mitchell. This is what happened earlier. Okay, there was a gentleman over here. I had asked him to move and go across the street, because—"

"Can I have my law back, please?"

"You'll get your law back."

"I have to stand at my table. Please talk to me at my table. I'm distributing written matter in accordance with the local law. I must stand with my materials."

"Mitchell, 'cause you and I are talking, you can leave the table. Nothing is going to happen to you. All right? Now, like I was saying previously, there was a gentleman here. I asked him to go across the street, because apparently they don't want anybody on Sixth Avenue today."

"Who?"

"Mitchell. Listen. All you have to do is listen."

"Okay, I'm listening. But you have to understand that I'm frustrated with you, because you said to me before that the law means nothing to you."

"Listen."

"Can I have my copy of the law back?"

"Are you gonna listen? Or are you just gonna ramble on?"

"I'll listen if you respect me. I want my copy of the law back."

At this moment, the officer who had been in the passenger seat of the car, whom I'll call Captain Y, approached us at the table.

"Here's your copy of the law back," said Officer X.

"Listen," said Captain Y. "Regardless of what that says [pointing to my copy of the law], *we* decide where you're allowed to vend and where you're not. So don't cop an attitude with the officer."

"I'm not."

"Listen to me carefully! Don't cop an attitude with them, because they know the law better than you know the law. And you can take this [pointing to the law] and bring it to Central Booking. You don't want to do that on Christmas. So just cooperate with the officers and don't cop an attitude. You understand? 'Cause the last thing they want to do is get tied up in court."

"Okay, Officer."

"And we don't want to put you in jail tonight."

"Okay, Officer."

"So I told him you can stay for now. Put your magazines and do what you got to do. But we decide, not you, where you stay. Do you understand that?"

"Can I ask you a question?"

"Surely."

"Do you have any idea why he came here and told me I had to move? I mean, I'm set up within the legal lines."

"Well, actually, it's so many feet from a doorway."

"It's measured out exactly," I said.

"How many feet is it?"

"It's supposed to be more than twenty, and this is more than twenty."

"No, it's not. From that door to here is not twenty feet," said the captain.

"You see these painted lines here? These are the vending lines that are set up by the police."

"Listen to me carefully! They've been changed!"

A number of vendors had crowded behind the captain to hear what he was saying. One man yelled, "Its twenty-one feet. The reason I'm listening is I'm a vendor, too."

"Listen to me," said the captain. "That door to this table is how many feet?"

"Twenty-one feet."

"Wanna bet? All right, the fact is, you can stay for now. All right? So the point is moot."

"Okay," I said.

"I don't want to argue with you on Christmas."

"Okay," I said.

"As long as you understand that!" said the captain. With that, the police left.

"I see he gave you back your paper," Al called out. "I think that was a point well made. Now Ishmael can put his stuff back there."

"Where is Ishmael?" I asked, looking to the corner. "Is he gonna put his tables back here?"

"He said he's waiting until you leave," said Hakim.

"Okay."

I left the table and approached Ishmael. "Here's my tape recorder if you want it." It had occurred to me that this scene with Officer X might not be Ishmael's last encounter with the police.

"Yeah, let me just keep it on." He took the machine and put it in the milk crate under his table, and I went inside an open coffee shop, the Bagel Buffet, to warm up.

*　*　*

As I sat by myself at a small table, I reflected on the events that had occurred on the block. Although I hadn't given careful thought to what might be gained by setting up in Ishmael's spot, I had long sought to understand the ways of the police as they used their discretion to enforce the municipal laws against written-matter vendors and unhoused people on Sixth Avenue. I had tried to interview police officers, but had always been told that to conduct an interview I would have to get permission from the New York City Police Department's Bureau of Public Information. When I finally did get such permission once, after months of waiting, the sergeant in charge of policing vendors sat with me in the back of the Sixth Precinct and answered all my questions, but somehow said nothing of any significance. This reminded me of what I had read of others' experiences, including that of Paul Chevigny, a leading American scholar of police. "It must be admitted that the NYPD is difficult to study," he writes. "Bureaucratized as it is, it turns a bland face to the public as well as to scholars. Everything has to be done through channels; hardly anyone in the department will talk to an outsider without approval from above, and once the approval is obtained, hardly anything of substance is revealed."[12]

As a sociologist, I would have liked to use as my example taped conversations between police and vendors when neither party knew they were being recorded. Likewise, I would have preferred to see Hakim and the vendors win or lose this battle without any interference or intervention on my part. Nevertheless, it seemed that my encounter with the police might have analytic value.

Because I possessed a copy of the local law and understood it, I had witnessed a striking example of the extent to which officers of the Sixth Precinct will use their discretion to circumvent the law, even when someone waves that very law before their eyes. But how did I *know* that this abuse of discretion was characteristic? It was possible, for instance, that the officer had tried especially hard to get me off the block because he wanted to prove to Ishmael and the other vendors that he wouldn't show favoritism toward a white vendor. Possibly, if one of the regular black vendors had waved the law in the officer's face, he would have been allowed to stay.

In the end, of course, I *was* allowed to stay, by the captain, even though this embarrassed the officer. There is no way for me to know if this was because I knew the law and had a copy handy, or because I was an educated white male. In everyday life, of course, race, class, and education are correlated: white middle-class people are more able to mobilize the law than poor people of color. An altogether thorough experiment would have required one more trial, with Hakim at the table, in order to test what happens when a person with education and a knowledge of the law, but a low social status, challenges

the police. Lacking this, the closest that I can come to such an experiment is some observations of the way Hakim was treated under similar circumstances.

In a letter he wrote to me after the passage of Local Law 45 in 1993, Hakim tells of setting up his table in front of Balducci's gourmet market. I quote from the letter with his permission:

Yesterday I came into New York and set up twenty feet from the entrance to Balducci's Supermarket and ten feet from the intersection.

There is nowhere else to work right now.

I knew that, if necessary, I was going to set up on the block where Balducci's is located a long time ago. I never told anyone that I studied the location and placement logistics for every block in the Village. I do not wait for other vendors to do anything. I act alone. No one is going to help me anyway. No one. I was holding on to my trump card for a long time. I knew there was a legal space in front of Balducci's Supermarket.

Within ten minutes a Puerto Rican Balducci's security guard with a cheap "March of the Wooden Soldiers" uniform says to me, "I am just trying to be nice. You can't stay here. You gotta leave."

"This is public space," I told him. "This is a *legal* location for vending. I do not want to be here, but I can't work down the street. So, you are gonna have to call the police."

Anyway the police come in an unmarked wine red car. Two patrol officers and the Sergeant in the back seat.

The measure tape comes out.

Are you ten feet from the intersection?

I'm more than ten feet and I'm twenty feet from the entrance to their store.

They measure. I got her ass! She has that "I'm tired of this smart-ass Nigger" look on her face.

One of the patrol officers says to me, "You know the law pretty well, huh?"

"Yeah, I read it like some people read *T.V. Guide*, but, I don't want to be here, Officer."

The sergeant had to get back in her car and leave. They *cannot* move me. They have no *legal basis* to move me without running the risk of being *sued*. She knows this.

The manager of Balducci's does not like this and I overhear him say, "That's ridiculous."

If the Sergeant thought she could "make it up" as she imagined it, she would have lied to force me to move. But she *recognizes* I have done my homework.

No *sane* African-American should ever trust what any police officer says. Get the law and look it up. Know your basic rights.

What have I found? That people down here do not know how to look up basic laws, and they cannot afford experts.

Because I am generally regarded as a Nigger, many white folks, even well meaning white folks, think I am stupid. Stupid means: The inability to achieve the tactical intelligence of a white person.

Hakim's letter strongly suggests that the crucial difference between Ishmael and me may not have been race alone, but level of education and confidence about the law. What seems more important is that if the officers will speak so cavalierly about the law with an educated middle-class white vendor—"this means nothing to me"—it seems reasonable to infer that their treatment of poor and uneducated black men who cannot cite the law chapter and verse is potentially far more arbitrary.

It is helpful to see this incident in the larger historical context of how skid rows used to be policed. In a classic sociological study of the mid-1960s, Egon Bittner shows that in skid-row districts the law was invoked somewhat arbitrarily, but mainly "as a resource to solve certain pressing practical problems in keeping the peace."[13] Patrolmen saw it as their goal to help people on skid row and to engage in service activities. Those officers whose "roughness is determined *by personal feelings* rather than situational exigencies, are judged to be poor craftsmen."[14] Officers did not expect or demand deference.[15] They used the law "to keep skid-row inhabitants from sinking deeper into the misery they already experience."[16] Officers kept the peace on skid row not merely by knowing names, but by having a detailed personal knowledge of

the people on the street. Supervisory personnel understood that such knowledge was crucial, so they exhibited "a strong reluctance to direct their subordinates in the particulars of their work experience."[17]

Some of the officers who regulate vendors on Sixth Avenue today know their names; others don't. Regardless, the police on Sixth Avenue today have less detailed knowledge than the patrolling officers on skid row did. They do not view it as their job to help salvage souls or to develop a detailed knowledge of the men on the beat, which they can draw upon in difficult situations. And their supervisors, having less respect for such detailed knowledge, give commands from far away.

NOTES

1. For a complete description of this movement, see George L. Kelling and Catherine M. Coles, *Fixing Broken Windows* (New York: Free Press, 1996).
2. Local Law 80 of 1996 "to amend the administrative code of the city of New York in relation to a prohibition against certain forms of aggressive solicitation."
3. For an excellent discussion, see Paul Stoler, "Spaces, Places, and Fields," *American Anthropologist* 98, no. 4 (1996): 776–88.
4. See Kelling and Coles, *Fixing Broken Windows*.
5. Bittner, *Aspects of Police Work*, p. 159: "Community policing recognizes that organizational structures and administrative processes that treat officers like factory workers have failed. Police work, unlike factory work, is not simple and routine, but complex; it is usually conducted by one or two officers in the field, without direct oversight, who must use considerable discretion in handling problems. When officers confront complex life and death decisions, success depends not on direct supervision or rote application of specific rules, but on the application of general knowledge and skill, obtained through prolonged education and mentoring, to specific situations. Community policing aims to develop administrative techniques that recognize this complexity in the work of police officers. Sergeants, for example, become mentors and coaches, not overseers. Their focus is on assisting officers in solving neighborhood problems, not adherence to organizational rules."
6. Given the level of pressure that is placed on police by the local community board and the Business Improvement District to control the behavior of what they call street people, the officer thinks he is speaking for the community when he takes such action.

7. I am made sensitive to this possibility, and was inspired to look for evidence to support it, after reading David Garland's monumental book *Punishment and Modern Society* (Chicago: University of Chicago Press, 1990). See also Joel Feinberg, "The Expressive Function of Punishment," in *Doing and Deserving* (Princeton: Princeton University Press, 1970).

8. As Donald Black notes in a classic article ("Crime as Social Control," *American Sociological Review* 48 [1983]: pp. 34–45), "A great deal of the conduct labeled and processed as crime in modern societies resembles the modes of conflict management . . . that are found in traditional societies which have little or no law (in the sense of governmental social control)." By taking Black's observation about crime in modern society and applying it to the police, we can better understand the way in which the quality of life is regulated.

9. I believe it would be inconsistent with the argument of this chapter to name the police officer involved. To use his name would suggest that these incidents are the fault of a particular individual, rather than the pernicious result of a system of policing.

10. Indeed, directly across the street, there was a newsstand in operation. This was the first comparison to the newsstands that I had heard during my years on the block. Here, a homeless-rights organization might be on more solid factual ground in arguing in court that singling out Ishmael's acts of selling on Christmas is irrational and fails equal-protection scrutiny. They also might argue that the police would confiscate Ishmael's magazines and belongings when he left his table unattended, but they would never confiscate the belongings of the newsstand when the attendant stepped out to use a washroom or went into McDonald's for a soda, which I have often seen him do. Both the newsstand attendant and Ishmael are using public land for the same purpose, distributing written matter, and an unattended table does not interfere with public use of the sidewalks any more than an unattended newsstand. The reason for treating Ishmael and the newsstand differently, it might be argued, is that seizing Ishmael's property achieves the purpose of punishing him for behavior that is disfavored by the community but not illegal. The behavior being punished is not that of distributing written matter, but the lifestyle of street homelessness. Punishing the lifestyle is certainly an illegitimate state objective. No doubt, the newsstand vendor would object to being compared to Ishmael on the grounds that he runs a licensed business, a permanent structure which cannot be built without the approval of five agencies.

11. I chose this periodical deliberately because at that time it was distributed through the mail (and not sold on newsstands), so it had no price marked on it. In the few months prior, officers of the Sixth Precinct had been routinely asking vendors to produce tax-identification numbers. When vendors could not, police told them to break down their tables. I had left my tax ID at home, because I hadn't expected to do any vending that day. I decided to put a sign on the table indicating that the magazines were free. It said, "Merry Christmas. Free Magazines. One per person."

12. Paul Chevigny, *Edge of the Knife: Police Violence in the Americas* (New York: New Press, 1995), p. 33.

13. Egon Bittner, "The Police on Skid Row: A Study of Peace Keeping," reprinted in Bittner. *Aspects of Police Work* (Boston: Northeastern University Press, 1990).

14. Ibid., p. 701.

15. Ibid., p. 708.

16. Ibid., p. 711.

17. Ibid., p. 715.

CHAPTER 7

The Corner

Life on the Streets

Peter Moskos

It's a different culture. You know, what is normal for us—like going to work, getting married—they don't understand that. Drugs are normal. Mommy did it. Daddy did it, not that he's around. But if people want to take drugs, there's nothing we can do. All we can do is lock them up. But even that is normal.

— A Baltimore City police officer

The drug-dealing block is a buzz of constant activity. Dealers hawk their wares, customers come and go, and addicts roam the street hustling for their next hit. Occasionally a police car will appear and the street crowd will disperse, slowly walking away from the police car. Being too fast or too slow can make one a conspicuous mark for police attention. So people walk, shuffle, and roll with a well-practiced nonchalance. Soon after the appearance of a police car, the street will be deserted. When the police car leaves, the crowd returns.

The Eastern District's 45,000 residents account for over 20,000 arrests every year.[1] Most arrests are drug-related.[2] Police officers patrol in their cars, respond to 911 calls, and clear corners. These officers, who by and large hate the ghetto, are frustrated to see those arrested go free in the revolving door of the criminal justice system: "justice for criminals," goes the well-worn police cliché. The cycle repeats. Police earn court overtime pay while residents get rap sheets. It's a horrible equilibrium, and police are the fulcrum.

The Baltimore Police Department estimates that 80 percent of homicides are drug-related. Most of these murders are not big news. A twelve-person shooting at an "RIP party" for a drug dealer who had himself been murdered was not even page-one news in the *Baltimore Sun*. The violence of Baltimore's drug trade may be extreme, but it is typical of drug-related violence: poor young men, usually black, with access to guns, involved in illegal public drug dealing.[3]

Police rarely witness the actual drug deal. Police see the signs and the aftermath of what occurs on the street, but in many ways know very little. After a year on the street, 94 percent of patrol officers believe that citizens know more about what goes on in an area than the officers who patrol there.[4] Police response to an active drug corner follows a standard modus operandi: a citizen calls 911, a responding police car approaches, drug activity stops, and people—dealers, friends, addicts, lookouts, and any "innocents" who happen to be walking by—will slowly walk away.

Most often, the suspects will go for a brief walk around the block and then, after police leave, reconvene on the same or a nearby stoop. Dispersing without being asked is considered a sign of criminal activity, or perhaps an outstanding warrant. But police also view quick and unprompted departure—walking, not running—as a sign of respect and a satisfactory resolution to most problems. On one such call, I pulled up to a stoop and two drug suspects walked without being asked. My partner happily said, "I love respectful drug dealers." We drove away.

Clearing the corner is what separates those who have policed from those who haven't. Some officers want to be feared; others, respected; still others, simply obeyed. An officer explained: "You don't have to [hit anybody]. Show up to them. Tell them to leave the corner, and then take a walk. Come back, and if they're still there, don't ask questions, just call for additional units and a wagon. You can always lock them up for something. You just have to know your laws. There's loitering, obstruction of a sidewalk, loitering in front of the liquor store, disruptive behavior." Police assume that if the suspects are dirty, they will walk away rather than risk being stopped and frisked. You *can* always lock them up for something, but when a police officer pulls up on a known drug corner, legal options are limited.

UNTOUCHABLES: DRUGS AND POLICE CORRUPTION

Temptation is everywhere. Given the prevalence of drug dealing and the fact that drug dealers hold hundreds and sometimes thousands of dollars in cash, police officers routinely face the opportunity for quick and illegal personal gain. Police could get away with stealing drugs or money, at least for a while. But robbed drug dealers can and will call Internal Affairs. And officers with criminal dealings will usually be ratted out by another criminal. Putting a dirty cop behind bars is as good a get-out-of-jail card as exists.

I policed what is arguably the worst shift in the worst district in Baltimore and saw no police corruption. I know there are corrupt police officers. After three years on the street, one Eastern District officer stopped a man who drove his motorized scooter through a red light. The man had $6,300 in his pocket.

The officer counted the money and allegedly returned $4,900 of it. The man called police to report the missing money and the officer was arrested and indicted on felony theft charges. One year later, these charges were dropped on condition that the officer resign from the police department and agree not to work in law enforcement again. When a cop is dirty, there is inevitably a drugs connection. Over a few beers after work, the subject of the drug squad came up. An older cop warned me to "stay away from drugs [in your dealings as a cop]. They'll just get you in trouble in the long run."

Incidents do happen, but the *police culture* is not corrupt. Though overall police integrity is very high, some will never be convinced. But out of personal virtue, internal investigation stings, or monetary calculations, the majority—the vast majority—of police officers are clean. A greater problem is that high-arrest officers push the boundaries of consent searches and turn pockets inside-out. Illegal (and legal) searches are almost always motivated by a desire to find drugs. In the academy, an officer warned the class, "Corruption starts six months to a year after you're out of the academy. When you're on the streets and you start shaking down drug dealers because they're worthless shits." Similarly a sergeant explained:

> You'll get out there, thinking you can make a difference. Then you get frustrated: a dealer caught with less than twenty-five pieces will be considered personal use. . . . Or you go to court and they take his word over yours. You're a cop and you're saying you saw something! . . . After it happens to you, you don't care. It's your job to bring him there [to court]. What happens after that is their problem. You can't take this job personal! Drugs were here before you were. And they'll be here long after you're gone. Don't think you can change that. I don't want you leaving here thinking everybody living in this neighborhood is bad, does drugs. Many [cops] start beating people, thinking they deserve it.

Police officers are often in a position to hold various amounts of drugs and money. Legally seized drugs and money are kept in one's pockets (carefully separated from personal belongings) before being taken to the station house and submitted in the proper fashion. Officers have to be careful not to make *honest* mistakes. They could put something in the wrong pocket. Something could fall out of a pocket. The night gets busy and they might forget to submit. Before each shift, police officers search the squad car for anything left behind.

Many residents, after repeated calls to police about drug dealers, assume that officers are either incorrigibly corrupt or completely apathetic:

> I understand what you [police] deal with. But you got to understand. People see police drive right by the dealers, don't even get out of the car. Or they [police] got them [dealers] with their legs spread [being searched]. Who's to say you ain't taking a little something on the side? You can't have drugs on this scale without somebody letting it happen.

Police discount such accusations:

> People get bad ideas from the media or from criminals that we're corrupt or brutal. But we're not. Or they refuse to think that their son could be involved with drugs. They want the corner cleared, but if we pick up their son it must be the racist cops picking on him because he's black. And with the amount of drugs you've got in this area, of course they aren't going to like police because we're trying to lock them up. Too many people here are pro-criminal.

Even financially, it pays to be straight. A New York City police officer explained:

> My pension is worth between one and two million dollars. I'd have to be a fool to risk that for $100, even $1,000. I'll tell you when I'll be corrupt: the day I walk into a room piled with drugs, five million dollars in cash, and every-

body dead. For five million, I'd do it. I'd leave the drugs and take the cash.

Some officers enter the police department corrupt. Others fall of their own free will. Still others may have an isolated instance of corruption in an otherwise honest career. But there is no natural force pulling officers from a free cup of coffee toward shaking down drug dealers. Police can omit superfluous facts from a police report without later perjuring themselves in court. Working unapproved security overtime does not lead to a life in the Mob. Officers can take a catnap at 4 am and never abuse medical leave.[5] There is no slope. If anything, corruption is more like a Slip 'N Slide. You can usually keep your footing, but it's the drugs that make everything so damn slippery.

STOP SNITCHING

While the police see good communication between the public and the police as essential to fighting crime, relations are quite poor. This shouldn't be surprising. Drug users are criminal. If they want to stay out of jail, they and those who care for them have every reason to be wary of police. One officer complained: "Nobody here will talk to police. Half the public hates us. The other half is scared to talk to us. I would be, too. But we can't do anything without the public. They know who's dirty and who's not. They know who's shooting who. We don't know. They live here. We just drive around in big billboards. How are we supposed to see anything? The public doesn't understand that nothing will ever go to court if nobody talks. We can only do so much. As long as nobody ever sees anything, things aren't going to change." Police cannot base their testimony, or even a legal stop, on the claims of an anonymous call from a citizen.

The desire to remain anonymous comes from a combination of common sense and fear. Yet our system of justice depends on the willingness of victims and witnesses to testify. The Sixth Amendment says, "In all criminal prosecutions, the accused shall enjoy the right . . . to be confronted with the witnesses against him." No witness means no conviction. The "stop snitching" phenomenon compounds the problem. Witness protection is minimal, and even when offered it is often turned down. Relocation is impractical when it involves moving away from home, family, friends, and babysitters.

The idea that "snitches get stitches" is not new, having roots going back at least to the Mob's code of Omertà. But wearing T-shirts to a criminal trial with "stop snitching" printed inside a red stop sign is a relatively new fashion statement. The campaign's rise to prominence and the public's awareness of the snitching issue grew largely out of basketball star Carmelo Anthony's cameo appearance in a 2004 amateur Baltimore DVD called *Stop Fucking Snitching*. The video was in part a reaction to increased police success in "flipping" low-level drug suspects. In 2000, Baltimore detectives were instructed to interrogate all arrested drug suspects. Minor offenders could potentially gain their freedom with useful information about guns, murders, or major drug dealers.

The DVD is an often amusing but too long and poorly edited collection of street-corner bravado. A motley collection of self-proclaimed thugs rap, smoke weed, flash guns, and flaunt money. Snitches are named and threatened. Two corrupt police officers were outed as being "in the game." The Baltimore Police Department made a short video in response to *Stop Fucking Snitching* called *Keep Talking*. In the end, many of the people featured in the video were arrested. The two named officers were arrested and convicted by a jury that did not believe their testimony that they were only playing by the informal rules of the narcotics game.

Yet overall, the significance of the "stop snitching" video is probably overblown. Quite simply, it's nothing new in the 'hood.

The distinction between those "in the game" and "civilians" has never been clear. In October 2002, the Dawson home on Oliver Street was firebombed, killing both parents and their five children. A drug dealer was angry because he believed that Mr. and Mrs. Dawson kept calling the police. When witnesses get killed, people don't need a video or T-shirt to tell them to keep quiet.

New or not, the impact of silence is hugely detrimental to police and prosecutors. Even without personal risks, there is little incentive to testify. Nobody gains through interaction with the criminal justice system. You don't get paid for it; there is no guarantee that testimony will result in conviction and jail time; and after the second or third postponement, a sense of civic duty usually fades. The hassles of court—passing through metal detectors, wasted days, close contact with crowds of criminals—combined with practical matters such as work and childcare make it far easier, even smarter, to see nothing, hear nothing, and mind your own business.

POLICE PERSPECTIVE

Because of these problems and the "victimless" nature of drug crimes, most drug arrests are at the initiative of police officers. On one occasion, while driving slowly through a busy drug market early one morning, I saw dozens of African American addicts milling about while a smaller group of young men and boys were waiting to sell. Another officer in our squad had just arrested a drug addict for loitering. I asked my partner, "What's the point of arresting people for walking down the street?" He replied: "Because everybody walking down the street is a criminal. In Canton or Greektown [middle-class neighborhoods] people are actually going somewhere. How many people here aren't dirty? ['None.'] It's drugs. . . . If all we can do is lock 'em up for loitering, so be it."

Police have diverse opinions about the drug problem. I asked my sergeant if it was more effective to arrest drug addicts or to remain on and patrol the street to temporarily disrupt drug markets. He surprised me by choosing the former:

Arresting someone sends a better message. Locking up junkies makes a difference. This squad used to have more arrests than five of the districts. We used to go out every night and just make arrest runs as a squad. Start with six cars, like a train. Fill one up, then you have five cars. Continue until you're out of cars. At 1 am, everybody on a drug corner is involved with drugs. We locked them up for loitering. Got lots of drugs, a few weapons, too. After a few weeks, everything was quiet. Eventually it got so that we had to poach from other districts. We ran out of people to arrest. You think the neighbors didn't like that?

Police are defined by arrests, so an arrest-based approach toward the drug problem is popular. Mocking a much disparaged comment attributed to a former commissioner, one officer said, "We're not 'social workers with guns.' We're PO-lice. . . . We're supposed to be locking up the drug addicts, not sending them for referral." Another officer simply said: "I lock up junkies." He explained:

Some people consider that a bullshit lockup. But fuck 'em. I don't see them locking up Al Capone. You bring your skanky white ass into East Baltimore and I'll send you right to C.B.I.F. [jail]. If I lock somebody up before they buy drugs, that's one less chance that they're going to get robbed. One less chance they're going to get shot. One less chance they're going to OD right before shift change. If everybody locked up all the junkies, eventually they'd give up. Plus I love [the overtime money from] court!

Another officer explained how a high-arrest strategy would make the streets safer:

I'll tell you how. Go out there and lock everybody up. If you're standing on the corner, you go to jail. If you've got drugs on you, you stay there [in jail]. We could clear up these streets. But people go crazy as soon as you lock up their baby. Some people out here actually do have jobs. And they want the corner cleared until they realize that it's their son standing out there.

Other police officers, however, questioned the benefit of repeatedly arresting addicts:

Locking up junkies isn't going to do it. They've got to go after the kingpin. The big man. The man with the moolah. But there's too much power up there. You go high enough and you never know who you're going to find. You think it's just here in Baltimore? They don't grow poppies in East Baltimore.

Another officer said:

They've got to keep people in jail. I'd like to see some of that "three-strikes-you're-out" here. We keep locking up the same people over and over again. And they get right out. They don't care if they go to jail: three hots and a cot. The whole system is a joke. What do you expect? People don't change.

A veteran sergeant proposed raising the risk of drug-related deaths as a means of scaring addicts into quitting:

You really want to know? I've got a plan, but you won't like this. What you've got to do is put bad drugs out there. Make people get sick. Kill a few. The only way a junkie is ever going to kick the habit is if he's afraid he's going to die. If every time somebody was shooting up, there was a good chance they'd die? You'd solve the drug problem in a month. Or at least people wouldn't start. People are dying now. You've seen 'em overdose. And it's good for business because all the other junkies want some of that "good shit."

Nobody believes that victory in the drug war is imminent. Nor do police believe that current tactics can do anything other than maintain the status quo. Some police blame the Constitution for limiting police officers' ability to arrest drug criminals: "Yeah, I think the Constitution should be unamended. If we could stop whoever we wanted, there would be a lot less crime. Criminals have all the rights. That's why they call it the *criminal* justice system." Many police offer some variation of this.

The majority of police do not want drug laws softened. One sergeant told me, "Look, we're out there doing what we can. Should we just throw in the towel? Legalization would send the wrong message. We don't legalize murder just because we can't stop it. If we weren't out there, the problem would be a lot worse." In survey data, one-fifth of officers agree that possession of small amounts of marijuana should be legal.[6] A smaller minority support complete legalization of all drugs. This support comes more from a libertarian philosophy of limited government than from a belief in harm reduction or effective policy. As one officer put it, "Fuck. I'd just legalize it all. I don't think it's the state's business telling people what they can and can't do anyway. Legalize it, regulate it, tax it. And then I'd go home and smoke a big doobie."

It may seem incongruous for police officers to see the futility of drug enforcement and simultaneously promote increased drug enforcement. But for many, the drug war is a moral issue and retreat would "send the wrong message": "It's a crusade for me. My brother and a cousin died from heroin overdoses. I know that on some level it's a choice they made. But there was also a dealer pushing it on them. I want to go out and get these drug dealers."

Another officer was more explicit: "You've got to see it [drugs] as evil. What do you think? It's good? When we're out there, risking our lives, we're on the side of good. Drugs are evil. It's either that or seeing half the people in the Eastern [District] as being evil. I like to think that I'm helping good people fight evil. That's what I'd like to think."

As long as drugs are illegal, someone on the corner will deal drugs. When police con-

front the public drug dealers, police will almost always win the individual battle. But there is no hope that the current system of policing will let us win the war on drugs. The failure of police to eliminate street-level drug dealing is nothing new. Berkeley professor and chief of police August Vollmer said it seventy years ago: "One notorious peddler stood on a corner and waited until his customer dropped money near a telephone pole. He picked it up, and one of his agents put the drug wanted, as indicated by the amount of money, in a crevice in the same telephone pole. Where money is taken by one person and the package is inserted by another, conviction is difficult if not impossible."[7]

The attitudes of police and criminal are largely controlled by a desire to protect their turf while avoiding unnecessary interactions. On each call for service, drug dealers generally do not wish to provoke the police and most police officers are not looking for adventure. At night, curfew violations can be enforced on minors. Open containers can be cited. People can be arrested for some minor charge. But arrests take officers off the street and leave the drug corner largely unpoliced while the prisoner is booked. Nothing police officers do will disrupt the drug trade longer than it takes drug dealers to walk around the block and recongregate. One officer expressed this dilemma well: "We can't do anything. Drugs were here before I was born and they're going to be here after I die. All they pay us to do is herd junkies."

NOTES

1. One arrest for every two people does not mean that every other person is arrested each year. There are a lot of repeat customers. Out of 108,000 arrests overall in Baltimore in 2005, there were 60,000 "unique individuals" (Greg Warren, director of substance-abuse treatment services for the Maryland Department of Public Safety and Correctional Services, quoted in Ron Cassie's March 22, 2006, *Baltimore City Paper*, "High and Inside").

   If the city ratio held true for the Eastern District, it would mean that 30 percent of residents get arrested each year. Almost certainly, given the large number of arrests for minor charges in the Eastern District, the percentage of individuals arrested multiple times is higher in the Eastern District than in the city overall.

2. Based on my own observations and Warner and Coomer's (2003) "Neighborhood Drug Arrest Rates."

3. Baltimore's homicide rate is more than seven times the national average. See Jacobs and Wright (2006) for an excellent description of both why and how violence so commonly occurs within the structure and culture of public drug dealers.

4. Author's survey data.

5. I say some of this speaking from experience.

6. Marijuana attitudes are based on the author's survey data. Fifteen percent of incoming officers and 20 percent of the same officers after one year on the street believe that possession of small amounts of marijuana should be legal. In the 1998 General Social Survey, 29 percent of the public agrees with the statement.

One growing group dedicated to the cause of drug legalization is Law Enforcement Against Prohibition (www.leap.cc). This organization consists of police officers, prosecutors, and judges who support drug regulation rather than prohibition.

7. Vollmer 1936, 111.

CHAPTER 8

Like Therapy

The Blues Club as a Haven

David Grazian

Third places the world over share common and essential features. As one's investigations cross the boundaries of time and culture, the kinship of the Arabian coffeehouse, the German *bierstube*, the Italian *taberna*, the old country store of the American frontier, and the ghetto bar reveals itself. . . . The wonder is that so little attention has been paid to the benefits attaching to the third place. It is curious that its features and inner workings have remained virtually undescribed in this present age when they are so sorely needed and when any number of lesser substitutes are described in tiresome detail. Volumes are written on sensitivity and encounter groups, on meditation and exotic rituals for attaining states of relaxation and transcendence, on jogging and massaging. But the third place, the people's own remedy for stress, loneliness, and alienation, seems easy to ignore.

—Ray Oldenburg, *The Great Good Place*

A CAST OF REGULARS

Thus far, we have explored the world of the blues club, and B.L.U.E.S. in particular, through the lens of the audience member, and in doing so, we have observed how out-of-towners seek out the symbols of authenticity suggested by fabricated images of blackness, ghetto life, and the city of Chicago itself. But while these consumers squeeze into the club's small interior on most Friday and Saturday evenings for their weekend kicks, during the rest of the week they are joined by a colorful cast of local regulars in search of a slightly different kind of authenticity. Now that we have peeled away some of its layers of manufactured authenticity, let us return to B.L.U.E.S. once again, but this time we will observe the club from the point of view of this cast of regulars, a collection of die-hard blues fans, professional musicians, amateur players, bartenders, and other locals who inhabit the club throughout the week not only to be entertained by the blues, but also as the following entry from my field notebook reveals, to check in with friends, schmooze with acquaintances, and gossip about everybody else.

"So, Robin, how do I look tonight?"

Robin, the Tuesday night bartender, looks confused and wants to know what Doug means, and why he is asking *her*. As for me, I've been at the bar since about 11 P.M., and from what I can gather, Doug, who is the harmonica player for the evening's headliner, has been spending the night confidently chatting up his date. But now that she has left the bar for the rest room, he is shifting from his ordinarily confident demeanor to more of an anxious backstage role, enlisting Robin for grooming tips.

As Doug explains his desire to impress his date, I peek around the bar in search of other members of the Tuesday night cast of regulars. Rob Hecko, the club owner, sips coffee at his perch on the raised platform by the front door, where he can survey his employees and customers while watching television; he chats with Mike, one of the club's bouncers enjoying an evening off. Mark, a local booking agent and former club owner, approaches the bar to order his usual glass of red wine. Chicago blues artist Dave Myers strikes up a conversation with a friend of the band at the back of the club as he sells and autographs his CD for any takers. Jay jokes at the bar with Aimee, the other Tuesday night bartender, and Patrick, the evening's bouncer. Louis, a local saxophonist and the organizer of the weekly jam session at B.L.U.E.S. Etcetera, makes his rounds at the club, greeting all familiar faces. Meanwhile, Karen, a local blues photojournalist snaps her flash down by the stage at Tail Dragger (the blues singer introduced in chapter 1).

As the night wears on, the banter among the regulars continues, and as I characteristically peel away the red-and-white label from my beer bottle, I try to fashion myself as a potential member of this cast of characters. I chat with Dizzy, asking him if he will be in attendance for the Wednesday night jam session, and he suggests that he might consider going if Jack, his current band mate, offers him a ride from his South Side apartment to the North Side club. Karen soon returns to the bar and casually smooches with her date as I exchange remarks with Suzanne, the Tuesday night waitress, about her social life in West Town's Wicker Park neighborhood. Later Aimee buys me my third beer as she relishes telling her tale of last Monday night's fun at Suzanne's Academy Awards party, after which several members of the staff headed out to Smoke Daddy for beer and music until early in the morning. She appears equally jovial as she details her plans to go with Hecko to catch her favorite blues artist, Lee Russell, at a show in the suburbs.

As the night progresses, Dizzy performs a few numbers on the fly, after which Tail Dragger resumes his spotlight at the front of the stage, growling in his best Howlin' Wolf imitation. He rhapsodizes mournfully about his latest stint in prison in his highly affected baritone blues voice as Jay remarks aloud to himself, "Oh, why was I in jail? Oh, I remember . . ." and he turns to Karen and adds, "because I shot somebody and killed them!" (In 1993 Tail Dragger murdered fellow Chicago blues performer Boston Blackie over a financial dispute and served four years in the Illinois State Correctional System for the crime.) Karen gestures that he shouldn't announce this news so loud, but he retorts that Tail Dragger didn't hear him and neither did anyone else . . . and the night continues on until closing.

Unlike many of the audience members who jump and shout alongside them at B.L.U.E.S., the members of this cast of regulars do not spend a lot of time thinking about the authenticity of black or white musicians, or whether their favorite B.B. King song will be performed during the second set, or how their experience at the club resonates with popular depictions of Chicago's urban nightlife. Instead, they experience the club through an alternative interpretive lens, and so they literally see a different kind of world when they enter the bar, a world populated by local acquaintances and familiar strangers. According to Marci, a bartender and manager at B.L.U.E.S.:

Oh, yeah, well, Saturday night is amateur night, you know, all tourists, people from the suburbs. During the week it's different. I mean, there are still some tourists, but not as many. Tuesday nights are more for locals, and lots of people here are friends with the band, and it's just great—lots of my friends come, and it's just cooler.

THE JAM SESSION AND THE SEARCH FOR AN AUTHENTIC SELF

In Chicago, New York, and other urban areas, jazz and blues musicians traditionally frequented certain after-hours clubs for intense jam sessions where they could practice their craft by improvising with fellow artists in settings removed from the more commercial world of public performance. Held in the back rooms and basements of private clubs, secret speakeasies, or other invitation-only gatherings, musicians and their hangers-on would congregate and play at the jam after their paid gigs in order to experiment with new ideas, learn about possible jobs, network and talk shop with fellow performers, and compete for in-group status among their peers. In this manner, the jam session provided them with an alternative space of leisure and work, a place where they could socialize with colleagues and rivals until the wee hours and simultaneously fulfill a set of professional needs and responsibilities.[1]

Because late-night jam sessions typically excluded nonmusicians, jazz and blues aficionados tended to regard these clandestine meetings as far more authentic than the concerts, dances, and other public appearances where music was performed. As a result, cultural entrepreneurs began staging commercial jam sessions in the late 1930s during which audiences would be permitted to witness these formerly private moments of improvisation. Of course, opening up these jam sessions to paying outsiders diminished their capacity to symbolize the same authenticity they once did in an earlier, less constraining environment.[2]

Today many blues jam sessions in Chicago operate as little more than open-mike nights where amateur and up-and-coming musicians are permitted to sit in with established house bands and take improvised solos for paying audiences on typically slow weeknights. However, in spite of the commercialized aspects of these latter-day jams, they continue to serve as an emotional outlet for young musicians and other bar regulars in search of community. At the former weekly jam session held every Wednesday night at B.L.U.E.S. Etcetera, Adam, a guitarist in his mid-twenties, emphasizes the scene's impact on his overall sense of well-being:

> Yeah, I can't wait for the Wednesday night jam. It's like I need my fix. I remember a year ago I had been playing in a bunch of rock and metal bands, and suddenly I got really into blues and started playing it alone in my apartment, and it was great, but I wanted to jam with other guys, and no one else I knew was into playing blues. Then I showed up at the jam, and it was like so great, you know? And now, I get really depressed if I miss it. It's like therapy.

Of course, like their more traditional counterparts, contemporary jam sessions also offer an alternative world for musicians to develop professionally by providing exposure and experience for new arrivals and amateurs, a meeting place for aspiring musicians to find potential band mates and accompanists, and a forum where they can learn about local employment opportunities. In fact, Adam met the members of his current band at a series of jam sessions throughout town, while Elliot, the aforementioned singer and guitarist from chapter 1, credits a local jam session for introducing him to the city's blues scene.[3] He owes much of his reputation to a contest held at the prestigious jam session at Buddy Guy's Legends, at which he garnered the top prize:

> Well, the jam sessions are really the places where you get your start if you're new . . . That's where you go to get known . . . I got my start at the jams, just going to the weekly jam session . . . making connections, networking . . . Music is just like a business in that way . . . And that helped open doors for us.

In addition, jam sessions provide a fertile ground for blues artists seeking to develop their artistic talents and professional skills. During encounters between musicians, advanced players often befriend their novice counterparts to teach them various techniques and tricks of the trade. In my own experiences at B.L.U.E.S. Etcetera's Wednesday night jam session, Jeffrey, a fellow saxophonist, would frequently take me aside to teach me basic playing techniques, such as using the blues scale to improvise while playing solos. (The blues scale consists of the root, 3rd, 4th, 4th, 5th, and 7th intervals of the major scale: for example, the blues scale in the key of C major [C-D-E-F-G-A-B-C] would be: C-E-F-F-G-B-C. By raising or lowering the notes of the major scale by half-intervals, thereby making them sharp or flat, musicians deliberately play "out-of-tune" to produce the "blue" notes indicative of blues and jazz melodies.) For many of the jam session participants, mentoring involves showing inexperienced players how to take solos and harmonize using these scales. These lessons often expand into general lectures on practicing, instrument maintenance, and artistic development: where to take private lessons and shop for equipment accessories, the importance of listening to old records and attempting to replicate solos at home, the merits of metallic and rubber mouthpieces over plastic ones, and so forth.

While some advanced musicians hold these impromptu lessons in their private encounters with less experienced players, others turn their onstage interactions into pedagogical opportunities. At B.L.U.E.S. Etcetera participation in the horn section offers such an opportunity. Sequestered at bar stools near the right side of the stage, brass and woodwind horn players congregate, harmonize softly to accompany the band, and switch off taking solos at the horn microphone. Their interactions provide opportunities for the passage of advice among musicians of varying degrees of ability.

I experience such an encounter one night when I assist James, a black semiprofessional trumpet player and regular at the jam, by helping provide harmonic accompaniment to the band's performance. At the stage James asks me to follow his lead and begins to play off the major third, which I simply imitate until the song's completion. Although we have grown acquainted through our interactions at the microphone for the past few months, we tend to confine our conversations to topics of music performance. On break between songs, James turns to me and remarks: "Yeah, I haven't seen you here for a couple of weeks, so I know you've been practicing. And it sounds good, man, it sounds real good. I can tell you've been practicing, man."

We begin chatting about music and harmony, and he suggests that we play the same rhythmic part to lend a strong accompanying base to the musicians onstage. He then runs down a chromatic scale of successive notes on his horn. (A typical chromatic scale consists of twelve tones played at half-step intervals in ascending or descending order. For example, the chromatic scale in C major includes the following notes: C-C-D-E-E-F-F-G-G-A-B-B.) As I echo James's trumpet by singing the notes aloud, he continues the impromptu lesson: "See, that's your best teacher, right there. You've got to sing it to yourself, and then you play it. . . ." We begin playing to the music, and suddenly he stops to implore: "Here, see, follow me. Listen!" and he holds the root note of the first chord of the progression, and then continues, "Then we just play down the chromatic scale, like this . . . Yeah, that's it . . . you've got it."

While James offers his impromptu lesson to facilitate the performance at hand, he also uses the opportunity to perform the role of the seasoned musician and mentor by displaying his knowledge of music theory and offering encouragement to a younger protégé. Meanwhile, younger players seek out the kind of instruction offered by James because it helps them to develop their craft in a supportive environment. In the end, these moments give blues musicians (amateurs as well as their more advanced counterparts) the pleasure associated with a distinctive nocturnal identity in the club's community of regulars.

In fact, while contemporary jam sessions bear scant resemblance to their celebrated Prohibition-era counterparts, they still provide an alternative forum for young performers to develop a highly stylized nocturnal self. By offering amateur musicians the opportunity to perform before paying audiences and chat with fellow players in a public world of strangers, jam sessions enable would-be superstars lacking in subcultural status the ability to act out roles compatible with their pursuit of an authentic sense of self. In this manner, the symbol-rich setting of the blues club provides the necessary dramaturgical backdrop for such persons to actually *become* blues artists.[4]

Of course, this art of "becoming" is much simpler to accomplish in musical settings than other established professional fields—after all, one can at least *claim* to be a blues or jazz player (although not necessarily a very good one) with a minimal degree of musical knowledge and experience more easily than one can appropriate the professional title of doctor or lawyer without proper training and public legitimacy. While institutions of higher learning and certification regulate the process by which such careerists become professionals, similar organizational structures rarely exist for urban musicians or their subcultures.[5]

On the way to becoming blues artists, young musicians sometimes create personae based on the fantasies provided by the myths of the stage. In their bombastic acts, musicians play characters familiar to the world of blues and jazz, and vocalists possess the expressive resources to use this strategy to the fullest extent. While men belt out their best "Sweet Home Chicago" or "Born Under a Bad Sign," their female counterparts enact highly stylized performances of torch songs like "Call It Stormy Monday." Adorned in sequined dresses and high heels, such singers whisper and coo into their microphones as they attempt to embody a sultry sensuality on the stage. By incorporating these dramatic strategies into their performances, they employ the theatrical resources of the club to great effect.

These strategies complement the more subtle performances maintained by amateur musicians during their *offstage* breaks from playing music. Some young players attempt to heighten their performance of authenticity by appropriating the timeworn role of the urban hipster and subcultural insider through fashion, slang, and other affectations of countercultural style.[6] Likewise, amateur performers try to exaggerate their insider credentials by directing liberal amounts of criticism at audience members and fellow musicians. At the same time, these players exude enthusiastic optimism regarding their *own* careers as they fix their sights on future stardom, imagining themselves as young mavericks and starlets on the verge of fame and inevitable professional success.

On Wednesday evenings at B.L.U.E.S. Etcetera, amateur musicians flaunt these roles in their attempts to impress peers, audiences, and skeptical professionals. Bill, a young but highly talented saxophonist, offers a case in point. A sophomore at a local college, his participation at B.L.U.E.S. Etcetera's jam session allows him the ability to act out a heavily affected urban identity. Augmented by gestures, demeanor, and a Black English speaking style, his self-conscious performance overemphasizes his struggle for subcultural status and urban authenticity: "Yeah, my man, well, you know how it is . . . Now I ain't gonna bullshit you, but I'm trying to get together a horn section . . . I'm in school now, but the minute I get that diploma—*Bam*, I am outta there, and this is gonna be it, know what I'm saying? Shit . . ."

Like Bill, Greg, a young white musician in his early twenties, appropriates the jam session as a backdrop for his expressive on- and offstage performance of a nocturnal identity. On most Wednesday nights, Greg, a singer, harmonica player, and bandleader, can be found in the back room of B.L.U.E.S. Etcetera shooting pool and slapping palms with his fellow band mates, buying rounds of beer for his friends, and watching the evening's basketball game on the overhead television set with a scattered assortment of the club's older black regulars and hired professional musicians. Greg moved from Washington, D.C., to Chicago in search of its blues scene after graduating from college and found a place where he could develop a new life as an artist. One evening over a game of pool, he leans on his cue stick, strokes his goatee, and explains his decision to move to the city:

Yeah, well, when I was sixteen, I had a job working as a clerk in the Senate, and after that I decided that I didn't want that kind of life.

So, after college I just decided that this was what I always wanted to do . . . Ever since I was a kid, I've wanted to play the blues. So I just came out here, and I've been going to clubs, and hanging out with the best musicians, and sitting in, and getting them to teach me something, anything . . . and it's been the best. I've learned more in the past four months then I ever thought I could. It's just the best.

As a newcomer to the Chicago scene, Greg idolizes the city's blues musicians and the clubs where they perform and incorporates their world into his own by forging a nocturnal identity for himself as a subcultural participant and by dreaming of stardom aloud, literally. Pointing to me, and then to himself and two of his fellow mates, he predicts: "Someday, like five years from now, I have no doubt that all of us, the four of us, are going to be running the whole show, and that's going to be *us* up there." He points to the stage and smiles.

In actuality, Greg recognizes the hardscrabble difficulties inherent in pursuing a career in music and realizes that, in all likelihood, he will eventually have to seek out an occupational life elsewhere. After sharing his dreams about achieving status as a bluesman, he acknowledges that he lacks alternative career goals and fears the uncertainty of his future. Meanwhile, Greg finds the financial instability of the musician's life unsatisfying and frightening, and he clearly dislikes his present blue-collar job working for the city. However, in spite of these realizations, Greg maintains his guise as a subcultural member and up-and-coming artist, insofar as it provides him with an affirmative self-image and the means to smoothly interact with his peers and role models at the club.

Although they possess status on account of their seniority and longstanding presence at the club, older nonprofessional musicians often rely on strategies of nocturnal roleplaying as much as their younger counterparts. For instance, Donny, a middle-aged black gentleman, enjoys plopping himself in the middle of the "action" at the club, invited or otherwise. He generally plays a proactive if obtrusive role at weekly jam sessions at B.L.U.E.S. Etcetera by approaching musicians on their break and imploring them to approach the stage by pointing and shouting: "Go on up! Play! Play!" As an "armchair" blues artist, he runs around to each of the musicians, offering his running commentary on their performances, and frequently attempts to "conduct" the horn section from a couch near the stage. At one Wednesday night jam session, Donny approaches me from his seat and signals me to follow his lead, belting out "Bop! Bop!" while furiously motioning with his hands. Later that same evening he tries to convince me to participate in another jam session in Rogers Park, where one of his acquaintances will be performing, and takes my phone number down as he runs back and forth between groups of established musicians at the club. When I mention this to Jeffrey, he warns: "Yeah, I've seen him around. He talks a lot and tries to tell you how many people he knows, but I just ignore him." Sure enough, I later overhear him listing all the local musicians he knows to a session bass player. The next week I run into Donny at B.L.U.E.S., and after reaching for a hug, he asks me if I have been to Kingston Mines, the club across the street.

"You should get a gold card, man—just tell them you play with a band. Now, *I* got one from my cousin, you know, *my cousin*, now *he* played until he was eighty-eight, and he died when he was eighty-eight. That was Sunnyland Slim, he played until the day he died . . . Hey, I'll show you his picture, it's up on the wall here . . ."[7]

If regulars like Donny attempt to accentuate their nocturnal status by playing up their strong (if embellished) connections to the club's subcultural elite, other musicians do so by cultivating more of an artistically elitist sense of self. An alto saxophonist in his midthirties, Jeffrey moved to the Chicago area several years ago from Germany and performs regularly at a number of local jam sessions on a weekly basis. One Wednesday evening in April, I spot him at B.L.U.E.S. Etcetera enjoying a beer along with any number of Marlboro cigarettes. I approach him, and after chatting for a few minutes about the jam, he leans over and pulls me close to holler into my ear above the clamor of the club. Barely audible, Jeffrey shouts:

"You know, you just have to play for yourself, that's the most important thing"—as he gestures toward the audience—"because these people don't care at all, and most of them hardly even listen. And it's really frustrating, because you play a solo, and they don't respond, and so you think it sucked . . . Now, I want to get to the point where I'm good enough so I can get gigs, and people will know who am I, and that way at least if you suck, you know. But now, they don't listen and they don't even know what a good solo is." As he points out two trumpet players, he continues: "Like, take these guys. These guys aren't that great, and what they are playing isn't very interesting, but the audience doesn't even notice! That's why you have to play for yourself, because most of these people can't tell a really great solo from just an OK solo . . ."

In other conversations Jeffrey develops his future plans by imagining a career trajectory before him, and months later he affirms: "See, what I want to do is spend the rest of the year really practicing until I'm really great, and then I want to put together a band. But I don't want to go out there until I'm ready." But unfortunately, as the owner of a suburban video rental store, his day job prevents him from touring with fellow musicians or establishing regular gigs on his own; consequently, his amateur status renders him unable to develop a truly professional identity. To compensate, he forges an artistic self at the club by criticizing not only the audience, but his fellow musicians as well.[8] In fact, Jeffrey often refuses to perform on especially slow evenings at the club when he does not approve of its lineup of amateur players. On one such occasion he even refuses to open his saxophone case, and instead of joining the performance, we chat in a corner of the club as he pokes fun at the predictability of the featured band's repertoire. As the evening passes on, he challenges me to a contest: "I'll bet you that the next song will be in concert G, and it will be . . . hmmm, let's see . . . 'Stormy Monday.' If I'm wrong, I will buy you a beer." He is correct.

THE STAGING OF SUBCULTURAL COOL

While local musicians obviously stress the importance of skill and technique when evaluating themselves and their fellow players, they develop their nocturnal identities as bar regulars by emphasizing more emotional faculties, such as an aggressive self-confidence and a heightened sense of subcultural cool. But although they may naturalize their own use of such affectations in the club's theatrical setting, musicians still remain highly aware of the performative aspects of artistic identity. At the club experienced players and club regulars try to socialize their novice counterparts into the social world of the blues by stressing the maintenance of self-confidence and subcultural style as integral to one's successful presentation of a nocturnal self. Accordingly, neophytes gradually become seasoned regulars through this process of acculturation.[9]

This socialization process became evident on my first night of performing at the B.L.U.E.S. Etcetera jam session. On a Wednesday evening I timidly walk from my apartment to the club at around 10 P.M. with my alto saxophone case in hand, nervous about confronting the club's community of regulars as an out-of-practice player. As Jack nods me into the club without asking for the nominal dollar charge expected of amateur jam participants, the sight of the relatively anonymous crowd of out-of-towners, as opposed to the usual gang of insiders, only slightly eases my fears. I sit at the bar and order a Budweiser from Robin (who, like Jack, works at both B.L.U.E.S. and B.L.U.E.S. Etcetera) while listening to Louis and his band play their obligatory first set before the jam begins. Near the end of the set, I finally gain the courage to head toward the stage, where I sit next to a guitar player, and we slowly nod to one another while watching the music together in silence. Meanwhile, other musicians casually chat over discounted $1.50 bottles of Leinenkugel's beer and lively billiard matches in the back room of the club.

After the set ends Louis grabs his clipboard and sign-up sheet and calls a handful of participants to the stage for the jam's first set.[10] The club seems fairly packed for a Wednesday evening, without a single empty table in sight. I head toward a group of musicians assembling and tuning their instruments at the side of the stage and slowly take out my saxophone, turning around to see if anyone is watching me. I try to feign confidence, but upon scanning the large audience, my stage fright only deepens, leaving me to wonder what possessed me to attempt this foolish endeavor in the first place.

Then suddenly, only moments later, Louis introduces the first jam, with *me* as the entire Wednesday night horn section. As the music begins, I stay fixed on my bar stool, unable to turn toward the microphone. Instead, I hunt around for the correct key, and at some point I actually duck into a corner of the club behind the video game machines to pull out the cheat sheet I've drawn up of the twelve major blues scales, just in case I get even more desperate than I already am. To my surprise, I stumble across a number of fellow players back there in the corner, including an elderly black gentleman toying with a harmonica. Caught red-handed, I show him my cheat sheet, but he denies that this consultation actually constitutes "cheating."

I eventually find myself heading out to the stage as the next song comes on, and I timidly approach the microphone to play along with the song, making up a riff until the next verse when the singer shouts "Saxophone!" and points to me. Taking my cue, I hesitate, take a deep breath, and plunge into a feeble attempt at improvisation, faltering with panic through each insecure beat. Nevertheless, I'm off, rushing through a blur of notes in the wrong key, and I'm so shaky that I'm really all over the map, jumping octaves at a squeaky pitch, then hitting a barrage of flat notes, and I polish it all off with an obese, sonic burp.

Meanwhile, as Ari, another young saxophonist, approaches the microphone, I return to my bar stool to gape in awe as he performs an impressive improvised solo with confidence and style. I spot Louis looking on, and I point to Ari and exclaim, "He's smokin' me!" but the bandleader quickly retorts, "Hey, that's *not* what it's all about. It's all about coming down and just playing, no matter *who* you are." As he walks away, I begin honking away at my seat, just trying to practice by playing along with the band, but at some point Ari turns to me and suggests that I should play into the microphone so the audience can actually hear me.[11]

The set ends as Louis reaches the stage to implore to the crowd, "Hey, if you like what you hear, please drop a ducat in our bucket and help keep the blues jam alive," and I take this as a cue to duck into the men's rest room, only to be accosted by the patron at the next urinal.[12] An audience member from Canada, he starts hammering away.

"How often do you guys jam? Is it open to everybody? Are there any callbacks?"—and after I briefly explain the organization of the jam, *he* offers me feedback on my playing: "You're shy," he tells me. "And now, you *are* good, but you are, well, a little *wobbly*. You have to just play through it and not worry if you hit a wrong note, just keep on with it." Frazzled, and even more embarrassed than earlier, I attempt to regain composure, when *another* customer turns to make a similar suggestion as we all exit the small rest room together.

At the jam session, brief encounters with musicians and audiences teach the uninitiated performer basic rules for handling oneself in the club and on the stage, and many of these lessons emphasize the importance of attitude and style, rather than musicianship and technical skill. This socialization process, through which advanced musicians attempt to transform "shy," "wobbly" newcomers into more assertive players, continues when amateurs accompany more established musicians during their gigs.

At half-past two in the morning at B.L.U.E.S., Jack, who leads his own local band in addition to his other many responsibilities at the club, invites me up to the stage with my saxophone to take a solo during the last song of his final set. I timidly approach the bandstand while Jack points to me and whispers, "Dave, just play off a shuffle in F major." But, as he awaits my improvised solo, I suddenly freeze. Most blues instruments are tuned to the key of C, but the alto saxophone is always tuned to the key of E. Consequently, when a bandleader requests a solo in a particular key, I always have to mentally transpose that key into the appropriate equivalent for the saxophone, which in this case would be D major. Most professional musicians either have the formula for this transposition committed to memory, or the talent and experience to enable them to figure it out immediately, playing by ear after listening for a few seconds. But for someone who possesses *neither* of these abilities, that process takes a little bit longer. And so, amidst all the excitement I forget the notes, and after running through the possible combinations in my head for what must seem like an eternity, I begin slowly fumbling through *all* the keys on my horn, evading the microphone as I hunt in vain for the appropriate sound.

Jack's face reveals concern as he mistakes my technical incompetence for stage fright—as does Jason, his guitarist, who leaves his post to lower the microphone into the bell of my horn. So, not wanting to disappoint, I start honking and squeaking out random notes as I search in noisy, out-of-tune desperation for the correct key. After another half a minute of poking around, I eventually stumble upon the appropriate blues scale and finish out the solo barely in tune. Surprisingly, the audience generously proffers its enthusiastic applause as prompted by Jack—"Let's hear it for Dave!" As I leave the bandstand for my bar stool, the German tourists at my cocktail table shake my hand and seem, astonishingly, impressed.

And then, just as my spirits begin to lift, Jack takes me aside. "OK, time for a lecture." I begin to shake.

"Dave, you play really good, man—you've got some chops." What? "You've obviously been playing for a while, and you've got some jazz influences that I heard in there, am I right?" Confused, I offer an uneasy nod when suddenly I realize that Jack has somehow mistaken my out-of-tune improvisation as an intentional use of complex harmonic structures suggestive of more avant-garde musical styles, like hard bop and free jazz.

"But, Dave, you've got to play into that microphone, man, you can't be afraid of it. I see you at the jam session, and you're always hiding in the corner. Man, you got to step up to the microphone, man, and just play, because that's the only way you'll get better. I mean, you play much better than most of those sax players they got there, man. You've got to just do it."

While musicians often assume the technical competence of their fellow players in spite of all evidence to the contrary, they tend to attribute their onstage foibles to more psychological barriers, such as stage fright. Since professional musicians are highly aware of these and other performative aspects of nocturnal identity, they try to socialize their novice counterparts into their social world by teaching them to manage their self-confidence while performing. From this constructive criticism, advice, and encouragement, amateurs gradually learn how to appropriately present themselves with a relaxed self-assurance and a seemingly natural kind of cool during their performances. As Willy, a tenor saxophonist and longtime regular at the jam, advises me one evening at B.L.U.E.S., "Well, the important thing about the jam is to just play, and feel good about it and get an emotional response from it. But sometimes, some guy who thinks he's a badass will show up and try to show up everybody and lay down a trip, but that's not what the jam is about, you know. It's all about emotion."

Experienced musicians also transfer these lessons in self-evaluation and impression management to less advanced players by recalling their own experiences as newcomers to the club and the advice their mentors gave them during their own amateur years. On the evening of my first jam session described above, I reveal my onstage fears to Jeffrey, but he takes me aside to reassure me.

"Oh, but you shouldn't feel intimidated at all. I mean, *that's not what this is about*, you know? We all play at different levels, and you've just got to do what you can. Like when I played at my first one of these things four years ago, my friend Lincoln took me here, and I played, and I hadn't been playing very long, and I sucked! And I was so frustrated that as I was leaving, I said I would not come back for a whole year, and Lincoln just shook his head and said, 'Oh no, you're coming back in two weeks!' And so I did, and I still wasn't good, but you play what you can, and you learn from the others, and that's how you get better. And now, there are still guys, you know, who are just like *here* compared to me," he says as he raises his hand above his head, "but you always have to learn, and you get better."

NOTES

1. Mezz Mezzrow and Bernard Wolfe, *Really the Blues* (New York: Random House, 1946); and DeVeaux, *The Birth of Bebop*, 202–35.

2. DeVeaux, *The Birth of Bebop*, 277–84. Of course, more clandestine jam sessions continued to attract jazz and blues players throughout the bebop era; see ibid., 202–35.

3. In September 1998 Adam's band invited me to rehearse and perform with them during their second set at a gig held at U.S. Beer Co., a local blues and rock bar. My own relationship with the band began with a series of unplanned encounters at B.L.U.E.S. Etcetera, particularly during its weekly jam session.

4. On the art of "becoming" an occupational self, see Donileen R. Loseke and Spencer E. Cahill, "Actors in Search of a Character: Student Social Workers' Quest for Professional Identity," *Symbolic Interaction* 9, no. 2 (1986): 245–58.

5. On the professionalization of occupational roles, see Andrew Abbott, *The System of Professions: An Essay on the Division of Expert Labor* (Chicago: University of Chicago Press, 1988).

6. On the use of argot and fashion as countercultural style, see Stuart Hall and Tony Jefferson, *Resistance through Rituals: Youth Subcultures in Post-War Britain* (London: Routledge, 1976); Paul Willis, *Learning to Labor* (New York: Columbia University Press, 1977), and *Common Culture*; Hebdige, *Subculture*; Grazian, "Uniform of the Party"; Thornton, *Club Cultures*; and Malbon, *Clubbing*.

7. While I could not ascertain whether or not Sunnyland Slim and Donny were actually cousins, a number of ethnographic accounts suggest that fictive kinship relations are regularly manufactured among friends and colleagues within the context of black neighborhood life. Thus, Donny's use of the term *cousin* to describe his relationship to Sunnyland Slim may, in fact, refer to an invented (but not necessarily less meaningful) relationship; on this practice of "going for cousins," see Elliot Liebow, *Tally's Corner: A Study of Negro Streetcorner Men* (Boston: Little, Brown, 1967), 170–73; and Anderson, *A Place on the Corner*, 17–23.

8. Jeffrey's strategy of constructing identity through boundary work resembles the tactics utilized by the jazz performers in Becker, *Outsiders*; however, although Becker's informants constantly forge distinctions between themselves and their audiences, they rarely extend that hostility to their discussions of fellow musicians.

9. Other urban subcultures acculturate new members in a similar manner; for example, see ibid., 41–58, on socialization within drug subcultures.

10. In Chicago, clubs organize their jam sessions differently according to their own particular rules and norms governing the centrality of the evening's house band, the professional status of the musicians permitted to perform, the scheduling of artists, and so forth. For example, the organizers of B.L.U.E.S. Etcetera's jam session gather random groups of musicians who take to the stage to perform impromptu songs together, while the Green Room at Macaw's, Winner's, and other venues

invite players to join the house band one at a time to join in on a song from a predetermined set list. In the first instance, participants maintain a great deal of autonomy over their performances, while the latter jams really just allow participants the chance to perform alongside the club's hired band.

11. Of course, by suggesting the irrelevance of "who you are" at the jam session, Louis obscures the status disparities that exist at the club. Indeed, these same musicians seek individual status by stratifying their world into *unequal* classes of amateurs and professionals, club newcomers and established regulars, beginners and advanced players, organizers and participants, voluntary and paid performers, and mentors and students, to say nothing of the relationship between musicians and their audiences. The mentoring processes of socialization described above integrates new members into the subcultural world of the jam while it simultaneously establishes and reproduces unequal relationships and identities between novices and their more seasoned counterparts. By successfully presenting "expert" selves, experienced musicians naturalize the hierarchical relations existing between themselves and less experienced players. As long as advanced musicians insist that the stratification of the subculture is "not what this is about" by punctuating a moral imperative based on "emotion" rather than experience, status, and subcultural capital, such an ethos masks the material and symbolic distinctions that characterize the stratified social world of the blues club. On mystification as a dramaturgical and ideological tool, see Goffman, *The Presentation of Self in Everyday Life.*

12. While Louis's request suggests that these tips will be paid out to the musicians for offering their free services, in fact, the evening collection—sometimes thirty-five or forty dollars—goes to Louis himself as *his* added compensation for hosting the jam in addition to his fee paid by the club owners. One night before a show, he explains that he uses the collection to pay for the upkeep of the jam session music equipment and shares a portion of the rest with the club's bartenders and waitresses.

CHAPTER 9

Guiding Practices

Storytelling Tricks for Reproducing the Urban Landscape

Jonathan R. Wynn

> Through stories about places, they become inhabitable. Living is narrativizing. Stirring up or restoring this narrativizing is thus also among the tasks of renovation. One must awaken the stories that sleep in the streets . . . Festivals, contests, the development of 'speaking places' in neighborhoods or buildings would return to narratives the soil from which they grow.
>
> (de Certeau, Giard and Mayol 1998, pp. 142–3).

INTRODUCTION

The walking tour guides of New York City are a diverse group of individuals who teach about the public histories, spaces, and cultures of Gotham. Like Aristotle, they are peripatetic—using walking and experience as a part of their teaching. Ancient Greek guides, called *exegetai* ('explainers'), were professional storytellers often posing the offer to sea-weary travelers, "Give me a copper coin, and I'll tell you a golden story." Such characters were approached with apprehension: they were colorful necessities, yet pesky and potentially deceptive. For dwellers and visitors of any age, a metropolis can be confusing and overwhelming; as a practice of reproducing a city's landscape of culture, history, and meaning, this study focuses upon how individuals use storytelling as a way in which tour guides explain the urban fabric to others (Suttles 1990).[1]

In today's New York City there are, for example, walking tours about the edible flora of Prospect Park, the Radical Left history of the East Village, the Native American History of Manhattan, and the filming locations of television shows like 'Sex and the City.' The walking tour, as a social form, has become ubiquitous: organizations like the Central Park Conservancy and the New School University use tours as a part of their educational programming, the city government has them for jurors on lunch break, as does the hip health club 'Crunch' as a way to "work out the mind and body." High school teachers use them, as do international artists like Janet Cardiff. It is because of this omnipresence and diversity that guiding is hard to weigh on the cultural scale. Guides themselves are torn between the more schlocky aspects and their own intellectual endeavors, keeping nearly forgotten histories alive and parlaying popular sentiments, all the while re-enchanting the urban world. Rather than locating them within a 'low culture' – 'high culture' dichotomy (Gans 1999; DiMaggio 1992), this study demonstrates their position in the middle: blending education and entertainment, knowledge with a little panache.

It is, then, the *how* of tour guiding that is at issue here—the tricks of this particular trade. Rather than a device that makes a task easier, Howard Becker writes that tricks "suggest ways of interfering with the comfortable thought routines . . . ways to turn things around, to see things differently, in order to create new problems" (1998, pp. 6–7). His *Tricks* examined how ethnographers could think reflexively about their work and how they represent that world to readers. Neither tricks nor thinking reflexively, however, are the sole purview of social scientists: they are a part of the practices of everyday folk as well.

CULTURE AND STORYTELLING

Every society has a need for contact with its own past . . . Where this cannot be provided by the powers of individual memory within the kinship group, historical chroniclers and antiquarians are required.

(Shils 1972, p. 4).

As one autodidactic guide said, "No place, and no people are without history." The wonder of urban culture is that, according to Suttles, it is a "vast, heritable genome of physical artifacts, slogans, typifications, and catch phrases . . . most appropriately called collective representations" (1984, p. 284). Through their storytelling, guides weave local knowledge and culture into a larger 'set' of cultural meanings.[7] To practice their craft, guides depend less upon a savant's storehouse of facts and figures than on their ability to manipulate these unruly elements into a varyingly coherent narrative. This is not necessarily an easy task, but guides are not without their resources.

In a dizzying blur of information, Mr. Harrison weaves together a fifteen-minute patchwork of facts in his dandyish elocution prior to setting out: Before the establishment of the railway system here at Grand Central, if one were to travel between New York City and Pittsburgh he would have to change his pocket watch six times.

He pulls pictures out of his tote to show the dirty, smoke-stained rail yards north of the Terminal, and then how they looked after they were covered by the soon-to-be-elite Park Avenue.

"Fifth Avenue is not an American street, it is where we prove that some are more equal than others."

He tells us that Manhattan is made of a particular rock known as Mica Schist, and that the mainland up north is composed of Gneiss, proving "That's why Westchester is really very Gneiss and Manhattan is full of Schist." "I always say, Brownstone was the Aluminum siding of the mid-19th Century."

Cole Porter said that Park Ave. is "Where bad women walk *great* dogs."

EIGHT TRICKS OF THIS TRADE

While Grey Line Bus Tours had such a poor appreciation of the narrative skills of its guides that the company attempted (but failed) to replace them with taped recordings, walking tours demand a storyteller with wit, knowledge, and charisma. Most of these tricks are well intentioned enough to mollify or good-naturedly razz a group, to educate and entertain, to establish authority without alienating, to attach local knowledge with popular culture, and to struggle with the tensions of consumerism and perceived 'inauthenticity.'[8] Swidler, in her pivotal essay on culture in action, sees culture as containing "diverse, often conflicting symbols, rituals, stories, and guides to action," and the practices of manipulating that culture as a 'tool-kit' (1986, p. 277). Guides might call it *shtick*. Similar to Grazian's attempt to explicate the "specific performance employed by producers attempting to pull off an event with as little apparent effort as possible" (2003, p. 140), the following are tools at a guide's disposal to be used, combined, and violated. Again, guides described a few of these tricks, but predominantly these devices have served as objects for ethnographic analysis.

Moving out on the sidewalk, Mr. Harrison yells over the 42nd Street traffic and holds against the midday current of pedestrians to tell us that Grand Central is a *Terminal*, not a *Station*, and traces this common misconception back to the introduction of an old radio show, that decided 'Station' sounded much better on air. He begins to move people's bodies around to get them physically involved. He sculpts a woman's arms around to mirror Athena's pose ("The Kitty Kelly of the Ancient World") in Jules-Alexis Coutan's sculpture, 'Transport,' that alights the adjacent façade. He lines us up into two rows and has two volunteers walk between them, waving, to show how architects wanted buildings with huge columns to make people feel special. Some people giggle, some move to the back of the group, afraid of being next.

Trick #1: The Conceit

Mr. Harrison was an obvious choice to provide the narrative thread that runs through this essay. Not only is he fascinating, but he is also is reflexive about his craft. When asked, he was quick to come up with one of his major devices:

> I try to sort of twist people. I sort of believe in John Donne's idea of 'the conceit:' taking an idea and turning it at a right angle into something totally different. And I do this based on what people know. So, I start with the familiar and then I get into the weirdness—leading to unfamiliarity. I try to make them look at something that they've seen, but maybe not seen the same way.

Another autodidactic guide proudly talks on his tours about how this research lead him to believe that the story about Dylan Thomas having 17 straight whiskies at the White Horse Tavern is possibly fiction, and that Hell's Kitchen derived its name from Davy Crockett—two examples of 'debunking.' While Jeffrey Harrison will talk about African- and Chinese-American cowboys, and another guide uses the tag line of "There are 10,000 people buried in Washington Square Park" on her brochure, both are used more than just to debunk a myth, but are used for the express purpose of tweaking the familiar. Guides like Mr. Harrison use the conceit to

draw participants into the tour, as well as to make them feel ownership of its interactive process, and the city itself.

The conceit works to de-mythologize commonly held beliefs. As Shils writes, part of intellectual work includes the rejection of an "inherited set of values," serving "the important function of molding and guiding the alternative tendencies which exist in any society" (1972, p. 7), and here, Mr. Harrison sees it less an outright refusal, than a teasing out of alternatives.[9] Put into practice it works: he feeds off of startled looks and puzzled expressions in order to draw the participant in.

Trick #2: The 'Perfect Tour Guiding Moment'

It seems that certain stories help to define a tour, a culture, a city. These moments are ideal in simplicity and wonder, yet speak beyond the story itself. Guides relish to tell such tales: allowing them to illustrate different layers of architecture, social forces, cultural changes, politics, and/or economics. One of those moments is the once unfinished back face of City Hall, because its architects failed to forecast the city's growth further north. This also stands in for the larger processes of sprawl and population shifts. As an academic guide told me:

> That story about, you know, the construction of City Hall, given the fact that it coincided with the establishment of the grid street system in New York, I think that it helps non-New Yorkers be more anchored in what they are going to see, what they are going to experience. (. . .) The Sara Delano Roosevelt Park story [about Eleanor Roosevelt's struggles against Robert Moses' unbridled urban planning, and how he snubbed her by naming a park after her mother-in-law] is another one that I tell all the time, because it is about Bob Moses, who I hate, and I want everybody else to hate him and imagine that the city might have been different without him. And it's funny.

The best of these are dramatic, include famous personae, have a twist, and are instructive. The most important thing for guides, however, is its multiple usage; that they are, in some fashion, 'universal' New York stories. The fight between Roosevelt and Moses is a guide favorite because it has everything: the public, parks, drama, fame, plight, power, and even disliked mothers-in-law. These moments resonate meaning, and are selected to provide a persuasive vision.

Mr. Harrison talks about how Grand Central was built from 1903 to 1913, and was the second transit hub built on the site. Because its architect was trained in the Beaux-Arts tradition (he spells it for us: "B-E-A-U-X-A-R-T-S"), the building is raised up on an elevated platform, like a sculpture on a pedestal.

On another tour of the same spot, a different guide told the story of how Coutan never saw his sculpture, which took seven years to build (three fewer than whole building), grace the top of the Terminal. Coutan proclaimed: "I'd rather die than go to New York!" To this, the crowd chuckles, and someone says loudly: "Boy, the French haven't changed."

Below 'Transport' he mentions again the bronze statue of 'Commodore' Vanderbilt, an infamous figure in the history of the Terminal, the railway industry, and New York. We're told his nickname originates from his first business of ferrying people between Brooklyn and New York—people said that he was so proud of his little boat that he fancied himself a commodore.

Trick #3: Happenstance

Great urban spaces, for Richard Sennett, are those wherein "to know too much might weaken the desire to know what will happen next . . . endowed with the possibilities of the unexpected" (1990, p. 195). One of the most wonderful things about a walking tour is that, unlike a bus tour, there is the potential of tapping into unexpected urban interactions. Guides love to report stories of being invited into old homes with antique interiors, how groups were offered afternoon tea, or

how a resident or homeless person will begin to contribute to, or argue over, a story. In an interview, Jeffrey told me:

It's also one of those blessings of New York. It is that serendipitous event of something you never expected, incalculable. And you never know when it is going to happen and it's a god-send. It's the woman—this will often happen on a tour—someone will come out with a wary ear [and want to debate me]. Crazy people are part of the magic of the city.

More academic guides show disbelief of such quixotic stories, but not without a tinge of envy. While autodidactic guides seem to scout out chance, New Apple guides are either too timid or uninterested, preferring changes to be in routes or emphases already within their stock of knowledge. Self-taught guides are more likely to understand that the tour is as much an *experience* as it is a *lesson*, and therefore prize an entertaining ad-libbing within the emergent urban world. They are comfortable in the unknown and changeable, and say that these moments are often the participant's favorite parts of the tour. It is frustrating too, because it is the *least* planned aspect.

Trick #4: Simulation

Unlike Colonial Williamsburg or Western Ghost Towns, walking tours are not 'reenactments' (see Fine and Speer 1985). There are, however, a few performance-oriented tours that attempt to simulate historical experiences or moments. Like any of these eight tricks, simulations can range from the ham-fisted to the sleight of hand.[10] Jeffrey Harrison physically involves people in his tours: molding them into the positions of statues or columns, and weaving them through crowds in a conga-line.

There are more involved simulations. One guide dresses like Abraham Lincoln. A group of guides recite poetry on their Greenwich Village Literary Pub Crawls. Another guide aspires to collect a whole gallery of guides dressed as 'vintage' characters to transport participants 120 years in the past. Wanting to develop this part-tour company, part-repertory troupe, Mike Auster rode the newfound interest in the Five Points area, leading tours costumed as 'Butcher Bill' O'Toole, and had a young woman portray 'Becky, the hot corn girl.' On one tour, she came up behind us singing her advertisement for corn right on cue (signaled with a tip of his hat). Having met Mike at a Renaissance fair, her part entails sweetly answering questions with a fake English accent with the accompaniment of a real pet rat on her bare shoulder.

Goffman makes a great deal of how the 'make-believe' is a significant part of our understandings of everyday life (1974, pp. 48–56), but the more scholastic guides wouldn't dare such theatrics. Jeffrey and Mike, both self-taught guides with divergent styles, would agree that this is shtick not without a pedagogical purpose. By trying to get participants involved, by balancing make-believe and real life, the trick of simulation is a delicate one that illuminates the tension in touring between education and entertainment. While it is no surprise that Jeffrey sees this trick as something to be sparingly deployed, Mike was singularly honest when he told me that, in the end, "if there are two different dates, or two different facts, go with the one that is the most interesting. Never let the information get in the way of a story."

> Before heading into the Terminal, Mr. Harrison takes us next door to the Lincoln Building. He asks us if we would have ever remembered Chrysler's or Woolworth's first name if they had not built a building for themselves (Answers: Walter, Frank), but this is uninteresting to the group. He tells us that in naming this building, they made a safe bet, to do so after a president that both parties claim as their own. He tells us that when this was built we were a country without any history: so we borrowed it, looking up to the Italian ceiling and ornamentation.

> Mr. Harrison brings us over to one of the five sculptures Daniel Chester French used as studies for the Lincoln Memorial, and points out the copyright mark with an outstretched pinky finger. Carefully, he explicates its composition: we often think Abe's eyes look promisingly into the future but that he is, in fact sullen, that he is not sitting on a throne but a plain seat, that he is dressed ragged and not regal, and that the ordinary coat ("The kind of coat you might leave in the trunk of your car") draped behind him on his right is placed in the same fashion as the flag on his left to indicate that the state and the everyman are equal.

Trick #5: The Duel

Some self-taught guides collaborate on debate-based tours. These events are often scripted and, despite antagonistic appearances, are a united effort to educate and attract participants. According to a guide who gave a 'capitalist vs. radical' tour of Wall Street:

> It was hysterical. A lot of fun. We did nine of them for about two years, he did the conservative side, I did the radical side. And we fought over Wall Street, which was perfect. (. . .) We didn't do too much preparation, but by the time we were finished I would think of jokes that he would say and we'd tell each other before hand, it was really well choreographed. (. . .) I'd talk about how a third of the founders were slave owners, and all the protests at the Stock Exchange, I'd talk about how this is 'great', and how anyone can make money, and blah blah blah, what a great institution, free market. I'd talk about all the corruption scandals at that time, and all the brokers getting arrested. (. . .) We'd end at Battery Park, but overlooking Ellis Island, I would talk about all the immigration restrictions and Bob would talk about all the immigrants coming over here in such large numbers and, "If it's so bad why'd they come?"

Jeffrey has done dueling tours on the Jewish Rialto, and another with an architecturally based format:

> I'm more 19th Century, he is a kid of the sixties, he's Mr. Modernism, I'm Mr. non-modernism,

and we speak to two different worlds, with similar levels of appreciation. So what would happen [was], when we would start doing the "I don't agree with you" routine, then we'd go back and forth, but the nice thing was that it made people realize that there's more than one way of looking at the world.

These tours, however, are not particularly cost-effective. The orchestration of debates, and dividing both the prep work and profits make this trick hard. For these reasons, guides might take advantage of more informal interactions with a feisty participant or stranger. The resulting banter allows the group to hear different opinions and offers guides an opportunity to establish their authority through demonstration of knowledge and their rhetorical ability to pacify critical missives. In a performance there are often "bonds of reciprocal dependence" that link a group together but that a team, such as the one between a guide and participant, helps to define the situation (Goffman 1959, p. 82). While Goffman saw open conflict as corrosive, here, the duel is affirming.

Back outside, in front of the unceremonious main entrance of the Terminal, Jeffrey starts talking about how "There is no evidence that Disney was ever caught reading a book." He asks what color Alice's hair was in Lewis Carroll's text (reminding us that it is called *Alice's Adventures Underground*, not *Alice in Wonderland*). When someone guesses blond, he pulls out a reproduction of an original illustration to show that her hair was, in fact, short and brown. Clucking his tongue, "See? He didn't even look at the pictures!" Because the architect was very careful to draw the visitor in viscerally, Jeffery sets up the experience. Why are sculptures placed high? Because when the chin is up the lungs get more oxygen, and the body feels good. But here, at the entrance, Mr. Harrison points out that the downward incline is intended to get our hearts racing, to lure us in. Right before we go through dull wood doors, he tells us that real life rabbit holes are actually quite boring, and in we go.

"Beaux-Arts was always about more than the practical." He corrals us into the entrance, and down the incline, and stops us there. He tells us there used to be two sets of doors here, for two sets of reasons: temperature control and pacing. Visitors get distracted and are surprised at the majesty of the room on the other side. To simulate the missing effect, Jeffrey shuffles in before us, sticks out his arms, and makes us bump through them one by one. The group giggles past, as he says, "The doors are the wrapping for the Christmas present of the interior!"

Trick #6: The Joke

A key to being entertaining is, of course, being able to tell a good joke. A few guides claim to be adamantly uninterested in being funny (and are successful at it, I might add), but most have a few standards (e.g., "Yes. Historic neighborhood, historic jokes"). The trick is in keeping it fresh, but even repetition itself can make a good gag. An autodidactic guide, an aspiring actor who studied Vaudevillian banter and conducts theater tours, will talk about how a critic once wrote that Neil Simon didn't have a good idea for a play this season, but he wrote one anyway. He'll then lean into the person next to him and repeat, *"He wrote one anyway."* A good joke doubles as a way to educate:

You are sugarcoating people's education (. . .) but, you try to make them informative jokes. You know? I mean, it's like this line that I do about Ladies' Mile: it was the only place in New York, in the old days, where a woman could walk unescorted. Now, I could go into an explanation of what that meant, in that usually, when woman went around unescorted, that you thought she was a prostitute. But I just throw in a line "Well, there were places where a woman could walk unescorted, down by the docks, but that doesn't matter." So, that's a joke, it gets a laugh, but also it explains to them what it meant to walk unescorted (. . .) You're working with less time, so you kinda come up with a way to hit it quicker (. . .) It puts the idea in their head, kinda snuck under the RADAR.

It is rather easy to find data to create a tour using public history, and it is therefore material of this nature that tends to be jealously guarded. The theater guide spoke of his anger not that someone stole a joke, but that she kept telling it *wrong*.

In fairness, some guides bristle at the notion that they tell jokes. According to one autodidactic guide: "Have you ever heard of Dorothy Parker? Oscar Wilde? Did they tell *jokes*? No, darling, they had *wit*. A joke can be anything. Wit has context. It is based on intellect. Don't call it a joke, it demeans my humor. You can put that as a footnote." This guide's point, obviously said for effect, still resonates with the notion that a guide's greatest attribute is that they are always working within a social context. It is fair to say that the ability to use most tricks involves wit.

> While another guide used the Waiting Room to point out the Botticino and Tennessee Marble (and how the walls are not French Limestone, not Limestone, and not even stone, but actually gypsum plaster molded to simulate French Limestone), Mr. Harrison talks about the social aspects. In particular, how a woman's traveling experience included elaborate powder rooms and resting areas. He tells us how travelers would arrive, grab their luggage, walk through these wonderful spaces, walk to one of the hotels within a few blocks, and be reclining in bed within ten minutes. He asks demurely, "Now, where were you ten minutes after arriving at JFK? In a cab on the BQE? Still waiting for your luggage?"
>
> He also takes time to demote two famous men: describing Frank Lloyd Wright as the most overrated 20th Century architect (but a passable 19th Century one), and Fredrick Law Olmsted as an amateur gardener with only two years experience before Central Park.

Trick #7: Fabrication

A myth told with good humor, or even inadvertently is one thing. But some guides, in order to maintain the face of authority, might manufacture a tale or a fact. Such lies are common enough in everyday life (Goffman 1974, pp. 10,15). As an autodidactic guide told me, the correct information isn't always there, but "a little schmaltz never hurt anyone—In fact, it could be good because it gets them thinking." For another guide: "There was a guy, who'd say, if he didn't know the address: 70 Pine Street. He didn't know the year it was built? 1892. Architects? Smith and Lewenski. He'd say it with complete confidence. It sounded good. [laughs] That's a trade secret by the way." There are also lies that, to no surprise of Goffman's, venture more than skin deep. Rebeccah Laurent admitted that she has constructed a whole identity as a non-practicing Jew from Brooklyn four years older, just to give herself credibility to clients on her Lower East Side tours:

> It seems that people *want* me to be Jewish. And they react very badly when they find out that I'm not. They act as if I've tricked them somehow. I have light eyes and dark curly hair. That's not a trick. It's very offensive to me the way that they react—as if I just sold them the Brooklyn Bridge. I mean, it's really unbelievable to me. Um, so I've started lying. It's easier to lie and create this persona that makes everybody happy, and it stops some of the questions and the more offensive stuff.

Perhaps this might be expected from an out-of-work actor guide, but this was an academic. Smaller embellishments are frequent for autodidactic guides too (e.g., faking a Brooklyn accent or wearing a Mets hat while having a distaste for baseball). It is, despite the rigor and intelligence of many self-taught guides, a measure of the stigma of the tourism industry—they feel that without the authority of the lectern and the legitimation of a university announced at the beginning of a tour, as so many academic guides disclose, that they find alternate ways to establish authority.[11]

> Making our way into the grand space of the Terminal, Jeffrey Harrison stops to tell us "Come on in." Sticking his chin out, he shows us how the

ramp arches our backs so that we face the ceiling mural (painted by Brooklynite Charles Basic, who died of gangrene while on vacation after a camel stepped on his toe). He reminds us of the visceral influence of architecture. He then bolts off into the crowd thirty paces, hopping between couples and commuters, to demonstrate the careful mass-ballet that occurs here every day. He grabs another volunteer, and shows that the floor blocks of Tennessee marble are the width of a single walking pace, and the length of a fast one. As we head further downstairs he stops halfway and talks about how the original brass railings were modeled on the size of a lady's wrist, and shows how the wall tiles are based upon the width of the human hand. Stairs, Jeffrey insists, ought to fit the stride of the average person, not a clumsy arithmetic of rise and span. Jeffrey stops to point out how easy it is for a passing woman wearing high heels—who is still well within earshot—to walk up the stairs without looking down. Then, with a flourish, he says that "Good French stairs are like great sex: it's a lot of fun, and you have no idea where it's going."

Trick #8: The Bridge

Often a guide will use one element of architectural detail to talk about the larger forces of the neighborhood or the city. This technique, when one aspect of a form is used to represent the whole (i.e., when the image of a crown represents the British monarchy), is called *metonymy*. Such a connection is popular, but difficult. A more modest use of this technique might look at iron columns to talk about the transition from light-industry to loft buildings to boutiques of Soho. There are ambitious uses too:

We'll start near City Hall (. . .) I have my own little story that I can tell them with an overarching meta-narrative about that tour, which is just my own thing. Other people could do something totally different. But, on that tour the story for me is when the bridge was being built, there were two cities: there was New York then there was Brooklyn. And Brooklyn had a certain urban vision. Brooklyn was founded on an urban vision, called the American City. So:

trees, parks, wide streets, and churches. American, Protestant, prosperous middle class, right? And they looked across the river and they saw New York: Tammany, immigrants, corruption. And the bridge as going to connect these two very, very different cities and ultimately form this cosmopolitan—both American and somehow not American—city. (. . .) Now I have a little meta-narrative for each tour.

While an expert in 18th Century France, this academic guide was particularly careful with his pedagogic technique for guiding. His reflexive and explicit development of a 'meta-narrative' for all his tours, was singular throughout this study.

Downstairs on the newly renovated concourse level, there are shops and food kiosks, waiting chairs, schedules, and ramps to train platforms. Mr. Harrison walks down to one of the ramps, and asks us why it was designed with an unnecessary incline. When no one guessed, he made his way up the ramp in a kind of slightly slow-motion run, to tell us that they wanted to prevent late commuters from bolting onto the concourse level. Ramps were a central part of the design of the building, not because of an Americans With Disabilities Act, but the architects wanted to moderate the flows of foot traffic and bodily experiences.

Checking the time, he shows us his favorite part of Grand Central: the Junior's Restaurant dessert case. Huddled up against the Plexiglas he teaches us two important lessons. The first is how to pick out good cheesecake: real cheesecake does not have a graham cracker crust, nor does it have that shmutz on the top, pointing to a lesser cousin with strawberries on top of it. Which brings up the second important lesson. He gets serious. "If you are going to be a New Yorker, you have to learn the second official language of New York City. Anyone? Yiddish."

NOTES

1. This essay is taken from a larger study and, therefore, cannot illuminate many key aspects of this social world. Analysis of tour content, the biographies, histories, and cultural capital of the guides, are not included. All names are pseudonyms.

2. Jeffrey Harrison and his tour were selected from over 50 interviews and over 160 hours of participant observation conducted from June 2001 to June 2005, because many of the 'tricks' that guides used are evidenced within his tour. It should be noted that this narrative thread is a linear description of his tour and, therefore, does not explicitly or directly correlate with its surrounding text in complete harmony. The intended result is an essay not dissimilar to a walking tour: weaving together multiple themes, ideas, stories, analysis, and imagery (for similar usage, see Wacquant 1995).

3. Most of these academic studies on thematizing spaces and the production of events focus on large-scale social forms—for example, how cities compete to host international events like the Olympics for their prestige and perceived economic growth potential (Judd 1999)—an overemphasis on structure ignores the smaller, phenomenological ways in which individuals create and come to understand this urban world. Despite their location in this field, evidence of guides arises only if they are somehow fraudulent or absent-minded (see Perrottet 2002; Sante 1992).

4. The larger ethnographic study engages in the literature on informal and service sector work in greater detail and, in particular, the ways that *affect* is a central component of this variety of labor (Hardt and Negri 2001; Lazzarato 1996).

5. *Cultural Studies* 16 (4) is devoted to these characters, and many of the essays call for research that supplements theoretical discussions with research on the *ways* through which these social actors present and manipulate knowledge and information.

6. Their biographical trajectories (i.e., laid off office workers, out-of-work actors, aspiring academics, and hobbyists) and their organization in the social field (i.e., affiliated with a touring company like New Apple, or independent) also affect their 'toolkits.'

7. Narrative is defined by Somers as "networks of patterned relationships connected and configured over time and space" (1999, p. 128). Just as everyday storytelling is a non-linear phenomenon, so too are stories of cities: full of metaphors, ironies, and juxtapositions.

8. The search for authenticity is central to current research on tourism and urban culture. Grazian's *Blue Chicago* describes that it is "based on a mix of prevailing myths and prejudices invested in the absence of actual experiences" (2003, p. 12).

9. Shils' point is not too small to restate: his intellectuals are, unlike guides, within established social institutions and have rejected inherited values. It is because they position themselves in the interstitial spaces of urban culture rather than within organizations that, in the larger project, I refer to guides as 'street intellectuals.'

10. Shields believes that representations blanket the city, and that, "in everyday life, we fashion and receive countless representations. Of course we all realize that a totally accurate representation—a perfect copy—is impossible. We are happy to settle for a good likeness . . . [yet they are] treacherous metaphors, summarizing the complexity of the city in an elegant model" (1996, pp. 228–229).

11. Concerns over fabrication are not just that of the tourism industry but are, in fact, a concern in everyday life, and concealment, deception, and manipulation are of importance to cultural intermediaries in general (Negus 2002, p. 508).

CHAPTER 10

'Tough Love'

Mediation and Articulation in the Urban Boxing Gym

Lucia Trimbur

> The only people out at that time of night are cops and robbers.
>
> (Jerry, boxing trainer)

Reclining in a plastic chair with his hands folded behind his neck, ankles crossed, and heels propped on a lopsided Formica table, Jerry, a trainer, is beginning to lecture Cedric, a tall, shy, 14-year-old boxer, in the quiet corner of a Brooklyn boxing gym. Today's lecture is inaugurated when Cedric innocently mentions he hurt his hand playing basketball at 1:30 am. With an injured wrist, Cedric cannot hit the heavy bag. But it is not the injury that concerns Jerry, it is Cedric's lack of a curfew. Assuming the authority of a parent, Jerry grills Cedric: why was he out so late? Who was he out with? And what time did his mother want him home? Cedric answers back: he is bored in the house; he was out with friends; his mother does not care when he returns home, and as his father is incarcerated, he cannot enforce curfews. Each answer produces an even more dramatic roll of the eyes from Jerry until he has heard enough. He proffers his analysis. Life in the projects is very dangerous for black men, far more than Cedric realizes. The only people out at 1:30 am are cops and robbers, and Cedric is likely to get shot, as much by the cops as by the robbers. He is also likely to get picked up by the police, and without identification, he will be sent to Rikers Island. If

Cedric doesn't believe Jerry, he should consult Kenny, another of Jerry's amateur boxers, who recently endured this very trauma.

Jerry then prescribes a remedy: Cedric must self-impose a curfew and find a summer activity. Jerry has been working on the latter by trying to locate Cedric employment, but he has not been able to secure anything yet. He promises to soon, since living in the projects stunts potential and hanging out will not help Cedric fulfill his dreams. Jerry will also show Cedric the world, and so the ultimate consequence of Cedric's curfew infraction is that if Jerry can put together enough money, he will take Cedric with him when he travels.

The lecture's conclusion is Jerry's rhetorical specialty. Does Cedric know why Jerry is so intimately acquainted with the dangers of street life? It is because Jerry *was* one of those late-lurking robbers. Jerry rehearses a history of drug use that culminated in a debilitating crack addiction. A parallel history of crime is detailed: pick-pocketing, robbery, and attempted murder in Brooklyn's social housing buildings. Jerry ends with a pronouncement: Cedric does not know the perils of project life because he cannot see beyond it. Jerry implores him to try.

Oration, like the speech bestowed on Cedric, is a technique that gym trainers frequently deploy when they work with amateur fighters. This particular lecture illuminates the kinds of problems—often not directly related to the sport of boxing—they mediate and illustrates some of the difficulties of addressing these problems. Jerry's vacillations, for example, between social-structural arguments that hold racial segregation responsible for Cedric's lack of opportunities and arguments that prize personal responsibility to overcome disadvantage reflect the tensions trainers manage when they mentor young men. Jerry's hopes for Cedric show the worth that trainers see in the men they train.

In the urban gym, trainers like Jerry coach amateur boxers both inside and outside the ring. In the ring, trainers prepare amateurs for competition and help their boxers develop masculine identities. Outside the ring, they provide desperately needed forms of social, psychological, and material support. As they engage these physical and social practices, trainers negotiate a discursive tension. When they work with amateur boxers, trainers draw upon discourses espousing individualism. And yet, when talking about the motivation for their work, trainers utilize a different discourse, one that acknowledges and critiques structural inequality and anti-black racism. This article examines the presence of these seemingly contradictory discourses. It analyzes how discourses advocating personal responsibility and discourses critiquing systemic injustice simultaneously find expression in the gym.

IN THE RING: TRAINING AND THE TROPE OF 'TOUGH LOVE'

A trainer's athletic goals are to teach boxers the sport's techniques, develop their skills, and prepare them for competition. Although most agree on the basics of boxing, it is up to an individual trainer to ascertain how to accomplish these goals with individual fighters.[1] Trainers take an enormous amount of time learning about their amateurs—what works for one will not always work for another—which requires determining when

and how far a fighter can be pushed. Not pushing a fighter may make for a comfortable training experience but inevitably produces a brutal wake-up call in a bout. Pushing an athlete too far will at best demoralize him and at worst place him in a life-threatening situation. But pushing a fighter just the right amount can precipitate a breakthrough in confidence, paving the way for pugilistic success.

One of the most important practices utilized to mold boxers is the spar. Sparring is typically done on Tuesdays, Thursdays, and Saturdays, when fighters are considered the most focused and rested.[2] Jerry's coaching in spars follows a formula. In the early rounds, Jerry gives very little praise and an almost overwhelming amount of criticism. When they err, the sparring partners are taunted for their lack of effort in the ring. They are feminized and degraded as 'women' or 'little girls' and mocked as 'sleeping together' when they clinch one another in exhaustion. If the boxers protest or offer excuses, including injury, they are chastised until silenced. In the middle of the spar when visible signs of exasperation and dejection present themselves—heads, shoulders, and hands drop while footwork slows—Jerry might threaten to drop them from his team if they do not comply with his instruction. With little choice, they rally, and more times than not succeed in throwing the number and quality of punches demanded. In the last rounds of the spar, as they push through fatigue and pain, their determination wins Jerry's approval. He compliments and encourages them, and when the spar is finished, they climb out of the ring drenched in sweat, bodies slumped in exhaustion, and faces beaming.

This pattern is demonstrated in a spar between Maurice and Ali:

Jerry: Come on, let your hands go! Let your hands go! Come on. Bend. Double your punches and work. Work! You waiting too long, you ain't fightin'.

You aren't fightin' amateur, move your head. Stop reaching! Bend your legs, jab. Come on, work, work, work! Both hands. Bend your legs and work. Work. Stop swinging wild and back him up. WORK. Back up his punch. Come on! You'd better not drop the right hand to the body. You wait too much, man. Why you wait?

This, like most of Jerry's questions, is intended to be rhetorical, but Maurice cannot resist the opportunity to explain himself:

Maurice: My hand hurts.
Jerry: What?
Maurice: My *hand* hurts.
Jerry: Then why are you boxing, Maurice, if you hand hurts? Look at me. Come here. Let me put some grease on your face, man. What are you going to tell the guy next week? That your hand hurts?
Maurice: [sulking] No.
Jerry: Right now forget about your hand. You ain't got one.

Maurice complies and boxes as if he has, quite literally, forgotten that he has a hand, dropping his right glove and using only his jab. He executes Jerry's instruction virtually word for word, which earns him praise. When the spar is over, Maurice descends from the ring with a big smile, and he and Jerry begin joking. Sitting on the ring's edge, they discuss how Maurice's accomplishment, produced through bodily trauma, will benefit him in his next fight.

In boxing training, trainers ask their athletes to disregard their assessments of the situation and context—that they are in pain because they have been injured—and instead take up their trainers' understandings—that boxers can fight through the pain. That is, rather than focusing on the *fact* of physical suffering, fighters are asked to respond *to* that

suffering by summoning a masculine will and determination. Joyce Carol Oates observes that 'The boxer must somehow learn, by what effort of will non-boxers surely cannot guess, to inhibit his own instinct for survival; he must learn to exert his "will" over his merely human and animal impulses, not only to flee pain but to flee the unknown' (Oates, 1994: 15). This process is not seamless. Maurice does not believe that he can execute Jerry's instruction; he gets angry and even challenges the soundness of Jerry's reason. But Maurice eventually capitulates, adopting Jerry's interpretation of the spar. He ignores his own reading (i.e. that he cannot fight because of a severely injured hand) and trusts Jerry. By the final rounds of the exercise, both are delighted when Maurice prevails.

This process can be troubling to watch. The amount of criticism a fighter sustains during a spar is crushing for any sporting activity but especially for one in which athletes endure significant bodily harm. I watched fighters break noses, fingers, and hands, dislocate shoulders, and twist ankles only to be blamed for their injuries and told to continue. Following Maurice's spar, I ask Jerry why he would demand that Maurice continue sparring when he is suffering:

> I want to put them in the frame of mind that if you hurt your hand in a fight, what are you going to do? You gonna quit? Or you gonna continue? Life is only over unless you give up and give into it. There's a thing called 'tough love.'

Tough love is the most often articulated trope of training practices. The trope bespeaks the care, devotion, and responsibility that trainers have for their amateurs while acknowledging the particular demands and realities of pugilism.

The 'love' in tough love derives from trainers' responsibility for their fighters' well-being in the ring. A boxer—especially an anxious or young boxer—often cannot judge a fight: how much injury he is sustaining, what punches are working, which combinations are not, where defenses are failing. Trainers say 'the corner wins the fight for you', meaning that a trainer can better assess the bout than the competitor: strategy, skill, and danger. Trainers take this evaluation seriously, and in order to keep their athletes safe, trainers assume control, dictating both fighters' actions as well as their understandings of those actions.

An exchange between Jerry and Kenny, an extremely talented amateur boxer, throws into sharp relief the gravity of trainer responsibility. After Kenny is hit too much for Jerry's liking, Jerry pulls him from the ring. Stopping a spar abruptly is unusual, and in this case, signifies that something is very wrong with Kenny's performance:

Jerry: Listen to me, come down. Come down for a minute. The reason why you're getting hit is that you're too tight. Relax. When you throw a jab, you're dropping your jab. Pop POP. POP POP. You know what I'm saying? Don't jab and do this [drops his hand to demonstrate]. The man going to hit you with a right hand. Jab, jab, and move your head from side to side. That's all you gotta do.

Kenny: But the first round, I always be cold, Jerry.

Jerry: I understand that, but you can't come out cold in boxing. People get knocked out in the first round. That's the most dangerous round of the fight—the first round. You gotta come out hot and smoking in the first round because that's how people get knocked out in the first round. You see first round knockouts? It's because people come out cold. You can't come out cold. This is not a sport when you can afford to come out cold. You understand what I'm saying? Because if you're

a slow starter, they ain't gonna wait for you to start. They gonna get off [on] you.

Jerry removes Kenny from the ring because his physical safety is at risk. He worries that Kenny is accustomed to warming up in the first round and, if not broken of this tendency, it will be a liability in competition. But Jerry's quote indexes another investment in tough love. Jerry fears that opponents will 'get off' on Kenny if Jerry does not get him into the best physical and mental shape possible. Thus trainers also see themselves as responsible for protecting their fighters from failure. The 'love' in tough love tries to shield amateurs from disappointment as much as from injury.

The 'tough' in tough love emerges from trainers' belief that their amateurs' general inclination is to back away from difficult situations. Their job is to teach them how to call up will while in physical agony.[3] This is a gendered, heteronormative process. Jerry frets that if he entertains his fighters' excuses, they will become weak and emasculated, losing some of the inherent masculinity deemed necessary for success in the gym:

If I make a way out for you, you gonna take an easy road. You don't pet grown men. I'm not saying men don't deserve hugs and stuff like that. But you can't treat a man like he a woman. You gonna ruin him. You gonna take what's naturally in him and turn it into something else.

Entertaining fighters' complaints of painful experiences—'petting' them—is demeaned as feminine. Jerry's reference to 'hugs' suggests that a particular type of physical intimacy threatens masculine toughness, and so the task of the boxing trainer is to ensure that the masculinity 'naturally' constitutive of men is not lost through feminine coddling. Racial, gender, and sexual aspects of subject formation coagulate in gym discourse as a way to regain and maintain power. Daniel Y. Kim argues that '. . . the effects of racism and the possibilities of its transcendence are often framed by a rhetoric of gender and sexuality' (Kim, 2005: xv).[4] These discursive practices construct a gender and sexual binary that often mirrors, even reproduces, the binary logic of neoliberal thought.

On the 'hard road' that Jerry references, fighters are held responsible for the injuries they sustain. When Cedric is hurt in a spar, Jerry casts it as Cedric's failure:

> I got this kid Cedric . . . and he got hit in the throat and the stomach. He fell down. 'I'm getting [out of the ring]—.' 'No you're not. Finish. Finish the round.' 'But my throat!' I say, 'Your throat is hurting because I always told you "stop picking your head up". And you won't. And your stomach hurt because you won't do no road work.'

Cedric was not injured because *another fighter* punched him in the throat and stomach. He was hurt because *he* failed to protect himself through rigorous aerobic training and defensive skill. He had a choice, exercised the wrong option, was injured, and is at fault.

Through tough love, the context of injury is naturalized and the individual response to injury prioritized. The fact of physical suffering is accepted as-is, as an inevitable feature of gym life, and fighters are constituted as having a choice in the midst of bodily trauma: either they can quit or they can continue.[5] Possibilities for expressing agony or even critiquing the exercise are structured out and the fighter's actions scrutinized. A dual-gender system polices this process; sexist and homophobic rhetoric function as demonizing and sanctioning devices, denigrating anything considered remotely feminine and instead encouraging heterosexual masculinity.

One could argue that prioritizing this commitment to individualism is necessary in a sport as highly individuated as boxing. A corner may coach, advise, and encourage, but it is up to the boxer to battle through the difficulties of the bout on his own. However, this same commitment to the *response* to suffering rather than the *fact* of injury presents itself outside the ring.

IN THEIR CORNER: THE SOCIAL PRACTICES AND RELATIONS OF MENTORING

The boxing experience is used as a theoretical template when trainers intervene in the social lives of their fighters. Trainers take seriously the idea of individuality and hold close the notion that 'anyone can do it'. Trainers often connect experiences in the ring with life outside it. Jerry, for example, likes to give boxing-related object lessons by linking performance in the ring with other aspects of a boxer's life in order to prove personal failings:

> What I'm telling you now, didn't I tell you both [his predictions about boxing and school]? It's the same situation you got in school. Your teachers tell you, 'If you don't do you work, you gonna fail.' I tell you 'If you don't do this, this will happen.' But I forewarned you.

But trainers go beyond merely drawing rhetorical parallels, and undertake a set of social practices distinct from boxing: from providing material resources to acting as educators and from imparting romantic advice to fulfilling the role of father. When engaging these sets of practices, trainers become the structure in their fighters' lives, and trainers and fighters develop relationships not centered on pugilism but rather focused on the need for support.

Trainers develop for their boxers a social network, which often involves finding athletes work. Because amateurs are usually unemployed or in insecure positions and trainers know their fighters will never make money from the sport, they are constantly on the lookout for suitable employment.[6] They discuss with other gym members job vacancies and consult with their white-collar clients about potential openings. When a popular home furnishings retailer moves into the area, Jerry urges Max, one of Jay's amateurs, to put in an application. Jay realizes that the manager of the store is a white-collar client and lobbies for Max, ultimately securing him the position. When Jerry learns that Scott is unemployed, he uses his connections in the neighborhood to locate a job, which is particularly difficult as Scott does not have work papers. Peter, one of the gym's most well-established trainers, routinely passes along episodic security and construction work to amateur fighters while William, a trainer who also works as a stunt double, frequently recruits them as extras in film and television.

Locating employment for fighters may require that trainers forgo the job themselves. When a Manhattan boxing gym offers Jay a position that pays $10 per hour and guarantees 20 hours per week, Jay is tempted to accept, as he is homeless at the time and trying to save money for an apartment.[7] However, knowing that Anthony has been searching for work for over six months and concerned the difficulty may be due to his criminal record, Jay passes him the job. After working with a Comedy Central comedian for almost a year and making a dependable salary, Jerry gives the position to Leon, an amateur he has trained for over 13 years. When I ask Jerry if he can afford to relinquish a job that adds roughly $10,000 to his income per year, he shifts the focus of the discussion to Leon: 'It's a good job for him.'

Possibly the most meaningful role trainers assume is confidante. Trainers spend a tremendous amount of time talking with and listening to their amateurs. When Scott needs to bring his middle-aged mother across the US–Mexico border, he discusses with Jay, at length, the difficulty of the impending journey. After crossing into California, Jay is the first person Scott calls from a payphone to say they are safe. Upon return to New York, he brings Jay a bottle of tequila to celebrate.

When Diego earns a high score on a practice GED test while confined on Rikers Island and again when he passes the exam, he calls Jay from jail with excitement. And when Max's partner has a baby, Max endlessly discusses fatherhood with Jay: how to burp the baby, how to get vaccinations, and how to change Pampers. Max calls Jay the father he never had, and anoints Jay his son's godfather. Jay is also confidante to several fighters who try to resist re-entering the drug trade but find making ends meet impossible on minimum wage.

Trainers think through each of their fighters' needs and lives, which can be manifested in small but crucial ways. Jay is asked to nominate a fighter from his team to the Police Boxing Association (PBA), which travels around the world competing with other police leagues, and he chooses Adrian because Adrian has not traveled outside New York and Pennsylvania. In addition to paying part of Leon's tuition, Jerry pays his utility and cell phone bills. Peter buried a fighter who died without leaving his family the resources to cover the cost of a funeral and fought successfully, although for seven years, to get another fighter, who was wrongly imprisoned, released.

As trainers care for their boxers, they utilize the same trope of tough love and express the same commitment to individualism as they do in the ring. When applied in the social world, personal responsibility narratives naturalize the inequality of social circumstances and refuse excuse-giving or complaining, demanding self-sufficiency instead. In particular, trainers look to work to solve problems and to instill discipline to overcome disadvantage.

When Max becomes a father, he has a difficult time adjusting to parenthood. His complaints about the pressure and his lack of energy provoke a hail of criticisms from Jay, who tells me:

I cursed him out three times yesterday and I gave him a long talk about discipline. Well, first of all I told him not to have a baby, and he had a baby. You have a baby, you have responsibility. Baby need Pampers, baby need milk, baby need Similac. Number two, you have to deal with the baby mother. Whether you like her or you don't like her, you still got to deal with her. Number three, you need to work now. He's bitching and moaning, 'I'm tired. I don't want to work.' Yeah, everybody—that's what everybody in the real world do. You wake up, you go to work, you try to get in your boxing and workout. You go home, you play with your baby. He's feeling the crunch of the real world. But before he was a teenager. He'd get up and hang out in the street and come into the gym and hang out in the gym for four hours and then go home. Now he can't do that, and it's a crunch on him and he gets whiney and I don't want to hear that shit. Be a man and do what you got to do.

'What you got to do' as a 'man' can be decoded as the expectation of breadwinning and heading the family. Through his prescription of employment—'you need to work now'—Jay demands Max participate in an institution that historically has served as a pillar of patriarchy. This is significant because Jay knows that this possibility is almost occluded in the postindustrial landscape of Brooklyn where finding adequate work for men of color without high school degrees is extremely difficult, never mind for men like Max, who also are marked by a criminal record (Pager, 2007). But the context of joblessness and mass incarceration is rarely integrated into Jay's mentoring. Despite knowledge about it—indeed life experience shaped by it—Jay ignores it and instead demands his amateurs fulfill the expectations of dominant masculinity through labor. Jay's sentiments belie the tension between the need for support, which is feminized as weakness, and the requirements of manhood, which demand self-sufficiency.

Jay takes a similar position on Adrian, a fighter who has a history of serious physical and psychological abuse. Jay will acknowledge that Adrian has suffered at the hands of parents, teachers, and major socializing institutions, but when talking about Adrian's future, he will focus only on Adrian's response. I express my concern to Jay that Adrian is, quite literally, starving, and Jay responds:

But eh, look, that's life. Look, let me tell you something. I'm not the most handsome motherfucker. I'm short, I'm chubby, I got fake yellow teeth. I'm going fucking bald, I got bumps on the back of my neck, and I have no fucking money. So I say, 'Well, I'm short, fat, bumps on the back of my neck, and I have no fucking money. But the other side: I'm smart. I'm charming. I make good fucking jokes, and I make people feel comfortable.' I have to use my brain. I can't match muscle for muscle, look for look. So Adrian gotta understand that. Yeah, he don't have the talent, so your endurance got to be incredible. Your will power gotta override this man's talent. And that might go farther. You gotta do dirty tricks. You gotta play mind games . . . He gotta *understand* that. You gotta work with what God gave you. And that's that. You can't get jealous. Yeah, I wish I was 6'2" and didn't have to sleep outside.

In Jay's assessment, hunger is part of life. It is not narrated as the product of antiblack racism and inequality but rather a feature of everyday existence. And, as Jay suggests, the only response to that 'fact' is individual; to adapt by drawing upon existing strengths and relying on 'endurance'.

As hinted at through Jay's reference to his own life—best exemplified by his experiences of homelessness—trainers construct and reference a hierarchy of suffering to deflect the suffering of the boxer they are working with to another person who is suffering or has suffered more. Trainers point to personal histories of deeper oppression than the pain at hand;[8] when amateurs, or ethnographers for that matter, make claims about the unmet promises of US citizenship, they are referred to others who do not enjoy those same promises. Boxers who live in the US without documentation are common figures for this comparison. Scott is used by several trainers as an example of 'heart' and 'courage' in the midst of suffering. After he crosses the US–Mexico border, he cements his heroism and instruction potential in the eyes of many gym trainers. That he also works 12-hour shifts in a minimum wage job without complaining only enhances his status. Jerry admires Scott's 'heart':

> I would love to see Scott become a world champion because he has a hell of a story to tell. Because of how he left and he came back, what he had to endure to get back here. He had to cross over the border and stuff like that. That's daring defeat when you do something like that. To get back under those circumstances, that's a guy who wants something out of life and who has a plan in life.

Trainers draw from the ideology of neoliberalism noted earlier and train their fighters to enact the same gendered, heterosexual normativity outside the ring as inside: focus on discipline and regimen; have courage and heart; be personally responsible; tackle any obstacles; if you perceive a barrier, there is no alternative except to overcome; failure is simply not an option. Trainers utilize discourses of personal responsibility and freedom of choice, which long have served as the bases of a patriarchal American capitalism and its corresponding Protestant work ethic (Sandlin, 2004).

ANTI-BLACK RACISM, SOCIAL INJUSTICE, AND SOCIAL CRITIQUE

If trainers espouse discourses of individualism when they work with boxers, they use a different discourse when discussing the motivations for working as boxing coaches and the opportunities for men of color in postindustrial New York. In these instances, trainers articulate critiques of anti-black racism and structural injustice and advance arguments about social rather than personal responsibility. Jerry and Jay voice sharp criticism about the life chances of their fighters and in very different ways.

Jerry's narrative of recovery from a crack cocaine addiction and a history of crime informs his athletic and social practices as he seeks to prevent young black men from making the mistakes he made. According to Jerry's own account, he fell in with the wrong crowd as a young man in Bedford Stuyvesant in the 1980s and embarked on a path of pot and cocaine use and then crack addiction. He began petty crime—low-level drug trading and robbery—to finance his habit until he shot a family member in a Brooklyn social housing unit. While serving a multiple-year sentence in Attica, he activated a radical transformation and vowed never to go back to prison. He kept to himself for the remainder of his term, studying for his GED, and then, when released, sought drug rehabilitation. He held various jobs during the day and coached in his spare time until he could afford to train fighters full-time. On becoming a trainer, he reflects, 'One thing led to another, and I fell in love with the sport all over again but from a different perspective, from a different view, from a different angle. I said "I can still make a difference."'

When discussing his history, Jerry locates his participation in crime and drugs in the socio-economic context of the 1980s and 1990s. In particular, Jerry argues that growing up in the racially segregated neighborhood of Bedford Stuyvesant during the height of the crack cocaine boom and living in deteriorating social housing shaped his life chances. Though he considers it his responsibility to respond to the conditions of racial oppression, largely through self-help, rehabilitation, and labor, Jerry believes in the importance of governmental and social responsibility and warns of the consequences of societal inaction. When talking about US public policy and anti-black racism, Jerry argues that the government has the responsibility to provide men with the means to support themselves with dignity. He will point out the contra-dictions of completing a prison sentence and being continually penalized for past crimes. And he will analyze the minimum wage in the context of New York City rent prices, warn-ing of the potential for race riots because of an inadequate affordable housing stock for residents of color.

Jerry's desire to make a difference is ani-mated not only by his past mistakes but also by a vision of society in which govern-ment and everyday people help each other more. Trainers fall into the latter category. When I ask if he thinks all trainers should give their amateurs the athletic, social, and psychological attention he devotes to them, he responds, 'Sure, because if everybody thought in those terms, you'd have bet-ter people.' Jerry often becomes frustrated with the amateurs with whom he works, but he will not give up on them. At one point he develops problems with Kenny, who is lying to people in the gym by boasting of a world championship. When Jerry con-fronts Kenny about the lie, Kenny clarifies that, '*in my heart* I'm a champion', and the aporia between Kenny's actual and existen-tial championship annoys Jerry. But though he stews over the incident for several days, he still maintains his basic tenet of social responsibility: 'I just can't close the door on people. To me, nobody closed the door on me [when addicted to crack]. There was always a door open no matter what.'

When asked why he does not discuss sys-temic white racism and social inequality with his amateurs, Jerry explains that he worries that anger at racial injustice will produce 'bitterness', which he considers a dead end, self-destructive, and unruly emotion. The assumption undergirding Jerry's concern is that critique can *only* end in bitterness and that there are no existing spaces—political, social, or otherwise—to actualize that cri-tique. His own battles with bitterness inform this apprehension:

The world don't owe me anything, so what's the point walking around bitter? You know? Every decision you made you made a conscious decision. You did it to yourself. You made your own decisions in life. You just have to learn to deal with it. Accept life for what it is. You understand what I'm sayin'? Cause if I walked around bitter all the time, believe me nobody would want to be around me, and nobody would want to deal with me.

And yet Jerry's argument about the primacy of individual decision-making is contra-dictory because Jerry does, in fact, believe that the world owes people certain things. His very work—physical and social—is an enactment of the belief that the world owes his amateurs—who have been demonized as drug dealers, hustlers, excons, juvenile delinquents, and social outcasts—better opportunities. But when training ama-teurs, he falls back on a self-help discourse that he believes contributed to his success in drug rehabilitation. His tough love simultane-ously occupies two contradictory positions: the belief that his amateurs should strive in life and anxiety about the consequences of their failure.

Jay did not face the same struggles with addiction or the long periods of forced con-finement, but as a black youth, his opportu-nities for education, decent employment, and escaping the poverty of his Crown Heights neighborhood were limited by institutional racism. Coming of age at the height of the crack boom presented him with economic possibilities, but after forays into the extra-legal economy, Jay found the consequences of criminality unappealing. He turned instead to boxing and then the armed forces. While proud of his athletic and military accomplish-ments, Jay believes anti-black racism blocked avenues for social and economic mobility. His work at the gym attempts to provide young men with the knowledge and oppor-tunities to which he did not have access. He tells me:

Nobody navigated me. If somebody had navigated me, I'd probably be in Harvard somewhere. Street navigator. Yeah, that's what kids need. That's the perfect word. They want to do right, but they haven't been navigated. They don't know what to do. You know what I mean? You counsel them on more things than this boxing shit. They don't know what to do. Baby stuff, how you do the baby stuff. Things like—even how to get the baby circumcised when he little. You gotta counsel them on everything—where to get a job, what to do.

Jay's instruction attempts to provide his fighters with the 'street navigation' he never had. He asserts that poor urban areas are so segregated that young men are not taught how to move out of them. They are not given basic information like how to apply to college, how to apply for a job, or even how to acquire basic documents, like a passport. Society's biggest failure is not mentoring and providing young black men with the resources to leave the ghetto. His work as a trainer is motivated by a critique of racial oppression and a need in the generations below him. He undertakes his work because other institutions have relinquished their responsibilities:

These kids get raised on the street, and they're not guided. Max is a smart guy, but he didn't know what to do. He had no guidance. Where I go to get my GED?' 'My girlfriend pregnant, where I go?' 'Where's health care?' 'How I fill out an application?' 'How you sign up for a lease?' 'What to wear on a job interview?' You know, *everything. These guys just don't know.* When they go do things kinda wrong and do a social faux pas, they get frustrated. They get in a corner. And most people—like almost my whole team is criminals. All of them went to jail at one period of time or another, and when you fill out an application, you're like ostracized. You did your fucking time, that's it. You can't get a job. You can't do this, you can't do that. Boxing is like, they embrace you.

To Jay, the gym is a makeshift institution for socialization and a place where men who are frustrated, excluded from full citizenship by criminal records, and unable to meet the expectations of dominant society can be supported and even embraced. Jay sees it as the last social space for homosocial bonding and where young men learn the rituals of masculinity:

I think this the last place where men get trained by men. There used to be outlets—like the army. There ain't no outlets anymore. They not used to dealing with men. I don't care—if you're a single mother, you can't raise no manchild.

However, at times, Jay can reveal hesitation about this role. After he has cursed Max out, I ask Jay how he responded:

Well, I don't *make* him. He kind of listened. I mean, that's the kind of talk his father should have with him. I shouldn't have to have that fucking talk with him. All these kids have no fathers. The majority of these boxers don't have no father figure so I have to step in, and I've got to have these talks. They don't understand that when you get older the choices you make affect you for 15 to 20 years. When you're younger maybe you'll get reprimanded for it, but now the choices you make affect your ass. You get used to working. Yeah it's hard going to the gym and working full-time and taking care of your baby. But that's what you got yourself into. You have to get that discipline in mind.

Like Jerry, Jay moves from acknowledging and critiquing the contexts of social and economic injury to demanding personal responsibility and determination. Jay analyzes injustice at the social-structural level, but still promotes a form of masculine individualism and, in particular, the transcendent power of labor. But unlike Jerry, Jay does not draw upon self-help discourses. His discourses of individualism emerge from an assessment of the postindustrial landscape and his belief that there are literally no other options. Anger at anti-black racism is justified, and bitterness at urban marginality is legitimate, but self-sufficiency and self-responsibility are still necessary to succeed. When I ask Jay why, like Jerry, he demands such magnificent acts of will from his amateurs, he responds, 'You can sit in the gym angry and depressed all you want. But it's not going to get you anywhere.' Jay's work, then, enacts a social critique while accepting the reality of current social conditions as unalterable.

NOTES

1. In this article I use the masculine pronoun to refer to trainers because during my field-work all of the gym's trainers were men. I want to note, however, that over the past several years, women have become gym trainers. I also use the masculine pronoun to refer to amateur boxers because this paper focuses on the distinctly homosocial relationships that develop between male trainers and fighters.

2. Many trainers believe that Mondays are bad days for sparring because fighters—both male and female—are likely to have partied or had sex on Saturday night, tiring out the athletes. Tired athletes will not be as alert in the ring, and thus it is considered dangerous to have them spar.

3. Joyce Carol Oates writes, 'A boxing trainer's most difficult task is said to be to persuade a young boxer to get up and continue fighting after he has been knocked down' (Oates, 1994: 13).

4. Kim writes:

> The origins of 'minority discourse,' according to David Lloyd and Abdul JanMohamed, are to be found in the 'damage' that racism inflicts on minoritized subjects: 'we must realize that minority discourse is, in the first instance, the product of damage—of damage more or less systematically inflected on cultures by the dominant culture.' But as a discourse, minority discourse is not only 'the product of 'damage,' but also the narratives, symbols, images and so forth that subjects of color might use to give representational shape to damage'. (Kim, 2005: 2)

5. Although physically and psychologically demanding, these sparring scenarios are not reckless but exist within the clearly demarcated and designed limits the trainer carefully constructs. Therefore I qualify 'almost' to specify that there are some injuries that trainers will not ask their fighters to fight through. Jerry explains: 'Certain situations, I pull them out. If you got a headache, you not boxing.' Trainers also know when a fighter is really hurt and when he is exaggerating in order to be pulled out of the ring. This is when a trainer's skill as well as intimate understanding of his fighter comes into play. Jerry tells me, 'It's all about your reaction. I know how to read their pain. I know how to read through their pain.'

6. For a sharp discussion on professional boxers' understandings of their social mobility as well as the relations of power imbrued in the labor of professional boxing, see Wacquant (1998).

7. Jay's clients and boxers did not know he was homeless.

8. These notions of suffering, sacrifice, determination, and will are deeply held among trainers, and they practice what they preach. When Jay became homeless he never complained about his exhausting routine roaming the streets at night and coaching in the gym during the day. Instead he joked about his weight loss as 'the homeless diet'. He would not stay with anyone from the gym because he felt it threatened his dignity and self-respect; his task was to endure. Jerry frequently discusses his own fight back from a serious crack addiction: prison, rehabilitation, relapse, and homelessness. One of the reasons that fighters do not challenge their trainers when they are being harsh or 'real' is because they know their trainers have suffered substantially. Jerry and Jay ask their fighters to overcome; it is probable that Jay and Jerry have faced a similar barrier themselves.

CHAPTER 11

What We Talk about When We Talk about Religion

Courtney Bender

TALK ABOUT RELIGION: RELIGIOUS SPEECH GENRES

Despite the varied ways volunteers practiced religion in the kitchen (through praying. counting containers, laughing, and so on), most *talk* about religion went on in several discrete ways: talk about going to church, preparing for holidays, and parody or satire. Talk about church and holidays cropped up when volunteers talked about their daily schedules, and they indulged in parody and satire when the media and political events focused on religious groups. Many volunteers were involved in churches and synagogues or other religious or spiritual groups. Most participated in religious traditions during holidays and family life events and elaborated on their often difficult and frustrating loyalties to family and tradition. Others parodied and satirized religious groups that were "bigoted," commenting on how some religions were more "religious" than others. This talk did not include theological reflection or discourse about moral behavior. Each, however, included some direct reference to religious or spiritual organizations, belonging, or identity. Each genre structured and suggested certain statements and responses and thus constituted expectations about the possibility and extent of talk about religion.

My interpretation of religious talk is based in Bakhtin's notion of speech genres. Speech genres, Bakhtin says, "include short rejoinders of daily dialogue (and these are extremely varied depending on the subject matter, situation, and participants) everyday narration, writing . . . the brief standard military command, the elaborate and detailed order."[1] In theory, genres are not merely an individual's utterance or statement. They anticipate, and help to shape, a certain kind of rejoinder and certain kinds of relationships. (When I greet the contractor fixing my roof with, "Hi, how are you," he responds, "Just fine, thanks," before we move onto practical issues. When I call my sister on the phone and ask the same question, I might expect a five-minute discourse on her miserable day at school.) Speech genres are relatively stable forms in theory, but they are not always consistent in use (the contractor might also tell me about his terrible day at work). People misunderstand each other. Individuals with different expectations and understandings of words, tones, and genres transform intended meaning into something new. Genres are probably best understood, then, not as fully structuring constraints, but as created and anticipated structuring points for conversations. They do not determine outcomes, but they do sketch out expectations for how a conversation might proceed. "Genres carry the generalizable resources of particular events; but specific actions or utterances must use those resources to accomplish new purposes in each . . . milieu."[2]

The simple religious genres I heard and recorded in the kitchen are not unique to it. If one pays attention, they can be heard in other spaces and settings in daily life. Likewise, these three genres do not exhaust the everyday religious speech genres that Americans regularly use. They were nevertheless the most common ones I recorded in the kitchen, and they were the ones volunteers used to build discursive relationships where they could also elaborate on religious ideas and values.

GOING TO CHURCH

Volunteers talked about going to church or synagogue by weaving their religious affiliations into the details of conversations about other things. They thus established their religious identities in everyday chatter about schedules and plans rather than by making declarative statements such as "I'm an Episcopalian." Even volunteers like Nancy who thought others might disparage their tradition's tenets mentioned their involvement from time to time. As far as I am aware, active members of religious groups did not censor their involvement from conversations.

Most volunteers did not associate their own or others' comments about "going to church" with meaning or faith. Religious participation was one of a number of things people did throughout the week. In this regard, going to church was similar to going to the gym. Nevertheless, talk about church-going placed volunteers within a web of institutional affiliations that, it seemed, mattered to them and to others. When I asked volunteers if they knew whether other volunteers attended religious services, they not only said yes but told me who was Protestant, who was Catholic, and who was Buddhist.

Talk about going to church was more complex than it first appeared, however. This genre also implicitly denoted appropriate and inappropriate religious affiliations. I became aware of this boundary when Tuesday morning volunteers made plans to attend the upcoming volunteer appreciation-party together. Tanya told us she wouldn't

be joining us because she was going to South America to see an "Indian spiritual guide." She was surprised when the other volunteers started to make jokes about the trip. They warned her not to be "brainwashed" and to watch out for hucksters and for anyone who offered her Kool-Aid.

Tanya was a dedicated and well-liked volunteer, and the others (I believe) did not intend to hurt her feelings. Nevertheless, their allusion to Jim Jones and the implication that she was less than rational insulted Tanya. She tried to explain that the guide was a recognized healer, but she got nowhere. Tanya's defense only made the others laugh more. Finally she said, "Well, I'm going to get a great suntan!" Julie changed direction and asked Tanya what vaccines she needed, helping her to reinterpret the trip as solely a "vacation." No further discussion followed about Tanya's guide or why he was important to her.

This interchange began quite simply, when Tanya mentioned why she would not be attending an upcoming volunteer event. Her trip was not unlike others' pilgrimages to Jerusalem, and thus similar to other conversations about going to church. Yet the others' reactions made it clear that her trip fell outside the boundaries of the "going to church" genre. Tanya had waded into murky and ill-defined spiritual commitments and energies (and curiosity).

Tanya's religious journey, in other words, brought to light spiritual experiences that defied normal boundaries of affiliation expected by others in the kitchen. Attending mass or synagogue was socially acceptable. Participating in less structured practices and quests was not so acceptable. Acceptability was structured in part by the genre, and Tanya's decision did not fit the genre in that it raised questions that went beyond what it could answer. What did Tanya believe? What would her relationship to the guide be? All those issues of authority and belief, "settled" in commonplace talk about church, were unsettled and ambiguous when volunteers began to talk about spiritual quests and novel religious affiliations.

The boundaries of "going to church" talk became clearer when a volunteer (incorrectly) interpreted the genre to signal a willingness to discuss religious experience. One morning Harrison caught Gloria off guard as she finished telling a funny story about her friend Ann, whom she identified as "my friend from church." Harrison asked what church she went to. "Unitarian," she answered.

"What do you get out of church?" he asked.

"Well, I'm really close to the people there—closer than to any other group of people—we just share so much!" Rather than telling Harrison how they had helped her and her family get through her sister's sudden death (as she had told Susan and me several months before), she said, "It's rare that you find a group of people you can talk to, and share so many things. And when you do, that's something you have to hang on to." Gloria had been attending her church for decades and considered it her extended family.

Harrison was looking for new things to do, Susan knew, because they had talked about rejoining the "singles scene" in Manhattan. Susan, who attended a progressive Presbyterian church in lower Manhattan "on and off," asked Harrison from across a heaping pile of yucca root, "Why? Are you thinking of attending somewhere? Church is a good place to meet people, you know."

He answered with a nonanswer. "It's just that recently I've been going through this rough time. I've been pretty depressed about it, you know. And one morning, I was just sitting, and thinking—and something came over me. It was like I was looking at my life and watching it go by. It was—just a detached, calm feeling. It was just this, well, it was this intensely spiritual thing, and that has never happened to me before." Susan nodded, encouraging but noncommittal. Gloria rolled her eyes.

He continued, "It was what the Buddhists call detachment. I didn't grow up religious, and that's part of my problem, you know." He chuckled and went on to say, "But I don't want to be a Buddhist. You know, to say that what happened was detachment—it's like, who cares. Everybody's a Buddhist these days, but that's really what it was, you know?"

"There's a Zen monastery I know of—maybe you should try it out," I offered, thinking that he might want a bit more encouragement, but he said no.

"With all the violence that's been in my life recently, I don't want to be in an organized religion. They just seem to be *violent*." I asked him what he meant (I had never heard Zen called violent before). He explained, "To me it seems that organized religions are just—well, they do violence to the experience. It's your experience, and they put it into something, contain it."

"Maybe, but a church can really be a support when things are rough in your life," Gloria offered.

"Yeah, maybe, but—" Harrison trailed off.

No one else said anything.

Gloria could not have expected that mentioning Ann "from church" would lead us into such a conversation. She shied away as it took shape: rather than giving him concrete examples, she used an abstract statement that could go "anywhere" Harrison wanted it to go. She didn't really answer his question.

Taking the little we knew about Harrison, the rest of the volunteers around the table suggested several reasons for going to church that fit more neatly within the contours of the genre. But Harrison rebuffed our suggestions that church would help him meet new people or offer a community to support him in time of trouble. When he started to talk about this experience, he was looking for a way to understand it, not for some affiliation or community. By the time we recognized that Harrison was not talking about finding a church to attend, we were not sure where he was headed.

Harrison labeled his experience Buddhist even though he immediately told us he was not Buddhist. Although he was familiar with a few Buddhist categories that might explain his feeling, he seemed bothered that it could be classified so easily (as in "everyone" is a Buddhist these days). My suggestion that he check out a monastery seemed to annoy him even more.

Talking about church did not propel volunteers toward talk about belief or religious experience. On the few occasions when it was misunderstood by someone to signal talk about belief, others were confused and resistant. They switched to other genres or at the very least alluded to them in their speech. Not all individuals could follow such switches without losing their place, however; some were more adept than others. Sean found this out one afternoon as we poured salad dressing into small plastic cups with Robert and Cherry, two African American volunteers. Sean asked Cherry why she hadn't come in on her regular day.

"I'm usually coming in here on Thursdays," she said, turning to Robert to clarify Sean's question. She told Sean, "On Mondays I go to the prison to do some prison visiting. There's a seminar for training tomorrow at Bethany Baptist, so I came in today. That's what I do. I do that one day, and this one day." She started prison visiting when a friend asked her to come along, and she enjoyed volunteering so much that she decided to take on a second project at God's Love We Deliver.

Robert then told us, "I found this on my own too. I didn't have a church that helped me find something to do, but here I am. I wish I could get them at my church involved in doing this kind of work. But they aren't interested."

Cherry looked surprised. "Isn't your church an *outreach church*?" she demanded, stressing each syllable.

"Sure," he said wryly. "It's an outreach church. They open up the doors every Sunday, and the preacher is preaching. That's the way they're reaching out to the people so they come in."

"But does it do *ministry*?" she wanted to know.

"My church—the money comes in, it don't flow out," said Robert, repeating as he demonstrated the flow with his hands. "You know what I'm saying, it comes in, it don't go out."

Cherry disapproved, pursing her lips and shaking her head in disgust.

"I come here on my own. I don't come through my church," he repeated.

"So who does the outreach?" Cherry persisted.

"Nobody but me."

"Well that's no church for me. If I were at that church, I would leave."

Sean, who had been silent, leaned in to add his two cents. 'You know what, I saw these churches in September when I was in Europe? They were these huge buildings, you know?" Robert and Cherry listened to him for a beat as he began to describe their cool stone interiors and stained-glass windows, then returned to their conversation. Sean then turned to me, "The buildings were just beautiful."

"I know," I said. "Too bad so few people attend them!" I thought maybe this comment would connect Cherry and Robert's conversation to Sean's interjection. But Sean just stared as if he didn't understand me. Robert and Cherry were still talking.

"Pray and stay, sister, that's what it's about," Robert was telling Cherry, still defending his church. "Pray and stay. I've got roaches, and I've got mice in my house. They come in, but that doesn't mean I go. Just the same as at church. You have to keep going, don't worry about *anyone else*."

I laughed at the metaphor. Seeing me smile, Robert leaned over the table toward Cherry, saying in a loud, clear voice, "You've got to know this, sister: Our Lord is a deliverer."

Cherry nodded in agreement, smiling as they each repeated several times in a cadence, putting the accent on different syllables, "Our Lord is a deliverer. Our Lord is a deliverer."

Even though Sean started this conversation, he was quickly cut from it. Cherry and

Robert found they had a common experience in coming to the kitchen on "their own," yet they argued about what was important about going to church.

Robert and Cherry moved easily from talk about "going to church" to a conversation that compared churches' ministerial and outreach methods. Sean, by contrast, had little experience attending religious services. He did not immediately catch the genre switch to an evaluation of different churches, and he interjected his experience, which fit better within the regular parameters of "going to church."

I was also a spectator, albeit a more knowledgeable one than Sean. Realizing he had failed to get back into the conversation, Sean tried to strike one up with me. Pained that I could not listen to Robert and Cherry (the data lost!), I attempted to craft a topical bridge to bring Sean's comments closer to theirs, but Sean's blank look told me my tack would not work. When I started listening to Robert and Cherry again and marked my renewed attention with a laugh, they closed the conversation with a confession they both agreed to: "Our Lord is a deliverer." Then Robert laughed and digressed into further conversation about the roaches in his apartment. Sean and I could both (unfortunately) relate to roach problems.

Although the genre seemed trivial when I first noted its use, I soon learned otherwise. Talk about going to church not only established religious identities but distinguished "normal" religious activity from less normal, personal kinds. It made space where the former could be discussed more easily and where the latter had to be translated if others were to respond favorably. Whether or not volunteers were religiously or spiritually tolerant, the genre excluded talk about less traditionally defined spiritual journeys.

PREPARING FOR HOLIDAYS

Talk about going to church was frequent. Talk about holidays punctuated kitchen conversation in seasonal spurts. Holidays structured the kitchen calendar, with its most festive and frantic time stretching between Halloween and New Year's Eve. Volunteers helped cook multicourse meals for Thanksgiving and Christmas (called the "Holiday Feast"), picking up extra shifts as they were needed. While talk about going to church often imparted facts about volunteers' identities and affiliations, talk about holidays positioned them in relation to their families, to traditions, and to religious observance in more detailed ways. In talking about holidays, they could voice their ideas about religious tradition, interweaving them with stories about family and about food.

In the ongoing holiday hubbub, volunteers discussed their own heroic preparations for their families and the inevitable strains that family get-togethers produced. We compared recipes and family traditions and sometimes discussed holidays' "meanings." These discussions let them talk about their religious beliefs in more open-ended ways than the genre of "going to church" presented.

A few weeks before Passover, Judy asked Sean for a recipe for a "vegetable dish" she could take to a seder. She groaned that she would rather be anywhere than at her sister-in-law's house that night. But she would go and would even bring a vegetable dish, though this wasn't what she usually brought. "Usually my sister-in-law just tells me to bring a fruit platter—real straightforward, just cut up the fruit and go. But this year she asked my other sister-in-law's daughter to do the fruit. She told me, 'Why don't you bring a vegetable?' At least I got it easier than my other sister-in-law. She has to bring 'something in a sweet potato'!"

Sean suggested a baked asparagus dish. As he explained how to make it she interrupted. "I can't do that, it's not kosher," she said.

Melinda asked why not. "The bread crumbs? You could leave those off you know," she offered.

"Yeah, but I wouldn't put them in anyway, too heavy," Judy said. "It's the Parmesan cheese. Not kosher. I'd like to take something lighter." She wrinkled her nose, turning to me. "The whole meal is usually casseroles. The last thing I want to see is another casserole. Yech."

Sean had walked away, so Melinda and I helped Judy decide on an asparagus dish that would be easy to make for thirty people, could be served cold—and was kosher. I mentioned that my family always had asparagus on Easter.

"Do you have it with ham?" Judy asked.

"No, we usually have lamb or salmon," I said, "and a little Virginia country ham on the side, but that's just because we're southern." Judy was surprised at our "traditional" Easter main course. "I thought everyone had ham at Easter."

"No, that's just the white bread Americans," Melinda broke in, amused at Judy's stereotype. "That's what we always had, with the pineapple slices and cherries and the whole works. But the Italians have lamb, I think."

"Ah, but Courtney's not Italian!" Judy noted.

We continued talking about Easter meals, with Judy quizzing Melinda and me on what we would do on Easter Sunday. "Well, I won't go to church," Melinda said after hearing that I would attend an early morning service with my extended family. "We used to go on Easter, but that's the only day we ever went, besides Christmas. After I got married again we just decided it was silly to go once a year. So we stopped."

"So you don't do anything—you don't even go to the Easter parade?" Judy probed.

"No—I don't know, do they still have the Easter parade?"

Judy made it clear that she was not happy to take part in her holiday. "Next year, Tahiti," she said, changing the traditional phrase "Next year in Jerusalem" to an even more remote location. (Judy followed through on this pledge: the following year she spent the week of Passover in the Caribbean. I asked her what, if anything, she had done to mark the holiday. "Oh, we observed it. We had our white wine, a piece of baguette, and toasted 'Next year in Jerusalem.' That was it!")

Judy participated because her husband and children expected her to, not because she was observant. She was told what to do and how to do it: in this case her sister-in-law dictated what she was to bring. Judy was annoyed that she was being bumped further up the ladder of responsibility for the meal. It was certainly more work to fix a "hot" vegetable as part of the meal than to make a platter of fruit for noshing. Judy compromised by preparing a vegetable that was "light" and that she could serve cold, subverting the unspoken expectation of family order that an array of hot and cold dishes helped reproduce. She told us later that "everyone" loved the asparagus, even though her sister-in-law was shocked that she had brought something cold.

Judy's gripes about Passover plans led not only to a more subtle interpretation of how religion, family, and food fit together in her life, but also to further commentary about how food factored in the ways Melinda and I celebrated the Easter season. Judy told us she thought Easter was "going to church and the Easter egg hunt—chocolate bunnies, y'know."

When I first told Judy that my extended family did not have a standard Easter meal, she gave me a knowing wink, incorrectly equating our "lack" of a set, traditional menu with a lack of observance. I continued by saying that my uncle and father prepared most of the meal. "I'm gonna come to your house," she said in disbelief. Reflecting that our menu changed from year to year, I also mentioned that a smaller family group also had a celebratory meal the night before Easter that we called "the rites of spring." Unlike the noon Easter "dinner" that we ate with my abstaining grand-parents, the rites of spring included excellent wine. The menu of shad roe with crabmeat and fresh asparagus had been set years before. Judy continued to ask questions about my family's "rites of spring" week after week. As she winked and grinned, I realized how surreptitious and secular the "rites" seemed when I talked about it (even the name connoted an illicit frolic in a starry field), especially when compared with the Easter meal shared after an early morning church service in the broad spring sunlight.

The easy confluence of holiday and food talk led others to discuss holidays' religious meanings (and often their confusion about those meanings). Charlene boasted, for instance, that she could teach us the "four questions" asked at a seder, but she blushed when she got stuck after the second. When Julie invited Mort "down to her place" for the second night of Passover, Mort asked no one in particular, "Why *are* there two nights of Passover?"

"I don't know either," Julie mused. She turned to ask Barbara, "Do you know why?"

Tamar broke in. "They only have one night in Israel."

"So why do we have two nights here?"

Tamar had the definitive answer; she was Israeli, and the others deferred to her on Jewish culture issues. "It's because of the Diaspora. The Jews in Europe didn't know which night it was because the calendars got confused. They did two nights to make sure they got the right time one of the nights."

"Really, that's quite interesting," said Barbara. "I always thought it was something religious. It wasn't originally that they had two nights?"

"No, it's not religious," repeated Tamar. "It's tradition."

"So now do we know the right day?" asked Julie, frowning.

"They do in Israel," answered Tamar.

"I wish we only did it once," Mort said.

"Come on—if we only did it one night then you couldn't come down to my house. Or you'd have to decide between your parents and me!" Julie laughed, patting him on the back.

Barbara mulled over Tamar's report, saying almost to herself, "Larry would probably do without the second night. But I've already invited everyone—I like to do it." Before she retired as a cooking instructor, Barbara taught countless Jewish women how to make brisket "like their mothers and grandmothers" and how to prepare gefilte fish and haroseth. She was not about to give up preparing her own table once a year, even on the "second night." Religious and ethnic or cultural reasons for celebrating holidays intertwined in exchanges like these, solidifying the importance of traditional and family rites.

Jewish volunteers—Julie, Judy, Mort, Barbara, and many others I met—volunteered on Christmas Day, recognizing that many Christian volunteers would be celebrating with family. Likewise, non-Jewish volunteers picked up the slack during the Passover season and around Yom Kippur and Rosh Hashanah. Hannah told me that volunteers' awareness of holidays, and their willingness to "pick up the slack" when others were observing, circumvented most scheduling problems. But it did not escape anyone's attention that GLWD paid more attention to Christian holidays. It sent Easter candy on Good Friday but not hamantaschen during Purim. It wrapped "Holiday" presents to deliver to clients on December 25 but did not tuck Hanukkah gelt into its deliveries.

Christian holidays thus presented situations where volunteers questioned the agency's "religiousness." According to the chefs and Barb, the client services coordinator, GLWD celebrated any day that it could, to make the clients' lives happier. So, in addition to birthday cakes for clients, the agency prepared elaborate celebrations on Thanksgiving and Christmas and delivered special treats on other holidays. It also delivered candy on Valentine's Day and Halloween and strawberry shortcake on the Fourth of July. Staff members maintained that the agency did not celebrate Christian holidays in a religious manner—or denied that they celebrated them at all.

One of my office duties was to coordinate and update the constantly changing client list for Thanksgiving and Christmas meal deliveries. When I was talking to Chris, a specials chef, about how many modified meals he would make at Christmas, we both became confused. Chris tried to convince me that GLWD had not prepared a special delivery for clients on Christmas Day in past years. "It's Thanksgiving that we celebrate here, Courtney," he told me. He was right, at least in some respects. Thanksgiving was the more prominent holiday. Religious meanings did not stick to Thanksgiving, allowing the agency to celebrate it without the sidestepping and reinterpreting that Christmas required. Nevertheless, the agency made a big deal of Christmas every year, albeit as the "Holiday Feast." I don't know why Chris forgot about the prime rib he carved on Christmases past, but our interchange highlighted some of the contradictions that holidays posed for kitchen workers.

These contradictions nonetheless made for fruitful and interesting conversations where GLWD's volunteers and staff tried to interpret the unsteady boundary between Christian holidays rooted in religious doctrine and the consumer and civic celebrations that accompanied (or engulfed) them. Whether God's Love We Deliver should deliver a full Christmas experience, replete with presents and a meal inspired by Scrooge's Christmas morning extravagance was another issue. Rather than asking staff directly why the agency celebrated these holidays, volunteers focused on the symbols themselves. Why all the *trimmings* for Christmas, and why notice Easter at all?

Faced with dyeing twelve hundred eggs during Easter week, Judy asked Bill, "What do eggs *symbolize*?" He said authoritatively, "Easter is a pagan holiday, it's the spring fertility feast. That's what it was originally. Eggs were a sign of fertility." She rolled her eyes, saying, "Yeah, yeah, I got you." The answer was not quite untrue, but Bill and Judy both knew it was not really an answer. The question of why we paid any attention to Easter was left dangling.

Earlier in the spring, on Valentine's Day, Barb, who came down for a piece of red velvet cake, mentioned in passing that she spent the previous evening clipping tracts off eight hundred Valentine's Day wreaths donated by a local florist. Emily asked what was in them. On hearing that they were Psalms, she said, "Why did you take them off? Maybe someone would have liked one!"

Barb replied, "Not all of our clients are Christian, you know. The meals are the only thing we send out. We don't send out anything that's Christian, Jewish, or whatever."

"So what about Christmas Day? Why do we do that?" Emily asked.

"That's our *Holiday Feast*," Barb answered, correcting Emily. "We send it out that day because it's when some of our clients expect to have gifts and stuff, and since it's such a big delivery, we can get the extra volunteers we need to do it." Barb continued to call the December 25 delivery a Holiday Feast, but everyone else called it Christmas. Barb was less vigilant in ferreting out the religious message one might decipher from a dyed Easter egg. And she worked diligently to make sure that GLWD delivered the fanciest Christmas gift basket of all New York's AIDS organizations.

Volunteers developed their understanding of their own and others' religious views and obligations as they talked about holidays. Similarly, GLWD's expression of holiday cheer prompted them to raise questions about how the agency should celebrate and, by extension, how it should mark the boundaries of the religious and the cultural. Talk about the place of religion in public life received more play, however, in conversations about the Catholic Church and the "religious right." These two groups received much attention in the kitchen, most of it as parody and cutting commentary.

NOTES

1. Bakhtin, *"Speech Genres" and Other Late Essays,* 60.
2. Speech genres, in Bakhtin's understanding, are socially and historically constructed categories and are "relatively stable types of utterances." However, they also help to "suggest the social relations between the speakers and their relation to outsiders; to indicate a set of values; to offer a set of perceptions; to outline a field of possible, likely, or desirable actions; to convey a vague or specific sense of time and space; to suggest an appropriate tone; to rule in or rule out various styles and languages of heteroglossia; and to negotiate a set of purposes" (Morson and Emerson, *Mikhail Bakhtin,* 293).

PART II

Relationships with Participants

SECTION I

Crossing Boundaries

We have already looked at readings that demonstrate themes and issues behind two data collection strategies of immersion, being there and being on the job. The sections in Part II feature readings that deal with two themes that relate to how ethnographers handle relationships with their participants. The first section focuses on the obstacles and challenges that ethnographers face when they try to gain entry, acceptance, and trust among the people they study, with reference to how their relationships enable and interfere with data collection and analysis. As several of this volume's pieces have already demonstrated, ethnographers regularly study people with different backgrounds from them. An important challenge for fieldworkers is to establish a degree of common ground with people in the field. Social distance could seriously impede communication between researchers and their participants as well as limit an ethnographer's ability to understand their participants' point of view. At the same time, close relationships could jeopardize a researcher's ability to objectively analyze a group. Ethnographers must always balance degrees of immersion and closeness with the detachment and critical distance that is necessary to analyze and explain the social phenomena under investigation. In other words, researchers conducting participant observation seek to understand others' interpretations of their own situation by getting close to them without getting so close that they glamorize them. The classic sociological dictum, "If men define situations as real, they are real in their consequences" (Thomas & Thomas 1928, 572) certainly applies to the experience of conducting ethnographic research. Socially constructed categories and meanings serve as both subjects of analysis as well as obstacles to forming relationships. These boundaries are defined and felt as real by ethnographers and participants alike. This makes overcoming and managing the social barriers that divide ethnographers from their participants, including race, ethnicity, social class, gender, sexual orientation, religion, or some combination of these or other salient characteristics, extremely important in ethnographic research.

Among the themes of establishing and managing relationships that ethnographers often discuss is the process of "getting in." At some point every participant observer must approach and ask a group's members, or a gatekeeper, if they can study them. For many researchers gaining entry means meeting a single person who introduces them to the rest of the group or to the setting. This person often serves as a guide or a main informant for ethnographers as they gradually learn about their social world. For Mitchell Duneier, from the previous section, this person was Hakim, the vendor whose sidewalk table had a copy of his first book on it. Along with balancing closeness and distance, as discussed above, a challenge for ethnographers in their relationships with main informants is not becoming dependent on them for access or information or excessively reliant on their perspective in their analyses. After Hakim read the book-length manuscript that Duneier wrote about him, he felt the analysis required the points of view from the other vendors to compose an accurate examination of life on the sidewalk. As they begin a research project and enter a setting, researchers should consider every participant to be an expert on their own lives and on the social group and not substitute generalized explanations about the group with the limited perspectives of key informants.

After getting in, ethnographers must achieve degrees of acceptance and trust among the people they study. Without these conditions researchers are at a tremendous disadvantage in terms of obtaining access to the lives of their participants, and therefore to learning how they interpret their situation. The barriers to this access, such as race, ethnicity, age, gender, and social class, threaten to weaken communication and understanding. Ethnographers experience conflicts along these social boundaries in the form of miscommunications, feelings of wariness, and even expressions of hostility from the people they study. They must carefully navigate the new social world so as not to offend anyone, to be understood as trustworthy, and to put themselves in an advantageous position to collect data. As the readings in this section demonstrate, there are various ways in which fieldworkers have crossed these boundaries and managed their relationships with people from different social backgrounds. Learning the codes and culture of the group, such as what topics to avoid in conversation and even when to speak and not to speak, is important for navigating and interacting with people in the field. Sometimes group members accept ethnographers for reasons that the latter did not consciously intend. Those fieldworkers who are successful in their relationships often learn from their interactions in the field how participants perceive them and why they accepted and trusted them.

Because of the extreme importance of crossing boundaries, fieldworkers regularly reflect on their experiences, miscues, and successes in striking this balance in their relationships and overcoming social barriers in methodological sections and appendixes, and this section features authors who have done so. The readings, however, do not come from these specialized methodological pieces. I briefly outline their discussions below, and leave it to readers to evaluate each author's social position vis-à-vis their participants on their own.

In this section I chose not to include examples of ethnographies on groups with whom their authors identify. "Insider research" has been a form of fieldwork since ethnography's inception in sociology (Anderson 1923; Baca Zinn 1979; Polsky 1967). These projects present their own methodological advantages for researchers, (such as getting in and gaining trust and acceptance with greater ease as a result of sharing a common identity and perhaps similar biographies) as well as obstacles, such as dealing with the pressures of speaking on behalf of a group. And fieldworkers may be insiders in some ways but not others, such as ethnographers who share a racial identity with their participants but are not in the same social class (see Smithsimon 2011, 29–32). I excluded such works here because crossing boundaries presents several issues and themes that are common to the fieldwork experience of both insider and outsider research. But readers will benefit from comparing the strategies and obstacles of authors who conduct insider research to those who conduct research on people who differ from them.

The first reading in this section is truly a classic in the field of urban ethnography. In fact, it is often considered the first major work of participant observation. First published in 1943, and expanded with an informative methodological appendix in 1955, William Foote Whyte's *Street Corner Society* examines life in the Italian immigrant slum of Boston's North End (or "Eastern City's" "Cornerville").[1] As we saw in this volume's Introduction, sociologists at the

Chicago School used the case study method, which included personal documents, life histories, mapping techniques, and statistical analyses, along with observational research in the field. While a student at Harvard, the upper-middle-class Whyte was heavily influenced by the immersive fieldwork of anthropologists. After hearing about the slum area and learning some of its statistics and stereotypes (e.g. a high crime rate, thriving racketeering and political corruption), he realized the actual lives and perspectives of the people themselves were left out:

> Those who are concerned with Cornerville seek through a general survey to answer questions that require the most intimate knowledge of local life. The only way to gain such knowledge is to live in Cornerville and participate in the activities of its people. One who does that finds that the district reveals itself to him in an entirely different light.
>
> (1943, xv–xvi)

Focusing on field notes of his own observations and experiences as a participant in the daily lives of Italians, Whyte set out to explain a working community that outsiders saw as a slum by understanding the insiders' point of view.

To do so Whyte had to overcome the ethnic and social class differences that separated him from the Italians in the North End. He fails several times to get in to the community because of his lack of local knowledge or understanding of the culture. Whyte finally meets and eventually befriends Doc, a young Italian man who becomes his main informant, through a settlement house. Doc runs the local Nortons street youth gang that hangs out on the corner, and Whyte learns how they are organized and the culture of the group. At first Doc vouches for Whyte to the members of the gang and gambling ring. While they all publicly accept this endorsement, privately they are curious about his intentions. They meet Whyte's academic explanation for his presence with silence. The people of Cornerville are content in thinking that he is merely writing a book about them, as vague an explanation as that is, and accept him based on how he handles his personal relationships. For instance, he learns the proper way to behave with women in the neighborhood, that arguing was important in conversations on the street corner (in contradiction to his training which taught him not to argue with participants), and when to ask and not ask certain types of questions. Over time Whyte learns that while the corner boys accept his presence, they continue to see him as different from them. He fell short in his attempt to completely immerse himself in the community. A particular incident demonstrates the limitations of crossing boundaries as a form of total immersion. One day Whyte uses an amount of obscenities and profanity that is uncharacteristic of him (1943, 304). He surprises the working-class Italians, who prefer him to act the way he normally acts, which is different from them. In this episode Whyte learns the importance of crossing boundaries to the point of acceptance, the shortcomings of doing so to the point of trying to completely blend in, and the difficulties of total immersion.

In this piece Whyte examines the importance of bowling in the Nortons' competition with the college boys and other gangs and in the determination of the group's social hierarchy. Whyte discovers that a member's social standing in the gang has a strong relationship with their bowling score, such as when those with low status were not allowed to play on Saturday nights despite their strong bowling ability. The corner boys use bowling to put and keep people in what they determine is their appropriate social position. When Whyte unexpectedly wins a competition between the members, he learns that they consider it a concession that they allow him to have, since he is not an official member of the gang. Unlike Grazian's saxophone playing, from the second section in Part I, Whyte's performance is not a form of socialization, but an event that highlights the group's social structure and the salience of social boundaries. Through detailed accounts and careful participant observation that hinges on the relationships that he created, Whyte reveals how the group reproduces their social ranking system through a seemingly insignificant activity.

Whyte was influenced by the work of anthropologists, but Elliot Liebow was a trained anthropologist who decided for his second major work to immerse himself in an impoverished African-American neighborhood in Washington, D.C. His classic *Tally's Corner* also focuses on the lives of streetcorner men in the 1960s. But Liebow's mission was not just to examine the social structure of this inner-city community. He wished to explore their lives to critique the culture of poverty thesis—or the notion that African-American families passed down poverty from generation to generation (1967, 5)—that had become popular in the 1960s. Through repeated site visits to the corner "Carry-out" and a key chance encounter with a man named Tally Jackson, Liebow gained the acceptance of most people in the area. Although he mentions a few residents who never seem to trust or like him, they recognize that he became so entrenched that they could not question his presence. In this sense it is not always necessary for ethnographers to achieve universal approval or establish closeness with everyone in the setting to get in and develop successful relationships. Liebow says that despite the close relationships he formed in the field, differences in terms of race as well as "occupation, education, residence, and speech" (1967, 252) "irrevocably and absolutely relegated me to the status of outsider" (1967, 248). In the book's reflective methodological appendix he uses the metaphor of a "chain-link fence" to describe his level of immersion and relationships with the men:

> despite the barriers we were able to look at each other, walk alongside each other, talk and occasionally touch fingers. When two people stand up close to the fence on either side, without touching it, they can look through the interstices and forget that they are looking through a fence.
>
> (1967, 250–251)

Still, Liebow maintains that the barriers were very real. He also speculates that being a white outsider meant that he was not a competitor to the African-American men in terms of employment or personal relationships, and was thus someone they could speak to honestly. This imagery of the chain-link fence serves as a powerful symbol of the limits of immersion in the field for ethnographers, and calls into question the extent to which urban ethnographers are accepted and trusted by their participants.

Liebow covers several topics of daily life, such as intimate relationships, fatherhood, and peer groups. In this piece he focuses on jobs, particularly the struggles the men go through to find and hold well-paying, steady employment. Liebow starts the chapter with a field note of a simple episode he probably observed on a regular basis: a pickup truck drives down the street, with the driver looking for day laborers, passing dozens of men hanging out on the street corners. Liebow assumes that the driver, who only gets a few men for the job, thinks of the men as lazy, because of what he has heard about this population of poor blacks and based on his own experience. Regardless of the driver's actual thoughts, the attitude that the poor and unemployed are incorrigibly lazy is not uncommon, and Liebow uses the episode to launch into an analysis of the varied work patterns and attitudes toward work that the men hold. He finds that the men view the mostly menial jobs that are available to them in the same manner as members of the middle class do: as low-paying, low-status, and difficult for gaining respect let alone making a living. As this piece demonstrates, Liebow's conversations with the men have a friendly tone, and his relationship with them reached the point where friends and the courts accept him as a spokesman for one of the men when he is arrested for violating his probation for a prior incident. However, they never stop understanding him as an outsider.

The next piece is also by an anthropologist and serves as a companion work in poverty research to Liebow's. In the late 1960s Carol Stack, who is white, moved with her young son into "The Flats," a poor black ghetto in a city in the Midwest. She intended to study families who had migrated from the rural south to the urban north in the mid-twentieth century. Stack soon discovered an extensive kinship network for the exchange of goods and services that people in The Flats used to survive. In her book, *All Our Kin*, she explores these "strategies for coping with poverty" (1974, 9) by living in The Flats, getting in with two families, and becoming a part of their kin networks. Stack learns from her participants of the salience of race as a social boundary, and discusses how she managed to overcome it. She recalls their reaction to a time when she helped one of the families fold newspapers for one of their son's paper route:

> Magnolia later told me that she had been surprised that I sat with them that first day to fold papers, and then came back to help again. "White folks," she told me, "don't have time, they's always in a rush, and they don't sit on black folk's furniture, at least no Whites that comes into The Flats."
>
> (1974, 10)

By embedding herself in the neighborhood and the kin network, Stack overcomes a very real social boundary between her and the black families.

But Stack also uses another of her social identities to overcome this salient social boundary, namely her identity as a young mother of a young child. In this piece Stack introduces her main informant, Ruby Banks, a young black woman with children. The family warns Stack that her "whiteness" may cause hostility in Ruby. The relationship is chilly when this white academic and black single mother first meet, with Ruby offering unsolicited critiques on how Stack is raising her son. But over time they form a strong friendship, based partly on their children and mutual interest in what they consider the other's peculiar tastes and attitudes toward life. They turn their racial and class differences and the conflicting ways in which their various social identities intersect into jokes that strengthen their relationship. While Stack immerses herself in the daily activities and exchanges of the kin network, she does not try to completely overcome the differences between her and her participants, as evidenced by her relationship with Ruby. Stack constantly reflects on her different attitudes from Ruby toward such matters as child-rearing and furniture and uses them to understand the perspectives of people in The Flats and the importance of kin in their daily lives.

As the works in this section already make evident, ethnographers often reflect in particular on their relationships with their participants and in general on the nature of researcher–participant interaction. Ethnography's overall mission is to generalize from the lives of the people they study and provide explanations for their perspectives and behaviors. But in this section's next piece Sudhir Venkatesh aims an analytical lens on ethnographers, who they are to their participants, and how such a reflective undertaking can illuminate the structures of meaning they reproduce. In the 1990s Venkatesh, who is of Indian descent, studied an African-American public housing project in Chicago. In his resulting book (2000) he focuses on the strategies that tenants use to meet their basic needs despite neglectful state practices, widespread unemployment, and the presence of street gangs, while also accounting for the attitudes of these street gang members. He learns that hustling, or various activities in the informal economy, is not just a way to make ends meet, but a set of practices that allow tenants to craft an identity and a meaningful existence.

In this article Venkatesh reflects not on how he understands his relationship with the people of the Robert Taylor Homes, but on how they understand him as an ethnographer among them. He "reconstruct[s] the informants' point of view" (2002, 92) toward his role in the field to highlight how "doin' the hustle" is a "dominant organizing principle" (2002, 93) in the housing project, even in the way in which tenants view his role. Venkatesh learns that the tenants understood his research as his way of getting what he needed to make ends meet, or running his own hustle just like them. They interpreted his practices in a manner that was consistent with how he came to understand theirs, which created a relationship that was mutually beneficial and reinforced his data analysis. To them, urban ethnography is a hustle, and Venkatesh, in a reflective section, somewhat agrees. However, this realization leads him to gradually reduce his fieldwork, which compromises their interpretation of his role. As this piece shows, reflecting on how their participants understand them provides ethnographers with a validity test for their own data at the same time as it helps them manage their relationships in the field.

Saloons were important field sites for urban ethnographers since even before Park's arrival at the University of Chicago (Mattson 2007), and we have thus far seen two examples of urban ethnographies that focus at least partly on behavior in nightlife establishments. This final example is a work that exclusively examines bar behavior. Sherri Cavan studied under the esteemed ethnographer and theorist Erving Goffman at the University of California, Berkeley. Goffman was a student of the "Second Chicago School" (Fine 1995) whose members examined and disseminated the theories of symbolic interactionism and practiced fieldwork methods throughout the country (Wynn 2011). Working in this tradition, Cavan examines the social order of the unserious setting of the public drinking establishment. In the early 1960s she studied nearly 100 bars in San Francisco. She went to the restroom to jot down notes like many researchers in bars. In a manner reminiscent of the first Chicago School, she also shows the distribution of bars in the city through an ecological analysis and a map (1966, 24–30).

Most relevant for this section is that Cavan often had to overcome and manage the social boundary of gender in the traditional male setting to play the role of bar patron. In fact, Cavan goes to bars from which women are either categorically excluded or at which are scarce without male accompaniment. To overcome this boundary Cavan relies on a male companion to gain access. Gender plays a key role in her analysis, such as when she discusses bar rituals and spatial organization. Cavan set out to strike up conversations with patrons and talk with them about their behaviors and thoughts on the bar. As a woman, however, she is susceptible to having men approach her first. For Cavan it became important to take control of the situation and assert her role as a participant observer to gather as much information from the interaction as possible. She also uses her gender in particular to examine the behavior of men toward women and test the tools of interaction that women have at their disposal for initiating or ending an encounter with a man in bars. Cavan describes "pickups," or sexually-oriented encounters, as social games with their own interaction rituals (also see Grazian 2008). Through observation and practice she learns how women use various strategies to declare their willingness to begin and their desire to end encounters, such as their spatial location and positioning within the bar.

Cavan creates a non-mutually exclusive typology of four bars based on the ways in which she discovered patrons use them. The type featured in this piece is the "marketplace bar," or places where services (chiefly sex, but also gambling) and goods (drugs, stolen merchandise) are exchanged. She focuses on the "B-girl," or a girl who is paid by the bar to act as a patron, flirt with men, and get them to spend money. Through several examples Cavan shows how patrons, B-girls, and other employees define the situation of the cross-sex encounter, and of those instances when a new definition is introduced. Overall, Cavan succeeds in examining bar behavior by offering an example of setting-based ethnographic research. She also demonstrates the importance of managing the social boundary of gender in the data collection process.

This section's final piece features several unique methodological strategies. In the mid-2000s sociologist Javier Auyero teamed up with Debora Swistun to study the people who live in Flammable, a shantytown surrounded by a petrochemical compound, a landfill, a hazardous waste incinerator, and a polluted river, in Buenos Aires. Auyero and Swistun seek to discover the meanings residents attach to their poisoned environment, and understand the relationship between their attitudes and their apparent collective inaction to improve their surrounding conditions. They roughly divide the research duties of this team ethnography in half. Since Swistun grew up in Flammable, she focuses on her neighbors, while Auyero interviews local officials, company personnel (the major corporate actor is the Shell oil company), activists, and lawyers. The people of Flammable tell heartrending stories of health problems and physical and psychological pain and suffering, with Swistun even realizing during the research that her own health concerns likely resulted from her exposure to the shantytown's hazards. Because of its high levels of toxicity Flammable is a destination for journalists, scientists, and doctors who wish to study it (and who wish to not spend much time there doing so). Sensitive to residents' extreme health problems, the stigma of illness they carry, and the effects of other visiting researchers who are only interested in them as test subjects, Auyero and Swistun make sure to foster relationships with Flammable's vulnerable residents and not misrepresent or distance themselves from them. Theirs is a most fragile community that requires plenty of care.

Auyero and Swistun use a broad array of data collection strategies to understand the lived experiences of the people of Flammable. When they learn that children and families are an important part of the shantytown, they realize the potential data collection problems they may confront vis-à-vis social boundaries. How can they, as adults, experience Flammable's situation from the perspective of children? What problems with communication will they have? To overcome these gaps in this piece, Auyero and Swistun use a popular qualitative method in visual sociology (Becker 1974; Harper 1987). They give a group of school children disposable cameras with a simple task: photograph things in their neighborhood that they like and things that they do not like. Auyero and Swistun then sit with them and their photographs and ask them to describe what they depict. They learn that the children take very few pictures of "good" places, and even their descriptions of them are negative. The places they do not like dominate the photos, and it becomes clear that hazardous conditions are the frame for their everyday reality. This strategy does not just provide them with vivid data on what everyday life in Flammable is like for its children, but it also bridges the age gap between adult researcher and child participant. Through photography Auyero and Swistun learn how Flammable's children define their environment and interpret their situation. Their results are an insightful but painful introduction to a threatening urban world.

Urban ethnographers are often most interested in populations that are misrepresented and misunderstood, either because of prevailing stereotypes or lack of accurate knowledge about them. But fieldworkers must also be careful about not misrepresenting their subjects, particularly in those cases when the social distance between them is substantial. Crossing social boundaries is a way to understand how field researchers attempt to bridge the distance that exists in the field and foster communication and relationships. As we will see in the next and final section in this volume, establishing and maintaining relationships contains an additional dimension of navigating the multiple standards of ethics.

NOTE

1. The North End was not far from Boston's West End, the Italian neighborhood that Gans conducted research in twenty years later.

REFERENCES

Anderson, N. 1923. *The Hobo: The Sociology of the Homeless Man.* Chicago: University of Chicago Press.

Baca Zinn, M. 1979. "Field Research in Minority Communities: Ethical, Methodological, and Political Observations by an Insider," *Social Problems,* 27: 209–219.

Becker, H.S. 1974. "Photography and Sociology," *Studies in the Anthropology of Visual Communication,* 1, 1: 3–26.

Cavan, S. 1966. "The Marketplace Bar," *Liquor License: An Ethnography of Bar Behavior.* Chicago: Aldine Publishing Company: 171–177; 193–200.

Fine, G.A. 1995. *A Second Chicago School? The Development of a Postwar American Sociology.* Chicago: University of Chicago Press.

Grazian, D. 2008. *On the Make: The Hustle of Urban Nightlife.* Chicago: University of Chicago Press.

Harper, D. 1987. "The Visual Ethnographic Narrative," *Visual Anthropology,* 1, 1: 1–19.

Liebow, E. 1967. "Men and Jobs," *Tally's Corner: A Study of Negro Streetcorner Men.* Boston: Little, Brown, and Company: 61–71.

Mattson, G. 2007. "Urban Ethnography's 'Saloon Problem' and its Challenge to Public Sociology," *City & Community,* 6, 2: 75–94.

Polsky, N. 1967. *Hustlers, Beats, and Others.* Chicago: Aldine Publishing Co.

Smithsimon, G. 2011. *September 12: Community and Neighborhood Recovery at Ground Zero.* New York: New York University Press.

Stack, C. 1974. "The Flats," and "Swapping: What Goes Around Comes Around," *All Our Kin.* New York: Basic Books: 11–16; 32–43.

Thomas, W.I., & Thomas, D.S. 1928. *The Child in America: Behavior Problems and Programs.* New York: Knopf.

Venkatesh, S.A. 2000. *American Project: The Rise and Fall of a Modern Ghetto.* Cambridge, MA: Harvard University Press.

Venkatesh, S. 2002. "'Doin' the Hustle': Constructing the Ethnographer in the American Ghetto," *Ethnography,* 3, 1: 91–92; 96–103.

Whyte, W.F. 1943. "Doc and His Boys," *Street Corner Society: The Social Structure of an Italian Slum.* Chicago: University of Chicago Press: 14–25.

Wynn, J.R. 2011. "From Hobo to Doormen: The Characters of Qualitative Analysis, Past and Present," *Ethnography,* 12, 4: 518–542.

CHAPTER 12

Doc and His Boys

William Foote Whyte

BOWLING AND SOCIAL RANKING

One evening in October, 1937, Doc scheduled a bowling match against the Italian Community Club, which was composed largely of college men who held their meetings every two weeks in the Norton Street Settlement House. The club was designed to be an organization of well-educated and superior men, although Doc was a member, and Angelo, Lou, and Fred of the Nortons had been voted in upon his recommendation. The other Nortons felt that the club was "high-toned," and around the corner it was known as the "Boys' Junior League." They were a little flattered that members of their group could mix with such a club, but their opinion was formed largely from the personalities of Chick Morelli, the president, and Tony Cardio, another prominent member, both of whom they considered snobbish and conceited. Consequently, the Nortons took this match very seriously.

Doc was captain of the Nortons. He selected Long John, Frank, Joe, and Tommy for his team. Danny and Mike were not bowling in this period. Chick and Tony led the Community Club team.

Feeling ran high. The Nortons shouted at the club bowlers and made all sorts of noises to upset their concentration. The club members were in high spirits when they gained an early lead but had little to say as the Nortons pulled ahead to win by a wide margin.

After the match I asked Frank and Joe if there was any team that they would have been more eager to beat. They said that if they could pick out their favorite victims, they would choose Chick Morelli, Tony Cardio, Joe Cardio (Tony's brother), Mario Testa, and Hector Marto. These last three had all belonged to the Sunset Dramatic Club.

Frank and Joe said that they had nothing against the other three men on the Community Club team but that the boys had been anxious to beat that team in order to put Chick and Tony "in their places." Significantly, Frank and Joe did not select their favorite victims on the basis of bowling ability. The five were good bowlers, but that was not the deciding factor in the choice. It was their social positions and ambitions that were the objects of attack, and it was that which made victory over the Community Club so satisfying.

Lou Danaro and Fred Mackey had cheered for the club. Although they were club members, the boys felt that this did not excuse them. Danny said: "You're a couple of traitors—Benedict Arnolds. . . . You're with the boys—and then you go against them. . . . Go on, I don't want your support."

Fred and Lou fell between the two groups and therefore had to face this problem of divided allegiance. Doc's position on the corner was so definitely established that no one even considered the possibility of his choosing to bowl for the Community Club against the Nortons.

This was the only match between the two

teams that ever took place. The corner boys were satisfied with their victory, and the club did not seek a return match. Tony Cardio objected to the way in which the Nortons had tried to upset the concentration of his team and said it was no fun to bowl against such poor sports. There were, however, clashes with individual members of the club. One night in November, Doc, Frank Bonelli, Joe Dodge, and I were bowling when Chick Morelli and Lou Danaro came in together. We agreed to have two three-man teams, and Chick and Doc chose sides. Chick chose Lou and me. The match was fairly even at first, but Doc put his team far ahead with a brilliant third string. Toward the end of this string, Chick was sitting next to Joe Dodge and mumbling at him, "You're a lousy bum. . . . You're a no-good bowler."

Joe said nothing until Chick had repeated his remarks several times. Then Joe got up and fired back at Chick, "You're a conceited—! I feel like taking a wallop at you. I never knew anybody was as conceited as you. . . . You're a conceited—!"

Doc stood between them to prevent a fight. Chick said nothing, and Doc managed to get the six of us quietly into the elevator. Joe was not satisfied, and he said to me in a loud voice: "Somebody is going to straighten him out some day. Somebody will have to wallop him to knock some of that conceit out of him."

When we were outside the building, Lou walked away with Chick, and the rest of us went into Jennings' Cafeteria for "coffee-ands." We discussed Chick:

Doc: It's lucky you didn't hit him. They'd be after you for manslaughter. You're too strong for the kid.

Joe: All right. But when somebody's too tough for me, I don't fool around. . . . He shouldn't fool around me. . . . If he's gonna say them things, he should smile when he says them. But I think he really meant it.

Doc: The poor guy, so many fellows want to wallop him—and he knows it.

Frank: I liked him all right until the other night. We went to the Metropolitan Ballroom. . . . He didn't mingle in at all. He just lay down on a couch like he wanted to be petted. He wasn't sociable at all.

After driving Chick home, Lou joined us in Jennings'. He said that Chick felt very bad about the incident and didn't know what it was that made people want to hit him. Lou added: "I know he didn't mean it that way. He's really a swell kid when you get to know him. There's only one thing I don't like about him." Then he told about a time when Chick had started an argument with a dance-hall attendant on some technicality involved in the regulations of the hall. Lou commented: "He was just trying to show how intelligent he was."

A few days later, when Joe's anger had subsided, Doc persuaded him to apologize.

Doc did not defend Chick for friendship's sake. Nor was it because they worked together in the Community Club. In the club Doc led a faction generally hostile to Chick, and he himself was often critical of the manner in which Chick sought to run the organization. But Doc had friends in both groups. He did not like to see the groups at odds with each other. Though friendship between the Nortons and Chick was impossible, it was Doc's function to see that diplomatic relations were maintained.

The Community Club match served to arouse enthusiasm for bowling among the Nortons. Previously the boys had bowled sporadically and often in other groups, but now for the first time bowling became a regular part of their social routine. Long John, Alec, Joe Dodge, and Frank Bonelli bowled several nights a week throughout the winter. Others bowled on frequent occasions, and all the bowlers appeared at the alleys at least one night a week.

A high score at candlepins requires several spares or strikes. Since a strike rarely occurs except when the first ball hits the kingpin properly within a fraction of an inch, and none of the boys had such precise aim, strikes were considered matters of luck, although a good bowler was expected to score them more often than a poor one. A bowler was judged according to his ability to get spares, to "pick" the pins that remained on the alley after his first ball.

There are many mental hazards connected with bowling. In any sport there are critical moments when a player needs the steadiest nerves if he is to "come through"; but, in those that involve team play and fairly continuous action, the player can sometimes lose himself in the heat of the contest and get by the critical points before he has a chance to "tighten up." If he is competing on a five-man team, the bowler must wait a long time for his turn at the alleys, and he has plenty of time to brood over his mistakes. When a man is facing ten pins, he can throw the ball quite casually. But when only one pin remains standing, and his opponents are shouting, "He can't pick it," the pressure is on, and there is a tendency to "tighten up" and lose control.

When a bowler is confident that he can make a difficult shot, the chances are that he will make it or come exceedingly close. When he is not confident, he will miss. A bowler is confident because he has made similar shots in the past and is accustomed to making good scores. But that is not all. He is also confident because his fellows, whether for him or against him, believe that he can make the shot. If they do not believe in him, the bowler has their adverse opinion as well as his own uncertainty to fight against. When that is said, it becomes necessary to consider a man's relation to his fellows in examining his bowling record.

In the winter and spring of 1937–38 bowling was the most significant social activity for the Nortons. Saturday night's intraclique and individual matches became the climax of the week's events. During the week the boys discussed what had happened the previous Saturday night and what would happen on the coming Saturday night. A man's performance was subject to continual evaluation and criticism. There was, therefore, a close connection between a man's bowling and his position in the group.

The team used against the Community Club had consisted of two men (Doc and Long John) who ranked high and three men (Joe Dodge, Frank Bonelli, and Tommy) who had a low standing. When bowling became a fixed group activity, the Nortons' team evolved along different lines. Danny joined the Saturday-night crowd and rapidly made a place for himself. He performed very well and picked Doc as his favorite opponent. There was a good-natured rivalry between them. In individual competition Danny usually won, although his average in the group matches was no better than that of Doc's. After the Community Club match, when Doc selected a team to represent the Nortons against other corner gangs and clubs, he chose Danny, Long John, and himself, leaving two vacancies on the five-man team. At this time, Mike, who had never been a good bowler, was just beginning to bowl regularly and had not established his reputation. Significantly enough, the vacancies were not filled from the ranks of the clique. On Saturday nights the boys had been bowling with Chris Teludo, Nutsy's older cousin, and Mark Ciampa, a man who associated with them only at the bowling alleys. Both men were popular and were first-class bowlers. They were chosen by Doc, with the agreement of Danny and Long John, to bowl for the Nortons. It was only when a member of the regular team was absent that one of the followers in the clique was called in, and on such occasions he never distinguished himself.

The followers were not content with being substitutes. They claimed that they had not been given an opportunity to prove their ability. One Saturday night in February, 1938, Mike organized an intraclique match. His team was made up of Chris Teludo, Doc,

Long John, himself, and me. Danny was sick at the time, and I was put in to substitute for him. Frank, Alec, Joe, Lou, and Tommy made up the other team. Interest in this match was more intense than in the ordinary "choose-up" matches, but the followers bowled poorly and never had a chance.

After this one encounter the followers were recognized as the second team and never again challenged the team of Doc, Danny, Long John, Mark, and Chris. Instead, they took to individual efforts to better their positions.

On his athletic ability alone, Frank should have been an excellent bowler. His ball-playing had won him positions on semiprofessional teams and a promise—though unfulfilled—of a job on a minor-league team. And it was not lack of practice that held him back, for, along with Alec and Joe Dodge, he bowled more frequently than Doc, Danny, or Mike. During the winter of 1937–38 Frank occupied a particularly subordinate position in the group. He spent his time with Alec in the pastry shop owned by Alec's uncle, and, since he had little employment throughout the winter, he became dependent upon Alec for a large part of the expenses of his participation in group activities. Frank fell to the bottom of the group. His financial dependence preyed upon his mind. While he sometimes bowled well, he was never a serious threat to break into the first team.

Some events of June, 1937, cast additional light upon Frank's position. Mike organized a baseball team of some of the Nortons to play against a younger group of Norton Street corner boys. On the basis of his record, Frank was considered the best player on either team, yet he made a miserable showing. He said to me: "I can't seem to play ball when I'm playing with fellows I know, like that bunch. I do much better when I'm playing for the Stanley A.C. against some team in Dexter, Westland, or out of town." Accustomed to filling an inferior position, Frank was unable to star even in his favorite sport when he was competing against members of his own group.

One evening I heard Alec boasting to Long John that the way he was bowling he could take on every man on the first team and lick them all. Long John dismissed the challenge with these words: "You think you could beat us, but, under pressure, you die!"

Alec objected vehemently, yet he recognized the prevailing group opinion of his bowling. He made the highest single score of the season, and he frequently excelled during the week when he bowled with Frank, Long John, Joe Dodge, and me, but on Saturday nights, when the group was all assembled, his performance was quite different. Shortly after this conversation Alec had several chances to prove himself, but each time it was "an off night," and he failed.

Carl, Joe, Lou, and Fred were never good enough to gain any recognition. Tommy was recognized as a first-class bowler, but he did most of his bowling with a younger group.

One of the best guides to the bowling standing of the members was furnished by a match held toward the end of April, 1938. Doc had an idea that we should climax the season with an individual competition among the members of the clique. He persuaded the owner of the alleys to contribute ten dollars in prize money to be divided among the three highest scorers. It was decided that only those who had bowled regularly should be eligible, and on this basis Lou, Fred, and Tommy were eliminated.

Interest in this contest ran high. The probable performances of the various bowlers were widely discussed. Doc, Danny, and Long John each listed his predictions. They were unanimous in conceding the first five places to themselves, Mark Ciampa, and Chris Teludo, although they differed in predicting the order among the first five. The next two positions were generally conceded to Mike and to me. All the ratings gave Joe Dodge last position, and Alec, Frank, and Carl were ranked close to the bottom.

The followers made no such lists, but Alec let it be known that he intended to show the boys something. Joe Dodge was annoyed to discover that he was the unanimous choice to finish last and argued that he was going to win.

When Chris Teludo did not appear for the match, the field was narrowed to ten. After the first four boxes, Alec was leading by several pins. He turned to Doc and said, "I'm out to get you boys tonight." But then he began to miss, and, as mistake followed mistake, he stopped trying. Between turns, he went out for drinks, so that he became flushed and unsteady on his feet. He threw the ball carelessly, pretending that he was not interested in the competition. His collapse was sudden and complete; in the space of a few boxes he dropped from first to last place.

The bowlers finished in the following order:

1. Whyte
2. Danny
3. Doc
4. Long John
5. Mike
6. Joe
7. Mark
8. Carl
9. Frank
10. Alec

There were only two upsets in the contest, according to the predictions made by Doc, Danny, and Long John: Mark bowled very poorly and I won. However, it is important to note that neither Mark nor I fitted neatly into either part of the clique. Mark associated with the boys only at the bowling alleys and had no recognized status in the group. Although I was on good terms with all the boys, I was closer to the leaders than to the followers, since Doc was my particular friend. If Mark and I are left out of consideration, the performances were almost exactly what the leaders expected and the followers feared

they would be. Danny, Doc, Long John, and Mike were bunched together at the top. Joe Dodge did better than was expected of him, but even he could not break through the solid ranks of the leadership.

Several days later Doc and Long John discussed the match with me.

Long John: I only wanted to be sure that Alec or Joe Dodge didn't win. That wouldn't have been right.

Doc: That's right. We didn't want to make it tough for you, because we all liked you, and the other fellows did too. If somebody had tried to make it tough for you, we would have protected you. . . . If Joe Dodge or Alec had been out in front, it would have been different. We would have talked them out of it. We would have made plenty of noise. We would have been really vicious. . . .

I asked Doc what would have happened if Alec or Joe had won.

They wouldn't have known how to take it. That's why we were out to beat them. If they had won, there would have been a lot of noise. Plenty of arguments. We would have called it lucky—things like that. We would have tried to get them in another match and then ruin them. We would have to put them in their places.

Every corner boy expects to be heckled as he bowls, but the heckling can take various forms. While I had moved ahead as early as the end of the second string, I was subjected only to good-natured kidding. The leaders watched me with mingled surprise and amusement; in a very real sense, I was permitted to win.

Even so, my victory required certain adjustments. I was hailed jocularly as "the Champ" or even as "the Cheese Champ" Rather than accept this designation, I pressed my claim for recognition. Doc arranged to have me bowl a match against Long John.

If I won, I should have the right to challenge Doc or Danny. The four of us went to the alleys together. Urged on by Doc and Danny, Long John won a decisive victory. I made no further challenges.

Alec was only temporarily crushed by his defeat. For a few days he was not seen on the corner, but then he returned and sought to re-establish himself. When the boys went bowling, he challenged Long John to an individual match and defeated him. Alec began to talk once more. Again he challenged Long John to a match, and again he defeated him. When bowling was resumed in the fall, Long John became Alec's favorite opponent, and for some time Alec nearly always came out ahead. He gloated. Long John explained: "He seems to have the Indian sign on me." And that is the way these incidents were interpreted by others—simply as a queer quirk of the game.

It is significant that, in making his challenge, Alec selected Long John instead of Doc, Danny, or Mike. It was not that Long John's bowling ability was uncertain. His average was about the same as that of Doc or Danny and better than that of Mike. As a member of the top group but not a leader in his own right, it was his social position that was vulnerable.

When Long John and Alec acted outside the group situation, it became possible for Alec to win. Long John was still considered the dependable man in a team match, and that was more important in relation to a man's standing in the group. Nevertheless, the leaders felt that Alec should not be defeating Long John and tried to reverse the situation. As Doc told me:

Alec isn't so aggressive these days. I steamed up at the way he was going after Long John, and I blasted him. . . . Then I talked to Long John. John is an introvert. He broods over things, and sometimes he feels inferior. He can't be aggressive like Alec, and when Alec tells him how he can always beat him, Long John gets to think that Alec is the better bowler. . . . I talked to him. I made him see that he should bowl better than Alec. I persuaded him that he was really the better bowler. . . . Now you watch them the next time out. I'll bet Long John will ruin him.

The next time Long John did defeat Alec. He was not able to do it every time, but they became so evenly matched that Alec lost interest in such competition.

The records of the season 1937–38 show a very close correspondence between social position and bowling performance. This developed because bowling became the primary social activity of the group. It became the main vehicle whereby the individual could maintain, gain, or lose prestige.

Bowling scores did not fall automatically into this pattern. There were certain customary ways of behaving which exerted pressure upon the individuals. Chief among these were the manner of choosing sides and the verbal attacks the members directed against one another.

Generally, two men chose sides in order to divide the group into two five-man teams. The choosers were often, but not always, among the best bowlers. If they were evenly matched, two poor bowlers frequently did the choosing, but in all cases the process was essentially the same. Each one tried to select the best bowler among those who were still unchosen. When more than ten men were present, choice was limited to the first ten to arrive, so that even a poor bowler would be chosen if he came early. It was the order of choice which was important. Sides were chosen several times each Saturday night, and in this way a man was constantly reminded of the value placed upon his ability by his fellows and of the sort of performance expected of him.

Of course, personal preferences entered into the selection of bowlers, but if a man chose a team of poor bowlers just because they were his closest friends, he pleased no one, least of all his team mates. It was the custom among the Nortons to have the losing team pay for the string bowled by the winners. As a rule, this small stake did not play an important role in the bowling, but no one liked to pay without the compensating enjoyment of a closely contested string. For this reason the selections by good bowlers or by poor bowlers coincided very closely. It became generally understood which men should be among the first chosen in order to make for an interesting match.

When Doc, Danny, Long John, or Mike bowled on opposing sides, they kidded one another good-naturedly. Good scores were expected of them, and bad scores were accounted for by bad luck or temporary lapses of form. When a follower threatened to better his position, the remarks took quite a different form. The boys shouted at him that he was lucky, that he was "bowling over his head." The effort was made to persuade him that he should not be bowling as well as he was, that a good performance was abnormal for him. This type of verbal attack was very important in keeping the members "in their places." It was used particularly by the followers so that, in effect, they were trying to keep one another down. While Long John, one of the most frequent targets for such attacks, responded in kind, Doc, Danny, and Mike seldom used this weapon. However, the leaders would have met a real threat on the part of Alec or Joe by such psychological pressures.

The origination of group action is another factor in the situation. The Community Club match really inaugurated bowling as a group activity, and that match was arranged by Doc. Group activities are originated by the men with highest standing in the group, and it is natural for a man to encourage an activity in which he excels and discourage one in which he does not excel. However, this cannot explain Mike's performance, for he had never bowled well before Saturday night at the alleys became a fixture for the Nortons.

The standing of the men in the eyes of other groups also contributed toward maintaining social differentiation within the group. In the season of 1938–39 Doc began keeping the scores of each man every Saturday night so that the Nortons' team could be selected strictly according to the averages of the bowlers, and there could be no accusation of favoritism. One afternoon when we were talking about bowling performances, I asked Doc and Danny what would happen if five members of the second team should make better averages than the first team bowlers. Would they then become the first team? Danny said:

> Suppose they did beat us, and the San Marcos would come up and want a match with us. We'd tell them, those fellows are really the first team, but the San Marcos would say, "We don't want to bowl them, we want to bowl you." We would say, "All right, you want to bowl Doc's team?" and we would bowl them.

Doc added:

> I want you to understand, Bill, we're conducting this according to democratic principles. It's the others who won't let us be democratic.

CHAPTER 13

Men and Jobs

Elliot Liebow

The man sees middle-class occupations as a primary source of prestige, pride and self-respect; his own job affords him none of these. To think about his job is to see himself as others see him, to remind him of just where he stands in this society.[1] And because society's criteria for placement are generally the same as his own, to talk about his job can trigger a flush of shame and a deep, almost physical ache to change places with someone, almost anyone, else.[2] The desire to be a person in his own right, to be noticed by the world he lives in, is shared by each of the men on the streetcorner. Whether they articulate this desire (as Tally does below) or not, one can see them position themselves to catch the attention of their fellows in much the same way that plants bend or stretch to catch the sunlight.[3]

Tally and I were in the Carry-out. It was summer, Tally's peak earning season as a cement finisher, a semiskilled job a cut or so above that of the unskilled laborer. His take-home pay during these weeks was well over a hundred dollars—"a lot of bread." But for Tally, who no longer had a family to support, bread was not enough.

"You know that boy came in last night? That Black Moozlem? That's what I ought to be doing. I ought to be in his place."

"What do you mean?"

"Dressed nice, going to [night] school, got a good job."

"He's no better off than you, Tally. You make more than he does."

"It's not the money. [Pause] It's position, I guess. He's got position. When he finish school he gonna be a supervisor. People respect him. . . . Thinking about people with position and education gives me a feeling right here [pressing his fingers into the pit of his stomach]."

"You're educated, too. You have a skill, a trade. You're a cement finisher. You can make a building, pour a sidewalk."

"That's different. Look, can anybody do what you're doing? Can anybody just come up and do your job? Well, in one week I can teach you cement finishing. You won't be as good as me 'cause you won't have the experience but you'll be a cement finisher. That's what I mean. Anybody can do what I'm doing and that's what gives me this feeling. [Long pause] Suppose I like this girl. I go over to her house and I meet her father. He starts talking about what he done today. He talks about operating on somebody and sewing them up and about surgery. I know he's a doctor 'cause of the way he talks. Then she starts talking about what she did. Maybe she's a boss or a supervisor. Maybe she's a lawyer and her father says to me, 'And what do you do, Mr. Jackson?' [Pause] You remember at the courthouse, Lonny's trial? You and the lawyer was talking in the hall? You remember? I just stood there listening. I didn't say a word. You know why? 'Cause I didn't even know what you was talking about. That's happened to me a lot."

"Hell, you're nothing special. That happens to everybody. Nobody knows everything. One man is a doctor, so he talks about surgery. Another man is a teacher, so he talks about books. But doctors and teachers don't know anything about concrete. You're a cement finisher and that's your specialty."

"Maybe so, but when was the last time you saw anybody standing around talking about concrete?"

The streetcorner man wants to be a person in his own right, to be noticed, to be taken account of, but in this respect, as well as in meeting his money needs, his job fails him. The job and the man are even. The job fails the man and the man fails the job.

Furthermore, the man does not have any reasonable expectation that, however bad it is, his job will lead to better things. Menial jobs are not, by and large, the starting point of a track system which leads to even better jobs for those who are able and willing to do them. The busboy or dishwasher in a restaurant is not on a job track which, if negotiated skillfully, leads to chef or manager of the restaurant. The busboy or dishwasher who works hard becomes, simply, a hard-working busboy or dishwasher. Neither hard work nor perseverance can conceivably carry the janitor to a sit-down job in the office building he cleans up. And it is the apprentice who becomes the journeyman electrician, plumber, steam fitter or bricklayer, not the common unskilled Negro laborer.

Thus, the job is not a stepping stone to something better. It is a dead end. It promises to deliver no more tomorrow, next month or next year than it does today.

Delivering little, and promising no more, the job is "no big thing." The man appears to treat the job in a cavalier fashion, working and not working as the spirit moves him, as if all that matters is the immediate satisfaction of his present appetites, the surrender to present moods, and the indulgence of whims with no thought for the cost, the consequences, the future. To the middle-class observer, this behavior reflects a "present-time orientation"—an "inability to defer gratification." It is this "present-time" orientation—as against the "future orientation" of the middle-class person—that "explains" to the outsider why Leroy chooses to spend the day at the Carry-out rather than report to work; why Richard, who was paid Friday, was drunk Saturday and Sunday and penniless Monday; why Sweets quit his job today because the boss looked at him "funny" yesterday.

But from the inside looking out, what appears as a "present-time" orientation to the outside observer is, to the man experiencing it, as much a future orientation as that of his middle-class counterpart.[4] The difference between the two men lies not so much in their different orientations to time as in their different orientations to future time or, more specifically, to their different futures.[5]

The future orientation of the middle-class person presumes, among other things, a surplus of resources to be invested in the future and a belief that the future will be sufficiently stable both to justify his investment (money in a bank, time and effort in a job, investment of himself in marriage and family, etc.) and to permit the consumption of his investment at a time, place and manner of his own choosing and to his greater satisfaction. But the streetcorner man lives in a sea of want. He does not, as a rule, have a surplus of resources, either economic or psychological. Gratification of hunger and the desire for simple creature comforts cannot be long deferred. Neither can support for one's flagging self-esteem. Living on the edge of both economic and psychological subsistence, the streetcorner man is obliged to expend all his resources on maintaining himself from moment to moment.[6]

As for the future, the young streetcorner man has a fairly good picture of it. In Richard or Sea Cat or Arthur he can see himself in his middle twenties; he can look at Tally to see himself at thirty, at Wee Tom to see himself in his middle thirties, and at Budder and Stanton to see himself in his forties. It is a future in which everything is uncertain except the ultimate destruction of his hopes and the eventual realization of his fears. The most he can reasonably look forward to is that these things do not come too soon. Thus, when Richard squanders a week's pay in two days it is not because, like an animal or a child, he is "present-time oriented," unaware of or unconcerned with his future. He does so precisely because he is aware of the future and the hopelessness of it all.

Sometimes this kind of response appears as a conscious, explicit choice. Richard had had a violent argument with his wife. He said he was going to leave her and the children, that he had had enough of everything and could not take any more, and he chased her out of the house. His chest still heaving, he leaned back against the wall in the hallway of his basement apartment.

"I've been scuffling for five years," he said. "I've been scuffling for five years from morning till night. And my kids still don't have anything, my wife don't have anything, and I don't have anything.

"There," he said, gesturing down the hall to a bed, a sofa, a couple of chairs and a television set, all shabby, some broken. "There's everything I have and I'm having trouble holding onto that."

Leroy came in, presumably to petition Richard on behalf of Richard's wife, who was sitting outside on the steps, afraid to come in. Leroy started to say something but Richard cut him short.

"Look, Leroy, don't give me any of that action. You and me are entirely different people. Maybe I look like a boy and maybe I act like a boy sometimes but I got a man's mind.

You and me don't want the same things out of life. Maybe some of the same, but you don't care how long you have to wait for yours and I— *want—mine—right—now.*"[7]

Thus, apparent present-time concerns with consumption and indulgences—material and emotional—reflect a future-time orientation. "I want mine right now" is ultimately a cry of despair, direct response to the future as he sees it.[8]

In many instances, it is precisely the street corner man's orientation to the future—but to a future loaded with "trouble"—which not on leads to a greater emphasis on present concerns ("I want mine right now") but also contributes importantly to the instability of employment, family and friend relationships, and to the general transient quality of daily life.

Let me give some concrete examples. One day, after Tally had gotten paid, he gave me four twenty-dollar bills and asked me to keep them for him. Three days later he asked me for the money. I returned it and asked why he did not put his money in a bank. He said that the banks close at two o'clock. I argued that there were four or more banks within a two-block radius of where he was working at the time and that he could easily get to any one of them on his lunch hour. "No, man," he said, "you don't understand. They close at two o'clock and they closed Saturday and Sunday. Suppose I get into trouble and I got to make it [leave]. Me get out of town, and everything I got in the world layin' up in that bank? No good! No good!"

In another instance, Leroy and his girl friend were discussing "trouble." Leroy was trying to decide how best to go about getting his hands on some "long green" (a lot of money), and his girl friend cautioned him about "trouble." Leroy sneered at this, saying he had had "trouble" all his life and wasn't afraid of a little more. "Anyway," he said, I'm famous for leaving town."[9]

Thus, the constant awareness of a future

loaded with "trouble" results in a constant readiness to leave, to "make it," to "get out of town," and discourages the man from sinking roots into the world he lives in.[10] Just as it discourages him from putting money in the bank, so it discourages him from committing himself to a job, especially one whose payoff lies in the promise of future rewards rather than in the present. In the same way, it discourages him from deep and lasting commitments to family and friends or to any other persons, places or things, since such commitments could hold him hostage, limiting his freedom of movement and thereby compromising his security which lies in that freedom.

What lies behind the response to the driver of the pickup truck, then, is a complex combination of attitudes and assessments. The streetcorner man is under continuous assault by his job experiences and job fears. His experiences and fears feed on one another. The kind of job he can get—and frequently only after fighting for it, if then—steadily confirms his fears, depresses his self-confidence and self-esteem until finally, terrified of an opportunity even if one presents itself, he stands defeated by his experiences, his belief in his own self-worth destroyed and his fears a confirmed reality.

NOTES

1. "[In our society] a man's work is one of the things by which he is judged, and certainly one of the more significant things by which he judges himself. . . . A man's work is one of the more important parts of his social identity, of his self; indeed, of his fate in the one life he has to live." Everett C. Hughes, *Men and Their Work*, pp. 42–43.
2. Noting that lower-class persons "are constantly exposed to evidence of their own irrelevance," Lee Rainwater spells out still another way in which the poor are poor: "The identity problems of lower class persons make the soul-searching of middle class adolescents and adults seem rather like a kind of conspicuous consumption of psychic riches" ("Work and Identity in the Lower Class," p. 3).
3. Sea Cat cuts his pants legs off at the calf and puts a fringe on the raggedy edges. Tonk breaks his "shades" and continues to wear the horn-rimmed frames minus the lenses. Richard cultivates a distinctive manner of speech. Lonny gives himself a birthday party. And so on.
4. Taking a somewhat different point of view, S. M. Miller and Frank Riessman suggest that "the entire concept of deferred gratification may be inappropriate to understanding the essence of workers' lives" ("The Working Class Subculture: A New View," p. 87).
5. This sentence is a paraphrase of a statement made by Marvin Cline at a 1965 colloquium at the Mental Health Study Center, National Institute of Mental Health.
6. And if, for the moment, he does sometimes have more money than he chooses to spend or more food than he wants to eat, he is pressed to spend the money and eat the food anyway since his friends, neighbors, kinsmen, or acquaintances will beg or borrow whatever surplus he has or, failing this, they may steal it. In one extreme case, one of the men admitted taking the last of a woman's surplus food allotment after she had explained that, with four children, she could not spare any food. The prospect that consumer soft goods not consumed by oneself will be consumed by someone else may be related to the way in which portable consumer durable goods, such as watches, radios, television sets or phonographs, are sometimes looked at as a form of savings. When Shirley was on welfare, she regularly took her television set out of pawn when she got her monthly check. Not so much to watch it, she explained, as to have something to fall back on when her money runs out toward the end of the month. For her and others, the television set or the phonograph is her savings, the pawnshop is where she banks her savings, and the pawn ticket is her bankbook.
7. This was no simple rationalization for irresponsibility. Richard had indeed "been scuffling for five years" trying to keep his family going. Until shortly after this episode, Richard was known and respected as one of the hardest-working men on the street. Richard had said, only a couple of month earlier, "I figure you got to get out there and try. You got try before you can get anything." His wife Shirley confirmed that he had always tried. 'If things get tough, with me I'll get all worried. But Richard get worried, he don't want me to see him worried . . . He will get out there. He's shoveled snow picked beans, and he's done some of everything. . . . He not ashamed to get out there and get us something to eat." At the time of the episode reported above, Leroy was just starting marriage and raising a family. He and Richard were not, as Richard thought, "entirely different people." Leroy had just not learned, by personal experience over time, what Richard had learned. But within two years Leroy's marriage had broken up and he was talking and acting like Richard "He just let go completely," said one of the men on the street.
8. There is no mystically intrinsic connection between "present-time" orientation and lower-class

persons. Whenever people of whatever class have been uncertain, skeptical or downright pessimistic about the future, "I want mine right now" has been one of the characteristic responses, although it is usually couched in more delicate terms: e.g., Omar Khayyam's "Take the cash and let the credit go," or Horace's "*Carpe diem.*" In wartime, especially, all classes tend to slough off conventional restraints on sexual and other behavior (i.e., become less able or less willing to defer gratification). And when inflation threatens, darkening the fiscal future, persons who formerly husbanded their resources with commendable restraint almost stampede one another rushing to spend their money. Similarly, it seems that future-timeorientation tends to collapse toward the persons are in pain or under stress. The point the label notwithstanding, (what passes for orientation appears to be a situation-specific rather than a part of the standard psychical Cognitive Lower Class Man.

9. And proceeded to do just that the following year when "trouble"—in this case, a grand jury indictment, a pile of debts, and a violent separation from his wife and children—appeared again.

10. For a discussion of "trouble" as a focal concern of lower-class culture, see Walter Miller, "Lower Class Culture as Generating Milieu of Gang Delinquency," pp. 7, 8.

CHAPTER 14

All Our Kin

Carol Stack

MY HOME BASE

The Jacksons' home with its seven children (living at home) became a home base, a place where I was welcome to spend the day, week after week, and where my year-old son Kevin and I could sleep, usually sharing a bed with children in the household. My personal network expanded naturally as I met those whom the Waters met or visited each day. My home base changed as I became personally accepted by others, and ultimately I was welcome at several unrelated households. These individuals and their personal networks radiated out to include more than three hundred people, whom I eventually visited, but I observed most intensively fifteen unrelated coalitions of kinsmen. In their homes my presence was least intrusive.

Through Magnolia and Calvin I met Magnolia's oldest daughter, Ruby Banks. Ruby was born in The Flats and raised "on aid" by her grandmother and Magnolia's sister, Augusta. Ruby is now raising her own children, also "on aid." Magnolia described Ruby's vitality and strong-headedness to me, warning that Ruby might be hostile to me, my whiteness, and my presence there. Nevertheless, I was anxious to meet Ruby, and Magnolia had become eager for us to meet.

The scene of our first meeting bristled with the tenseness of our anticipation. That very morning Magnolia and I had been casually chatting about the days before she met Calvin,

and her relationship with James Henderson, the father of her oldest children. Ruby walked into Magnolia's house "cussing," "putting down" the mess and the dirt on the floor, and the clothes Magnolia's younger children had on that day. Then she saw me on the couch and my year-old son on the floor. "The dirt on the floor could kill a white baby," she said. Paying no attention, Magnolia continued our conversation, telling me how much Ruby looked like her father. Ruby pulled up a stool, sat down, and lectured to me in a high-pitched voice, "James Henderson, he's no father to me! I don't even speak to him. I don't really own him because of the way he did me. The only father I know is my stepfather Calvin, and there's no better man in the world."

Ruby was angry at Magnolia. Her description of the world in which Ruby lived was not Ruby's. She shook her head and shouted, "Don't you believe a word of what she says. If that's what Magnolia been telling you, you better come over to my house and get things straight the way I see them." At that point Magnolia chuckled to herself, grabbed my son's bottle, and yelled at one of the children to fill it. Ruby looked at my son, grunted, and said, "That boy should have been off the bottle six months ago."

When I visited Magnolia the following afternoon, she asked me to take Ruby's youngest daughter, who spent the night at her house, back over to Ruby's. Remembering Ruby's "invitation," I was happy to run the errand. Ruby shared a house with Magnolia's sister, Augusta, across town. This was the first of hundreds of trips I made across town as I began to participate in daily visiting patterns in The Flats.

When I arrived Ruby was wringing out hand-washed clothing in an old handwringer. Her five-year-old daughter was changing a baby's diaper, and her two younger children were playing on the porch. Ruby called me into the kitchen and together we finished wringing out at least ten pounds of wet clothing. When we sat down to rest, Ruby talked about her father.

"I first met my father when I was in the third or fourth grade. I was in a grocery store and my mother introduced me to him and he looked at me and said, 'You sure have grown,' and patted me on the head. I looked up at him and asked, 'Is that really my father?' Magnolia said yes. Easter was coming so I said to him, 'How about buying me a pair of shoes since you never have given me nothing in your life and you never did nothing for me?' He told me to come over to his house on Bell Street and ask for him and he would give me the money for the shoes. When I went it so happened he wasn't there. His wife came out and pushed me off the porch. I was small and she shook me and called me all kinds of low-down names and told me that I didn't have no father. Then she hauled off and hit me and pushed me in the car and told me never to come back there again.

"My mother knew my father's people and my Aunt Augusta is real good friends with Aunt Ann, my father's sister. Some of my father's people really took to me. Uncle Leon came around the house to see me when I was really small and that's how I got to know him. Aunt Ann welcomed me to her house anytime I got ready to go over there. She's the only one I go and see now, she and Aunt Betty. The rest of them are snobs and they don't care nothing about me. I have a half brother by my father and he cares lots for me. Whenever he sees me, if he got money he give it to me. My other half brother, he's just like his mother. He thinks he so much.

"I don't speak to my father, but when he sees me he still tells his friends that he own me—but he tells his wife that he don't have a daughter. I know I'm a Henderson, and there's no way that the law and nobody else can say differently, but my mother put her name on my birth certificate because she knew that I would hate my father when I grew up. Right today I wish that she had never told me who my father was.

"A child wants a father to play with, to laugh with, and to hug. I wouldn't give my stepfather up for anybody in this world. I really appreciate what he did for me. It reminds me of a record that came out called 'Color Him Father.' It's about a man who ran away from his wife and left her with their children. Then another man came into the picture and helped them out so much that they called him 'color him father.' That record speaks of my life. It reminds me of my real father and how he treated me and my mother. My mother couldn't hardly get him to buy a light bulb. But, he tells a different story about how much he loved my mother, so who's to say."

We began to talk about the difference between Magnolia's, Ruby's, and Ruby's father's explanations of their relationships. Ruby told me that to learn anything about her family, or family life in The Flats—in order to interpret any single event—I would have to talk to many people. I took her advice and it turned out to be wise.

During the following months Ruby and I began to spend a great deal of time together and with our children. Ruby's attitudes toward men, kin, friends, and children shook many of my views, and I am still in the process of reshaping them today. For her part Ruby would get mad, amazed, and amused at some of the views I held. Whenever I expressed hesitation or uneasiness about my own ability to make it alone, with my child, Ruby would get very angry, providing me with numerous examples of women around The Flats who were doing so. Ruby was probing, observing, and interpreting my perceptions just as I was doing with hers. At times over the three years of our friendship, we would find many ways to test our perceptions of one another.

Ruby and I enjoyed comparing our attitudes and approaches toward everything. Although she asked me to bring my white friends over to her house, she was always hypercritical in assessing whether they were anti-Black or whether they "put on airs." Some of my friends she liked very much, yet she encouraged me to break up some friendships, especially if she had reason to doubt a friend's loyalty to me. It seemed at times, by the circumstances and demands that she contrived, that she was testing the loyalty of my friends—using her own standards, of course—just as she tested her own friends. For example, she insisted that I ask my friends to take care of Kevin or to loan me money. She was in fact teaching me how to get along.

Ruby and I also enjoyed comparing our culturally acquired tastes in furniture and dress. With no intention of buying, we loved to go to the local used furniture store to mock one another's preferences. Ruby admired new, vinyl and Masonite, tough, fake wood modern furniture. I was only interested in finding old turn-of-the-century oak furniture. She laughed at my love for old, used furniture, often warped with age. To her, aged and worn stood for poverty.

Sometimes when Ruby and I were alone we would act out a parody of one another, imitating one another's walk or dancing style, and sometimes this mime would be continued in front of friends. She and I went to white "hilly-billy" taverns not frequented by Blacks with our boyfriends. We dressed "white" in dressy dresses, the men in ties, and we danced the fox-trot to an electric guitar. The reaction to us was silence. People thought we were imitating them. At the next dance, we broke into "black" dance. Ruby and her friends took John[1] and me to

black nightclubs to observe the reaction of their black friends to us. They bought us outfits so we would dress "black." At times the reaction at the clubs was patronizing or even hostile, but Ruby was amused.

Most of our day was spent in The Flats in the company of Ruby's friends and kin. Occasionally, when Ruby and I were with individuals who did not know me or who were apparently hostile, Ruby would cuss, tease, or "signify" to my face. If my response was equally insulting or foul, this would put people at ease. After such a scene Ruby would frequently scold me for not coming up with as good a response as she could have given herself. There is no doubt in my mind that meeting Ruby and gaining an entree into social relationships in The Flats through her made much of this study possible. Ruby had a quick, affirmative way of letting others know my presence was acceptable to her, and that it "damn well better be acceptable to them." At one large family gathering, relatives came from out of town to see Ruby's stepfather, who was sick. Ruby sensed their hostility and insecurity toward me. She turned to me and said, "What is your white ass doing sitting down when there is so much cooking and work to do in my kitchen?" I responded, "My white ass can sit here as long as your black ass can." With that, we both got up, went into the kitchen and got to work.

My mode of transportation varied with the weather. During the first spring and summer of my field work, I walked or rode my bicycle. People in The Flats walk year-round and ride bicycles in good weather. In the process of shopping, visiting, washing clothes, and paying bills, many walk more than five miles a day. Time consumed in walking often involves more than one trip to the same place. If the laundry has been washed, and clothes are ready at the cleaners, and a daily shopping has to be made, one or two or three members of a household, including younger children, may make three or four trips during the day to carry the load of goods home. Walking across town, sharing a work load, carrying packages, riding in a cab, and visiting kin and friends showed me about the pace of life in The Flats and the patience with which the residents endured pain, misfortune, and disappointment. Early in the morning, for example, people in a household might get excited about a large house they heard was for rent or a decent refrigerator that was for sale. A large group of us, including five to ten children, would take a walk to see the house or refrigerator, only to arrive too late.

Picking through piles of clothing at the local Goodwill or at the Salvation Army Store was another frustrating job made even more difficult without a car. Toward the end of the summer many of the women and their children in The Flats began to make daily trips to these second-hand stores, which were located outside The Flats in the Jackson Harbor business district, to pick out enough clothes for all of their children to begin school. For three consecutive summers I spent most of the month of August walking to secondhand stores with families, helping find the right size dresses, shirts, pants, socks, coats, and shoes for their children. The children would look for clothes for themselves and their brothers, sisters, and cousins. They seemed enthusiastic when they found a piece of clothing that would fit someone, but I gained more insight into their real attitude toward these ventures one afternoon when a woman I knew well, Ophelia, asked me to take her eleven-year-old son to Goodwill because "he didn't have a shirt to cover his back." She told us to buy three shirts. Sam and I walked to the store and began the search. We found five shirts his size. Sam seemed pleased. I told him to pick out the three shirts he liked best. He shook his head and said, "Caroline, to tell the truth, I don't like any of them. You pick out three and then let's go show Mama that we got the job done." Sam's response was a mature, resigned response to the necessities of life.

SWAPPING

"What Goes Round Comes Around"

Ruby Banks took a cab to visit Virginia Thomas, her baby's aunt, and they swapped some hot corn bread and greens for diapers and milk. In the cab going home Ruby said to me, "I don't believe in putting myself on nobody, but I know I need help every day. You can't get help just by sitting at home, laying around, house-nasty and everything. You got to get up and go out and meet people, because the very day you go out, that first person you meet may be the person that can help you get the things you want. I don't believe in begging, but I believe that people should help one another. I used to wish for lots of things like a living room suite, clothes, nice clothes, stylish clothes—I'm sick of wearing the same pieces. But I can't, I can't help myself because I have my children and I love them and I have my mother and all our kin. Sometimes I don't have a damn dime in my pocket, not a crying penny to get a box of paper diapers, milk, a loaf of bread. But you have to have help from everybody and anybody, so don't turn no one down when they come round for help."

Black families living in The Flats need a steady source of cooperative support to survive. They share with one another because of the urgency of their needs. Alliances between individuals are created around the clock as kin and friends exchange and give and obligate one another. They trade food stamps, rent money, a TV, hats, dice, a car, a nickel here, a cigarette there, food, milk, grits, and children.

Few if any black families living on welfare for the second generation are able to accumulate a surplus of the basic necessities to be able to remove themselves from poverty or from the collective demands of kin. Without the help of kin, fluctuations in the meager flow of available goods could easily destroy a family's ability to survive (Lombardi 1973). Kin and close friends who fall into similar economic crises know that they may share the food, dwelling, and even the few scarce luxuries of those individuals in their kin network. Despite the relatively high cost of rent and food in urban black communities, the collective power within kin-based exchange networks keeps people from going hungry.

As low-skilled workers, the urban poor in The Flats cannot earn sufficient wages and cannot produce goods. Consequently, they cannot legitimately draw desired scarce goods into the community. Welfare benefits which barely provide the necessities of life—a bed, rent, and food—are allocated to households of women and children and are channeled into domestic networks of men, women, and children. All essential resources flow from families into kin networks.

Whether one's source of income is a welfare check or wages from labor, people in The Flats borrow and trade with others in order to obtain daily necessities. The most important form of distribution and exchange of the limited resources available to the poor in The Flats is by means of trading, or what people usually call "swapping." As people swap, the limited supply of finished material goods in the community is perpetually redistributed among networks of kinsmen and throughout the community.

The resources, possessions, and services exchanged between individuals residing in The Flats are intricately interwoven. People exchange various objects generously: new things, treasured items, furniture, cars, goods that are perishable, and services which are exchanged for child care, residence, or shared meals. Individuals enlarge their web of social relations through repetitive and seemingly habitual instances of swapping. Lily Jones, a resident in The Flats, had this to say about swapping, "That's just everyday life, swapping. You not really getting ahead of nobody, you just get better things as they go back and forth."

The obligation to give

"Trading" in The Flats generally refers to any object or service offered with the intent of obligating. An object given or traded represents a possession, a pledge, a loan, a trust, a bank account—given on the condition that something will be returned, that the giver can draw on the account, and that the initiator of the trade gains prerogatives in taking what he or she needs from the receiver.

Mauss's (1954) classic interpretation of gift exchange in primitive societies stresses the essence of obligation in gift giving, receiving, and repaying. A gift received is not owned and sometimes can be reclaimed by the initiator of the swap. A person who gives something which the receiver needs or desires, gives under a voluntary guise. But the offering is essentially obligatory, and in The Flats, the obligation to repay carries kin and community sanctions.

An individual's reputation as a potential partner in exchange is created by the opinions others have about him (Bailey 1971). Individuals who fail to reciprocate in swapping relationships are judged harshly. Julia Rose, a twenty-five-year-old mother of three, critically evaluated her cousin Mae's reputation, "If someone who takes things from me ain't giving me anything in return, she can't get nothing else. When someone like that, like my cousin Mae, comes to my house and says, 'Ooo, you should give me that chair, honey. I can use it in my living room, and my old man would just love to sit on it,' well, if she's like my cousin, you don't care what her old man wants, you satisfied with what yours wants. Some people like my cousin don't mind borrowing from anybody, but she don't loan you no money, her clothes, nothing. Well, she ain't shit. She don't believe in helping nobody and lots of folks gossip about her. I'll never give her nothing again. One time I went over there after I had given her all these things and I asked her, 'How about loaning me an outfit to wear?' She told me, 'Girl, I ain't got nothing. I ain't got nothing clean. I just put my clothes in the cleaners, and what I do have you can't wear 'cause it's too small for you.' Well, lots of people talks about someone who acts that way."

Degrees of entanglement among kinsmen and friends involved in networks of exchange differ in kind from casual swapping. Those actively involved in domestic networks swap goods and services on a daily, practically an hourly, basis. Ruby Banks, Magnolia Waters' twenty-three-year-old daughter, portrays her powerful sense of obligation to her mother in her words, "She's my mother and I don't want to turn her down." Ruby has a conflicting sense of obligation and of sacrifice toward her mother and her kinsmen.

"I swap back and forth with my mother's family. She wouldn't want nobody else to know how much I'm doing for her, but hell, that's money out of my pocket. We swap back and forth, food stamps, kids, clothes, money, and everything else. Last month the AFDC people had sent me forty dollars to get a couch. Instead of me getting a couch, I took my money over to Mama's and divided with her. I gave her fifteen dollars of it and went on to wash because my kids didn't have a piece clean. I was washing with my hands and a bar of face soap before the money come. I took all the clothes I had, most of the dirty ones I could find, and washed them. It ran me up to six dollars and something with the cab that my sister took back home. I was sitting over at the laundry worrying that Mama didn't have nothing to eat. I took a cab over there and gave her ten more dollars. All I had left to my name was ten dollars to pay on my couch, get food, wash, and everything. But I ignored my problems and gave Mama the money I had. She didn't really have nothing after she paid some bills. She was over there black and blue from not eating—stomach growling. The craziest thing was that she wouldn't touch the rent money. I gave the last five dollars out of the rent money. She paid her sister her five and gave me five to get the kids something to eat. I said, 'What about my other ten?', but she put me off. She paid everybody else and I'm the one who's helping her the most. I could have most everything I needed if I didn't have to divide with my people. But they be just as poor as me, and I don't want to turn them down."

Close kin who have relied upon one another over the years often complain about the sacrifices they have made and the deprivation they have endured for one another. Statements similar to Ruby's were made by men and women describing the sense of obligation and sacrifice they feel toward female kin: their mothers, grandmothers, or "mamas." Commitment to mutual aid among close kin is sometimes characterized as if they were practically "possessed" or controlled by the relationship. Eloise, captured by the incessant demands of her mother, says, "A mother should realize that you have your own life to lead and your own family. You can't come when she calls all the time, although you might want to and feel bad if you can't. I'm all worn out from running from my house to her house like a pinball machine. That's the way I do. I'm doing it 'cause she's my mother and 'cause I don't want to hurt her. Yet, she's killing me."

When Magnolia and Calvin Waters inherited a sum of money, the information spread quickly to every member of their domestic network. Within a month and a half all of the money was absorbed by participants in their network whose demands and needs could not be refused.

The ebb and flow of goods and services among kinsmen is illustrated in the following example of economic and social transactions during one month in 1970 between participants in a kin-based cooperative network in The Flats. As I wrote in my field notes:

Cecil (35) lives in The Flats with his mother Willie Mae, his oldest sister and her two children, and his younger brother. Cecil's younger sister Lily lives with their mother's sister Bessie. Bessie has three children and Lily has two. Cecil and his mother have part-time jobs in a cafe and Lily's children are on aid. In July of 1970 Cecil and his mother had just put together enough money to cover their rent. Lily paid her utilities, but she did not have enough money to buy food stamps for herself and her children. Cecil and Willie Mae knew that after they paid their rent they would not have any money for food for the family. They helped out Lily by buying her food stamps, and then the two households shared meals together until Willie Mae was paid two weeks later. A week later Lily received her second ADC check and Bessie got some spending money from her boyfriend. They gave some of this money to Cecil and Willie Mae to pay their rent, and gave Willie Mae money to cover her insurance and pay a small sum on a living room suite at the local furniture store. Willie Mae reciprocated later on by buying dresses for Bessie and Lily's daughters and by caring for all the children when Bessie got a temporary job.

The people living in The Flats cannot keep their resources and their needs a secret. Everyone knows who is working, when welfare checks arrive, and when additional resources are available. Members of the middle class in America can cherish privacy concerning their income and resources, but the daily intimacy created by exchange transactions in The Flats insures that any change in a poor family's resources becomes "news." If a participant in an exchange network acquires a new car, new clothes, or a sum of money, this information is immediately circulated through gossip. People are able to calculate on a weekly basis the total sum of money available to their kin network. This information is necessary to their own solvency and stability.

Social relationships between kin who have consistently traded material and cultural support over the years reveal feelings of both generosity and martyrdom. Long-term social interactions, especially between female kin, sometimes become highly com-

petitive and aggressive. At family gatherings or at a family picnic it is not unusual to see an exaggerated performance by someone, bragging about how much he has done for a particular relative, or boasting that he provided all the food and labor for the picnic himself. The performer often combines statements of his generosity with great claims of sacrifice. In the presence of other kin the performer displays loyalty and superiority to others. Even though these routines come to be expected from some individuals, they cause hurt feelings and prolonged arguments. Everyone wants to create the impression that he is generous and manipulative, but no one wants to admit how much he depends upon others.

The trading of goods and services among the poor in complex industrial societies bears a striking resemblance to patterns of exchange organized around reciprocal gift giving in non-Western societies. The famous examples of reciprocal gift giving first described by Malinowski (1922), Mauss (1925), and Lévi-Strauss (1969) provided a basis for comparison. Patterns of exchange among people living in poverty and reciprocal exchanges in cultures lacking a political state are both embedded in well-defined kinship obligations. In each type of social system strategic resources are distributed from a family base to domestic groups, and exchange transactions pervade the whole social-economic life of participants. Neither industrial poor nor participants in nonindustrial economies have the opportunity to control their environment or to acquire a surplus of scarce goods (Dalton 1961; Harris 1971; Lee 1969; Sahlins 1965). In both of these systems a limited supply of goods is perpetually redistributed through the community.

The themes expressed by boasting female performers and gossiping kin and friends resemble themes which have emerged from black myth, fiction, and lore (Abrahams 1963; Dorson 1956, 1958). Conflicting values of trust and distrust, exploitation and friendship, the "trickster" and the "fool," have typically characterized patterns of social interaction between Blacks and Whites; notions of trust and distrust also suffuse interpersonal relations within the black community. These themes become daily utterances between cooperating kinsmen who find themselves trapped in a web of obligations. But the feelings of distrust are more conspicuous among friends than among kin.

Many students of social relations within the black community have concluded that friendships are embedded in an atmosphere of distrust. However, intense exchange behavior would not be possible if distrust predominated over all other attitudes toward personal relations. Distrust is offset by improvisation: an adaptive style of behavior acquired by a person using each situation to control, manipulate, and exploit others. Wherever there are friendships, exploitation possibilities exist (Abrahams 1970, p. 125). Friends exploit one another in the game of swapping, and they expect to be exploited in return. There is a precarious line between acceptable and unacceptable returns on a swap. Individuals risk trusting others because they want to change their lives. Swapping offers a variety of goods and something to anticipate. Michael Lee, a twenty-eight-year-old Flats resident, talks about his need to trust others, "They say you shouldn't trust nobody, but that's wrong. You have to try to trust somebody, and somebody has to try to trust you, 'cause everybody need help in this world."

A person who gives and obligates a large number of individuals stands a better chance of receiving returns than a person who limits his circle of friends. In addition, repayments from a large number of individuals are returned intermittently: people can anticipate receiving a more-or-less continuous flow of goods. From this perspective, swapping involves both calculation and planning.

Obtaining returns on a trade necessarily takes time. During this process, stable friendships are formed. Individuals attempt to surpass one another's displays of generosity; the extent to which these acts are mutually satisfying determines the duration of friendship bonds. Non-kin who live up to one another's expectations express elaborate vows of friendship and conduct their social relations within the idiom of kinship. Exchange behavior between those friends "going for kin" is identical to exchange behavior between close kin.

The Rhythm of exchange

"These days you ain't got nothing to be really giving, only to your true friends, but most people trade," Ruby Banks told me. "Trading is a part of everybody's life. When I'm over at a girl friend's house, and I see something I want, I say, 'You gotta give me this; you don't need it no way.' I act the fool with them. If they say no, I need that, then they keep it and give me something else. Whatever I see that I want I usually get. If a friend lets me wear something of theirs, I let them wear something of mine. I even let some of my new clothes out. If my friend has on a new dress that I want, she might tell me to wait till she wear it first and then she'll give it to me, or she might say, well take it on." Exchange transactions are easily formed and create special bonds between friends. They initiate a social relationship and agreed upon reciprocal obligations (Gouldner 1960; Foster 1963; Sahlins 1965).[2]

Reciprocal obligations last as long as both participants are mutually satisfied. Individuals remain involved in exchange relationships by adequately drawing upon the credit they accumulate with others through swapping. Ruby Banks' description of the swapping relationship that developed between us illustrates this notion. "When I first met you, I didn't know you, did I? But I liked what you had on about the second time you seen me, and you gave it to me. All right, that started us swapping back and forth. You ain't really giving nothing away because everything that goes round comes round in my book. It's just like at stores where people give you credit. They have to trust you to pay them back, and if you pay them you can get more things."

Since an object swapped is offered with the intent of obligating the receiver over a period of time, two individuals rarely simultaneously exchange things. Little or no premium is placed upon immediate compensation; time has to pass before a counter-gift or a series of gifts can be repaid. While waiting for repayments, participants in exchange are compelled to trust one another. As the need arises, reciprocity occurs. Opal Jones described the powerful obligation to give that pervades interpersonal relationships. "My girl friend Alice gave me a dress about a- month ago, and last time I went over to her house, she gave me sheets and towels for the kids, 'cause she knew I needed them. Every time I go over there, she always gives me something. When she comes over to my house, I give her whatever she asks for. We might not see each other in two or three months. But if she comes over after that, and I got something, I give it to her if she want it. If I go over to her house and she got something, I take it—canned goods, food, milk—it don't make no difference.

"My TV's been over to my cousin's house for seven or eight months now. I had a fine couch that she wanted and I gave it to her too. It don't make no difference with me what it is or what I have. I feel free knowing that I done my part in this world. I don't ever expect nothing back right away, but when I've given something to kin or friend, whenever they think about me they'll bring something on around. Even if we don't see each other for two or three months. Soon enough they'll come around and say, 'Come over my house, I got something to give you.' When I get over there and they say, 'You want this?', if I don't want it my kin will say, 'Well, find something else you like and take it on.'"

When people in The Flats swap goods, a value is placed upon the goods given away, but the value is not determined by the price or market value of the object. Some goods have been acquired through stealing rings, or previous trades, and they cost very little compared to their monetary value. The value of an object given away is based upon its retaining power over the receiver; that is, how much and over how long a time period the giver can expect returns of the gift. The value of commodities in systems of reciprocal gift giving is characterized by Lévi-Strauss (1969, p. 54), "Goods are not only economic commodities, but vehicles and instruments for realities of another order, such as power, influence, sympathy, status and emotion. . . ."

Gifts exchanged through swapping in The Flats are exchanged at irregular intervals, although sometimes the gifts exchanged are of exactly the same kind. Despite the necessity to exchange, on the average no one is significantly better off. Ruby Banks captured the pendulous rhythm of exchange when she said, "You ain't really giving nothing away because everything that goes round comes round in my book."

These cooperating networks share many goals constituting a group identity—goals so interrelated that the gains and losses of any of them are felt by all participants. The folk model of reciprocity is characterized by recognized and urgent reciprocal dependencies and mutual needs. These dependencies are recognized collectively and carry collective sanctions. Members of second-generation welfare families have calculated the risk of giving. As people say, "The poorer you are, the more likely you are to pay back." This criterion often determines which kin and friends are actively recruited into exchange networks.

Gift exchange is a style of interpersonal relationship by which local coalitions of cooperating kinsmen distinguish themselves from other Blacks—those low-income or working- class Blacks who have access to steady employment. In contrast to the middle-class ethic of individualism and competition, the poor living in The Flats do not turn anyone down when they need help. The cooperative life style and the bonds created by the vast mass of moment-to-moment exchanges constitute an underlying element of black identity in The Flats. This powerful obligation to exchange is a profoundly creative adaptation to poverty.

NOTES

1. John Lombardi, a fellow anthropologist, energetically joined the field study for over two years.
2. Foster's (1963) model of the dyadic contract includes two types of dyadic contractual ties: colleague ties between individuals of approximately equal socio-economic positions and patron-client ties between individuals of unequal social position. The underlying principles of exchange transactions discussed in this chapter approximate features of the dyadic model of colleague ties. According to Foster's model, colleague ties are expressed by repeated exchanges; they are informal and exist as long as participants are satisfied; they are usually of long duration and exact or perfectly balanced reciprocity between partners is never achieved.

CHAPTER 15

'Doin' the Hustle'

Constructing the Ethnographer in the American Ghetto

Sudhir Venkatesh

It is not altogether surprising that the ethnographer studying the American ghetto has become a curio for American sociology. Indeed, he (nearly all are male) is nothing short of a fetish. Hearing the factors that enabled him to enter the heart of the ghetto has become as interesting a tale as the 'ghetto specific' behavior lurking in the emergent narratives. There are certainly interesting and curious dimensions of fieldwork practice in the American ghetto, particularly since most ethnographers are male and non-minority, while the subjects are blacks and Latinos. But the sociological interest in the fieldworker–informant relation has not gone much further than veiled voyeurism. It has not received the critical scrutiny or self-reflection of its counterparts in anthropology (see, for example, Clifford and Marcus, 1986; Comaroff and Comaroff, 1992). Indeed, one aspect of ethnographic practice has received almost no attention at all, namely, what was the informants' experience of having an ethnographer in their midst?

For nearly a decade, I have been conducting ethnographic research in poor, urban, predominantly African-American communities in Chicago, Illinois. In order of frequency, the three most common fieldwork-related questions presented to me by other scholars are: 'Were you scared?' 'Did they *know* you are an Indian?' 'What kind of illegal acts did you have to commit in order to gain entrée?' I sometimes mention that I am equally busy studying the drug consumption patterns among rich, white 20-year-olds in New York who come from elite families, but I am never questioned about their capacity for intelligent reasoning, my fear or issues of legality and ethical compromise in the field.

This article examines the social production of the ethnographer, in the sense of how they are viewed by informants—a critical moment in any observational study—by reconstructing the status and identity of the researcher from the informants' point of view. It is an exercise in 'reflexive science' (Burawoy, 1998) and is meant to investigate the conditions that made possible the completion of one particular ethnographic study on the American urban poor (Venkatesh, 2000). I argue that if we take seriously the proposition that relations between fieldworker and informant form a constitutive part of ethnographic research, then reconstructing the informants' point of view—in this case the perceptions of the fieldworker and the research initiative—can aid the researcher in the more general objective of determining patterns of structure and meaning among the individual, group, and/or community under study. The 'data' of an ethnography, then, should not be restricted solely to conventional informational documents, such as fieldworker observations of subjects' behavior and interactions, interview data, earnings and expenditure surveys, etc. The interaction of fieldworker and informant is itself potentially revealing of the local properties of social structure and may also be mined to illuminate chosen research questions.

THE ACADEMIC HUSTLER

The 'hustle' was a social-structural attribute of 'project living', so it would be mistaken to think that over time, by gaining the trust or confidence of tenants, my relations with the tenants could escape or transcend its mediating influence. However, my role in the local landscape did change significantly during my fieldwork tenure and, importantly, each of the personas attributed to me was shaped in some way by the prevalence and importance of hustling in social reproduction. This was apparent even in the early phases of my fieldwork, when tenants tended to perceive me as either a gang member or a sympathizer. Tenants, particularly parents, grandparents, and guardians, questioned my motives because 'students' (usually in college or high school) who visited the community usually tutored schoolchildren. They did not take up quarter in a household, and they remained in the housing development for hours, not continuously for months at a time.

My extended stay in the community and my preference for observation (read: notetaking usually outside tenants' gaze) over interview-based elicitation gradually reconfigured tenants' perceptions of me. Over time public accusations that I was a gang member ceased, but my extended tenure in several households continued to provoke questions: Why did I choose to document practice rather than ask scripted questions about attitudes? Why was it necessary for my research to stay overnight with families? The local Black King's gang members knew that I myself was not purchasing large quantities of narcotics; however, many assumed I was hoping to use my ties to gang leaders in order to purchase drugs and establish an underground business that catered to the University of Chicago student body. Some discreetly offered to work with me to expand the gang's markets, hoping that they might personally benefit from the increased revenue. Local stakeholders and tenant leaders also began using me for their own purposes. Some asked whether I was a friend of the 'Spanish Cobras', a local Puerto Rican gang that had developed ties to the city's African-American street gangs, in the hope of using my good offices to reduce conflicts and to stabilize their drug-trafficking operations. Having observed me passing the time in local parks and parking lots reading Spanish newspapers (I was enrolled in university Spanish-language classes), a few tenants suspected that I was gang-affiliated. A few willingly offered a rendition of my biography, one that wove together 'student', 'gang member', and 'immigrant'. It was rumored that I had come to America with my family to work in the strawberry fields; in Chicago I became a college student and member of a Latino gang; I was trying to supply narcotics to the housing development and, thus, I was interested in the local Black King gang.

In one particularly telling incident, tenant leaders and local gang leaders summoned me to a meeting to address recent conflicts between citywide black and Mexican street gangs. The latter were rumored to be planning a drive-by shooting on the local Black King gang. I was asked to provide assistance.

'Yo Julio, we need your help,' an elderly man barked at me as I entered the room. I thought his invocation of 'Julio' was in jest.

'Yeah, why don't you call your friends,' another tenant said. 'Tell them, Julio. Tell them to get off our backs. You were running with these Mexicans. Tell them we don't need no trouble.'

'Running with them?' I muttered. 'My name's not Julio.'

'Julio, yo, Julio! What's this sign mean,' one Black King member said, contorting his fingers in an awkward position. 'Does that mean they're coming? Does that mean they're coming after us? You speak Spanish, what does that mean?! We have a meeting with these niggers tonight, so you'd better come with us, tell them to back off.'

(from fieldnotes)

This incident demonstrated clearly that I could not occupy a disinterested role. I brought resources to the neighborhood and also offered an avenue to the wider world, not necessarily in ways I could foresee or liked. I tried to counter local perceptions that I had ties to local gangs, black and Latino. I looked to other ethnographies for techniques to handle informants' perceptions of the fieldworker. These texts offered a standard chronology of fieldwork: initial awkward moments in which the role of the fieldworker required clarification were inevitable but, once 'access' was gained, the subjects' world would reveal itself. Few mentioned that informants might place me squarely in local social organization; in the case of the urban poor, that I would be quickly incorporated into a landscape defined by the continuous need to find any and all available means to ensure social order and to make ends meet on a daily basis.

As I moved through the broader populace, new constructions of my role in the community congealed, each shaped by the contours of the 'hustle'. Most important, I needed to look no further than my own ethnographic labor—reconstructed from the tenants' point of view—to understand that the 'hustle' was not only a practice with particular salience in ghetto spaces but also a perceptual frame. Tenants would make clear over the next few years that they understood quite well that the ghetto was a source of value to me, many opining that I was 'making my money' by translating their lives into presentable, titillating stories for 'the folks who read books all day and who just want to hear stories of black folk killing each other'. They made clear not only that I could not avoid getting involved in their 'hustles', but that in many ways, my own art form, the ethnographic craft, was an exemplary 'hustle'.

'A NIGGER, JUST LIKE US'

After my first two years of fieldwork, which had focused on the local street gangs, I wanted to situate their behavior in a wider context. In particular, I wanted to learn more about the overall workings of the underground economy and about the many other actors who hid their income and who sought illegal opportunities for revenue generation. But developing relationships with other segments of the Robert Taylor community was not easy because of my two-year association with the gang. To that point my interactions with tenants had been dominated by attempts to allay their fears that I was a state agent or gang member. I now needed to appease them *and* solicit their involvement in my study. I needed information on their lives and their experiences in Robert Taylor.

Accessing other sites of underground trading was difficult because tenants viewed me as a 'friend of the Black Kings'. Importantly, the Black Kings regulated underground economies, a role they had taken over from the elected tenant leaders in the mid 1980s. While tenant leaders suspected that I might be an advocate of the local group that had usurped one base of their power and a source of extra income, those in the general tenant body feared that I would report their hidden work to the gang leaders—who would then extort 'street taxes' from them.

Over the next year I sought ways to signal my independence from the gang—usually, by spending less time with its members—and I spent little time attending gang meetings and gang-sponsored social events. Instead, I concentrated my attention on the sites at which tenants traded goods and services with one another. On several occasions I participated in the informal economy by buying some food or bringing my car to a local mechanic who worked clandestinely in a local parking lot. On occasion, I brought my friends' cars to get repairs and maintenance. Having befriended more non-gang affiliated tenants, over time I managed to gain some independence from the gang.

One particular event precipitated the change. A summer basketball tournament involving several factions of the local Black King's gang had reached the championship game. As in most inner-city basketball contests (whether formal tournaments or spontaneous 'pick up' games), the players acted as the referees, calling fouls on one another. With no third party arbiter, disputes could produce lively debate as players jostled verbally and, less frequently, to defend and challenge fouls physically. Near the end of the game, with the score tied, a number of questionable calls by players led to a search for an impartial referee—an unusual occurrence signifying the importance of the contest in the minds of players. Players and fans were nervous partly because the prizes included bragging rights for tenants (each team represented a set of residential buildings); to heighten the public interest, the gang leaders had waged several thousand dollars on the outcome. According to tradition, part of the winnings funded a community-wide party that evening.

> 'Yo, Sudhir,' Anthony, the Black King leader, yelled to me, waving his arms.
> 'Come over here nigger and referee this game. It's almost over, so hurry up.'
> 'OK, fine, let him ref. He's *fair*,' a member of the opposing team concurred.
>
> (from fieldnotes)

The thought of refereeing the game frightened me. I had little experience refereeing. To that point, I had refereed one game in which I called so many fouls on one team that there were no substitutes left—a feat that led them to physically accost me en masse.

I decided to minimize my presence, running up and down the court appearing to be attentive and authoritative. This was a fanciful strategy; within the first few seconds it was clear that players would make their own calls and look to me for affirmation. Indeed, I was asked at each turn not simply to adjudicate the alleged infraction, but to state my allegiance for one or the other segment of the community. Players and fans asked not whether I saw a violation occur, but, 'whose side are you on, who are you with?' On one of these occasions, as a player drove to the basket and was struck in the head by an opponent, I was asked to call a foul. In response to a cry from the crowd, 'Who are you going for?', I replied inexplicably, 'Whoever's losing, that's the side I'm on, I'm making *all* calls for the losers.' This declaration was met with a roar of laughter, which added much-needed levity, and for the remainder of the contest and into the evening I repeated my subaltern leanings by saying how much I identified with 'losers' in the context of the American class structure.

The invocation of 'loser' and the discussions that evening about politics and class, where I made clear my own left political proclivities, proved to be significant in the months ahead. As I have indicated, I sought ways to signal my independence from the gangs and in my use of 'loser' I had meant to demonstrate my affinity for the excluded and the underdog. Tenants shared this meaning, but many understood my use of the term as signaling empathy for—and perhaps even proximity to—their own social standing. In the coming days, the word 'nigger' increasingly colored their greetings. I thought that 'nigger' was an in-group designation. In America the word has two powerful historical roots and associated uses. It is a derogatory term used by whites to insult blacks. But it has also appeared among African-Americans in uses intended to have more affectionate connotations, indexing a common social status premised on a racialized and outcast subjectivity. I asked Ottie Davis and Kenny Davenport, two tenants who had been supportive when I had encountered problems earlier in my fieldwork, about this change in my treatment and the reasons for the increasing use of 'nigger'. Their reply was revealing of my own ignorance and the fact that the 'hustle' remained the modal framework in which my behavior was framed:

'Do you think that people like me more now than before?' I said to Ottie and Kenny, wanting to understand the significance of my new label. 'Is that why they're calling me nigger and acting different?'

'You're a nigger, Sudhir,' said Ottie, putting his hand on my back. 'Ain't nothing wrong with that. You don't work, you ain't making much money, you living with families in the projects. You trying to get by. You're a nigger just like us.'

'You see, Sudhir, we don't discriminate, man,' Kenny chimed in. 'If you struggling, you struggling. And, look at you, hair all messed up, you ain't had no new clothes since I known you. You poor, just like us. Tell me that ain't the truth.'

'It's like we was talking about before,' continued Ottie, recalling our discussion of the distinctions among the city's African-Americans. 'You got African-Americans, folks that got money, you know, but that forget where they came from, and you got niggers. Niggers ain't just folks who ain't got nothing. It's folks who never forget where they came from.'

(from fieldnotes)

I could hardly deny that my economic circumstances might warrant this new interpretation. When people asked, I told them that I was earning approximately $12,000 per year as a graduate student, slightly more than the average income of local households. At that point, I was taking public transportation nearly everywhere, I dressed with bohemian tones and, perhaps most important, I spoke often of a professional desire to find a full-time teaching job. In other words, I was unemployed and perceived to be an active hustler in my own way, searching for any available means to supplement my income like the majority of the tenant body.

In subsequent days, fewer underground entrepreneurs actively hid their illegal entrepreneurial activity when I passed by. I spent more time with older segments of the community, which allayed tenant fears that I supported the gang's taxation of local entrepreneurs. In addition, I had helped nearly two dozen residents find employment in the neighborhoods surrounding Robert Taylor, which, to some tenants, meant that I was probably receiving some type of monetary 'payoff' from the employer. And there had been no surprise police busts for the long stretch during which I had been intimately observing local underground entrepreneurs. This helped erase suspicion that I was working undercover for law enforcement purposes. As a consequence, I entered hitherto unrevealed arenas of non-state regulated trading, such as prostitution, illegal sales of food stamps and government-issued social security cards, and car theft rackets. I do not think that tenants simply trusted me more than in the past; they merely thought I had my own 'hustle going on'. In other words, in relentlessly seeking information on mundane as well as extraordinary aspects of their lives, I was 'hustling' like them. They assumed that data collection was part of my world of work, one of the many ways I gained income. And for those who understood that data on the urban poor was in fact a sought-after commodity in social science, their speculations were 'on the money'.

Owing to my connections with actors and organizations in the wider world I was seen as a special type of local 'hustler' (Stack, 1974: 20). Tenants tried to enlist me in countless entrepreneurial schemes, typically requesting that I find clients for small-scale services such as house painting or auto care and, on occasion, soliciting support for more elaborate ventures such as drug sales and the resale of stolen weapons. I knew that if I avoided collusion in their schemes entirely, doors would close in front of me quickly. I decided to be selective in my involvement. I would offer token support for those entrepreneurs who sold *licit* goods and services, such as a gypsy cab driver or a car mechanic. But I refused to participate in the drug trade and would not find prospective 'johns' for prostitutes. What harm was there, I thought, in bringing a friend's car to the housing development for repair? What was immoral about buying boxed lunches from a leaseholder earning off-the-books income? Doing so would demonstrate my empathy with their struggle to survive harsh material circumstances.

But the ethical and practical lines I drew between the world of licit and illicit commodities did not match those of the tenants who labored in the underground economy. Assistance to entrepreneurs, however irregular, only increased my reputation as a hustler and, when I refused to help certain tenants (because of time constraints or unwillingness to support their specific schemes), I met with hostility. When I explained my calculus for patronizing licit over illicit commodities, many tenants were startled. Did I not understand that the 'shady' entrepreneurs (Drake and Cayton, 1945) also needed to survive like their counterparts who fixed cars and sold lunches? One young woman chastised me for refusing to help her locate prospective johns from the University of Chicago student population: 'What's the matter, you think you're better than us? You're just a nigger, Sudhir, don't forget it.'

Once again, I turned for counsel to Ottie and Kenny. I asked the two young men why people were growing angry at my selective assistance to local entrepreneurs.

'You got to be hustling. You can't understand until you walk in those shoes,' said Ottie, 'It don't really matter if you selling shorts and tee-shirts like my Auntie does or if you slanging dope, man. It's about survival, it's about hustling, getting your shit on, so you can feed your family.'

'Fuck that,' I said impatiently, 'I'm not going to help Peanut find a john. I'm not her pimp. I just don't want to do that around here.'

'You know what it's like? I'm going to tell you, but you ain't gonna like it,' Kenny instructed, sighing as if this required considerable patience. 'You come around here asking lot of questions, getting in folks' business all the time. What you give a fuck if this person dying or if their families are really messed up? You just care if they selling dope, right, 'cause that's what you want to understand? Am I right? You don't care about all these poor niggers. You got to write your book or you don't get your money. You ain't got time to worry what folks think about you, you just got to take care of your hustle. You think they don't know what you doing [with the book you're writing], [that] you gonna make a lot of money. Same thing with these niggers. They just looking out for themselves. You can't just come around here helping who you want, thinking that's OK and shit, that you doing good for folks. Don't work like that around here, man.'

'That's what we call a power thing, right?' added Ottie. 'Folks just see you acting like you a little prince or something. But, who says you the big dog?'

(from fieldnotes)

Once I heard the parallel between my own fieldwork and tenants' day-to-day 'hustles', I could not help thinking of my own ethnographic labor as yet another 'hustle'. The commonalities were concrete; aspects of my work resonated with their own schemes to supplement income. I had explained my student role as being 'paid' to write a thesis until I found a full-time academic position. This description did not match their profile of 'student'. Instead it appeared to be an opportunistic temporary arrangement similar to those sought after by tenants. Although I did not pay people who participated in my study,[1] I gave rent money to families with whom I stayed and I found employment for others. All this gave the impression that there were material benefits for speaking with me, and it was not far-fetched for tenants to speculate that I paid money for information.

The reconfiguration of my identity as 'nigger' and 'hustler' may have revealed localized systems of meaning, but my immediate reaction was to reduce my ethnographic 'engulfment' in the underground arena (Pollner and Emerson, 1983: 252). Sensing that I had gained sufficient information for a dissertation, I tried to extricate myself from the underground economy—and eventually from active fieldwork entirely. I refused nearly every invitation to help tenants with their underground schemes, and I altered my fieldwork considerably by limiting visits to families to life-historical interviewing. And as tenants saw me less often, my image as 'hustler,' as a 'nigger . . . who's trying to survive . . . just like us', was put to the test.

NOTES

1. In his ethnography, *People and Folks*. Hagedorn (1988) draws our attention to the 'collaborative nature of the research'. He is not referring to any dialectical relationship between fieldworker and informant or to any moment in which the fieldwork helped to shape the development of the conceptual apparatus. Instead, he is informing the researcher that market mediation can be appropriated to serve the ends of data collection. By 'paying for interviews', Hagedorn writes, he was able to inject a 'principle of reciprocity: the gang founder had something of value for us and we insisted on giving back something of value'.

CHAPTER 16

The Marketplace Bar

Sherri Cavan

Some public drinking places derive their special character from their use as centers of exchange for various goods and services, as well as clearing houses for certain kinds of information. Other than liquor, perhaps the commodity most frequently handled in the public drinking place is sex, on either a commercial or a noncommercial basis. But there are also bars that deal in narcotics, stimulant drugs, gambling, stolen merchandise, and a variety of other illicit goods.

Like the general category of marketplaces, the bar itself is in most instances merely the physical setting where the transactions are carried out. Except in the case where heterosexual encounters are to be sold for cash rather than drinks alone, the sellers generally have no official position as such within the bar; they are simply present with their wares. In this sense, then, the bartender who makes book does so outside of his official position in the bar, and from the standpoint of the activity of making book, his official position within the bar is irrelevant; the same activity could be carried on as well by a patron, and often is.

Where the exchange of heterosexual conversation is ultimately to be translated into monetary terms, the seller must establish some contractual agreement with the establishment to convert the drinks bought for her during the evening into cash at the end of the evening. Thus the B-girl is usually a salesman paid on a commission in the marketplace bar, rather than an independent entrepreneur.

Some marketplace bars require buyers and sellers to be accredited or vouched for by someone before they can enter into the activities of the bar, since, like the home territory bar, the characteristic features of the marketplace bar can be disrupted by outsiders. According to one informant, a person desiring narcotics or information about where narcotics can be obtained in one area in the city must first become a familiar face, not only by having been seen around the area for six or seven months but also by displaying the proper language, the proper taste in music, and the proper knowledge of the world in general; he must be able to cite having been in the right places at the right time, both in the city and outside the city.

A similar accreditation procedure is necessary where one desires a contractual selling relation within the establishment. As one B-girl is quoted as saying,

> A girl just can't walk off the street and tell a bartender she wants to be a B-girl. . . . She wouldn't get anything but a cold shoulder. There might be a half dozen girls sitting at the bar waiting for a sucker to walk in, but the bartender would tell her he didn't know what she was talking about. . . . Once you get to know the joints, and get known in them, or know another B-girl, then it's easy.[1]

The same type of validation also must take place when one desires intangible goods that can be used as tangible evidence by the police. Thus, even in bars in which it may be "common knowledge" that information about prostitutes can be obtained, patrons walking into the bar cannot always receive such information, since it can be used by the police as evidence of pimping, even though the one giving the information may be getting no fee from any transaction that may take place. The following examples come from the notes of a male field worker in two areas of the city generally known as places where such contact can be made:

The two men on either side of me were busy talking. In the middle of my second drink I asked the bartender, "Johnny, where could I get a girl for tonight?" He was leaning with both hands on the back bar counter looking at me and then said, as if trying to find out if he heard me correctly, "Where could you get a g-i-r-l?"

"Yes."

He paused and then said, "I don't know." Then he resumed bar-type movements of adjusting things and said, "I'm not interested in that sort of thing."

I said, "But couldn't you help a stranger in town?"

"I haven't the faintest idea," and then he moved down the bar and started talking with another customer.

When I left I said to him again, "Hey Johnny, couldn't you point me in the right direction?"

"I haven't the faintest idea. I've never cared for those types of people and I don't know. . . . I'm just not interested in that sort of thing."

"But you're depriving your customers. . . ."

"Well, I can't help that."

I called the bartender over and asked him where I might find a girl for the night. He didn't reply directly to this remark but rather said, "Right now they are all gone."

"They've all gone on vacation?"

"No, it's real tight right now."

"The mayor putting pressure on because of election year?"

"It's hot right now."

I asked the bartender where I could get a young girl tonight but instead of answering he walked back down to where I had been sitting, saying, "Don't leave your money with her" (indicating the woman I had been sitting with).

When I went back to my seat he said, "You have to look."

"That's what I've been doing," I said, but he just smiled.

SEXUAL MARKETPLACES

Whether bartered or bought, straight or gay, the number of establishments that can be counted as sexual marketplaces[2] is probably second only to the number of establishments that can be counted as home territory bars.

One important differentiation among sexual marketplace bars is whether the transactions that take place within them involve any form of financial consideration—whether there is an actual "buyer" and "seller" or whether the exchange is to take place in the form of bartering, where each party is both buyer and seller. The former type of establishment is found where B-girls, prostitutes, and male hustlers utilize the facilities of the public drinking place as their work setting; the latter type, probably more numerous, is found where the sexually unaffiliated congregate in search of temporary, or perhaps even permanent, companionship. This section focuses primarily on the establishment of noncommercial, sexually oriented encounters between strangers, or as they are more commonly called, "*pickups*." In the next section some features are given of the commercial, sexually oriented encounters in public drinking places.

Bars that are used by the patrons as sexual marketplaces vary in the extent to which this definition forms a part of their "*reputation*" or, in other words, in the extent to which the activity is a matter of public knowledge. Some establishments may be known as such only after they are patronized and others may be imputed to be sexual marketplaces only because they are located in areas where such activity could be expected to take place.

The following examples come from bars in three different areas of the city; the first four come from bars in two different more-or-less middle-class, residential neighborhoods, and the last comes from a bar in the downtown area. Although the field worker asked the question of the bartender, such information is available from other patrons as well (as the last example indicates).

B. J.:	"Where do you go for fun around here?"
Bartender:	"To eat?"
	"No, to find a girl."
	"Oh, you might try the Z—— up the street. Sometimes there are some there, sometimes not. Depends on the night. You know what I mean?"
B. J.:	"Where should I go to have some fun, get a girl and such?"
Bartender:	"Well, stay away from Market Street. They'll slip you a mickey and roll you. You might try North Beach, but it's very expensive, entertainment and all. You should just look around, look around."
B. J.:	"Where's the action in this town?"
Bartender:	"North Beach, it's really crowded on weekends. You can hardly walk on the streets."
	"Can I find a girl down there?"
	"Well, I think so, but you might look in a bar too."
	"You know any place else I might go?"
	"I'd tell you if I knew, but I don't. I'd tell you."
	"North Beach my best bet, eh?"
	"Well, you might try."
	We discussed how to get there and I left.
B. J.:	"Where can I go to find some fun and a girl?"
Bartender:	"Well, I go to North Beach. It's expensive, you know . . . a drink and cover charges . . . but it's the best and you won't get hustled."
	"What about Market Street?"
	"No, stay off Market and the tenderloin. There's nothing there that you'd be interested in. It's dangerous. Do you have a car?"
	"No."
	"Well, North Beach is across town. Take a streetcar and ask directions. North Beach is the place to go."
B. J.	"Where's the action?"
Bartender:	"Try P—— and A—— streets, off Market. All you want."
	"Go to C—— Street, too," a bystander said.
	"No, not C——," the bartender replied.
	"Try the E—— hotel," another bystander said.
	A short conversation about the hotel between the bystander and the bartender ensued.

At the same time, there are some bars that are known sexual marketplaces to at least a limited clientele:

B. J.:	"Where do I go to find the action in this town?"
Bartender:	"The action, uh. Well, go up N—— Street on the left hand side. Skip the bars in the first block and go into those on the second block. If there's nothing doing there, go up to R——— Street and turn left. Stick to the right hand side of the street. Try any of the piano lounges and in particular the A—— and the D——, but any of them will do."

He then left to talk to some of the other customers and I went to the restroom. On returning I couldn't remember the names of the bars he had given me, so I asked him again. He told me, and then somebody down the bar said I should try the J—— as well. "No," said the bartender. "He's just looking for a good time; he doesn't want to be taken."

Other bars are so established with respect to their use that their reputation transcends city, state, and in at least one establishment, national boundaries.

One of the male patrons told P. C. that he was in San Francisco on business, that he lived in New York. He went on to say that friends in New York had given him a long list of bars to see in San Francisco, bars which he said are "places that swing." He then mentioned seven or eight such places, all of which have a general reputation within the city as sexual marketplaces.

One of the patrons told me that although he now lives in the city, he had first heard about the present bar "in St. Louis, where a guy from Philadelphia said that this was a place where you see humanity in action."

I had been talking with two patrons who had very decided accents. They said that they were Australian and that they were in San Francisco on business. When I asked them where they heard of the present bar, they said that it had been while they were in Australia, but to my question of what they had heard about the bar, they replied, "Oh, that it was a nice place." Later, however, P. C. asked them the same question and was told, in a man-to-man fashion, that they heard it was a "body exchange."

In the same sense, some homosexual bars are known as "cruisy gay bars" and others are not, which is to say, some are known as sexual marketplaces and others as home territories.

B-GIRLS

The pickup is one form of sexually oriented exchange which may be transacted within the public drinking place, a form in which, at least ideally, neither participant expects any financial remuneration from the exchange. Sexually oriented exchanges can also be on a commercial basis so that at some point in time one participant can expect, either directly or indirectly, a monetary payoff from the encounter. As one B-girl is quoted, "You really don't have to ask a guy to buy you a drink . . . just sit there and he'll send one over. I figured since guys were always making passes, why not collect on it?"[5]

Like the casual bar pickup, B-girls enter into sexually oriented encounters with strangers in the public drinking place. But unlike the casual pickup, for the B-girl the bar is a work setting and the flirtatious sociability in which she engages with the patrons is a source of financial remuneration. Although she sits at the bar like those who are present as patrons, the B-girl, unlike the female patron, is not unconditionally open for interaction. Rather, she is available only to those who are willing to pay for the encounter.

Ginny (the B-girl) had one drink when she came on, around noon, and after that, Connie, the bartender, fixed her coffee. When a new man came into the bar, she would push the coffee cup away and sit twirling her empty glass, saying nothing unless the male offered to buy her a drink. Once a drink was bought for her, she would smile, laugh, and chat with the buyer until he either left or ceased buying her drinks.

Although the drinks in the bar cost the patrons fifty cents, her drinks cost a dollar. Each time a patron bought her a drink, Connie would put a penny into one of the empty sections in the cash register. At 5 p.m., when her husband came to pick her up, sixteen or seventeen pennies had accumulated. Just before she left, she and Connie went down to the end of the bar, where Connie handed her some folded bills. When I looked in the cash register later, the section where the pennies had been was empty again.

When business was slow, Ginny would go out for periods of five or ten minutes. On one of these occasions she came back with a young man in tow. He bought her two drinks and stayed about half an hour.

One of the male field workers writes:

There were two women sitting at the bar, each by herself. I came in and obviously avoided the empty stools to sit next to the blond. I immediately ordered a drink for myself and, after it came, said to the blond, "Why is it so lively tonight?"

"All the dead end kids are here," she answered.

"How can you tell which end is dead?"

She just shrugged. About this time, one of the men at the entrance end of the bar bought a drink for himself and one of the male patrons seated at his left. The latter appeared to be a new acquaintance. When the blond saw this, she downed her drink, said *C'est la vie* to me, got up, and walked down and sat next to the patron who had bought the drinks, saying to him, "I'll have a drink, too." She ordered it from the bartender, who brought it and then indicated that the patron should pay. He took a dollar from the patron and rang up the drink. There was no change (although the patron's drinks cost only fifty cents) and he put a penny in a glass by the cash register to tally the drink. Before I left, the patron had bought the blond three drinks, each time at her request.

While the B-girl is present in the bar in the guise of a patron, in some marketplace bars flirtatious sociability may be purchased by the drink from women who are explicitly employed in the establishment, such as cocktail waitresses, bar maids, and entertainer. While such bar functionaries are, in fact, expected to carry out the tasks that are associated with their occupational role, in the marketplace bar they are also present to provide cross-sex sociability for patrons who are willing to pay for it by the purchase of a drink.

I answered an ad for a cocktail waitress, no experience necessary. The ad and the address had been in the paper about every two to three months for over a year.

The bar was located on skid row. It was a very small place, with perhaps twenty to twenty-two seats along the bar and two booths in the back, but these were piled with beer crates and miscellaneous items and apparently were not used. When I asked the bartender why he needed a cocktail waitress, he said, "If these guys walk by and see me behind the bar, they don't want to come in and talk to me. . . . All you have to do is serve soft drinks and beer and talk with the guys—you know."

A similar example comes from the notes of one of the male field workers:

I had been buying drinks and talking with one of the strippers for about twenty minutes or so. When she said she had to leave to do her act, the bartender suggested to Lolly (one of the other strippers sitting next to the first girl) that she move down and sit with me, which she did.

I bought Lolly a couple of drinks and we talked for a while. At first she allowed me to suggest buying her a drink, but after a while she became increasingly aggressive about suggesting that I buy her a drink, finally asking me outright. At one point she offered me a cigarette. It was her last one and she said that I would "have to" buy her more. I did so at the cost of fifty cents.

About this time I was running out of money and told her I would have to leave. As I excused myself, she requested that I go out and buy some mints for her, saying that she could not leave the place.

Whether the B-girl is in the bar in the guise of a patron or whether she is available for cross-sex encounters in addition to other duties, her problem of working efficiently (by maximizing the number of drinks purchased for her) is aggravated by the fact that all present, whether they are there as patrons or employees, are defined as open for interaction to anyone, regardless of whether a drink has been bought for them or not. Defined by the patrons as unconditionally open and by her employer as conditionally open, her solution usually rests upon making overtures with promises. She uses her open character either to instigate a conversation or to permit a conversation to be instigated with her, but once she has shown her interest in an encounter, she makes herself unavailable, either physically or socially, to continue the encounter without the purchase of a drink.

The following examples come from the notes of two male field workers:

> I had been at the bar for twenty minutes or so when one of the girls sat down two stools from me. I watched her for a few minutes and then introduced myself. I did not offer to buy her a drink.
>
> "My name's Bruce. What's yours?"
>
> "Janie."
>
> "I'm from Fresno."
>
> "Oh." She turned her head away.
>
> "Not much to do down there," I said.
>
> "I imagine not," she said, turning her head away again.
>
> The conversation continued in this manner: question or statement by me and a brief answer, with her turning her head away or using some other gesture of avoidance. Finally I asked her if she would like a drink.
>
> "Yes, thanks. What do you do for a living?"
>
> Once the drink was bought for her, she seemed much more willing to enter into a conversation with me.

> I picked up my drink and moved down to the other end of the bar where the brunette was sitting. When I sat down I said to her, "Why so sad?"
>
> She answered, "I need a drink. Want to buy me one?"
>
> "I'm short on funds this week. How much is it going to cost?"
>
> "A dollar."
>
> "That's a little high. Can't I buy you a fifty-cent drink?"
>
> "No."
>
> "Can you go down to the V—— Club with me? It's a little livelier there."

> "Sorry, I have to stay here. Do you like the V—— Club?"
>
> "It's okay. Tonight's the first time I've ever been there."
>
> At this point she got up and went behind the bar, where she fixed a straight pineapple drink for herself. Then she picked up a newspaper, seated herself at the far end of the bar (moving about three stools away from me), and began reading.

Similarly, ongoing encounters with the B-girl are characteristically viable only so long as drinks are forthcoming from the male. Thus one of the male field workers writes,

> I had bought Nancy two drinks. When the bartender came around for the third drink I told him that I wanted no more. Nancy cut off the conversation and became very restless. I could no longer keep a conversation going. Finally she said that she had to get ready for her act, and she prepared to leave. At this point I asked her if she would like another drink. She accepted and talked for another ten minutes or so.

Similarly, while I was working as a barmaid, as long as the patron was buying drinks for me there would be no other duties that I had to attend to. However, once my drink was finished and no other offer was made to me by the patron, the bartender would typically find an assortment of minor tasks that needed my attention, tasks which could be immediately dropped if the patron offered me another drink.

Many who buy the services of B-girls do so with full realization that they are, in fact, buying the cross-sex encounter as a commodity,[6] and that they are getting no more than they are paying for, although they may well demand that they get at least as much as they pay for.

> Marv said that last night he went to the T—— (a bar just a few doors away from this one) and "dropped" five dollars with May, one of the B-girls. "It was sort of a waste," he said,

"because she drank it so fast that I couldn't even talk to her."

Lunt said that Julie (another B-girl at the same bar) "at least left the drink in front of her long enough for you to know that she had got it."

Marv and Lunt then started discussing the merits of the various girls along the street, and Kenny joined them with some of his own experiences. The consensus appeared to be that the girls who drank their drinks too fast were not only unsatisfactory, but unfair as well: if a fellow was paying for conversation he was entitled to it. Lunt said, "If I just wanted to look at her I could do it for free."[7]

Where the purchase of sociability is taken as a normal pattern for cross-sex interaction, there is no stigma attached to being a buyer and like the Don Juan in an arena of noncommercial sex, the exploits of heavy buyers may be treated as though they were feats of a culture hero.

After Marv, Lunt, and Kenny were finished with their evaluations of the B-girls along the street, there was some general conversation about the men who patronize them as well. Everyone had some story to contribute, mainly about how much various people had dropped with the girls on one occasion or the other.

Connie, the bartender, told a very long, elaborate story about a horse trainer from Colorado who dropped almost $3,000 in the various bars along the street one night. Connie said that at one point in the evening the horse trainer had asked him to bring some fresh girls in, not because he was tired of the ones that were there, but because he wanted to pass the money around to all the girls equally.

Everyone laughed at the stories, but it did not appear that they were laughing at the men involved in them.

In addition to those for whom transactions with the B-girls are a matter of course, there are also customers who may treat the interaction as something different or something more than what it is expected to be from the standpoint of the B-girl. Thus, there are those who may enter into an encounter with a B-girl believing it to be a noncommercial bar pickup, and those who may enter into an encounter believing it to be a commercial encounter, but one which offers more than mere sociability. In either situation, such patrons may make trouble for the B-girl and the bartender as well, the former because the patron must be made to pay for what he believes he is getting free and the latter because he feels he is not getting as much as he believes he is paying for. The complaints that are made to the official agencies about B-girls' activity may come from either source.

NOTES

1. *San Francisco Chronicle*, April 27, 1963.
2. Evelyn Hooker defines the term "sexual market" as "a place where agreements are made for the potential exchange of sexual services, for sex without obligation or commitment—the 'one night stand'" ("The Homosexual Community," paper read at the XIVth International Congress of Applied Psychology, Copenhagen, Denmark, August 14, 1961). I should prefer to use only the first part of her definition—that is, "a place where agreements are made for the potential exchange of sexual services"—and to define "sexual services" in a very broad way to include everything from flirtatious sociability to sexual intercourse. To define the sexual marketplace only in terms of sex without commitment, or as one-night stands, ignores the fact that a long-term relationship can ensue out of an initial encounter, and while the marketplace may be populated with those in search of temporary encounters, it may also contain others in search of more durable goods.
3. A similar problem exists for homosexuals with respect to dancing: who is to lead? The problem here again is not merely a question of who is to act feminine and who is to act masculine, but rather, how is the distribution of activity for a joint endeavor to be allocated without a predetermined answer such as in terms of biological sex characteristics. *Cf.* D. W. Cory and J. P. LeRoy, *The Homosexual and His Society* (New York: The Citadel Press, 1963), p. 115.
4. *Ibid.*, pp. 112–113.
5. *San Francisco Chronicle*, April 27, 1953. There is, in many respects, a good deal of similarity between the B-girl and the taxi dancer. Of the taxi-dance halls, Cressy writes, "Young women and girls are paid to dance with all comers, usually on a fifty-fifty commission basis. Half of the money spent by the

patrons goes to the proprietors . . . while the other half is paid to the young women themselves. The girl employed in these halls is expected to dance with any man who may chose her and to remain with him on the dance floor for as long a time as he is willing to pay the charges. Hence the significance of the apt name 'taxi-dancer' . . . like the taxi-driver with his cab, she is for public hire and is paid in proportion to the time spent and the services rendered" (Paul G. Cressy, *The Taxi-Dance Hall* [Chicago: University of Chicago Press, 1932], p. 3).

6. Analogous situations exist for the patrons of the taxi-dance hall as well. See Cressy, *op. cit.*, pp. 109 ff.

7. It might be noted that one of the typical items of "evidence" that ABC agents and the police put forth in support of a charge that a woman is engaged in B-girl activities is the speed at which she consumes her drinks. For example, one agent is quoted as testifying that a girl "drank eight champagne cocktails at $1.50 each in 33 minutes." (*San Francisco Chronicle*, June 6, 1953.)

CHAPTER 17

The Compound and the Neighborhood

Javier Auyero and Debora Swistun

Flammable shantytown is located in the district of Avellaneda, right on the southeastern border of the city of Buenos Aires, adjacent to one of the largest petrochemical compounds in the country—Polo Petroquímico y Puerto Dock Sud. The Shell Oil refinery opened here in 1931.[1] Since then, other companies have moved into the compound. At the time of this writing, Shell refinery is the most important plant in the Polo. There is another oil refinery (DAPSA), three plants that store oil and its derivatives (Petrobras, Repsol-YPF, and Petrolera Cono Sur), several plants that store chemical products (TAGSA, Antívari, and Solvay Indupa among them), one plant that manufactures chemical products (Meranol), one dock for containers (Exolgan), and one thermoelectric plant (Central Dock Sud).

The name "Flammable" is quite recent On June 28, 1984, there was a fire in the *Perito Moreno*, an oil ship that was harbored in a nearby canal. The ship exploded and produced what one elderly resident noted as the "highest flames I've ever seen." After the accident, companies in the compound built a new (and, according to experts, safer) dock exclusively for flammable products. The label "Flammable" carried over to the adjacent community—formerly known simply as "the coast."[2]

FLAMMABLE THROUGH YOUNG EYES

A year into our fieldwork, we provided a group of students at the local school with disposable cameras. We asked them to take half of the pictures of things they liked about the neighborhood and half of things they did not like.[3] Although a few of them stated that it was difficult to take pictures of the things they liked ("because there's nothing nice here . . ." "How can we take photos of the things we like if there's nothing pretty here?"), the concurrence among the groups was striking: among the things they like were people (most of the pictures classified by them as "good" portrayed friends and family) and institutions (pictures of the church, the school, the health center). Yet, even when they placed the school among the "good" pictures, during the interviews they did not fail to notice its dilapidated condition. Many of them took pictures of the health center and included them among the "good" pictures, but not for reasons they would consider worthy: they routinely use the center when they get sick or when there is an emergency. During our interviews, those who pictured the center stressed how well they are treated. Among the things they dislike, they all mentioned: the dispersed garbage and debris, the stagnant and filthy waters, the smokestacks, and the building of the main company within the petrochemical compound (Shell-Capsa). They all abhor the contamination of the water, the soil, and the air, and they emphasize that pollution is the only reason they consider leaving the neighborhood. Before we move to the pictures two forewarnings are in order. Note that we never mentioned pollution to them during the week we did the exercise; we told them we were interested in their views of their barrio. The issue of pollution is something they introduced in our conversations. Note also that it is not our purpose at this point to evaluate the truth value of their statements: whether the high-voltage wires or the coke plant causes cancer is not as important here as the fact that they resolutely believe this to be the case and that they grabbed the opportunity given by the proposed photographic exercise to express these beliefs. In other words, in what follows we simply want to introduce the reader to the physical space of Flammable (and, to the extent it is possible in a written text, to its sounds and smells) with the help of the images and voices produced by local youngsters.

The "Good" Pictures: The (Few) Things They Like

Photos 17.3 and 17.4 (The Health Center): "There's an ambulance there, and they take good care of you." "If something happens, you can go there and they treat you very well."

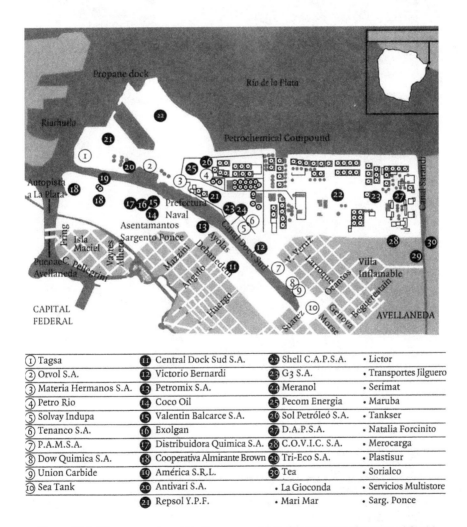

① Tagsa	⑪ Central Dock Sud S.A.	㉒ Shell C.A.P.S.A. • Lictor
② Orvol S.A.	⑫ Victorio Bernardi	㉓ G3 S.A. • Transportes Jilguero
③ Materia Hermanos S.A.	⑬ Petromix S.A.	㉔ Meranol • Serimat
④ Petro Rio	⑭ Coco Oil	㉕ Pecom Energia • Maruba
⑤ Solvay Indupa	⑮ Valentin Balcarce S.A.	㉖ Sol Petróleo S.A. • Tankser
⑥ Tenanco S.A.	⑯ Exolgan	㉗ D.A.P.S.A. • Natalia Forcinito
⑦ P.A.M.S.A.	⑰ Distribuidora Quimica S.A.	㉘ C.O.V.I.C. S.A. • Merocarga
⑧ Dow Quimica S.A.	⑱ Cooperativa Almirante Brown	㉙ Tri-Eco S.A. • Plastisur
⑨ Union Carbide	⑲ América S.R.L.	㉚ Tea • Sorialco
⑩ Sea Tank	⑳ Antivari S.A.	• La Gioconda • Servicios Multistore
	㉑ Repsol Y.P.F.	• Mari Mar • Sarg. Ponce

Figure 17.1 "The companies within the compound and Flammable" (Courtesy of Clarín)

Photo 17.1 "The barrio, the wall, and the compound." (Photo taken by Javier Auyero)

Photo 17.2 "Mi barrio." (Photo taken by Divina Swistun)

Photos 17.5 and 17.6: "The school building is falling apart. It's damn cold in the winter, we can't attend classes because of the cold. If you turn the [electric] heating on, the lights go off. And in our classroom there's a broken window, and it's very cold (*nos recagamos del frío*)."

The "Bad" Pictures: The (Many) Things They Don't Like

Overall, school students stress they didn't like the "bad" pictures because they show how dirty and contaminated their barrio is: "We

Photo 17.3

Photo 17.4

Photo 17.5

don't like any of these pictures because there's a lot of pollution, a lot of garbage"; "I like the neighborhood, all my friends are here. But I don't like pollution." In their minds pollution is associated with smoke (represented in the pictures of smokestacks, most of them taken late in the afternoon when the smoke can be better seen and thus excluded for their poor quality),[4] garbage, mud, and debris (represented in the pictures they took of the front of their houses, their backyards, and the streets they traverse daily). Pollution is also associ-ated with the main company within the petrochemical compound and particularly with the coke processing plant that was installed a decade ago (environmental organizations and some community activists tried unsuccessfully to stop the opening of the plant, arguing that it was potentially carcinogenic).

Photo 17.7: "This is the street where Yesica lives."

Photo 17.8: "And this is in front of her house."

Photo 17.6

Photo 17.7

Photo 17.8

Photo 17.9: "This is right in front of our house. There's a man living there, poor guy . . . you feel sorry for him. The rats are all around."
Photo 17.10: "This is my aunt's backyard."
Photo 17.11: "This is my backyard."

All of them see themselves as living amid waste and debris, en el medio de la basura, surrounded by stagnant and stinking waters, and by refuse that feeds huge, menacing rats. In several conversations during our fieldwork, mothers told us that they feared their babies would be eaten by rats "which are this big!"

Photos 17.12 and 17.13: "When you walk by, the stench kills you . . . you can see the rats

Photo 17.9

Photo 17.10

there, they are huge, like monsters." "Look at the river . . . it is all contaminated . . . I wish the neighborhood were cleaner."

Photo 17.14: "This is where we play soccer (in gym classes). . . . I wish it were cleaner."

One of the most revealing dialogues was the one we had with Manuela (who is now sixteen). One of the photos (Photo 17.15) she took shows the site where unmarked trucks dump garbage. Many neighbors scavenge

Photo 17.11

Photo 17.12

in the garbage and, according to Manuela, "they make a lot of money." In Photo 17.16, probably the one that best encapsulates students' concerns about their dirty surroundings, Manuela caught a cat eating from the garbage. And she uses the same word that she used to refer to her neighbors (*ciruja*, a scavenger): "Check out this cat . . . He is looking for something to eat. He is a scavenger cat (*un gato ciruja*)." One would hardly need sophisticated interpretive skills to realize that in matters of survival strategies and of surrounding dirt, neighbors and animals are, in Manuela's eyes, quite similar.

Pollution is not solely out there—in dirty streets, backyards, and playgrounds—but inside their own bodies where "contamination" has, in their view, a very precise name:

Photo 17.13

Photo 17.14

lead. In 2001, an epidemiological study detected high levels of lead poisoning among young children in the neighborhood (see below). The study received a lot of media attention—in the written press, which school students don't read, and on TV, which they do watch. Teachers also inform them about lead, and some of them or their relatives were themselves tested for the study. When speaking about pollution, they used the interviews and the pictures to talk about their loved ones and themselves as poisoned *persons*: "I would like to leave because everything is contaminated here. I don't know how much lead my cousin has in his blood . . . all of my cousins have lead inside" (Laura). "I have lead inside. . . . I had my blood tested because some lawyers said they were going to eradicate us" (Manuela).

Photo 17.15

Photo 17.16

Photo 17.17: "We don't like the factories because of all the smoke."

Photo 17.18: "This is all polluted. It's all coming from Shell."

Photo 17.19: "I don't like Shell because it brings pollution. . . . I don't know how much lead we have in our blood."

Many of the students have visited Shell's plant (Photo 2.20). Miguel liked it; as he puts it: "It's really cool . . . full of trucks." Carolina, who took a two-week-long computing course inside the company's premises, says, "It is ugly inside, machines, smoke, lots of smoke." Romina tells us that she and others "don't like it [Shell-Capsa] because at night there's a lot of smoke coming out. We once went to visit. They treated us really well, but they contaminate everything. . . . [Pointing to the coke plant] In front of my place, there's a woman who came to live to the neighborhood with her daughter. After a couple of years, they were all contaminated because of the coke. . . . Most people are contaminated by that." As Samantha Duts it: "There's a lot of disease here (*acá hay mucha enfermedad*)."[5]

Photo 17.17

Photo 17.18

Photo 17.19

Photo 17.20

In the pictures they took and in the opinions they expressed in conversation, it became quite evident that these youngsters blame Shell (and the petrochemical compound by extension) for the smoke and the lead that affect their health. As they see it, Shell and the high-voltage wires (see Photo 17.21) that were put up in 1999 are the source of most of the community's health problems. As Miguel describes, referring to Photo 17.21, "These wires carry lots of watts. I've been told they are really dangerous. They bring skin cancer." Nicolás's picture (Photo 17.22) summarizes this generalized perception: "This picture shows what we don't like. The coke plant, the wires."

Many students took pictures of Dock Oil, an abandoned factory that was the site of the most recent community tragedy. On May 16, 2005, three youngsters, one of them a classmate of the students we interviewed, broke into the premises of the abandoned building to scavenge for iron bars. Apparently, a wall fell down after one of the teenagers pulled the wrong beam. Two were injured, and the third died. When asked, the students were straightforward about the reasons why

they included so many pictures of Dock Oil among the "disliked" aspects of their neighborhood: "Because that's where one of our classmates died," they all said. As we looked at the pictures and transcribed these youngsters' voices, we couldn't help but think that the reason they included so many pictures of that (ugly) building is related to the shaky ground on which they live—both literally and figuratively. No image, and certainly no words, can better convey the sense of insecurity that, based on unsafe terrain, is widespread among these youngsters.

Where does this visual journey leave us? Youngsters' images and voices serve us well to introduce the reader into the physical and symbolic space of Flammable. These lives do not unfold on the head of a pin but in polluted waters, poisoned soils, and contaminated air, surrounded by garbage where rats, as one of the students unambiguously put it invoking his worst nightmares, "look like monsters." Youngsters think and feel about the surroundings not as something to be occasionally reckoned with but as something oppressively present. To quote from Kai Erikson (1976), they see the

Photo 17.21

Photo 17.22

Photo 17.23

Photo 17.24

environment as "a sample of what the universe has in store for them." In presenting a single, almost monolithic, point of view on their surroundings, these pictures and youngsters' critical comments misrepresent what is a far more complicated (confused and confusing) experiential reality.[6]

NOTES

1. www.shell.com.ar.
2. The local improvement association is still called Sociedad de fomento pro mejoramiento de la costa.
3. We asked thirteen ninth-grade students of the local school to divide themselves into groups (five groups of two students each and one of three students) and we gave them disposable cameras containing twenty-seven exposures each. They were told to use half the film to take pictures of things they liked about the neighborhood and half of things they did not like. We gave them no further instructions. They all returned the cameras providing a total number of 134 pictures. We then selected the pictures that better represent the themes that were recurrent in the whole group.
4. "The factories release a lot of smoke," Manuela tells us. "It's all full of oil. I didn't take a picture (of the smokestacks) because the sun was in front of me."
5. Though technically outside the petrochemical compound, the incinerator of hazardous waste (Trieco) was also mentioned as a source of pollution: "People say that at night, they burn things at Trieco, and it's very, very ugly" (Romina).
6. The youngsters we interviewed have a view on their surroundings that is more uniform than that of the adults for two reasons: (a) they use the public space of the neighborhood (streets, plazas, open fields) much more frequently than do adults; and (b) many of their teachers (who do not live in the neighborhood) have a homogenous view on contamination and its sources, and they communicate it to their students. As we were told by two school principals and two teachers in almost identical ways: "This place is all contaminated because of Shell. Contamination is killing the kids." Their homogenous view might also have been the outcome of the conditions under which our interviews with them were carried out. These interviews were closer to one-time encounters than to the kind of conversations, based on long-term acquaintance, that we had with adults—we met with them three times: when we presented the photography project, when we gave them the cameras and minimal instructions, and when we reviewed their pictures and interviewed them. Alas, these students may have seen us as "outsiders," with the biased results that we described in the beginning of chapter 4.

SECTION II

Doing the Right Thing

The theme for this volume's final section of readings is the broad and sometimes controversial topic of ethics in ethnographic research. When designing their projects and while in the field, all researchers must consider four sources of ethical standards of conduct: the standards of their own institutions (colleges, universities, and research centers through Institutional Review Boards, or IRBs), their discipline's ethical standards, their own personal ethical standards, and the ethical standards of their participants. These sources can sometimes overlap with each other, and they can sometimes conflict. In a more recent piece, Ruth Horowitz (2009) reflects on her fieldwork in a Mexican neighborhood with gangs and illegal activities in the 1970s (1983), in a time before institutional ethics committees. She explains how the ethical conduct that she followed, such as telling herself that she would never turn her field notes over to the police and always using code words for illegal activities and pseudonyms, would never be accepted by today's IRB. Indeed, it is likely that many of the practices used by ethnographers in the past, such as studying minors without their parents' permission, would not meet contemporary ethical standards. We can debate the extent to which institutional standards place limits on fieldwork, as Horowitz laments they do, but this level of institutional regulation remains a reality for fieldworkers. Ultimately, ethnographers are the designers of their projects and authorities over their research in the field. We have seen how fieldworkers must cross social boundaries and manage relationships with their participants. They bear the responsibility to ensure that they do not cause them harm by designing their projects with their participants' specific needs in mind and by being conscientious of these sources of ethical standards and alert to unexpected events and situations while in the field. Ethnographers especially bear this responsibility when they study vulnerable populations, or groups that are particularly susceptible to harm by participating in a research project.

Examples of harm from participating in an ethnographic research project include psychological and emotional damage from discussing certain topics or from having one's life analyzed. Participants can also have their reputations damaged, such as in the case of people who engage in compromising activities behind the backs of their employers or families. Their life situations may also be further compromised, as in cases of people who engage in illegal activities. Fieldworkers attempt to minimize the harm they may cause by following such strategies as obtaining informed consent from participants and maintaining confidentiality. Both of these strategies include active communication with people in the field over the purposes of the research, the sensitivity and dissemination of the information, and the level of participation that the researcher plans on reaching. Ethnographers also use strategies that aim specifically at their relationships with participants. These strategies alter the traditional research–participant dynamic for the sake of improving the analysis as well as preemptively handling situations from which ethical conflicts may arise. Some attempt to minimize the gap between researcher and participant through compensation, most commonly financial. Duneier from Part I, Section II, for instance, agreed to share all royalties from his book with the vendors he studied. Since the project and book would not have existed without their agreement to share their lives, Duneier included the men in his book's earnings, compensated them for their time for interviews, and gave them any profits he made from his time working as a vendor. Fieldworkers also share their findings with their participants, such as by bringing a manuscript back to them for their comments on the analysis. Along with finding out from participants if any ethical standards were compromised, this strategy also serves as a validation technique, with the people under investigation determining the accuracy of an ethnographer's explanations about them (Bloor 1997). Whyte, from the previous section, documents that he grew so close with Doc—his main informant and guide through the world of the corner boys—that he regularly spoke with him about his sociological findings. Such a practice serves not just to avoid issues of misrepresentation, but also strengthen the communication between ethnographers and participants over the research process. This strategy can help avoid any ethical breaches, especially once field research has completed and the work has been published. Fieldworkers also make participants co-researchers in their projects. The best example of this strategy is participatory action research, or "PAR," which seeks to empower research participants by making them active contributors in the examination of their own situation (see Cahill 2007). However, all preplanned safeguards against causing harm could become compromised instantaneously while in the field, where any situation could arise and any type of encounter could unfold. Researchers remain the final authorities over their research, how it is presented, and how it is disseminated. They have a professional duty to consider the potential consequences their work could have on others and make every attempt to prevent and minimize them.

An important concern for ethnographers is when ethical issues arise in the field during data collection. These issues take several forms. Fieldworkers develop many types of relationships with their participants, some of which are stronger, closer, and more intimate than others. Ethnographers are attentive listeners and are interested in hearing the details of people's personal lives, thoughts, and experiences. Close relationships can lead participants to become overly dependent on researchers in terms of emotional and psychological, and even monetary and material, support and comfort. This adds another dimension to balancing closeness and distance in relationships in the field. In his work from Part I, Section II, for example, Venkatesh compensated his participants for the time he spent sleeping in their apartments in the housing project and helped them gain employment by finding them clients for such services as car repair. He refused to participate in helping them in drug transactions or prostitution, thus managing his relationships according to ethical principles. However, he reduced his "ethnographic engulfment" (Pollner and Emerson 1983, 252) by scaling back his involvement in the underground economy and site visits once he realized that he had entered into their system of exchange, acquired the expectation to participate in their hustles, and recognized his own behavior through their interpretations of it as a hustle itself. After they have spent some time in the field, participants also often understand ethnographers as sources of information and gossip about others in the group. In these cases researchers can face pressure from participants to expose certain details of what others in the group have told them in confidence. Ethnographers also face ethical issues when they are in the writing process. How best to represent a participant within a text without compromising ethical agreements, such as over their identities? As mentioned, for some scholars one solution is to bring a writing sample in which participants appear to them for their comments. This strategy raises the questions, however, of the extent to which ethnographers should cede authority over their work to their participants and how fieldworkers should respond to participants' concerns.

The three readings in this section each deal with several important questions that urban ethnographers must keep in mind when designing their projects and behaving in the field. As mentioned, fieldworkers have an ethical responsibility to obtain informed consent from their participants, which entails informing them of the project's aims, intentions, duration, their level of participation, and the amount of risk involved. But to what extent can ethnographers anticipate how a project, particularly one that is exploratory, will unfold? How can they predict the ways in which their relationships will develop? If they cannot always inform their participants of their research goals, to what degree should deception be permitted? As we have seen, fieldworkers wishing to immerse themselves in people's worlds often live among them and engage in their activities. But what level of involvement should urban ethnographers have if the activities are illegal? Showing empathy and a non-judgmental attitude is important not just for researchers to gain the trust of their participants but also to not cause them harm. But what if urban ethnographers find their participants' behavior morally wrong and find themselves in a struggle to maintain objectivity? The following pieces address these questions. As with such issues as getting in and crossing boundaries, ethnographers often reflect on the ethical implications of their research, and the situations in which they faced an ethical dilemma. As in the previous section, these readings do not feature discussions by the authors on the ethical decisions they made or the moral dilemmas they faced. I discuss the ethical implications of each work, while each piece presents the data that the authors obtained and the conclusions that they drew.

There are several studies that are regularly cited in social science research methods courses and textbooks as historical examples of ethically unsound projects that eventually led to the creation of IRBs. Some of these are the Tuskegee syphilis study, the experiments the Nazis conducted on the Jews during World War II, the Zimbardo prison experiment, and the Milgram experiment on authority. The first two represent studies that caused physical harm to participants while the second two represent studies that caused psychological and emotional harm. The most common sociological study that gets cited among these works is *Tearoom Trade*, by Laud Humphreys. Since its first publication, in 1970, this notorious work remains salient for ethnographers because of the numerous controversies and ethical debates it raises.

Before becoming a graduate student in sociology at Washington University, in St. Louis, Humphreys was an Episcopal priest with training in psychiatric counseling. During the 1950s and 1960s, a time when homosexuals and homosexual activity were tremendously persecuted, Humphreys counseled many of his gay parishioners, and he learned much about their plights and personal struggles. While a graduate student Humphreys wrote a research paper on homosexuality. After reading it, his adviser asked him, "But where does the average guy go just to get a blow job?" (1975, 16). In 1965 Humphreys set out to explore those public places, known as "tearooms," where men go to have impersonal sex with other men. Such places were and still are quite common in cities for homosexual acts. To learn more about this behavior, Humphreys studied the tearoom of a public bathroom in a park.

Humphreys devotes an entire chapter early in the book to discussing his methods, which consisted of two phases. First he immersed himself in the homosexual subculture by regularly going to gay bars and parties in the city. Over time the community's members began to view him as one of them. Humphreys intentionally kept his research aims a secret and "passe[d] as deviant." He argues, "I am convinced that there is only *one* way to watch highly discreditable behavior and that is to be in the same boat with those engaging in it" (1975, 25). But Humphreys only achieved total immersion in the group by passing as a group member and disguising his role as a participant observer. He discovered a way to continue his covert research in the tearoom: by serving as the "watchqueen," or the person who monitors the door for any authority figures and alerts the participants in the stalls if one approaches. As with the larger subculture, he did not reveal his identity as a researcher to the tearoom's participants, playing the role of "sociologist as voyeur." Even when police arrested him, Humphreys did not reveal his true identity. In this role Humphreys documented the tearooms' activities without disturbing the action.

But urban ethnographies based solely on unobtrusive observation and brief informal conversations lack the perspectives, attitudes, and detailed backgrounds of others that are necessary to understand and explain their observed behavior. To remedy this, Humphreys approached a dozen participants, revealed his identity, and received permission to interview them. However, he felt this would not be a representative sample of participants. He therefore recorded the license plate numbers of many tearoom participants during his role as watchqueen, and then obtained their contact information from the police, claiming he was conducting market research. Coincidentally a research center was conducting a social health survey of men in the city, and Humphreys was permitted to add his tearoom participants' names to the list. With the social health questionnaire in hand, he allowed some time to pass, changed his appearance, clothing, and car, and went into the homes of the men who he observed in the tearooms a year prior to interview them. Everything fell into place for Humphreys to conduct the seemingly perfect unobtrusive study.

The backlash against *Tearoom Trade* was tremendous. Critics railed against the deception and misrepresentation Humphreys used, chastised him for the potential breaches in confidentiality and harm toward participants—emotional, psychological, and reputational—that he risked without their informed consent, and even said that such a subject should not be studied. The faculty of Washington University threatened to rescind his degree. Citing the notion of "situational ethics," or the idea that ethics must be considered on a case-by-case basis, rather than set in stone, Humphreys defended his methods by saying that he was a legitimate participant in a public setting characterized by anonymity, and ensured the confidentiality of his participants by using pseudonyms and by protecting and then destroying his master list of their identities. In the 1975 edition of his book he includes a postscript on ethics, a section featuring several essays on his methods by both supportive and critical social scientists and journalists, and Humphreys' own response to their comments.

Unfortunately, *Tearoom Trade* is a work that is more commonly discussed for its ethical implications than for its substantive arguments, and overall it is rarely actually read. (Of course, some would say that the work should be discredited for the very fact that Humphreys obtained his data unethically.) But Humphreys presents an important exploration of an underground population and examination of social deviance, albeit one that depends on data that was obtained in an ethically dubious manner. With this background of the research methods in mind, the following piece presents some of the study's data and analysis. Combining the two main phases of his research, Humphreys discusses who the men who visit the tearoom are, what they do for a living, what their family life is like, and what sorts of activities they engaged in and meanings they constructed about their selves in the bathroom. He learns that many of the men who visit the tearooms lead publicly heterosexual lives with wives and children, which provides insightful evidence for the existence of distinct public and private selves along the lines of sexuality. Such a finding cast homosexual behavior in an entirely new light for the time period. Based on their backgrounds, activities, and interpretations Humphreys creates a typology of the tearoom visitor. Despite the insight it provides, however, important debates on such ethical questions as the extent to which urban ethnographers can or should disclose their research goals or the appropriate role they should play in the field will always lurk beneath it.

Ethnographers have studied a large number of subcultures that are seen by the mainstream as "deviant." An example that several have examined is graffiti scenes. While modern graffiti writing and organized graffiti crews originated in New York City in the 1960s and 1970s, they quickly spread to other cities through alternative media, where they took on their own local styles. Meanwhile, authorities in these cities responded to graffiti's emergence with swift action and harsh penalties, criminalizing it and its practitioners. Jeff Ferrell set out to study how graffiti writing spreads in urban environments, how graffiti writers organize and understand their behavior, and how graffiti writing is understood as both a creative and criminal activity (also see Snyder 2009). In his book, *Crimes of Style*, Ferrell examines the "Syndicate," or a loose association of graffiti writers in Denver in the early 1990s. He discovers that graffiti writers in Denver have constructed a subcultural community based on their definitions of style. They write on walls and buildings to gain the attention and respect of their fellow artists, attempting to stylistically push their work beyond that of their peers.

Ferrell does not just follow these artists to learn the importance of style in their construction and definition of community, he also learns how to write graffiti and regularly joins the Syndicate's members in making their tags and pieces. Ferrell readily admits that he directly and regularly broke the law in his research. In fact, referencing Ned Polsky's (1967) discussion of his classic research on such subcultural deviants as pool players and hustlers, he points out that "the researcher becomes an 'accessory' to crimes simply by witnessing and failing to report them" (1993, 28). Ferrell claims that while sociologists are justified in getting involved in the lives of their subjects in their field work for the purposes of understanding how they construct their social world, he admits that there are limitations to such involvement, such as when the activities are sexual assault or suicide. He explains that graffiti writing is a non-violent property crime and justifies his involvement methodologically by stating the importance of investigating the claims his participants made about the "rush" you get from combining creativity and illegality, and of directly confronting the structures of legality that label graffiti writing as a crime. This is quite an interesting interpretation of and justification for engaging in an illegal activity, or of conducting fieldwork "at the edge," as he comments elsewhere (Ferrell and Hamm 1998). On the one hand, Ferrell is engaging in the same activities as his participants to experience their social world and test their claims. However, as Ferrell admits, there are limits on an urban ethnographer's involvement in such activities. The difficulty is in determining what those limits are and respecting them while balancing the ethical standards of multiple sources. While the law is often clear on the legality and illegality of certain activities, ethnographers must navigate the murkier territory of ethics, which often offers conflicting guidance for behavior.

This section's final piece points toward the issue of demonstrating empathy and maintaining objectivity when confronted with behavior or attitudes that fieldworkers find morally wrong. Participants often hold views and engage in behaviors that ethnographers will disagree with or that compromise their own moral beliefs. We have seen in the example of Bourgois's crack dealers from this volume's first section how he reacted to their physical abuse of a mentally disabled boy in school (Bourgois also cannot help but react strongly to their tales of rape). The concern is that moral judgments threaten the relationships that ethnographers must form. Ethnographers are often interested in people who hold divergent perspectives from them and for whom morally suspicious behaviors are a reality. They often hear stories and witness behaviors that violate their own moral principles. In his research on drug robbers in the South Bronx, Randol Contreras is confronted by just such a situation. After a decade in which drug-related violence and death proliferated with the crack epidemic, in the 1990s drug markets in many cities like New York underwent a dramatic shift as crime declined, urban economies improved, law enforcement policies targeted street-level drug sales, and sentencing laws became stricter. In many places drug dealing was for the most part eliminated from street corners and schoolyards and went underground, through more private channels, thus shrinking the market. Many dealers who sold crack and cocaine on the streets reacted to this shift by turning to drug robberies, or robbing dealers of their money and drugs. Doing so usually consists of attacking dealers in their homes, and then threatening, physically abusing, and even torturing them. As Contreras documents in this piece, one of the strategies they use to gain access to dealers' apartments is "The Girl," or a young, attractive woman who plays on the masculine identity of male dealers and seduces them into getting ambushed and robbed.

Such a group is not just highly difficult to gain access to, but also highly susceptible to being adversely harmed by taking part in a research project. They risk their freedom by agreeing to share their criminal activities and tactics that could be seen by the police, as well as their safety and lives by publicizing their violent behavior against and theft from other criminals. Contreras does not have any problems getting in since he grew up with many of them in the South Bronx and resided there during his fieldwork. He says that when he was growing up he witnessed many friends and acquaintances turn to a life of drug dealing and eventually drug robbing. An example of "insider research," Contreras used his shared background, ethnic identity, and familiarity with the drug robbers to gain their trust and convince them that he would uphold standards of ethics in his research, which is especially important for them as a vulnerable population. As opposed to Ferrell, Contreras states that he "*did not participate in any illegal activities*" (2009, 473; emphasis in original) during his research. (He does not justify his methodological decision or the effect this may have had on his work in this article.) Instead, he would regularly hang out with the drug robbers on the streets and in local bars before and after robberies, where he learned about their plans and got reports on how they went. He therefore often heard stories of the physical violence that the robbers would perpetrate on their drug dealer victims. Contreras's participants, who are people he has known for much of his life, trusted him not to reveal their identities or crimes to authorities or, perhaps worse, to present their lives in a manner that will reveal them to the people they are robbing. But Contreras must also regularly hear stories of self-justified violence, as well as of the mistreatment of "The Girl" by the robbers. In fact, such accounts and the interpretations that the social actors make of them are crucial to his analysis since he does not observe the behaviors firsthand. Contreras exemplifies the participant observer's role as interpreter of his participants' understandings and not as judge of them. With knowledge of criminal behavior that leads to laws being broken and physical pain being inflicted on others, he neither betrays the trust his participants show in him nor intervenes in their behavior in any way that would negatively impact their lives.

This section has only introduced the subject of ethics in fieldwork. While informative these three studies do not cover the wide range of ethical issues that emerge in ethnographic work, nor do they provide any universal codes of conduct. Each ethnographer's research decisions primarily pertain to their own projects on a specific group of participants. Because of the potential for unpredictable events happening in the field, we can say that ethnographic work will always be influenced to some degree by situations that emerge. The decisions that other fieldworkers have made to avoid and minimize the chances of harm occurring provide ethnographers with guidance on how to manage these situations when they do.

REFERENCES

Bloor, M. 1997. "Techniques of Validation in Qualitative Research: A Critical Commentary," in G. Miller & R. Dingwall (eds.), *Context and Method in Qualitative Research*. London: Sage: 37–50.

Cahill, C. 2007. "Doing Research with Young People: Participatory Research and the Rituals of Collective Work," *Children's Geographies*, 5, 3: 297–312.

Contreras, R. 2009. "'Damn, Yo—Who's That Girl?' An Ethnographic Analysis of Masculinity in Drug Robberies," *Journal of Contemporary Ethnography*, 38, 4: 465–466; 474–483.

Ferrell, J. 1993. "Denver Graffiti and the Syndicate Scene," *Crimes of Style: Urban Graffiti and the Politics of Criminality*. Boston: Northeastern University Press: 21–26; 49–53.

Ferrell, J. & Hamm, M.S. (eds.) 1998. *Ethnography at the Edge: Crime, Deviance, and Field Research*. Boston: Northeastern University Press.

Horowitz, R. 1983. *Honor and the American Dream: Culture and Identity in a Chicano Community*. New Brunswick: Rutgers University Press.

Horowitz, R. 2009. "The Chicago School and the Roots of Urban Ethnography: An Intergenerational Conversation with Gerald D. Jaynes, David E. Apter, Herbert J. Gans, William Kornblum, Ruth Horowitz, James F. Short, Jr., Gerald Suttles and Robert E. Washington," *Ethnography*, 10, 4: 375–396.

Humphreys, L. 1975. "The People Next Door," *Tearoom Trade: Impersonal Sex in Public Places*. Piscataway: Aldine Transactions: 106–111; 114–122.

Pollner, M. & Emerson, R.M. 1983. "The Dynamics of Inclusion and Distance in Fieldwork Relations," in R.M. Emerson (ed.), *Contemporary Field Research: A Collection of Readings*. Boston: Little, Brown: 235–252.

Polsky, N. 1967. *Hustlers, Beats, and Others*. Chicago: Aldine Publishing Co.

Snyder, G. 2009. *Graffiti Lives: Beyond the Tag in New York's Urban Underground*. New York: New York University Press.

CHAPTER 18

The People Next Door

Laud Humphreys

THE ROLE RELATIONSHIP
OF TOM AND MYRA

This handsome couple live in ranch-style sub-
urbia with their two young children. Tom is
in his early thirties—an aggressive, muscular,
and virile-looking male. He works "about
seventy-five hours a week" at his new job
as a chemist. "I am *wild* about my job," he
says. "I really love it!" Both of Tom's "really
close" friends he met at work.

He is Methodist and Myra a Roman Catholic, but each goes to his or her own church.
Although he claims to have broad interests in
life, they boil down to "games—sports like
touch football or baseball."

When I asked him to tell me something
about his family, Tom replied only in terms
of their "good fortune" that things are not
worse:

> We've been fortunate that a religious problem
> has not occurred. We're fortunate in having
> two healthy children. We're fortunate that we
> decided to leave my last job. Being married has
> made me more stable.

They have been married for eleven years, and
Myra is the older of the two. When asked
who makes what kinds of decisions in his
family, he said: "She makes most decisions
about the family. She keeps the books. But I
make the *major* decisions."

Myra does the household work and takes
care of the children. Perceiving his main

duties as those of "keeping the yard up" and
"bringing home the bacon," Tom sees as his
wife's only shortcoming "her lack of discipline in organization." He remarked:

> She's very attractive . . . has a fair amount of
> poise. The best thing is that she gets along well
> and is able to establish close relationships with
> other women.

Finally, when asked how he thinks his wife
feels about him and his behavior in the family, Tom replied: "She'd like to have me
around more—would like for me to have a
closer relationship with her and the kids."
He believes it is "Very important" to have
the kind of sex life he needs. Reporting that
he and Myra have intercourse about twice
a month, he feels that his sexual needs are
"adequately met" in his relationships with
his wife. I also know that, from time to time,
Tom has sex in the restrooms of a public
park.

As an upwardly mobile man, Tom was
added to the sample at a point of transition in
his career as a tearoom participant. If Tom is
like others who share working class origins,
he may have learned of the tearoom as an
economical means of achieving orgasm during his Navy years. Of late, he has returned to
the restrooms for occasional sexual "relief,"
since his wife, objecting to the use of birth
control devices, has limited his conjugal
outlets.

Tom still perceives his sexual needs in the symbolic terms of the class in which he was socialized: "about twice a month" is the frequency of intercourse generally reported by working class men; and, although they are reticent in reporting it, they do not perceive this frequency as adequate to meet their sexual needs, which they estimate are about the same as those felt by others of their age. My interviews indicate that such perceptions of sexual drive and satisfaction prevail among working class respondents, whereas they are uncommon for those of the upper-middle and upper classes. Among the latter, the reported perception is of both a much higher frequency of intercourse and needs greater in their estimation than those of "most other men."

THE AGING CRISIS

Not only is Tom moving into a social position that may cause him to reinterpret his sexual drive, he is also approaching a point of major crisis in his career as a tearoom participant. At the time when I observed him in an act of fellatio, he played the insertor role. Still relatively young and handsome, Tom finds himself sought out as "trade."[1] Not only is that the role he expects to play in the tearoom encounters, it is the role others expect of him.

"I'm not toned up anymore," Tom complains. He is gaining weight around the middle and losing hair. As he moves past thirty-five, Tom will face the aging crisis of the tearooms. Less and less frequently will he find himself the one sought out in these meetings. Presuming that he has been sufficiently reinforced to continue this form of sexual operation, he will be forced to seek other men. As trade he was not expected to reciprocate, but he will soon be increasingly expected to serve as insertee for those who have first taken that role for him.

In most cases, fellatio is a service performed by an older man upon a younger. In one encounter, for example, a man appearing to be around forty was observed as insertee with a man in his twenties as insertor. A few minutes later, the man of forty was being sucked by one in his fifties. Analyzing the estimated ages of the principal partners in 53 observed acts of fellatio, I arrived at these conclusions: the insertee was judged to be older than the insertor in forty cases; they were approximately the same age in three; and the insertor was the older in ten instances. The age differences ranged from an insertee estimated to be twenty-five years older than his partner to an insertee thought to be ten years younger than his insertor.

From the interviewed respondents, for whom the ages are known rather than estimated, a like picture emerges: 78 per cent of those age twenty-four or less were observed taking the insertor role: 63 per cent of those in the twenty-five to thirty-four age range were inserters; but only 46 per cent of men in the thirty-five to forty-four range were inserters when observed, as were only 8 per cent of those forty-five and older.

Strong references to this crisis of aging are found in my interviews with cooperating respondents, one of whom had this to say:

Well, I started off as the straight young thing. Everyone wanted to suck my cock. I wouldn't have been caught dead with one of the things in my mouth! . . . So, here I am at forty—with grown kids—and the biggest cocksucker in [the city]!

Similar experiences were expressed, in more reserved language, by another man, some fifteen years his senior:

I suppose I was around thirty-five—or thirty-six—when I started giving out blow jobs. It just got so I couldn't operate any other way in the park johns. I'd still rather have a good blow job any day, but I've gotten so I like it the way it is now.

Perhaps by now the writings of Hooker, Hoffman, and others have dispelled the idea that men who engage in homosexual acts may be typed by any consistency of performance in one or another sexual role. Undoubtedly, there are preferences: few persons are so adaptable, their conditioning so undifferentiated, that they fail to exercise choice between various sexual roles and positions. Such preferences, however, are learned, and sexual repertories tend to expand with time and experience. This study of restroom sex indicates that sexual roles within these encounters are far from stable. They are apt to change within an encounter, from one encounter to another, with age, and with the amount of exposure to influences from a sexually deviant subculture.

It is to this last factor that I should like to direct the reader's attention. The degree of contact with a network of friends who share the actor's sexual interests takes a central position in mediating not only his preferences for sex role, but his style of adaptation to—and rationalization of—the deviant activity in which he participates. There are, however, two reasons why I have not classified research subjects in terms of their participation in the homosexual subculture. It is difficult to measure accurately the degree of such involvement; and such subcultural interaction depends upon other social variables, two of which are easily measured.

The first of these characteristics is marital status. In his study of jazz musicians, Becker pointed out that "the musician's family (both the one he is born into and the one he creates by marrying) has a major effect on his career."[2] Family status has a definitive effect on the deviant careers of those whose concern is with controlling information about their sexual behavior. The married man who engages in homosexual activity must be much more cautious about his involvement in the subculture than his single counterpart. As a determinant of life style and sexual activity, marital status is also a determinant of the patterns of deviant adaptation and rationalization. Only those in my sample who were

divorced or separated from their wives were difficult to categorize as either married or single. Those who had been married, however, showed a tendency to remain in friendship networks with married men. Three of the four were still limited in freedom by responsibilities for their children. For these reasons, I have included all men who were once married in the "married" categories.

The second determining variable is the relative autonomy of the respondent's occupation. A man is "independently" employed when his job allows him freedom of movement and security from being fired; the most obvious example is self-employment. Occupational "dependence" leaves a man little freedom for engaging in disreputable activity. The sales manager or other executive of a business firm has greater freedom than the salesman or attorney who is employed in the lower echelons of a large industry or by the federal government. The sales representative whose territory is far removed from the home office has greater independence, in terms of information control, than the minister of a local congregation. The majority of those placed in both the married and unmarried categories with *dependent* occupations were employed by large industries or the government.

Median education levels and annual family incomes indicate that those with dependent occupations rank lower on the socioeconomic scale. Only in the case of married men, however, is this correlation between social class and occupational autonomy strongly supported by the ratings of these respondents on Warner's Index of Status Characteristics. Nearly all the married men with dependent occupations are of the upper-lower or lower-middle classes, whereas those with independent occupations are of the upper-middle or upper classes. For single men, the social class variable is neither so easily identifiable nor so clearly divided. Nearly all single men in the sample can be classified only as "vaguely middle class."

As occupational autonomy and marital status remain the most important dimensions along which participants may be ranked, we shall consider four general types of tearoom customers: (1) married men with dependent occupations, (2) married men with independent occupations, (3) unmarried men with independent occupations, and (4) unmarried men with dependent occupations. As will become evident with the discussion of each type, I have employed labels from the homosexual argot, along with pseudonyms, to designate each class of participants. This is done not only to facilitate reading but to emphasize that we are describing persons rather than merely "typical" constructs.

TYPE I: TRADE

The first classification, which includes nineteen of the participants (38 per cent), may be called "trade," since most would earn that appellation from the gay subculture. All of these men are, or have been, married—one was separated from his wife at the time of interviewing and another was divorced.

Most work as truck drivers, machine operators, or clerical workers. There is a member of the armed forces, a carpenter, and the minister of a pentecostal church. Most of their wives work, at least part-time, to help raise their median annual family income to $8,000. One in six of these men is black. All are normally masculine in appearance and mannerism. Although fourteen have completed high school, there are only three college graduates among them, and five have had less than twelve years of schooling.

George is representative of this largest group of respondents. Born of second-generation German parentage in an ethnic enclave of the midwestern city where he still resides, he was raised as a Lutheran. He feels that his father (like George a truck driver) was quite warm in his relationship with him as a child. His mother he describes as a very nervous, asthmatic woman and thinks that an older sister suffered a nervous breakdown some years ago, although she was never treated for it. Another sister and a brother have evidenced no emotional problems.

At the age of twenty he married a Roman Catholic girl and has since joined her church, although he classifies himself as "lapsed." In the fourteen years of their marriage, they have had seven children, one of whom is less than a year old. George doesn't think they should have more children, but his wife objects to using any type of birth control other than the rhythm method. With his wife working part-time as a waitress, they have an income of about $5,000.

"How often do you have intercourse with your wife?" I asked. "Not very much the last few years," he replied. "It's up to when she feels like giving it to me—which ain't very often. I never suggest it."

George was cooking hamburgers on an outdoor grill and enjoying a beer as I interviewed him. "Me, I like to come home," he asserted. "I love to take care of the outside of the house. . . . Like to go places with the children—my wife, she doesn't."

With their mother at work, the children were running in and out of the door, revealing a household interior in gross disarray. George stopped to call one of the smaller youngsters out of the street in front of his modest, suburban home. When he resumed his remarks about his wife, there was more feeling in his description:

My wife doesn't have much outside interest. She doesn't like to go out or take the kids places. But she's an A-1 mother, I'll say that! I guess you'd say she's very nice to get along with—but don't cross her! She gets aggravated with me—I don't know why. . . . Well, you'd have to know my wife. We fight all the time. Anymore, it seems we just don't get along—except when we're apart. Mostly, we argue about the kids. She's afraid of having more. . . . She's afraid to have sex but doesn't believe in birth control. I'd just rather not be around her! I won't suggest having sex anyway—and she just doesn't want it anymore.

While more open than most in his acknowledgement of marital tension, George's appraisal of sexual relations in the marriage is typical of those respondents classified as trade. In 63 per cent of these marriages, the wife, husband, or both are Roman Catholic. When answering questions about their sexual lives, a story much like George's emerged: at least since the birth of the last child, conjugal relations have been very rare.

These data suggest that, along with providing an excuse for diminishing intercourse with their wives, the religious teachings to which most of these families adhere may cause the husbands to search for sex in the tearooms. Whatever the causes that turn them unsatisfied from the marriage bed, however, the alternative outlet must be quick, inexpensive, and impersonal. Any personal, ongoing affair—any outlet requiring money or hours away from home—would threaten a marriage that is already shaky and jeopardize the most important thing these men possess, their standing as father of their children.

Around the turn of the century, before the vice squads moved in (in their never ending process of narrowing the behavioral options of those in the lower classes), the Georges of this study would probably have made regular visits to the two-bit bordellos. With a madam watching a clock to limit the time, these cheap whorehouses provided the same sort of fast, impersonal service as today's public restrooms. I find no indication that these men seek homosexual contact as such; rather, they want a form of orgasm-producing action that is less lonely than masturbation and less involving than a love relationship. As the forces of social control deprive them of one outlet, they provide another. The newer form, it should be noted, is more stigmatizing than the previous one—thus giving "proof" to the adage that "the sinful are drawn ever deeper into perversity."

George was quite affable when interviewed on his home territory. A year before, when I first observed him in the tearoom of a park about three miles from his home, he was a far more cautious man. Situated at the window of the restroom, I saw him leave his old station wagon and, looking up and down the street, walk to the facility at a very fast pace. Once inside, he paced nervously from door to window until satisfied that I would serve as an adequate lookout. After playing the insertor role with a man who had waited in the stall farthest from the door, he left quickly, without wiping or washing his hands, and drove away toward the nearest exit from the park. In the tearoom he was a frightened man, engaging in furtive sex. In his own back yard, talking with an observer whom he failed to recognize, he was warm, open, and apparently at ease.

Weighing two hundred pounds or more, George has a protruding gut and tattoos on both forearms. Although muscular and in his mid-thirties, he would not be described as a handsome person. For him, no doubt, the aging crisis is also an identity crisis. Only with reluctance—and perhaps never—will he turn to the insertee role. The threat of such a role to his masculine self-image is too great. Like others of his class with whom I have had more extensive interviews, George may have learned this sexual game as a teen-age hustler, or else when serving in the army during the Korean war. In either case, his socialization into homosexual experience took place in a masculine world where it is permissible to accept money from a "queer" in return for carefully limited sexual favors. But to use one's own mouth as a substitute for the female organ, or even to express enjoyment of the action, is taboo in the trade code.[3] Moreover, for men of George's occupational and marital status, there is no network of friends engaged in tearoom activity to help them adapt to the changes aging will bring. I found no evidence of friendship networks among respondents of this type, who enter and leave the restrooms alone, avoiding conversation while within. Marginal to both the heterosexual and homosexual worlds, these men shun involvement in any form of gay subculture. Type I participants report fewer friends of any sort than do those of other classes. When asked how many close friends he has, George answered: "None. I haven't got time for that."

It is difficult to interview the trade without becoming depressed over the hopelessness of their situation. They are almost uniformly lonely and isolated: lacking success in either marriage bed or work, unable to discuss their three best friends (because they don't have three), en route from the din of factories to the clamor of children, they slip off the freeways for a few moments of impersonal sex in a toilet stall.

Such unrewarded existence is reflected in the portrait of another marginal man. A jobless Negro, he earns only contempt and sexual rejection from his working wife in return for baby-sitting duties. The paperback books and magazines scattered about his living room supported his comment that he reads a great deal to relieve boredom. (George seldom reads even the newspaper and has no hobbies to report.) No wonder that he urged me to stay for supper when my interview schedule was finished. "I really wish you'd stay awhile," he said. "I haven't talked to anyone about myself in a hell of a long time!"

TYPE II: THE AMBISEXUALS

A very different picture emerges in the case of Dwight. As sales manager for a small manufacturing concern, he is in a position to hire men who share his sexual and other interests. Not only does he have a business associate or two who share his predilection for tearoom sex, he has been able to stretch chance meetings in the tearoom purlieu into long-lasting friendships. Once, after I had gained his confidence through repeated interviews, I asked him to name all the participants he knew. The names of five other Type II men in my sample were found in the list of nearly two dozen names he gave me.

Dwight, then, has social advantages in the public restrooms as well as in society at large. His annual income of $16,000 helps in the achievement of these benefits, as does his marriage into a large and distinguished family and his education at a prestigious local college. From his restroom friends Dwight learns which tearooms in the city are popular and where the police are clamping down. He even knows which officers are looking for payoffs and how much they expect to be paid. It is of even greater importance that his attitudes toward—and perceptions of—the tearoom encounters are shaped and reinforced by the friendship network in which he participates.

It has thus been easier for Dwight to meet the changing demands of the aging crisis. He knows others who lost no self-respect when they began "going down" on their sexual partners, and they have helped him learn to enjoy the involvement of oral membranes in impersonal sex. As Tom, too, moves into this class of participants, he can be expected to learn how to rationalize the switch in sexual roles necessitated by the loss of youthful good looks. He will cease thinking of the insertee role as threatening to his masculinity. His socialization into the ambisexuals will make the orgasm but one of a number of kicks to be found in such sexual encounters.

Three-fourths of the married participants with independent occupations were observed, at one time or another, participating as insertees in fellatio, compared to only one-third of the trade. Not only do the Type II participants tend to switch roles with greater facility, they seem inclined to search beyond the tearooms for more exotic forms of sexual experience. Dwight, along with others in his class, expresses a liking for anal intercourse (both as insertee and insertor), for group activity, and even for mild forms of sadomasochistic sex. A friend of his once invited me to an "orgy" he had planned in an apartment he maintains for sexual purposes. Another friend, a social and commercial leader of the community, told me that he enjoys having men urinate in his mouth between acts of fellatio.

Dwight is in his early forties and has two sons in high school. The school-bound offspring provide him with an excuse to leave his wife at home during frequent business trips across the country. Maintaining a list of gay contacts, Dwight is able to engage wholeheartedly in the life of the homosexual subculture in other cities—the sort of involvement he is careful to avoid at home. In the parks or over cocktails, he amuses his friends with lengthy accounts of these adventures.

Dwight recounts his first sexual relationship with another boy at the age of "nine or ten":

> My parents always sent me off to camp in the summer, and it was there that I had my sexual initiation. This sort of thing usually took the form of rolling around in a bunk together and ended in our jacking each other off. . . . I suppose I started pretty early. God, I was almost in college before I had my first woman! I always had some other guy on the string in prep school—some real romances there! But I made up for lost time with the girls during my college years. . . . During that time, I only slipped back into my old habits a couple of times—and then it was a once-only occurrence with a roommate after we had been drinking.

Culminating an active heterosexual life at the university, Dwight married the girl he had impregnated. He reports having intercourse three or four times a week with her throughout their eighteen married years but also admits to supplementing that activity on occasion: "I had the seven-year-itch and stepped out on her quite a bit then." Dwight also visits the tearooms almost daily:

> I guess you might say I'm pretty highly sexed [he chuckled a little], but I really don't think that's why I go to tearooms. That's really not sex. Sex is something I have with my wife in bed. It's not as if I were committing adultery by getting

my rocks off—or going down on some guy—in a tearoom. I get a kick out of it. Some of my friends go out for handball. I'd rather cruise the park. Does that sound perverse to you?

Dwight's openness in dealing with the more sensitive areas of his biography was typical of upper-middle and upper class respondents of both the participant and control samples. As was mentioned in Chapter 2, actual refusals of interviews came almost entirely from lower class participants; more of the cooperating respondents were of the upper socioeconomic ranks. In the same vein, working class respondents were most cautious about answering questions pertaining to their income and their social and political views.

Other researchers have encountered a similar response differential along class lines, and I realize that my educational and social characteristics encourage rapport with Dwight more than with George. It may also be assumed that sympathy with survey research increases with education. Two-thirds of the married participants with occupational independence are college graduates.

It has been suggested, however, that another factor may be operative in this instance: although the upper class deviants may have more to lose from exposure (in the sense that the mighty have farther to fall), they also have more means at their disposal with which to protect their moral histories.[4] As noted in Chapter 5, some need only tap their spending money to pay off a member of the vice squad. In other instances, social contacts with police commissioners or newpaper publishers make it possible to squelch either record or publicity of an arrest. One respondent has made substantial contributions to a police charity fund, while another hired private detectives to track down a blackmailer. Not least in their capacity to cover for errors in judgment is the fact that their word has the backing of economic and social influence. Evidence must be strong to prosecute a man who can hire the best attorneys. Lower class men are rightfully more suspicious, for they have fewer resources with which to defend themselves if exposed.

This does not mean that Type II participants are immune to the risks of the game but simply that they are bidding from strength. To them, the risks of arrest, exposure, blackmail, or physical assault contribute to the excitement quotient. It is not unusual for them to speak of cruising as an adventure, in contrast with the trade, who engage in a furtive search for sexual relief. On the whole, then, the action of Type II respondents is apt to be somewhat bolder and their search for "kicks" less inhibited than that of most other types of participants.

Dwight is not fleeing from an unhappy home life or sexless marriage to the encounters in the parks. He expresses great devotion to his wife and children: "They're my whole life," he exclaims. All evidence indicates that, as father, citizen, businessman, and church member, Dwight's behavior patterns—as viewed by his peers—are exemplary.

Five of the twelve participants in Dwight's class are members of the Episcopal church. Dwight is one of two who were raised in that church, although he is not as active a churchman as some who became Episcopalians later in life. In spite of his infrequent attendance at worship, he feels his church is "just right" for him and needs no changing. Its tradition and ceremony are intellectually and esthetically pleasing to him. Its liberal outlook on questions of morality round out a religious orientation that he finds generally supportive.

In an interview witnessed by a friend he had brought to meet me, Dwight discussed his relationship with his parents: "Father ignored me. He just never said anything to me. I don't think he ever knew I existed." [His father was an attorney, esteemed beyond the city of Dwight's birth, who died while his only son was yet in his teens.] "I hope I'm a better father to my boys than he was to me," Dwight added.

"But his mother is a remarkable woman," the friend interjected, "really one of the most fabulous women I've met! Dwight took me back to meet her—years ago, when we were lovers of a sort. I still look forward to her visits."

"She's remarkable just to have put up with me," Dwight added:

> Just to give you an idea, one vacation I brought another boy home from school with me. She walked into the bedroom one morning and caught us bare-assed in a 69 position. She just excused herself and backed out of the room. Later, when we were alone, she just looked at me—over the edge of her glasses—and said: "I'm not going to lecture you, dear, but I do hope you don't swallow that stuff!"

Although he has never had a nervous breakdown, Dwight takes "an occasional antidepressant" because of his "moodiness." "I'm really quite moody, and I go to the tearooms more often when my spirits are low." While his periods of depression may result in increased tearoom activity, this deviant behavior does not seem to produce much tension in his life:

> I don't feel guilty about my little sexual games in the park. I'm not some sort of sick queer.... You might think I live two lives; but, if I do, I don't feel split in two by them.

Unlike the trade, Type II participants recognize their homosexual activity as indicative of their own psychosexual orientations. They think of themselves as bisexual or ambisexual and have intellectualized their deviant tendencies in terms of the pseudopsychology of the popular press. They speak often of the great men of history, as well as of certain movie stars and others of contemporary fame, who are also "AC/DC."[5] Goffman has remarked that stigmatized Americans "tend to live in a literarily-defined world."[6] This is nowhere truer than of the subculturally oriented participants of this study. Not only do they read a great deal about homosexuality, they discuss it within their network of friends. For the Dwights there is subcultural support that enables them to integrate their deviance with the remainder of their lives, while maintaining control over the information that could discredit their whole being. For these reasons they look upon the gaming encounters in the parks as enjoyable experiences.

A physician (not included in my sample) whom I visited repeatedly outside the tearooms says that his day is not complete without a visit to the public johns. His children are raised; he loves his wife "dearly"; he enjoys stature in his profession; normally masculine in appearance, he has never been publicly labeled as deviant. His sexual aberrance is a routinized part of his life, isolated from the rest chiefly by means of information control, much as a surreptitious gambling habit might be hidden from his family and neighbors. As long as knowledge of his ventures in public

sex is kept from his mate (whom he believes to be sexually inadequate), it is possible that the sexual activity in his favorite tearoom may actually be functional for the maintenance of his marital stability.

NOTES

1. In the homosexual argot, "trade" are those men who make themselves available for acts of fellatio but who, regarding themselves as "straight," refuse to reciprocate in the sexual act.
2. Howard S. Becker, *Outsiders* (New York: The Free Press, 1963), p. 103.
3. Albert J. Reiss, Jr., "The Social Integration of Queers and Peers," *Social Problems,* Vol. 9, No. 2 (Fall, 1961), p. 114.
4. The author is indebted to John I. Kitsuse for this valuable suggestion, giving rise to the analysis of types in terms of their resources for information control.
5. Because these men label themselves as Ambisexual, I call them that; however, most of those in other categories may also engage in heterosexual as well as homosexual behavior.
6. Erving Goffman, *Stigma* (Englewood Cliffs, New Jersey: Prentice-Hall, 1963), p. 25.

CHAPTER 19

Denver Graffiti and the Syndicate Scene

Jeff Ferrell

It's about 7:30—nearly dark—on a September Saturday evening in Denver, and I drive by Scooters, the neighborhood liquor store, to pick up a six pack of cheap beer. A few minutes later I arrive at the P. Gallery, an alternative gallery/living space across from the homeless shelters in the "worst" part of downtown Denver. Waiting for me out on the roof are Eye Six, Mac (also known as Xerox), and J., a young woman who photographs graffiti and "hangs" with members of the subculture. After a couple of beers, we head out by car, first to "Wino Willy's" down the street for a twelve pack of cheap beer and a pocket-size bottle of Yukon Jack, and then on to a parking lot near Denver's lower downtown railyards.

Leaving the car, we walk down an alley to the abutment of a viaduct which spans the railyards, and scramble down into the yards. We're cutting crosswise though the yards, heading for what graffiti writers call the "Towering Inferno." An abandoned grain mill and warehouse, the Inferno is home not only to hoboes and the homeless, but to graffiti in a variety of forms. Up and down its seven floors, amateur writers have sprayed names and phrases, and on a couple of floors, quotations from philosophers. The Bloods and Crips (the "B's and C's," as some graffiti writers call them) have also been here, and have left various gang markings and symbols, including crossed out "b's" and "c's," and the image of a "B-Boy." Skinhead graffiti—

swastikas, white power slogans—adorns the rooftop. The more elaborate graffiti of Denver's graffiti subculture is also here. On an outer wall, above an old loading platform, is an unusual Eye Six throw-up of some years ago; it combines a painted eye, looking out over the word "SIX" in block letters, with a series of stylized Oriental letters. Beneath this is one of Rasta 68's tags—in this case tagged as ":Rasta:"—and around the corner one of his early murals, now tagged over by other writers. A few floors up, on an inside wall, Top has painted an elaborate, stylized "TOP!" mural in red, orange, pink and blue, and tagged "Syndicate"—the name of his crew—above it.[1] Tonight, as discussed back at P. Gallery, we plan to paint a mural on the roof.

As we walk, though, Eye Six and Mac spot a wall which borders the yards, consider the graffiti pieces along some stretches and the lack of pieces along others, and decide to paint a section of the wall, instead. A half mile later, we arrive at a stretch of the wall which wraps around the back of a storage yard, and which can be seen—in the daylight, anyway—from another of the viaducts.

Now we light cigarettes, open beers, and get to work. Eye Six and Mac pull from their bags cans of spray paint, some the more expensive Krylon brand, others cheaper off-brands; an old gallon can of pale green house paint, a paint tray, and a roller and Eye Six's piecebook. J. hunkers down to keep watch over the railyards. I go off looking to scrounge equipment, and come back with two old beverage cases and a piece of sheet metal.

Eye Six pours the house paint—which has, with age, turned the consistency of cottage cheese—into the tray, and he and I take turns rolling it onto the wall. Standing on the beverage cases for added reach, we eventually manage to cover an area roughly nine feet high by 25 feet long. As the paint begins to dry, Eye Six and Mac start outlining the piece, painting with light Krylon colors and referring often to a sketch of the piece in the piecebook. As designed in the piecebook, the piece is to be a large, elaborate "3XB," the name of one of the two graffiti crews—the other being Syndicate—to which Mac and Eye Six belong. Eye Six suggests that they make the letters "3XB" "the size of a New York subway car, top to bottom." For the most part, Eye Six and Mac work together. At times, they paint side by side, discussing the piece, the night, and graffiti generally. At other times, while one paints, the other stands back and checks the proportions of the piece as it unfolds on the wall. When Eye Six is unsure of his work, he asks Mac to "spot my dimensions for me"; when Eye Six notices a mistake or misdirection in Mac's painting, he tells him, or occasionally grabs a can of Krylon and begins to fix it.

As the outline begins to take shape, I also help with "erasing" the mistakes which Mac or Eye Six point out to me. I "erase" by spraying over sections of the outline with white spray paint—not Krylon, but one of the cheaper, "trash paint" brands. Though the work requires close attention, especially in the near-darkness illuminated only by some security lights across the rail yards, we maintain a sense of our surroundings. Those that are painting turn often to check the railyards, the sky, or real and imagined sounds; those that are not sit, squat, or stand so as to see behind and around us. When a police helicopter flies nearby with its searchlight scanning the ground, we press against an unpainted section of the wall and wait. And when a railyard security truck passes within a hundred yards or so in the course of checking trains, we hunker down in the grass and wait. The piece is further interrupted when J. notices the way in which the security lights cast our shadows on the wall, and suggests that we outline them in black spray paint. The resulting outlines form an oddly sinister group portrait of the night's crew.

As the elaborate outlines of the "3" and "X" are completed, the work of filling in the piece begins. The Krylon cans have long since been separated from their color-coded plastic tops, so Eye Six and Mac squint to ascertain the paint's color from the fine print on the cans' bottoms, occasionally risking a quick flash of light from a lighter or match. As they fill in the letters, they also pay attention to and discuss the amount of paint remaining, which they determine by the weight and feel of the can; at one point, Mac complains that there is only "about an inch" of paint left in the can he is using. I now move from "erasing" to another sort of work appropriate for a "toy," or inexperienced, writer: I fill in large, undifferentiated sections that Eye Six or Mac mark off for me.

During this process, we notice that four people—as best we can tell, two women and two men—walk by a few yards away in the railyards. A while later, two women—the same two as before?—walk up and, shyly and casually, begin to comment on the piece. Fifteen minutes later, two men arrive, and now we are sure that they must be the same four who passed earlier. And, during this process of introduction and negotiation, I realize that I recognize one of the women from an earlier encounter. Now I know who they are and why they are here. They're huffers.

A few days before, I had been photographing graffiti near the Platte River, which borders the yards opposite the wall where we now paint. As I approached the area beneath a viaduct, I noticed a young woman holding a can of spray paint. Given the scarcity of women in the Denver graffiti subculture, the fact that the paint was a cheap off-brand, and that I didn't recognize her, I wondered if she were a writer. Despite this, I asked, "What's up? Are you piecing?" but got no response. Instead, she walked slowly towards me, and as she came closer, I could see that her eyes were glazed. I could also see the rag into which she sprayed the paint before inhaling, and then I understood. She was a paint sniffer, a "huffer," and she was far gone on the fumes.

Now she and her three friends have found us, and as they sit around the edge of the scene, they begin to ask for, and occasionally grab for, cans of paint. Busily at work on their piece, Eye Six and Mac resist, both on ethical grounds ("No, man, you're gonna fry your brains on that stuff") and practical grounds ("Hey, man, leave that Flat Black alone, I'm using it"). The huffers counter that they will be happy to make do with our empty spray cans, since even those still contain enough fumes to be useful. So, the four newcomers take our empty spray cans, spray the residual fumes into our empty beer cans, and hold the beer cans to their noses while they sit and watch us paint. We talk a while—Eye Six pretends to know one woman's brother, and kids that he will tell him about her huffing—and then the huffers get up to leave. As they do, one of the men uses a can of paint not to sniff, but to scrawl some amateur graffiti—"California"—on the wall near the piece.

Despite the interruptions, most of the fill-in work is now done, and Mac and Eye Six turn to the more detailed styling of the piece. Mac uses the piece of sheet metal which I found earlier as a straight edge to sharpen angles and lines within the piece. He and Eye Six both add star-bursts, circles, and other stylized touches. Mac kids Eye Six about the "bubbles" he is adding to the piece, and hints that they are now passé; Mac chooses to paint in squares and other geometric patterns. As this is completed, Eye Six and Mac outline again the borders of the piece, this time using Krylon black to set the piece off from its background of pale green housepaint.

It's now almost midnight; the paint, beer, and Yukon Jack are running low; and enthusiasm for painting is being replaced by talk about police patrols and missed dinners. Despite the police helicopter, the railyard security, and the huffers, the piece has been completed, except for one thing: the "B" in "3XB" never made it onto the wall. So, although the crew name is "3XB," and although this is how the piece was designed in Eye Six's piecebook, it now stands as the "3X" piece. As we gather our gear to go, we again check the paint cans, keeping those with paint, and tossing empties out into the railyards. Before we throw away the empties, though, we carefully remove the spray nozzles and put them in pockets or bags.

We walk back-streets and alleys to the car, carrying both the pleasure and excitement of a piece well done and a few left-over cans of paint. This coincidence of attitudes and resources leads, without much discussion or planning, to tagging. As we walk, we tag bridge supports, loading docks, and back walls. In almost every case, the tags are those of crews rather than individuals; "3XB" at one spot, "SYN" or "SN" at another as a shorthand for "Syndicate." Mac even pauses long enough to execute an "SN" throw-up on the side of a warehouse. Back in the car, we drop Mac off at his house, and then head to a cheap, all-night cafe for dinner.

As this and the following chapter show, each moment in this night of wandering, piecing, and tagging illuminates the dynamics of the Denver graffiti subculture, and the social process of doing graffiti in Denver. The P. Gallery and Wino Willy's, the Towering Inferno and the railyards sketch the physical and social environments of graffiti work, the urban ecology of the subculture. Eye Six and Mac, 3XB and Syndicate hint at the social organization of graffiti writing, and the subcultural identities that evolve from it. The conversations between Mac and Eye Six, the on-the-spot evolution of "3XB" into "3X," point to the shared conventions, the negotiated sense of style, by which graffiti is produced. And the helicopter overhead, the railyard patrol nearby, the shadows thrown by the security lights across the way, all reflect the legal, political, and economic context of graffiti work.

SUBCULTURAL DYNAMICS

Even a quick examination of Denver graffiti begins to reveal the subcultural dynamics out of which graffiti writers and graffiti writing evolved. As already seen, a graffiti subculture—a "scene," in the writers' argot—began to emerge as writers started seeing each others' work, meeting, and forming crews. And as this scene grew, it not only created a collective context in which young writers like Fie and Rasta could develop, but redeveloped the graffiti career of an "older" writer like Z13. Drawing on shared aesthetic resources taken from the worlds of art, media, and hip hop culture, writers within the scene began to collaborate on designs, pieces, and identities—and did so with a sort of shared intensity beyond what many of them had experienced in traditional art worlds. For these writers, graffiti writing began to take on the many dimensions of collective activity.

At the core of this collective activity were the locations where writers came to piece together, and in so doing to create collective bodies of work. These were locations in which the scene became physically and symbolically real—in which the style and meaning of the place and the pieces transcended individual writers and tapped the subcultural production of graffiti. The original "wall of fame" defined the early configuration of the scene; it consolidated the efforts of "kings," encouraged the participation of "toys," and ensured the scene's increasing visibility in the very heart of downtown Denver. At the corner of Broadway and Colfax—the city's

center point at the southern edge of downtown—writers also began early on to meet and tag at what they called "writers' corner."[2] Fie remembers that "it was real popular to tag right there," as well he might, since he was arrested after an undercover police officer spotted his tagging there. Writers have subsequently utilized other, less visible locations—like a second "wall of fame" southwest of downtown, a third "wall of fame" evolving along a stretch of railyards wall, and the "Towering Inferno"—to meet and piece together.

Certainly one of the locations most deeply enshrined in the folklore of Denver's subculture is what came to be called, in a play on the subcultural term for graffiti writing, the "Bomb Shelter." During the late 1980s many of Denver's top writers painted elaborate pieces inside the Bomb Shelter—a large, abandoned railroad maintenance building in the railyards. Now bulldozed into splintered wood and broken, painted bricks—some of which have been collected as mementos by writers and graffiti aficionados—the Bomb Shelter became what Eye Six calls a "graffiti art gallery" (in Ferrell, 1990a: 10), and what others have dubbed the "unofficial Denver Museum of Graffiti" (*Point*, 1990).

Places like the first wall of fame and the Bomb Shelter constitute settings for stylistic interplay and social interaction, and in turn become part of the collective texture, the feel, of the local scene. As the number of places, pieces and tags has grown, and as writers have become more aware of and involved with the work of other writers, the dynamic among them has begun to build on itself. With the development of an active subculture, writers piece and tag not only with each other, but *for* each other; they increasingly define themselves and their activities in terms of other writers, and the larger scene. Thus, even when they piece or tag alone, they draw on the subculture's vitality and style—and on their sense of involvement with a larger enterprise—and engage in collective action.

Among those active in the scene, tagging is an inherently social activity. Surely hundreds, perhaps thousands of the city's residents regularly scribble nicknames, slogans, or declarations of love in back alleys and on bus benches; but they should not be confused with the relatively few taggers who account for the majority of the city's tags. These taggers tag within a context of subcultural meaning; they tag for each other. As the following chapter will show, such tagging in some cases directly draws more tagging from within the subculture. Even when it does not, though, it is embedded within a system of visibility, response, and status. Talking about Mac and other prolific subcultural taggers, Eye Six says:

Why do you tag? Well, you think, "I can't quit," you know. What he basically got down to was that he wanted fame and he wanted respect from the others. I mean, when you get down to it, there's twelve or thirteen people actively tagging the graffiti in Denver at any given time. He was interested in the respect of the other twelve.

Eye Six goes on to note, in regard to piecing, that "for me, too, it's to gain respect. . . . If you're painting on the street, I think in any art form, you want the respect of other artists." When writers piece, as when they tag, other writers make up their primary audience. Though they may hope that a piece will be seen and appreciated by the public, they can be sure that it will be seen and evaluated by members of the subculture.

Writers thus emphasize that the subculture functions to accelerate the technical precision and style of their work, and to create a sort of collective aesthetic energy on which they all draw. Voodoo remembers that in Baton Rouge, "everyone kept spray painting bullshit . . . 'cause there's no big scene. There's no cooperation . . . It's not like there's any kind of competition." Upon arriving in Denver, however, he found that

there was a good sense of competition, it was real healthy. And you had so many people involved to where it just moved me to go out twice a week, and carry a big load of spray paint on my skateboard to the railyard. I'd burn. It was like really inspiring . . . If there hadn't been the competition, I probably wouldn't have gotten as good as I did. The fact that it was like a scene sort of, an art scene. Everyone helped each other out.

Z13 likewise recalls that he was drawn back into piecing not only because "now there's like a scene going on," but because "there was competition in town, too, so that's always a part of it. . . . You know, seeing what you can do with the other guy." And Eye Six recalls that, after he "got on the grapevine" and organized the Progreso/"Denver Throw Down" show,

It was like a common energy thing. That was when everybody got real productive. That competitive edge . . . you're only as good as your competitor, in a lot of ways. It kind of pushes you to your best ability.[3]

If the subculture's "competitive edge" pushes writers to develop and hone their style, though, so does cooperation among them, as they learn new techniques and share stylistic innovations. Piecing together in the railyards, sketching designs in each others' piecebooks, or even arguing the merits of recently completed pieces over six packs of beer, writers negotiate a shared sense of style at the same time they elaborate their own. This cooperative development of individual and subcultural style goes on within and between crews. Fie, for example, points out that Eye Six has "really helped a lot as far as style and technique and all that stuff" not only in Eye Six's crews, Syndicate and 3XB, but throughout the Denver scene. Z13 adds that, as a member of Syndicate, his earlier "solo project" approach to piecing—which evolved largely out of necessity—has changed:

Now that I know these people, I like working with them. . . . Everybody's got their own unique style. Then I can see a little bit in their thing, you know. It always helps to learn new things from other people. So, I never turn down a chance to learn something from somebody else.

Although present throughout the subculture's activities, this collective stylistic process is perhaps most clearly manifested in the "art sessions" which Syndicate members hold. As Rasta says:

Me and [HL86] used to have art sessions. And I learned, you learn off each other. 'Cause I learned how [HL86] draws this certain thing, and then I'll see how Eye Six draws this certain thing, and then I'll see how Z13 like breezes through shit. And you just, you learn, you know. So that's what keeps the Syndicate, sort of holds it together, I guess.

As participants in an emerging "scene," Denver graffiti writers thus draw on common stylistic resources and in turn evolve new, collective notions of style as they do graffiti with and for one another. As they add pieces to a new wall of fame, or tag their way down a dark alley, they not only alter the face of the larger community, but develop an aesthetic community among themselves. As subsequent chapters will show, graffiti writing must be understood in terms of crime, power, and resistance; but it must also be understood as an activity embedded in the aesthetic imperatives which develop among the writers. Graffiti writing is not generic criminality, simple trespass and vandalism, with a stylish overlay of Krylon colors. It is an inherently stylish activity, organized around the interplay of writers' individual and collective artistry.

Denver writers make this manifest, talking about themselves and each other in terms of style. Style is the medium in which they move, the standard against which they measure themselves and their work. Z13, for

example, notes his pleasure at first meeting Eye Six because "I always liked his style," compliments Fie on having "a real, real good style," and defines his own style as character-oriented, "illustrative graffiti." Voodoo attributes his "fame, I'd guess you'd say, or my notoriety" to the fact that other writers appreciated that "my style . . . came from another direction," with its "organic" inclusion of roses and vines. And Eye Six points out the "long, drawn-out process" through which Denver writers must go in developing a distinctive Denver style that moves away from "New York style or L.A. style." [4]

In doing graffiti, then, Denver writers engage in crimes of style—crimes which must be located within the aesthetic operations of an emerging subculture. The next chapter will explore the elements of practical style which make these crimes possible, along with the specific dynamics of tagging, piecing, and other criminally stylish activities. Subsequent chapters will show how, for economic and political authorities, graffiti writing also presents itself as a crime of style.

NOTES

1. As of fall 1991, local graffiti writers—and especially the members of Syndicate—had added a number of new murals to the inside walls of the Inferno, and had made plans to paint still more. Despite these plans, though, Syndicate had temporarily suspended mural painting in the Inferno. A body was found at the bottom of an Inferno elevator shaft, and members feared increased police surveillance as a result. On this incident, see the *Rocky Mountain News*, October 14, 1991: 167.
2. Castleman, 1982, and Lachmann, 1988, provide interesting discussions of New York City "writers' corners."
3. Rasta 68 refers to this competitive process in terms of "daring people to take their piecing further."
4. A similar emphasis on style shows up in the comments of New York City graffiti writers, as recorded in Lachmann, 1988: 237, 239, 241: "I'm famous 'cause I ain't scared of the cops and I got the style." "I get it with my style, I don't got to fight." "No clerk, no . . . schoolteacher can say if I got style. Only someone who's out there . . . [doing murals] on the subways, in the parks can know to judge what I done."

CHAPTER 20

"Damn, Yo—Who's That Girl?"

An Ethnographic Analysis of Masculinity in Drug Robberies

Randol Contreras

On a drizzling, summer day, a young Dominican woman walks down Broadway in Washington Heights. The neighborhood is in *Quisqueya* land, a northern section of Manhattan with the largest concentration of Dominicans in the United States. It once supported a satiated drug market, a drug bazaar that featured drug sellers congregating on corners, on sidewalks, on stoops, competing desperately, dangerously, for the attention of drug consumers from all over New York City and nearby New Jersey. Still, like many other New York City neighborhoods, community backlash, crack's cyclical downturn, changing demographics, and police intervention, all reduced outdoor drug activities (Karmen 2000). A smaller market emerged, one dominated by less flash and arrogance; a furtive market involving patience and caution.

And Melissa from the Bronx, an attractive caramel-colored eighteen-year-old, with thick thighs, wide hips, large buttocks, a tiny waist—a body like a dense guitar that strums the imaginations of men with Dominican cultural tastes—is a part of the neighborhood drug market today. She walks toward a Dominican man, a drug dealer, hanging in front of a stoop with a friend. He looks to be in his forties; an old timer—a man too ancient for her tastes. But she continues toward him, reaches him, stops, asks: *Do you know where I can get some good weed?*

Melissa is The Girl.[1]

In illegal drug markets, dealers suffer from a peculiar apprehension; they worry about not only police, but also drug robbers (Bourgois 2003; Jacobs 1999, 2000). Haunted by images of being tied, interrogated, tortured, and faced with a harsh financial loss, drug dealers are cautious—extremely cautious—about their drug supplies and cash: paranoid, they triple-lock doors, repeatedly sneak peaks through curtained windows, and ponder the "true" identities of door knockers and ringers, passing pedestrians, and drivers. But rarely do they ponder the identity of The Girl who, in distress, knocks on the door, and asks for help; The Girl who flashes a smile in the street, slows her walk for an invitation; The Girl who they consider as easy sex—an easy "in and out"—that poses no threat to their drugs and cash.

But they should.

Drug robbers interpret this naiveté as a biological and social weakness in male dealers: it is natural, they reason, for men to want to mate with attractive women; it is men—all men—they reason, who compete in a masculinity contest, where they create male status through conquering women sexually. Many drug robberies, then, depend on The Girl, on how she contributes to this Cat and Mouse game—on how she plays on the masculinity of male dealers, seducing and luring them into a drug robbery, into getting them taken for their drugs and cash.

PLAYING ON THE MASCULINITY OF DRUG DEALERS

Drug robberies consist of stages: Pick a Target. Access the Target. Torture the Target. Get the Drugs and Cash. Split the Profits. *Adios*. The Girl is essential for getting to the target, the second stage in a drug robbery. Capturing a drug dealer, however, requires stealth; dealers are often cautious about the people they encounter daily—the "thug lookin'" guy glancing at them as they walk past in the street; the clean-shaven stranger meeting their eye as they scurry in and out of elevators; the mail deliverer; the Con Ed meter reader; the Jehovah's Witness who wishes to discuss the true meaning of happiness, the gospel of Jesus, of God, the oncoming Armageddon. But coming across an attractive girl, sometimes any girl, and catching her eye, in the street or through a peephole, takes a different meaning. A girl means potential sex, a romp in the bedroom, in an alley or a rooftop; sex means potentially bragging about it later, demonstrating masculinity and manliness; manliness means potentially gaining admiration, earning respect—all of it means potentially raising status, a rise of rank in the drug world, in the world of men. And as Melissa (who I introduced in the introduction), approached the dealer, smiling, she worked under these assumptions: the drug dealer could not afford to miss an opportunity to have sex with her, he could not afford to pass up added distinction among his peers.

After some small talk, and serious flirting, Melissa persuaded the dealer to a later date that evening. For the date, Melissa and the dealer remained in Washington Heights, going to a small social club around his neighborhood. Inside, Melissa tried to get the dealer drunk, ordering Hennessy cognac, insisting that he drink the same.

Melissa told me: "I was like, 'if that's what I'm gonna drink, you gonna drink that too. Fuck that. If I'm gonna get fucked up, you gonna get fucked up too.' So for every drink that I drank, he had two drinks." Perhaps because of masculine pride, the dealer gave in to her drinking demands, which now included drinking shots of rum. "I'll be like, yo, '*Papi, bébete un chin de 'to.*' [Papi, drink a little of this.] *Y yo me tiro ensima del* [and I'll throw myself on him], and he'll drink."

After a few rounds of liquor, they started dancing *merengue*. The dealer took this opportunity to get close to Melissa. He pressed his body against her. In her ear, he whispered: "I want to get to know you. I like you a lot. I'm glad we getting to know each other more." As a former underground stripper, Melissa was accustomed to rubbing her body against men, giving them lap dances and close-ups of her body. So when he pressed his body against her, and whispered in her ear, Melissa did not feel too uncomfortable. But then he pressed his lips on hers—"and I *kissed* him," Melissa says, disgustedly. However, she was so "fucked up" from drinking heavily, Melissa did not care then. "He was kissing me and I was like, 'Yeah,' I was kissing him too." I asked Melissa if she felt uncomfortable with people watching them. "Well, I was feeling nice and I wasn't really paying attention to anybody around me like that. But thinking about it now . . . now I have a problem with it. I feel disgusting!"

So, it was an evening of heavy drinking and kissing, slow dancing, and sensuous whispers; of later regret, of shame—but a fleeting regret and shame, for the thought of earning money had erased any regret on Melissa's part.

At about five o'clock in the morning, Melissa asked the dealer to take her home, in the Bronx, offering him to stay the night. A cab drove them to her apartment—which really wasn't hers—they went up in the elevator, reached the door, opened it . . .

Boom—he got bagged.

One summer afternoon, Pablo and Tukee, both Dominican drug robbers, explained to me how drug dealers often relax around women, setting aside their business interests.

"All niggas think about is pussy, bro," Pablo explained. "Look, man, I heard some place that men, they think about sex about every eight seconds or something like that, bro. You know what's every eight seconds, bro? I think that's almost like a thousand fucking times every hour! Trust me, Ran, niggas will open the door to get some pussy. And then to say that they fucked some bitch they just met, and that the bitch was a dime [a ten] at that, forget it, bro, they gonna open that door. [Pretending to a be a lucky dude] '*Oye, loco, si tu 'biera vi'to la chamaca que yo se lo metí, tu me llama el campeón. Yo soy el campeón, Ha-ha-ha.*' [If you would've seen the girl that I had sex with, you would call me the champion. I am the champion.] Trust me, they gonna open that door. Yo, how many men you know gonna turn down a fly-ass bitch, a bitch that's a dime, bro, a bitch that got a super fat ass? How many niggas? Man, I don't give a fuck who you are. If you see a fly-ass bitch, you gonna try to fuck her."

"Bitches be making niggas do a lotta shit," added Tukee. "They make niggas talk about shit they have, all the shit they moving—'Look, baby, I got this, this, and that over here, in my house, in my man's house, you know what I'm saying?' They talk about all that shit . . . shit they have in they house or shit that they gonna get, like how much dough they rolling with, all type of shit, B."

"Bitches even make niggas talk about shit they don't got," joked Pablo.

"For real, B, ha-ha-ha," Tukee said, laughing. "Niggas be moving only two ounces [of cocaine] a week, and they be like, 'Yo, you know what I'm saying, I be moving two kilos, three kilos a week . . . '"

"'I'm moving ten kilos, twenty kilos, ha-ha-ha!'" Pablo added, while laughing hysterically. "They be some broke ass niggas talking shit when they not supposed to. Especially to some stupid bitch they just met. That's why them dumb niggas get bagged."

As for The Girl, Pablo said:

"All she gotta do is say something like, 'Excuse me, I got a leak coming downstairs and I think it's coming from up here.' Then it's over, bro. They gonna open that door wanting to get that ass."

I pretended to be skeptical, telling Pablo that it seemed too easy: an attractive woman knocks on a door, says that she lives in the apartment downstairs and there's a leak coming down—that will make a drug dealer stashing a lot of drugs and cash open the door?

"Look, man," Pablo said, exasperated, "that shit works, bro. For real, man. Yo, one time we had this fucking bitch knock on a door, bro, and that's what she said. All she said was that there was like a leak or a lot of water or something going down into her apartment, where she lives downstairs. Randy, believe it or not, niggas opened the door, bro. And right there, boom, we just went in. Yo, Ran, man, believe me it works, bro."[2]

To Pablo and Tukee, male dealers reveal too much around women, exaggerating their drug status and earnings. The desire for sex and admiration is so powerful that dealers create a precarious situation, which makes them potential drug robbery targets. The more they reveal to women, they believe, the higher their sex appeal. The more they reveal to women, however, the more likely they are to get "bagged."

The Logic: as Melissa's example shows, when drug robbers set up a dealer, they sometimes have The Girl approach them in the street, an area where the dealer is around male friends or co-workers. For The Girl, this makes it easier to approach him, to bait him—his "boys" are watching. This strategy is a clever play on notions of masculinity upheld by most men, especially in the criminal world. Men often portray themselves as strong, aggressive, and virile

(Bourgois 2003), which means not spurning an attractive woman, a "dime," while around other men. Doing so may make them appear effeminate, worsen criminal social networking or job possibilities, and attract criminal predators searching for victims to strong-arm, bang-up, and "punk." So descriptive, colorful decorations—"this nigga's [an] ass," "he ain't nothin' but a chump," "he's a bitch-ass nigga"—are earned in and out of criminal activities (Copes and Hochstetler 2003; Mullins 2004). Therefore, rejecting a woman's advances, rejecting her obvious flirting and attention—technically, an action unrelated to business sense or courage in the drug market—can be used to mark a person's identity: "he's pussy." However, if he welcomes a woman's advances, well, now he's the "motha fuckin' man," "a player"—someone who has opportunities searching for him.

The Marijuana Line: when a woman buys marijuana from a street peddler, it often leads to sexualized readings of her character. Her boldness (she doesn't need a male to accompany her) can lead dealers to call her "a freak," a "hoe" [whore], or as Pablo saw it, "she's a whole lot of fun"; Tukee, "that bitch is open" [to anything]; and Gus, "easy pussy"—in other words, she is perceived to have no sexual inhibitions. Stickup kids, then, understand this—they understand themselves enough to guess how a dealer would sexualize a simple request from a female—"You know where I could find some good weed?" If the request extends to an invitation ("You want to smoke with me?")—Jackpot. However, the triumph—the certainty of easy sex ("she's getting high, so she's gonna give it up, son," Tukee tells me)—is short-lived if the dealer is a robbery target. The true Jackpot, then, was struck by The Girl and the robbery crew.

REPRODUCING MASCULINITY IN DRUG ROBBERIES

"Afterwards, I was like, 'Arrggh!'" Melissa said, breaking into a laugh. "I kissed a *viejo* [old

man] in my lips and all that. Arghhh!" Sensing her disgust, I asked if she would do it again.

"Yeah," Melissa said, smiling.

"Why?" I asked, surprised.

"Why not? For the money. It's easy and fast." We laughed.

To Melissa, the money was fast and easy; drug robberies could be done over and over again, nonstop, continuing the cash flow, uninterrupted.[3] However, I knew something she was clueless to: she could not play The Girl forever; the men did not respect her and trivialized her role; and after a big score, the crew would lie to her, cheat her, and pay her little. So, while The Girl was busy outfoxing potential drug robbery victims, drug crew members were outfoxing her out of pay. For instance, Pablo admitted that after using a Girl to enter an apartment, he lied to her about the score.

> "I don't tell them what's really involved," Pablo said, with a slick grin. "I let them think something else. I'll gas them, I'll lie to them. You understand? Like, for example, one time I said, 'My girlfriend is in there with this guy and, you know, I just want to beat him up.' And the girl just went and I didn't even have to pay her. And the door opened."
>
> "And she just left?" I asked, incredulously.
>
> "And she just left," Pablo said, "and let us do what we had to do. You see, there's a lot of little tricks you can use."

Pablo had deceived her: although the crew had found several ounces of cocaine and heroin, Pablo never revealed his true intentions for getting into the apartment. So, he never paid her.

Negro, another drug robber, admitted that he had also short-changed a female crew member.

> "I remember that one time we had a *muchacha* [girl] outside waiting for a guy that we were going to rob. He was supposed to come out of a building where he had an apartment with drugs—because he sold cocaine—and she was

supposed to tell us that he left the building. She was supposed to call us. The guy left the building, she called us, we went after him on foot. In a backpack, like the ones kids use for school, he had almost six hundred grams. We told her that we found forty grams, that we made a mistake, that we got him on the wrong day. We gave her a hundred dollars. If we would have told her that we got the six hundred [grams], we would have to give her almost a thousand dollars. Imagine that, giving her a thousand dollars for just telling us that he came out of the building. You're crazy if you think that we going to give her a thousand dollars. I'll put that one thousand to better use, ha-ha-ha."[4]

I asked him about why he did not want to pay her in full.

"*Imaginate*, if you don't have to pay someone . . . if you could tell somebody that you only found a thousand dollars, and you found ten thousand, you would do it. Anybody would do it. Any of these *tigueres* [guys] would do it. Even you would do it."

I asked Negro if he did it because she was a female.

"Look, I'll do it to whoever, whoever. But a woman is easier, she doesn't know anything about this business. You tell her anything and she'll believe it . . . because a woman is like that. Women are *boba* [stupid]. They're like children. They believe anything you say."

What if she doesn't believe you, I asked, and she finds out that you lied?

"I don't care if she knows. What can she do to me? I'll just keep telling her that she doesn't know what she's talking about. What can she do to me?"

Gus, another drug robber, explained in more detail how The Girl is manipulated and short-changed.

"Like a lot times," Gus informed, "The Girls would want like an equal cut of what we did. We were like, 'Nah, all you did was knock on a door. It's just a thousand dollars, just for that.' But without her knocking on the door, we would'a never got into the apartment."

"Can you think of an example?"

"One time we took like our boy's girl—he was locked up and his girl needed the money—so we took her. But she knew a lot about, you know, stickups from him. But she was like, 'Yo, I want an equal cut of what ya' got from that apartment. Fuck paying me a thousand dollars. I want a cut.' So it happens. But it doesn't happen unless it's that, unless The Girl really knows about what's going on. A lot of times, you know, The Girls would be happy with whatever—two hundred dollars, five hundred dollars—they'll be happy with whatever."

"Did you ever end up giving your boy's girl an equal cut?"

"N-a-a-a-w."

"How much did you give her?"

"We ended up getting like four or five hundred grams of crack. We gave her like forty—like a thousand dollars."

"And that was less than everyone else?"

"Of course."

"How much do you give [The Girl], in general, for drug robberies, knocking on a door?"

"If everything goes the way it's supposed to, we give them a thousand dollars, regardless what we got. Unless, you know, we didn't get enough to pay them. It happens sometimes. Sometimes you go somewhere and you don't find nothing. Or you don't find the right amount. It happens. But we try to make it seem like their role isn't that important—'Naw, you just knocking, you not doing anything, you not risking anything.' Try to make it seem like it's not that important. But it is."

"Suppose it was a guy knockin' on the door," I asked, "would you pay him as much if he was part of the crew?"

"Yeah, you right," Gus answered. "Yeah, if he would've asked for an equal cut. I guess women they don't—not all women—but most women don't question that. They don't question that their role isn't that important. But a man would think, 'Hold on. I knock on the door—without me, they can't get in.' A woman, it's not in her character like to question that. Like they would go by like what we would tell them—'Yo, go knock on the door'—they not even gonna see, or whatever, that it's important. But a man, he would question that."

"So what is it about women that . . ."

"I mean, it's just not natural for men to look at women as equals. That's basically it. It's natural for that."

"So why aren't they looked at as equal?"

"They're women. It just goes back to how we were brought up to look at women, whatever, you know."

"So how are women? Like what is it about women that makes them less than men?"

"It's just how society looks at things. Like let's say you go somewhere to fix your car or whatever, you see a man mechanic and a woman mechanic. You automatically go to the man. The woman could be better qualified, but it's just how it is."

"So why do you think women don't take another role in drug robberies?"

"They can't fit in another role. That's about all they can do. They could meet the guy somewhere; go somewhere where we could get him; they could knock on the door, get them to open the door—that's about it. They can't really do anything else."

"How about in the drug robbery where the guy's ear was cut off, did you ever pay The Girl?"

"Yeah."

"Did she get an equal cut?"

"Naw, she got five hundred dollars. Everybody else got . . . we had cut the dope and the coke . . . but that's all she got. Five hundred."

"She didn't complain about that?"

"Naw. Like I said, unless a Girl knows how important she actually is, they won't question."

"Did she actually know how much was found?"

"Yeah. Well, I don't think she actually understood like how much it was worth."

Pablo also gave a similar account, but did not want to concede the importance of The Girl:

"They just don't get the same cut," Pablo said, explaining how The Girl is paid.

"Why not?"

"Because they just never do. 'Cause all they do is just open doors. You know what I mean?"

"Well, how about if I argue that without them you couldn't have done it?" I asked.

Pablo paused; he was in deep thought. Then: "There's always a way, man."

"But from what you've told me, this is the easiest way," I said.

"They never get the same cut, though, Ran," Pablo answered, avoiding an admission that The Girl is important. "To be honest with you," Pablo continued, "they never get the same cut that the dudes do. The dudes always get more than The Girls. The girls get like chump change compared to the men."

"So, why do you think that is?"

"Maybe because the chick might be down with one of the guys who's doing it. Usually it's like that. Usually you don't go, 'Let me go pick this chick . . . Hey, you want to go do this?' It's usually somebody that's messing with somebody, or going out with somebody, you know what I mean? But she's never gonna get the same cut because the dudes ain't gonna respect her like that. They feel like she's not . . . she's not . . . equal or something like that."

"But what if a guy could open the door, you think he'll get a better cut than her?"

"Probably, because the guy would argue more. The female, if she knows her man, or whoever she's messing with, is doing it, she's getting the cut anyway, so she's getting something. So, I guess they feel that it's alright. But it's never that the girl gets fifty-fifty or whatever, whatever."

"So, you're saying if the boyfriend is getting a cut, that's her cut too."

"Yeah. She's gonna get something, but it's not like . . . for example, for argument sake, let's say there's a thousand dollars. There's two dudes and one chick. She's never gonna get three hundred and thirty-three dollars. She might get a hundred or a hundred and fifty, and it's a wrap. Like the woman is always down, you know what I mean? They use the women, put it like that. The women are used."

"Why?"

"Because that's the way it is. I don't know, I can't explain it, man. I can't break it down to you, but that's just the way it is. I guess because they're females and they're not gonna argue with you. I don't know. I don't know what it is."

Male drug robbers, the accounts show, believe that women are weak, unintelligent, and unaware of their worth. Because of this, they believe that men can convince The Girl that knocking on a door and getting a male dealer to open up, that spending a night out receiving fondles from strangers, that standing on a corner looking casual while surveying the scene, all are insignificant. Even if The Girl understands her role and worth, duping her causes no caution, no concern. Like their criminal counterparts in other settings (Mullins, Wright, and Jacobs 2004), and even male regulars in the mainstream (Anderson and Umberson 2001; Hollander 2001), these men often see women as harmless, as wielding laughable violence. In contrast, male drug robbers present men as rational criminals, who understand that securing a dealer is a robbery's most valuable act. Like the beginning scene in a drama, opening the door sets the robbery in motion, into a sequence of events ending in an applaudable outcome: a lot of money and drugs. So, they believe that any duplicity or double-dealing—like being lied to, like being paid nothing—is harder to do with men.

However, these male representations reinforce, reproduce, and reconstruct masculinity. Like in most masculinities, men are defined as powerful and competent, violent and bold; women, as weak and inept. Even when men see a possible truth, that The Girl is integral to their work, they become purposely obstinate and dense, declining to examine the situation under a different lamp, scope, or angle. Like a corporate CEO confronted with Marxist pamphlets, male drug robbers refuse to see an alternative logic, an alternative relation between men and The Girl. They want—or need—to see the sex setup as natural. A lot of money and masculinity are at stake.

I asked Gus about why women appeared relatively unconcerned with their share, why sometimes even girlfriends risked a lot despite getting little in return. I asked this because, like in other stories I had heard, and like what Pablo had just described, women drug market participants often become the girlfriends of male partners. And Gus and Melissa—like Gus and the mother of one of his children—had started seeing each other intimately.

"You told me some of your girlfriends used to transport drugs for you," I stated.

"Right."

"How did that happen?"

"A lot of times they were willing to do it," Gus responded. "That's the difference between men and women. Women want to make themselves feel needed. So they would do stuff just to show you, or prove to you, like they worth it. A lot of times a girl would do it for free to show you that, like, you would need her for something, so she could feel needed. Like Melissa, like if I told her to go do something for me, like go knock on a door, or whatever, she would—for free. I wouldn't have to pay her at all. She would do it just because I asked her to do it. That's the difference between men and women. Women deal with a lot more emotion, more than men."

"Do you think that's a weakness?"

"Of course."

"Why?"

"I mean, I wouldn't take a risk of spending whatever amount of years in jail just to prove to somebody that I'm worth it, or that I'm needed, that you need me."

On this point, Pablo agreed, but added another emotional distinction between men and women.

"For example," Pablo explained, "let's say you're with a chick, and you kill somebody, right. You hide him in your yard. You happen to smack this bitch one time or twice or whatever, or get into a fight with the bitch. That bitch is gonna be real quick to say, 'Yo, there's somebody dead back there.'"

"But what is it about her that would make her say that?" I asked.

"Because, yo, that's just the way they are," Pablo answered, as though it were logical. "It's alright when you're fucking them, it's all good and gravy, bro. But the minute you do something to them, bro, it's a wrap. Feel me? It's a wrap . . . Women are the type of people that just think about the moment; they don't think about the consequences or whatever. Like if they in love, you know what I'm saying, if they in love forget it, bro. Those bitches is crazy. They'll do anything. And I mean anything."

According to Pablo and Gus, women are intrinsically caring and insecure, inclinations that compel them to do anything for love and appreciation. Therefore, they perceive women as foolish accomplices, who are willing to transport illegal drugs or guns, a mule-like labor that reaps small rewards, and who are willing to lure a drug dealer into a robbery, a torturous event that can be fatal. So, women take risks not for money, but for love, ignoring the potential consequences of becoming an accomplice (such as physical harm or death, arrest and imprisonment, losing children, acquiring stigmas, ruining life chances for future job and school success).

This logic implies that men are smart, cool, and rational; that men are more likely to weigh crime risks and rewards. In other words, they perceive men as having a natural, rational leaning, an innate understanding that there is more in it for them than love— there is cold, hard cash. Women, on the other hand, are portrayed as warm, soft—unable to separate emotions from action. However, this sexist logic glosses over how women can sincerely assist in crime for financial reasons: earning a thousand dollars, or even its half, in a day, is much more than one or two weeks of legitimate pay for marginal women, the ones at the labor market's periphery, the ones likely to work at low-skilled, low-waged jobs (Edin and Lein 1997).

The sexist reasoning extends to how women can, in an emotional snap of the fingers, become vengeful and betray confidences. Like the stereotypical scorned woman undermining her lover vehemently, for a real or imagined wrong, Pablo characterizes women as vicious, as having a bottomless pit of revenge. This implies that men, unlike women, will be less inclined to "snitch" or "rat" on crime partners or friends, to reveal the whereabouts of illegal drugs, weapons, cash—or a buried corpse. Although Pablo is clearly exaggerating this male code of silence—most drug robbers I met do not follow this code (Rosenfeld, Jacobs, and Wright 2003; Topalli 2005)—this is a moment where he creates the masculine and feminine distinction, where men, not women, are reliable, trustworthy, and emotionally stable.

NOTES

1. My description of Melissa as attractive and enticing comes from discussions with the drug robbers I studied, and observations of how other neighborhood males reacted toward her. Furthermore, the label The Girl is a name male drug robbers created to describe her role; thus, I will use this term throughout the article when I refer to her and the role.

2. Throughout the accounts, participants will refer to other men as "nigga." However, it is not used pejoratively; it is a street replacement for casual terms like "guy" or "dude" that men often use to refer to each other. Sometimes, it is used as a term of endearment, such as when some of the participants referred to me as "my nigga, Ran."

3. During my fieldwork, drug robberies were attempted often, sometimes more than once per week.

4. Negro, like some other drug robbers, spoke only Spanish; thus, this is an English translation of his account, which, unfortunately, loses some of the nuances and flavor of his speech.

REFERENCES

PART I: DATA COLLECTION STRATEGIES

Section I: Being There, Up Close

Chapter 1

Gans, H.J. 1962. "Redevelopment of the West End," *The Urban Villagers: Group and Class in the Life of Italian-Americans*. NY: The Free Press: 281; 288–298.

Boston Housing Authority. 1956. "West End Progress Report." Boston: The Authority.

Fried, M. & Gleicher, P. 1961. "Some Sources of Residential Satisfaction in an Urban 'Slum,'" *Journal of the American Institute of Planners*, 27, 4: 305–315.

Fried, M. 1963. "Grieving for a Lost Home," in Duhl, L.J. (ed.), *The Urban Condition*. NY: Basic Books: 151–171.

Chapter 2

Bourgois, P. 1995. "Families and Children in Pain," *In Search of Respect: Selling Crack in El Barrio*. Cambridge, UK: Cambridge University Press: 259–267; 272–276.

Community Service Society. 1956. "Interim Report on Jefferson Site Service Pilot Project." Manuscript. File in Box 347 of the Community Service Society Archives, Butler Library, Columbia University.

Farrington, D. 1991. "Childhood Aggression and Adult Violence: Early Precursors and Later-Life Outcomes," in Pepler, D. & Rubin, K. (eds.), *The Development and Treatment of Childhood Aggression*. Hillsdale, NJ: Lawrence Erlbaum: 5–29.

Marsh, M.C. 1932. "The Life and Work of the Churches in an Interstitial Area." Ph.D. dissertation, New York University.

Chapter 3

Lloyd, R. 2006. "The Celebrity Neighborhood," *Neo-Bohemia: Art and Commerce in the Postindustrial City*. NY: Routledge: 123–143.

Adorno, T.W. & Horkheimer, M. [1944] 1994. *Dialectic of Enlightenment*. NY: Continuum.

Baudrillard, J. 1989. *America*. NY: Verso.

Clark, T.N. 2000. "Trees and Real Violins: Building Postindustrial Chicago," working paper, University of Chicago.

Clark, T.N., Lloyd, R., Wong, K., & Jain, P. 2002. "Amenities Drive Urban Growth," *Journal of Urban Affairs*, 24, 5: 517–532.

Clark, T.N. & Rempel, M. 1997. *Citizen Politics in Postindustrial Societies*. Boulder, CO: University of Colorado Press.

Eco, U. 1986. *Travels in Hyperreality*. NY: Harcourt Brace Jovanovich.

Eeckhout, B. 2001. "The Disneyfication of Times Square: Back to the Future?," *Critical Perspectives on Urban Redevelopment*, 6: 379–428.

Fairbanks, R. 2003. "A Theoretical Primer on Space," *Critical Social Work* 3: 131–154.

Grazian, D. 2003. "Like Therapy: The Blues Club as a Haven," *Blue Chicago: The Search for Authenticity in Urban Blues Clubs*. Chicago: University of Chicago Press: 87–90; 105–116.

Hannigan, J. 1998. *Fantasy City: Pleasure and Profit in the Postmodern Metropolis*. NY: Routledge.

Jacobs, J. 1961. *The Death and Life of Great American Cities*. New York: Basic Books.

Jameson, F. 1991. *Postmodernism: or, the Cultural Logic of Late Capitalism*. Durham, NC: Duke University Press.

Judd, D. 1999. "Constructing the Tourist Bubble," in Judd, D. & Fainstein, S. (eds.), *The Tourist City*. New Haven, CT: Yale University Press: 35–53.

Lloyd, R. & Clark, T.N. 2001. "The City as an Entertainment Machine," *Critical Perspectives on Urban Redevelopment*, 6: 359–380.

Lyotard, J. 1979. *The Postmodern Condition*. Minneapolis: University of Minnesota Press.

Murger, H. [1848] 1988. *Scènes de la Vie de Bohème*. NY: Schoenhof.

Naremore, J. 1998. *More Than Night: Film Noir in Its Contexts*. Berkeley: University of California Press.

Nevarez, L. 2003. *New Money, Nice Town*. NY: Routledge.

Peterson, R.A. & Kern, R. 1996. "Changing Highbrow Taste: From Snob to Omnivore," *American Sociological Review*, 61, 5: 900–907.

Sassen, S. 2001. *The Global City: New York, London, Tokyo*. Princeton, NJ: Princeton University Press.

Sorkin, M. (ed.) 1992. *Variations on a Theme Park: The New American City and the End of Public Space*. NY: Hill and Wang.

Thomas, J. 1998. "Transitional Areas Attracting Renters," *Chicago Sun-Time* Sept. 20: NC2.

Wright, E.O. 1985. *Classes*. NY: Verso.

Zukin, S. 1995. *The Cultures of Cities*. Oxford: Blackwell.

Chapter 4

Pattillo, M. 2007. "The Black Bourgeoisie Meets the Truly Disadvantaged," *Black on the Block: The Politics of Race and Class in the City*. Chicago: University of Chicago Press: 86–100.

Billingsley, A. 1992. *Climbing Jacob's Ladder: The Enduring Legacy of African-American Families*. NY: Simon & Schuster.

Brown-Saracino, J. 2004. "Social Preservationists and the Quest for Authenticity," *City & Community*, 3, 2: 135–156.

Burnham, L. 1998. "Home for Him is Harvard Square," *Colorlines* 1. http://www.arc.org/C_Lines/ CLArchive/story1_2_12.html (accessed December 1, 2005).

Cose, E. 1993. *The Rage of a Privileged Class*. New York: HarperCollins.

Dawson, M.C. 1994. *Behind the Mule: Race and Class in African-American Politics*. Princeton, NJ: Princeton University Press.

Dawson, M.C. 2001. *Black Visions: The Roots of Contemporary African-American Political Ideologies*. Chicago: University of Chicago Press.

Demo, D.H. & Hughes, M. 1990. "Socialization and Racial Identity among Black Americans," *Social Psychology Quarterly*, 53, 4: 364–374.

Dyson, M.E. 2005. *Is Bill Cosby Right? Or Has the Black Middle Class Lost Its Mind?* NY: Basic Civitas Books.

Gates, Jr., H.L. 1998. "The Two Nations of Black America," *Brookings Review*, 16: 4–7.

Gay, C. 2004. "Putting Race in Context: Identifying the Environmental Determinants of Black Racial Attitudes," *American Political Science Review*, 98, 4: 547–562.

Heflin, C.M. & Pattillo, M. 2006. "Poverty in the Family: Race, Siblings and Socioeconomic Heterogeneity," *Social Science Research*, 35, 4: 804–822.

Hochschild, J.L. 1995. *Facing Up to the American Dream: Race, Class, and the Soul of the Nation*. Princeton, NJ: Princeton University Press.

Hughes, M. & Thomas, M.E. 1998. "The Continuing Significance of Race Revisited: A Study of Race, Class, and Quality of Life in America, 1972 to 1996," *American Sociological Review*, 63, 6: 785–795.

Hughes, M. & Tuch, S. 2000. "How Beliefs about Poverty Influence Racial Policy Attitudes," in Sears, D., Sidanius, J., & Bobo, L. (eds.), *The Debate about Racism in America*. Chicago: University of Chicago Press: 165–190.

Jackson, J.L. 2001. *Harlemworld: Doing Race and Class in Contemporary Black America*. Chicago: University of Chicago Press.

Jackson, J.L. 2005. *Real Black: Adventures in Racial Sincerity*. Chicago: University of Chicago Press.

Metro Chicago Information Center. 1999. Community Capacity Survey Questionnaire. Provided to author by MCIC staff.

Pattillo-McCoy, M. 1999. *Black Picket Fences: Privilege and Peril among the Black Middle Class*. Chicago: University of Chicago Press.

Raley, R.K. 1995. "Black-White Differences in Kin Contact and Exchange among Never Married Adults," *Journal of Family Issues*, 16, 1: 77–103.

Schuman, H., Steeh, C., Bobo, L.D., & Krysan, M. 1997. *Racial Attitudes in America: Trends and Interpretations*. Cambridge, MA: Harvard University Press.

Simpson, A.Y. 1998. *The tie That Binds: Identity and Political Attitudes in the Post-Civil Rights Generation*. NY: New York University Press.

Tate, K. 1993. *From Protest to Politics: The New Black Voters in American Elections*. New York: Russell Sage Foundation.

White, L. & Riedmann, A. 1992. "Ties among Adult Siblings," *Social Forces*, 71, 1: 85–102.

Wilson, W.J. 1987. *The Truly Disadvantaged: The Inner City, the Underclass, and Public Policy*. Chicago: University of Chicago Press.

Chapter 5

Pérez, G.M. 2004. "*Los de Afuera*, Transnationalism, and the Cultural Politics of Identity," *The Near Northwest Side Story*. Berkeley: University of California Press: 92–110.

Alicea, M. 1990. "Dual Home Bases: A Reconceptualization of Puerto Rican Migration," *Latino Studies Journal*, 1, 3: 78–98.

Alicea, M. 1997. "'A Chambered Nautilus'": The Contradictory Nature of Puerto Rican Migration," *Gender & Society*, 11, 5: 597–626.

Anderson, B. 1983. *Imagined Communities: Reflections on the Origin and Spread of Nationalism*. London: Verso.

Bourgois, P. 1995. *In Search of Respect: Selling Crack in El Barrio*. Cambridge, UK: University of Cambridge Press.

Chávez, L.R. 1992. *Shadowed Lives: Undocumented Immigrants in American Society*. Fort Worth, TX: Harcourt Brace Jovanovich Publishers.

Duany, J. 2002. *The Puerto Rican Nation on the Move: Identities on the Island and the Mainland*. Chapel Hill, NC: University of North Carolina Press.

Ellis, M., Conway, D., & Bailey, A. 1996. "The Circular Migration of Puerto Rican Women," *Quarterly Review*, 34, 1: 31–64.

Flores, J. 1993. *Divided Borders: Essays on Puerto Rican Identity*. Houston, TX: Arte Publico Press.

Flores, J. & Yudice, G. 1983. "Living Borders/*Buscando America*: Languages of Latino Self-Formation," *Social Text*, 24: 57–84.

Glasser, R. 1997. *Aquí Me Quedo: Puerto Ricans in Connecticut*. Middletown, CT: Connecticut Humanities Council.

Glick Schiller, N., Basch, L., & Blanc-Szanton, C. 1992. *Towards a Transnational Perspective on Migration: Race, Class, Ethnicity and Nationalism Reconsidered*. New York: New York Academy of Sciences.

Goldring, L. 1992. "Blurring Borders: Community and Social Transformation in Mexico–U.S. Transnational Migration." Paper presented at New Perspectives on Mexico–U.S. Migration Conference, University of Chicago, October 23–24.

Goldring, L. 1998. "The Power of Status in Transnational Social Fields," in Smith, M.P. & Guarnizo, L.E. (eds.), *Transnationalism from Below*. New Brunswick, NJ: Transaction Publishers: 165–195.

Grasmuck, S. & Pessar, P. 1991. *Between Two Islands: Dominican International Migration*. Berkeley: University of California Press.

Hagan, J. 1998. "Social Networks, Gender, and Immigrant Incorporation: Resources and Constraints," *American Sociological Review*, 63, 1: 55–67.

Hollinger, D.A. 1993. "How Wide the Circle of the 'We'?: American Intellectuals and the Problem of the Ethnos since World War II," *American Historical Review*, 98, 2: 317–337.

Hondagneu-Sotelo, P. 1994. *Gendered Transitions: Mexican Experiences of Immigration*. Berkeley: University of California Press.

Kerkhof, E. 2000. *Contested Belonging: Circular Migration and Puerto Rican Identity*, Ph.D. diss., University of Utrecht, The Netherlands.

Kerkhof, E. 2001. "The Myth of the Dumb Puerto Rican: Circular Migration and Language Struggle in Puerto Rico," *New West Indian Guide*, 75, 3–4: 257–288.

Kibria, N. 1993. *Family Tightrope: The Changing Lives of Vietnamese Immigrants*. Princeton, NJ: Princeton University Press.

Levitt, P. 2001. *The Transnational Villagers*. Berkeley: University of California Press.

Mahler, S.J. 1995. *American Dreaming: Immigrant Life on the Margins*. Princeton, NJ: Princeton University Press.

Mahler, S.J. 1999. "Engendering Transnational Migration: A Case Study of Salvadorans," *American Behavioral Scientist*, 42, 4: 690–719.

Massey, D. 1994. *Space, Place, and Gender*. Minneapolis, MN: University of Minneapolis Press.

Menjívar, C. 2000. *Fragmented Ties: Salvadoran Immigrant Networks in America*. Berkeley: University of California Press.

Negrón-Muntaner, F. 1997. "English Only Jamas but Spanish Only Cuidado: Language and Nationalism in Contemporary Puerto Rico," in Negrón-Muntaner, F. & Grosfoguel, R. (eds.), *Puerto Rican Jam: Essays on Culture and Politics*. Minneapolis: University of Minnesota Press: 257–286.

Pessar, P. 1986. "The Role of Gender in Dominican Settlement in the United States," in Nash, J. & Safa, H. (eds.), *Women and Change in Latin America*. South Hadley, MA: Bergin and Garvey.

Ramos-Zaya, A.Y. 2003. *National Performances: The Politics of Class, Race and Place in Puerto Rican Chicago*. Chicago: University of Chicago Press.

Rivera-Batiz, F.L. & Santiago, C.E. 1996. *Island Paradox: Puerto Rico in the 1990s*. NY: Russell Sage Foundation.

Rúa, M. 2001. "Colao Subjectivities: PortoMex and MexiRican Perspectives on Language and Identity," *CENTRO: Journal of the Center for Puerto Rican Studies*, 13, 2: 117–133.

Sánchez, L.R. 1994. *La Guagua Aéra*. San Juan: Editorial Cultura.

Sandoval Sánchez, A. 1997. "Puerto Rican Identity Up in the Air: Air Migration, Its Cultural Representations, and 'Cruzando el Charco,'" in Negrón-Muntaner, F. & Grosfoguel, R. (eds.), *Puerto Rican Jam: Essays on Culture and Politics*. Minneapolis, MN: University of Minnesota Press: 189–208.

Smith, M.P. 2001. *Transnational Urbanism: Locating Globalization*. New Brunswick, NJ: Transaction Publishers.

Smith, M.P. & Guarnizo, L.E. 1998. *Transnationalism from Below*. New Brunswick, NJ: Transaction Publishers.

Souza, C. 2000. "Welfare Debates and Puerto Rican Teenage Mothers in New York City," *Economic and Political Weekly*, 35, 20–21: 24–32.

Stinson Fernández, J.H. 1994. "Conceptualizing Culture and Ethnicity: Toward an Anthropology of Puerto Rican Philadelphia," Ph.D. diss., Department of Anthropology, Temple University.

Uriciuoli, B. 1991. "The Political Topography of Spanish and English: The View from a New York Puerto Rican Neighborhood," *American Ethnologist*, 18, 2: 295–310.

Uriciuoli, B. 1996. *Exposing Prejudice: Puerto Rican Experiences of Language, Race, and Class.* Oxford: Westview Press.

Whalen, C.T. 2001. *From Puerto Rico to Philadelphia: Puerto Rican Workers and Postwar Economics.* Philadelphia: Temple University Press.

Zentella, A.C. 1990. "Returned Migration, Language, and Identity: Puerto Rican Bilinguals in Dos Worlds/Two Mundos," *International Journal of Social Language*, 84: 81–100.

Zentella, A.C. 1997. *Growing Up Bilingual: Children in El Barrio.* NY: Basil Blackwell.

Section II: Being on the Job

Chapter 6

Duneier, M. 1999. "A Christmas on Sixth Avenue," *Sidewalk.* NY: Farrar, Straus and Giroux: 253–256; 260–279.

Bittner, E. 1990. *Aspects of Police Work.* Boston: Northeastern University Press.

Black, D. 1983. "Crime as Social Control," *American Sociological Review*, 48: 34–45.

Chevigny, P. 1995. *Edge of the Knife: Police Violence in the Americas.* NY: New York Press.

Feinberg, J. 1970. "The Expressive Function of Punishment," in *Doing and Deserving: Essays in the Theory of Responsibility.* Princeton, NJ: Princeton University Press: 95–118.

Garland, D. 1990. *Punishment and Modern Society.* Chicago: University of Chicago Press.

Kelling, G.L. & Coles, C.M. 1996. *Fixing Broken Windows.* NY: Free Press.

Stoler, P. 1996. "Spaces, Places, and Fields," *American Anthropologist*, 98, 4: 776–788.

Chapter 7

Moskos, P. 2008. "The Corner: Life on the Streets," *Cop in the Hood: My Year Policing Baltimore's Eastern District.* Princeton: Princeton University Press: 64–66; 77–88.

Jacobs, B.A. & Wright, R. 2006. *Street Justice: Retaliation in the Criminal Underworld.* NY: Cambridge University Press.

Vollmer, A. 1936. *The Police and Modern Society.* Berkeley: University of California Press.

Warner, B.D. & Coomer, B.W. 2003. "Neighborhood Drug Arrest Rates: Are They a Meaningful Indicator of Drug Activity? A Research Note," *Journal of Research in Crime and Delinquency*, 40, 2: 123–138.

Chapter 8

Grazian, D. 2003. "Like Therapy: The Blues Club as a Haven," *Blue Chicago: The Search for Authenticity in Urban Blues Clubs.* Chicago: University of Chicago Press: 87–90; 105–116.

Abbott, A. 1988. *The System of Professions: An Essay on the Division of Expert Labor.* Chicago: University of Chicago Press.

Anderson, E. 1976. *A Place on the Corner.* Chicago: University of Chicago Press.

Becker, H.S. 1963. *Outsiders: Studies in the Sociology of Deviance.* NY: The Free Press.

DeVeaux, S. 1997. *The Birth of Bebop: A Social and Musical History.* Berkeley: University of California Press.

Goffman, E. 1959. *The Presentation of Self in Everyday Life*. Garden City, NY: Doubleday.

Grazian, D. 1994. "Uniform of the Party: The Impact of Fashion on Collegiate Subcultural Integration." Henry Rutgers honors thesis, Department of Sociology, Rutgers University.

Hall, S. & Jefferson, T. 1976. *Resistance through Rituals: Youth Subcultures in Postwar Britain*. London: Routledge.

Hebdige, D. 1979. *Subculture: The Meaning of Style*. London: Routledge.

Liebow, E. 1967. "Men and Jobs," *Tally's Corner: A Study of Negro Streetcorner Men*. Boston, MA: Little, Brown, and Company: 61–71.

Loseke, D.R. & Cahill, S.E. 1986. "Actors in Search of a Character: Student Social Workers' Quest for Professional Identity," *Symbolic Interaction*, 9, 2: 245–258.

Malbon, B. 1999. *Clubbing: Dancing, Ecstasy, and Vitality*. London: Routledge.

Mezzrow, M. & Wolfe, B. 1946. *Really the Blues*. NY: Random House.

Oldenburg, R. 1989. *The Great Good Place*. NY: Paragon House.

Thornton, S. 1996. *Club Cultures: Music, Media, and Subcultural Capital*. Hanover, NH: Wesleyan University Press.

Willis, P. 1977. *Learning to Labor*. NY: Columbia University Press.

Willis, P. 1990. *Common Culture*. Boulder, CO: Westview.

Chapter 9

Wynn, J.R. 2005. "Guiding Practices: Storytelling Tricks for Reproducing the Urban Landscape," *Qualitative Sociology*, 28, 4: 399–400; 404–413.

Becker, H. 1998. *Tricks of the Trade*. Chicago: University of Chicago Press.

Certeau, M. de, Giard, L., & Mayol, P. 1998. *The Practice of Everyday Life, Volume 2*. Minneapolis: University of Minnesota Press.

DiMaggio, P. 1992. "Cultural Boundaries and Structural Change: The Extension of the High-Culture Model to Theatre, Opera, and the Dance," in Lamont, M. & Fournier, M. (eds.), *Cultivating Differences: Symbolic Boundaries and the Making of Inequality*. Chicago: University of Chicago Press: 1900–1940.

Fine, E.C., & Speer, J.H. 1985. "Tour Guide Performances as Sight Sacralization," *Annals of Tourism Research*, 12, 1: 73–95.

Gans, H.J. 1999. *Popular Culture and High Culture: An Analysis and Evaluation of Taste*. NY: Basic Books.

Goffman, E. 1959. *The Presentation of Self in Everyday Life*. Garden City, NY: Doubleday.

Goffman, E. 1974. *Frame Analysis*. Boston: Northeastern University Press.

Grazian, D. 2003. *Blue Chicago: The Search for Authenticity in Urban Blues Clubs*. Chicago: University of Chicago Press.

Hardt, M. & Negri, A. 2001. *Empire*. Cambridge, MA: Harvard University Press.

Judd, D.R. 1999. "Global Forces, Local Strategies and Urban Tourism," in Judd, D.R. & Fainstein, S.S. (eds.), *The Tourist City*. New Haven: Yale University Press: 1–20.

Lazzarato, M. 1996. "Immaterial Labor," in Virno, P. & Hardt, M. (eds.), *Radical Thought in Italy: A Potential Politics. Theory Out of Bounds (Vol. 7)*. Minneapolis, MN: University of Minneapolis Press: 133–147.

MacCannell, D. 1973. *The Tourist: A New Theory of the Leisure Class*. Berkeley: University of California Press.

Negus, K. 2002. "The Work of Cultural Intermediaries and the Enduring Distance between Production and Consumption," *Cultural Studies*, 16, 4: 501–515.

Perrottet, T. 2002. *Pagan Holiday*. New York: Random House.

Sante, L. 1992. *Low Life*. New York: Vintage Books.

Sennett, R. 1990. *The Conscience of the Eye*. NY: Knopf.

Shields, R. 1996. *Cultures of Internet: Virtual Spaces, Real Histories, Living Bodies*. London: Sage.

Shils, E. 1972. *The Intellectuals and the Powers and Other Essays*. Chicago: University of Chicago Press.

Somers, M.R. 1999. "The Privatization of Citizenship: How to Unthink a Knowledge Culture," in Bonnell, V.E. & Hunt, L. (eds.), *Beyond the Cultural Turn*. Berkeley: University of California Press: 121–164.

Suttles, G. 1984. "The Cumulative Texture of Local Culture," *American Journal of Sociology*, 90, 2: 283–304.

Suttles, G. 1990. *The Man-Made City*. Chicago: University of Chicago Press.

Swidler, A. 1986. "Culture in Action: Symbols and Strategies," *American Sociological Review*, 51, 2: 273–286.

Wacquant, L. 1995. "The Pugilistic Point of View: How Boxers Think and Feel about Their Trade," *Theory and Society*, 24, 4: 489–535.

Chapter 10

Trimbur, L. 2011. "'Tough Love': Mediation and Articulation in the Urban Boxing Gym," *Ethnography*, 12, 3: 334–6; 339–43; 346–50.

Kim, D.Y. 2005. *Writing Manhood in Black and Yellow: Ralph Ellison, Frank Chin, and the Literary Politics of Identity*. Palo Alto, CA: Stanford University Press.

Oates, J.C. 1994. *On Boxing*. Garden City, NY: Dolphin/Doubleday Press.

Wacquant, L. 1998. "A Fleshpeddlar at Work: Power, Pain, and Profit in the Prizefighting Economy," *Theory and Society*, 27, 1: 1–42.

Chapter 11

Bender, C. 2003. "What We Talk about When We Talk about Religion," *Heaven's Kitchen: Living Religion at God's Love We Deliver*. Chicago: University of Chicago Press: 92–103.

Bakhtin, M. 1986. *"Speech Genres" and Other Late Essays*. Austin, TX: University of Texas Press.

Morson, G.S. & Emerson, C. 1990. *Mikhail Bakhtin: Creation of a Prosaics*. Stanford: Stanford University Press.

PART II: RELATIONSHIPS WITH PARTICIPANTS

Section I: Crossing Boundaries

Chapter 12

Whyte, W.F. 1943. "Doc and His Boys," *Street Corner Society: The Social Structure of an Italian Slum*. Chicago: University of Chicago Press: 14–25.

Chapter 13

Liebow, E. 1967. "Men and Jobs," *Tally's Corner: A Study of Negro Streetcorner Men*. Boston: Little, Brown, and Company: 61–71.

Hughes, E.C. 1958. *Men and Their Work*. London: The Free Press of Glencoe.

Miller, S.M. & Riessman, F. 1961. "The Working-Class Subculture: A New View," *Social Problems*, 9, 1: 86–97.

Miller, W. 1958. "Lower Class Culture as a Generating Milieu of Gang Delinquency," *Journal of Social Issues*, 14, 3: 5–19.

Chapter 14

Stack, C. 1974. "The Flats" and "Swapping: What Goes Around Comes Around," *All Our Kin*. NY: Basic Books: 11–17; 32–43.

Abrahams, R. 1963. *Deep Down in the Jungle: Negro Narrative Folklore from the Streets of Philadelphia*. Hatboro, PA: Folklore Associates.

Abrahams, R. 1970. *Positively Black*. Englewood Cliffs, NJ: Prentice-Hall.

Bailey, F.G. 1971. *Gifts and Poison: The Politics of Reputation*. NY: Schocken Books.

Dalton, G. 1961. "Economic Theory and Primitive Society," *American Anthropologist*, 63, 1: 1–25.

Dorson, R. 1956. *Negro Folktales in Michigan*. Cambridge, MA: Harvard University Press.

Dorson, R. 1958. *Negro Tales from Pine Bluff*. Bloomington, IN: Indiana University Press.

Foster, G. 1963. "The Dyadic Contract in Tzintzuntzan II: Patron-Client Relationships," *American Anthropologist*, 65, 6: 1280–1294.

Gouldner, A.W. 1960. "The Norm of Reciprocity: A Preliminary Statement," *American Sociological Review*, 25, 2: 161–178.

Harris, M. 1971. *Culture, Man, and Nature: An Introduction to General Anthropology*. NY: Thomas Y. Crowell.

Lee, R.B. 1969. "Kung Bushman Subsistence: An Input-Output Analysis," in Vayda, A.P. (ed.), *Environment and Culture Behavior: Ecological Studies in Cultural Anthropology*. NY: Natural History Press: 47–79.

Lévi-Strauss, C. 1969. *The Elementary Structures of Kinship*. Boston: Beacon Press.

Lombardi, J.R. 1973. "Exchange and Survival." Preprint.

Malinowski, B. 1922. *Argonauts of the Western Pacific*. NY: Dutton.

Mauss, M. 1925. Essai sur le don: Forme et raison de l'échange dans les sociétés archaïques," *Année Sociologique*, n.s., I: 30–186.

Mauss, M. 1954. *The Gift*. NY: The Free Press.

Sahlins, M.D. 1965. "On the Sociology of Primitive Exchange," in Banton, M. (ed.), *The Relevance of Models for Social Anthropology*. A.S.A. Monograph I. London: Tavistock Publications; New York: Praeger.

Chapter 15

Venkatesh, S. 2002. "'Doin' the Hustle': Constructing the Ethnographer in the American Ghetto," *Ethnography*, 3, 1: 91–92; 96–103.

Burawoy, M. 1998. "The Extended Case Method," *Sociological Theory*, 16, 1:4–32.

Clifford, J. & Marcus, G.E. (eds.) 1986. *The Poetics and Politics of Ethnography*. Berkeley: University of California Press.

Comaroff, J.L. & Comaroff, J. 1992. *Ethnography and the Historical Imagination*. Boulder, CO: Westview Press.

Drake, S. & Cayton, H. 1945. *The Black Metropolis*. Chicago: University of Chicago Press.

Hagedorn, J. 1988. *People and Folks: Gangs, Crime, and the Underclass in a Rustbelt City*. Chicago: Lake View Press.

Pollner, M & Emerson, R.M. 1983. "The Dynamics of Inclusion and Distance in Fieldwork Relations," in R.M. Emerson, ed., *Contemporary Field Research: A Collection of Readings*. Boston: Little, Brown: 235–252.

Stack, C. 1974. *All Our Kin*. NY: Basic Books.

Venkatesh, S.A. 2000. *American Project: The Rise and Fall of a Modern Ghetto*. Cambridge, MA: Harvard University Press.

Chapter 16

Cavan, S. 1966. "The Marketplace Bar," *Liquor License: An Ethnography of Bar Behavior*. Chicago: Aldine Publishing Company: 171–7; 193–200.

Cory, D.W. & LeRoy, J. P. 1963. *The Homosexual and His Society*. NY: The Citadel Press.

Cressey, P.G. 1932. *The Taxi Dance Hall: A Sociological Study in Commercialized Recreation in City Life*. Chicago: University of Chicago Press.

Chapter 17

Auyero, J. & Swistun, D. 2009. "The Compound and the Neighborhood," *Flammable: Environmental Suffering in an Argentine Shantytown*. Oxford: Oxford University Press: 28–31; 32–44.

Erikson, K. 1976. *Everything in Its Path: Destruction of Community in the Buffalo Creek Flood*. New York: Simon & Schuster.

Section II: Doing the Right Thing

Chapter 18

Humphreys, L. 1975. "The People Next Door," *Tearoom Trade: Impersonal Sex in Public Places*. Piscataway: Aldine Transactions: 106–111; 114–122.

Becker, H.S. 1963. *Outsiders: Studies in the Sociology of Deviance*. NY: The Free Press.

Goffman, E. 1963. *Stigma: Notes on the Management of Spoiled Identity*. Englewood Cliffs, NJ: Prentice-Hall.

McIntosh, M. 1968. "The Homosexual Role," *Social Problems*, 16, 2: 182–192.

Rainwater, L. 1965. *Family Design: Marital Sexuality, Family Size, and Contraception*. Chicago: Aldine.

Reiss, Jr., A.J. 1961. "The Social Integration of Queers and Peers," *Social Problems*, 9, 2: 102–120.

Chapter 19

Ferrell, J. 1993. "Denver Graffiti and the Syndicate Scene," *Crimes of Style: Urban Graffiti and the Politics of Criminality*. Boston: Northeastern University Press: 21–26; 49–53.

Ferrell, J. 1990a. "Bomber's Confidential: Interview with Eye Six and Rasta 68" (Part Two). *Clot*, 1: 10–11.

Castleman, C. 1982. *Getting Up: Subway Graffiti in New York*. Cambridge, MA: MIT Press.

Lachmann, R. 1988. "Graffiti as Career and Ideology," *American Journal of Sociology*, 94, 2: 229–250.

Point. 1990. Denver: Alternative Arts Alliance (September).

Chapter 20

Contreras, R. 2009. "'Damn, Yo—Who's That Girl?' An Ethnographic Analysis of Masculinity in Drug Robberies," *Journal of Contemporary Ethnography*, 38, 4: 465–466; 474–483.

Anderson, K.L. & Umberson, D. 2001. "Gendering Violence: Masculinity and Power in Men's Accounts of Domestic Violence," *Gender and Society*, 15, 3: 358–380.

Bourgois, P. 2003. *In Search of Respect: Selling Crack in El Barrio*. 2nd ed. NY: Cambridge University Press.

Copes, H. & Hochstetler, A. 2003. "Situational Construction of Masculinity among Male Street Thieves," *Journal of Contemporary Ethnography*, 32, 3: 279–304.

Edin, K. & Lein, L. 1997. *Making Ends Meet: How Single Mothers Survive Welfare and Low-Wage Work*. New York: Russell Sage.

Hollander, J.A. 2001. "Vulnerability and Dangerousness: The Construction of Gender through Conversation and Violence," *Gender and Society*, 15, 1: 83–109.

Jacobs, B.A. 1999. *Dealing Crack: The Social World of Streetcorner Selling.* Boston: Northeastern University Press.

Jacobs, B.A. 2000. *Robbing Drug Dealers: Violence beyond the Law.* NY: Aldine de Gruyter.

Karmen, A. 2000. *New York Murder Mystery: The True Story behind the Crime Crash of the 1990s.* NY: New York University Press.

Mullins, C.W. 2004. "Masculinities, Streetlife, and Violence: A Qualitative Secondary Examination," Unpublished Ph.D. dissertation, University of Missouri-St. Louis.

Mullins, C.W., Wright, R., & Jacobs, B.A. 2004. "Gender, Streetlife and Criminal Retaliation," *Criminology,* 42, 4: 911–940.

Rosenfeld, R., Jacobs, B.A., & Wright, R. 2003. "Snitching and the Code of the Street," *Criminology,* 43, 2: 291–309.

Topalli, V. 2005. "When being Good is Bad: An Expansion of Neutralization Theory," *Criminology,* 43, 3: 797–836.

Copyright Acknowledgments

The editor thanks the following authors and publishers for generously permitting the republication of their work:

FLAMMABLE: ENVIRONMENTAL SUFFERING IN AN ARGENTINE SHANTYTOWN by Auyero & Swistun (2009) 2400w from pp. 28–44. By permission of Oxford University Press, Inc.

Bender, C. 2003. "What We Talk about When We Talk about Religion," *Heaven's Kitchen: Living Religion at God's Love We Deliver*. Chicago: University of Chicago Press: 92–103. © 2003 by The University of Chicago. Reprinted with permission from the University of Chicago Press.

Bourgois, P. 1995. "Families and Children in Pain," *In Search of Respect: Selling Crack in El Barrio*. Cambridge, UK: University of Cambridge Press: 259–267 & 272–276. © Cambridge University Press 1995. Reprinted with permission of Cambridge University Press.

Cavan, S. 1966. "The Marketplace Bar," *Liquor License: An Ethnography of Bar Behavior*. Chicago: Aldine Publishing Company: 171–177 & 193–200. Reprinted with kind permission from the author.

Contreras, R. 2009. "'Damn, Yo—Who's That Girl?' An Ethnographic Analysis of Masculinity in Drug Robberies," *Journal of Contemporary Ethnography*, 38, 4: 465–466 & 474–483. Reprinted with permission from Sage Publications.

Excerpts from "A Christmas on Sixth Avenue" from SIDEWALK by Mitchell Duneier. Copyright © 1999 by Mitchell Duneier. Reprinted by permission of Farrar, Straus and Giroux, LLC.

Ferrell, J. 1993. "Denver Graffiti and the Syndicate Scene," *Crimes of Style: Urban Graffiti and the Politics of Criminality*. Boston, MA: Northeastern University Press: 21–26 & 49–53. Reprinted with the permission of Taylor and Francis, Ltd., www.informaworld.com

Gans, H.J. 1962. "Redevelopment of the West End," *The Urban Villagers: Group and Class in the Life of Italian-Americans*. NY: The Free Press: 281 & 288–98. Reprinted with the permission of Free Press, a Division of Simon & Schuster, Inc., from THE URBAN VILLAGERS: Group and Class in the Life of Italian-Americans by Herbert J. Gans. Copyright © 1962 by The Free Press. Copyright © 1982 by Herbert J. Gans. All rights reserved.

Grazian, D. 2003. "Like Therapy: The Blues Club as a Haven," *Blue Chicago: The Search for Authenticity in Urban Blues Clubs*. Chicago: University of Chicago Press: 87–90 & 105–116. © 2003 by The University of Chicago. Reprinted with permission from the University of Chicago Press.

Humphreys, L. 1975. "The People Next Door," *Tearoom Trade: Impersonal Sex in Public Places*. Piscataway, NJ: Aldine Transactions: 106–11 & 114–22. Reprinted with permission from Transaction Publishers.

Liebow, E. 1967. "Men and Jobs," *Tally's Corner: A Study of Negro Streetcorner Men*. Boston, MA: Little, Brown, and Company: 61–71. Reprinted with permission from Roman & Littlefield Publishing Group.

Lloyd, R. 2006. "The Celebrity Neighborhood," *Neo-Bohemia: Art and Commerce in the Postindustrial*

City. NY: Routledge: 123–143. Reprinted with the permission of Taylor and Francis, Ltd., www. informaworld.com

MOSKOS, PETER; *COP IN THE HOOD.* © 2008 by Princeton University Press Reprinted by permission of Princeton University Press.

Pattillo, M. 2008. "The Black Bourgeoisie Meets the Truly Disadvantaged," *Black on the Block: The Politics of Race and Class in the City.* Chicago: University of Chicago Press: 86–100. © 2003 by The University of Chicago. Reprinted with permission from the University of Chicago Press.

Pérez, G. M. 2004. "*Los de Afuera,* Transnationalism, and the Cultural Politics of Identity," *The Near Northwest Side Story.* Berkeley: University of California Press: 92–94 & 96–110. © 2004 by the Regents of the University of California. Reprinted with permission from the University of California Press.

Stack, C. 1974. "The Flats," and "Swapping: What Goes Around Comes Around," *All Our Kin.* NY: Basic Books: 11–16 & 32–43. Reprinted with kind permission from the author.

Trimbur, L. 2011. "'Tough Love': Mediation and Articulation in the Urban Boxing Gym," *Ethnography,* 12, 3: 334–6, 339–43, & 346–50. Reprinted with permission from Sage Publications.

Venkatesh, S. 2002. "'Doin' the Hustle': Constructing the Ethnographer in the American Ghetto," *Ethnography,* 3, 1: 91–92 & 96–103. Reprinted with permission from Sage Publications.

Whyte, W.F. 1943. "Doc and His Boys," *Street Corner Society: The Social Structure of an Italian Slum.* Chicago: University of Chicago Press: 14–25. © 2003 by The University of Chicago. Reprinted with permission from the University of Chicago Press.

Wynn, J. 2005. "Guiding Practices: Storytelling Tricks for Reproducing the Urban Landscape," *Qualitative Sociology,* 28, 4: 399–400 & 404–413. © 2005. Reprinted with kind permission from Springer Science+Business Media B.V.

INDEX

Note: Page numbers in **bold** are for figures and those in *italics* are for tables.

University Readers™
Reading Materials Evolved.

Introducing the

SOCIAL ISSUES COLLECTION

A Routledge/University Readers Custom Library for Teaching

Customizing course material for innovative and excellent teaching in sociology has never been easier or more effective!

Choose from a collection of more than 300 readings from Routledge, Taylor & Francis, and other publishers to make a custom anthology that suits the needs of your social problems/ social inequality, and social issues courses.

All readings have been aptly chosen by academic editors and our authors and organized by topic and author.

Online tool makes it easy for busy instructors:

1. Simply select your favorite Routledge and Taylor & Francis readings, and add any other required course material, including your own.

2. Choose the order of the readings, pick a binding, and customize a cover.

3. One click will post your materials for students to buy. They can purchase print or digital packs, and we ship direct to their door within two weeks of ordering!

More information at www.socialissuescollection.com

Contact information: Call your Routledge sales rep, or
Becky Smith at University Readers, 800-200-3908 ext. 18, bsmith@universityreaders.com
Steve Rutter at Routledge, 207-434-2102, Steve.Rutter@taylorandfrancis.com.

Routledge
Taylor & Francis Group
an **informa** business